ROCKMONT COLLEGE LIBRARY

JOHN DEWEY:
PHILOSOPHER OF SCIENCE
AND FREEDOM

JOHN DEWEY:

PHILOSOPHER OF SCIENCE AND FREEDOM

A Symposium • Edited by SIDNEY HOOK

GREENWOOD PRESS, PUBLISHERS
WESTPORT, CONNECTICUT

Library of Congress Cataloging in Publication Data

Hook, Sidney, 1902-   ed.
   John Dewey, philosopher of science and freedom.

    Reprint of the ed. published by Dial Press, 1950.
   "A Selected bibliography of publications by John Dewey": p.
    Bibliography: p.
    1. Dewey, John, 1859-1952--Addresses, essays, lectures
I. Title.
B945.D44H473   1976   191   76-7567
ISBN 0-8371-8840-7

ROCKMONT COLLEGE LIBRARY
34516

Copyright, 1950 by Dial Press Inc.

Originally published in 1950 by The Dial Press, New York.

Reprinted with the permission of The Dial Press.

Reprinted in 1976 by Greenwood Press,
A division of Congressional Information Service, Inc.
88 Post Road West, Westport, Connecticut 06881

Library of Congress catalog card number 76-7567
ISBN 0-8371-8840-7

Printed in the United States of America

10 9 8 7 6 5 4 3 2

Preface

THIS SYMPOSIUM is tendered to John Dewey as he enters the tenth decade of his life. He is the only major philosopher to have lived beyond his ninetieth year. Longevity, however, is not a philosophical achievement. It is a natural gift. Not the length of his life but the nature of his ideas makes John Dewey important for our time and explains why on four occasions he has been honored by his colleagues with a volume of commemorative studies.

The present volume seeks to give some evidence of the extent to which the intellectual climate of our time has been influenced by Dewey's ideas. Something of their scope may be inferred from the fact that it requires experts from so many different fields to survey them; and something of their depth by the analytical character of the contributions. Technically, Dewey is a philosopher's philosopher, but the impact of his philosophy has been general. He is the one professional philosopher of our age whose ideas have touched the common man through institutional changes in education and social action, broadly conceived, to which they have contributed. The essays which constitute the volume are valuable as an introduction to Dewey's thought: but they are indispensable to an understanding of the total effect of that thought on the intellectual history of our times.

There is good reason to believe that his significance as a thinker will extend beyond our own times. It has often been observed that philosophers are most effectively refuted not by argument but by being ignored. John Dewey has certainly lived long enough to be ignored, to become part of a history so much accepted as a matter of course that it seems more remote in time than it actually is. But instead, he still looms as large as ever in the intellectual life of the nation, not only in virtue of his own continuing contributions but as part of the liberal heritage of American culture in relation to which each new generation feels called upon to define its position. Whether we turn to the philosophy of law or science or art, it is instructive to note how often the issues raised by Dewey come to the fore in the latest discussions and the newest beginnings. John Dewey is continually being rediscovered even by those who have taken him for granted. He is continually being refuted, but the necessity of refuting him does not seem to abate. Strong differences exist about the validity of his ideas but none about their relevance.

The central reason for the vitality of Dewey's ideas is their concern with two main themes which are uniquely related to the distinguishing features of modern culture. They are, first, the nature of scientific inquiry and its implications for man's conception of himself, and the cosmos; and, second, the aspiration for a world of free men and free societies which despite the triumphs of totalitarian regimes in the world is stronger in popular consciousness than ever before in human history. These themes give the book its title.

The original suggestion for this volume developed in conjunction with the activities of the National Committee to Celebrate the 90th Birthday of John Dewey, which sponsored a public dinner to him on October 20th, 1949, and organized several meetings to discuss his views. The editor was requested to accept the full responsibility of organizing and carrying out the project. He wishes to thank the contributors and publishers for their cooperation in making this public tribute possible.

SIDNEY HOOK
New York University

New York, N. Y.
January 1, 1950

Contents

PREFACE		v
John Dewey and the Spirit of Pragmatism	HORACE M. KALLEN	3
Dewey and Art	IRWIN EDMAN	47
Instrumentalism and the History of Philosophy	GEORGE BOAS	66
Culture and Personality	LAWRENCE K. FRANK	88
Social Inquiry and Social Doctrine	HORACE L. FRIESS	106
Dewey's Theories of Legal Reasoning and Valuation	EDWIN W. PATTERSON	118
Dewey's Contribution to Historical Theory	SIDNEY RATNER	134
John Dewey and Education	JOHN L. CHILDS	153
Dewey's Revision of Jefferson	MILTON R. KONVITZ	164
Laity and Prelacy in American Democracy	HERBERT W. SCHNEIDER	177
Organized Labor and the Dewey Philosophy	MARK STARR	184
The Desirable and Emotive in Dewey's Ethics	SIDNEY HOOK	194
John Dewey's Theory of Inquiry	FELIX KAUFMANN	217
Dewey's Theory of Natural Science	ERNEST NAGEL	231
Concerning a Certain Deweyan Conception of Metaphysics	ALBERT HOFSTADTER	249
Dewey's Theory of Language and Meaning	PAUL D. WIENPAHL	271
Language, Rules and Behavior	WILFRID SELLARS	289

The Analytic and the Synthetic: an Untenable Dualism	Morton G. White	316
John Dewey and Karl Marx	Jim Cork	331
Dewey in Mexico	James T. Farrell	351

APPENDICES
- Notes on the Contributors 379
- A Selected Bibliography 381
- Some Publications 383

JOHN DEWEY:
PHILOSOPHER OF SCIENCE AND FREEDOM

John Dewey and the Spirit of Pragmatism

by HORACE M. KALLEN

WILLIAM JAMES was almost twenty-one and John Dewey three years and two months old that December of 1862 when President Lincoln called for a national day of prayer. The immediate occasion of the call was the country's depression after the terrible defeat of the Union forces at Fredericksburg. The continuing need was the crisis of civil war which at last consummated the chronic division over Liberty and Union that had strained the nation's life from birth. Daniel Webster had stated in an apothegm the ideal of those who had voted abolitionist Abraham Lincoln into the Presidency. *Liberty and Union,* Webster had cried, in the famous debate over nullification, *Liberty and Union, one and inseparable, now and forever.* True, the liberty the voters chose was not the liberty Webster had argued for. He had in mind the liberty of local government as set over against the general freedom of individuals. The liberty Americans voted for, in electing Lincoln, was the equal liberty under federal guarantee of each and every human being with every other, whatever his color, his religion, his race, his sex, his occupation, his national or cultural origin.

In the traditions of a large section of the American people, as to the generations of the privileged everywhere else in the world, such equal liberty had been anathema. Those Americans were used to devising and elaborating arguments of religion, of philosophy, of science, of culture, of economics, of politics and of history demonstrating that such equal liberty was impossible, or if possible, fraught with evil consequences alike for those who would concede it and those who would acquire it. They claimed the weight of all authority and all tradition for their side. Never, they argued, had there been, never could there be, equality of the unequal. It was God Himself who had divided mankind into elect and unelect, saved and condemned, masters and servants, rulers and subjects, leaders and followers, free men and bond. To take the affirmations of the Declaration of Independence in good faith, was to defy Providence, to propose anarchy in place of the good God's hierarchical order of the universe. If, then, equal liberty had to be the price of union, they would rather serve God by seceding from the Union, and defending with their blood his divinely-ordained order of rank and station. And secede and fight they did.

For a long time it looked as if Providence would reward their obedience to its commands with victory. Unlike the servants of God, their foes, the champions of liberty in union had always been men of peace, they and their fathers before them, without taste for the organization of warlike might, without the ideals or skills that rendered such organization effective. The force with which they undertook to impose union and to compel liberty at first suffered defeat after defeat. The battle of Fredericksburg was one such defeat, and, some urged, the decisive one. So, calling the people to prayer, Lincoln told them: "The dogmas of the quiet past are inadequate to the stormy present. The occasion is piled high with difficulty, and we must rise to the occasion. As our case is new, so must we think anew and act anew. We must disenthrall ourselves, and then we shall save our country."

Well, the soldiers of liberty did win the final victory for the Union, and their victory wrote liberty in the terms of the thirteenth, fourteenth and fifteenth amendments anew into the national Constitution. But the equal liberty in free union for which they sweated and suffered and bled and died is still remote from achievement. In the perspectives of history, the struggles to live and to grow of the "new nation, conceived in liberty and dedicated to the proposition that all men are created equal," have come upon new occasions piled high with new difficulties, and the need of its people to disenthrall themselves, to think anew and to act anew, is repeatedly as urgent as it ever was. The doubt has not died, even among its true friends, whether a nation so conceived and so dedicated can long endure. The doubt, indeed, attended its birth, and enthralls its growth to this very day. There have always been those who were fire for national sovereignty and independence and ice to personal liberty, fire for tradition and ice for new thought and new action, and they have never been among the least in the land. To disenthrall ourselves from the dogmas of the past to which those spirits would shape the future, has ever been the *sine qua non* of the innovations by which salvation comes.

As Thomas Jefferson had understood it, the very creation of "government of the people, for the people, by the people," which brought freedom to new birth in a new way, had been a prime act of disenthralment. In the year 1826 Jefferson was eighty-three years old. It was the fiftieth since the signing of the Declaration of Independence. It was the seventeenth since its author had retired from public affairs, and gone from enacting to communicating the democratic ideal. The chief architect of democracy in America had made himself its chief philosopher. In both roles Jefferson found that he was at war with enemies of the democratic way at home and abroad. His whole life long he had to fight at home on behalf of the First Freedom with the wall of separation this requires between Church and State; and on behalf of the universal, free public education and of the abolition of slavery and the slave trade implied by this freedom. As President, he had inherited a cold war with Great Britain which became hot in 1812 nor ended in a genuine peace until after the Civil War. He had had to fight for his country's liberties with the France of the Revolution and the France of Napoleon, while at home he had had to counter the men afraid of freedom, vested interests of church and privilege, a "tinsel aristocracy," who wanted America to be but a new name for old ways of spiritual and material bondage and not the free and fluid society where free men freely think their own thoughts and make their own places. Few were the occasions he had faced not piled high with difficulty and demanding reflection unthrottled by authority and action untrammeled by precedent.

This, and much else like this, must have been in Jefferson's mind when he wrote to the Mayor of Washington regretting his inability to participate in the festivities of the fiftieth anniversary of the signing of the Declaration of Independence. That action, he said, had called for a "bold and doubtful election between submission and the sword." Consequences had justified the hazard at home, and he firmly believed that the Declaration would be to the entire world—"to some parts sooner, to others later, but finally, to all, the signal of arousing men to burst the chains, under which Monkish ignorance and superstition has persuaded them to bind themselves, and to assume the blessings and security of self-government. The form which we have substituted restores the free right to the unbounded exercise of reason and freedom of opinion. All eyes are opened or opening to the rights of man. The general spread of the light of science has already laid open to every view the palpable truth that the mass of mankind have not been born with saddles on their backs, nor a favored few booted and spurred ready to ride them legitimately by the grace of God. These are grounds for hope for others. For ourselves, let the annual return of this day forever refresh our recollection of those rights and an undiminished devotion to them."

The letter was read at that Fiftieth Anniversary Celebration. Together with letters from Jefferson's disciples and successors, James Madison and James Monroe, and two other still living signers of the Declaration, it was at once printed and published. The future fathers of William James and John Dewey, both then youths of fifteen, could well have known and remembered and somehow assimilated it to their experiences of the annual Fourth of July celebrations at which the Declaration was once again read. William James's father, indeed, was the orator of the celebration which the citizens of Newport held on the tragic July 4 of 1861 when Congress was meeting, at President Lincoln's call, to face the threat of secession and war, and to preserve the Union. His subject was

"The Social Significance of Our Institutions," and the Declaration was undoubtedly in his mind, and the spirit of it a potent unconscious force in all his generous expression of his democratic religion.[1]

Indeed, until the nation's cities became too many and too large, all the nation's children were witnesses to the Fourth of July ceremonies and heard the Declaration read. It, and other perennial components of the nation's birthday celebration, acquired the quality of joyous religious symbols. They signalized the momentous American difference in the multitudinous confrontations of experience which growing up in the United States presented. Together with the tasks of the frontier, they were the elements of spiritual novelty. The rest was traditional. The rest—the relations between men and women and parents and children, between employers and employees or masters and slaves, between clergy and laymen and teachers and pupils—were continuous with the folkways and mores of Europe. The rest were extensions of the doctrines and disciplines of the dominant European culture, with its sacerdotal and aristocratic orders, its hierarchy of birth, rank and vocation.

Not that the affirmations of the Declaration themselves lacked a European derivation and parentage. They were the very distillation of what is known as the Enlightenment. In Europe, however, they were only the ways of thinking and talking of a small cosmopolitan society of illuminati. They were visions of the heart's desire in whose light such clear spirits as Voltaire and Diderot and Condorcet could appraise the horror which established rule, asserting authority from God, perpetrated upon the souls and bodies of the subject multitudes. Their achievement was aspiration and criticism, not reconstruction: it was *Candide* at one pole and the *Sketch for a History of the Progress of the Human Spirit* at the other. Men of sensibility without status and of vision without power, they could escape exile, the Bastille, the hangman or the Inquisition only as they masked their defiance by apparent conformation and their con-

---
[1] See *The Literary Remains of the late Henry James,* edited with an introduction by William James. Boston: James R. Osgood and Company, 1885.

demnation by ironic approval. They were allegorists paramount.[2] The Frenchmen of the next generation did make the French Revolution, but failed to build the liberty, equality and fraternity which the Enlightenment had envisioned into a way of life. In fact, they degraded the vision from a plan to be realized into a dogma to be asserted; they transvalued a programmatic into a compensatory ideal. But the history of all Europe, France included, and of all the world since, vindicates Jefferson. It has been the history of a blood-drenched labor to bring the ideal to actuality as fact.

Such, inevitably, has also been the history of the United States. But with this difference: that somehow aspirations and ideas which stayed compensatory or otiose or frustrate in Europe did become instruments for the reordering of interpersonal and institutional relationships in America. On the edges of the American wilderness neither peasant skill nor noble privilege could avail as in Europe. The occasions were new, the difficulties high and the thoughts and actions had to be new. Ancient dogma, established habit or mere brute strength were alike insufficient. A man was on his own. His family were on their own. To stay alive they had to study out new

[2] Voltaire was of course the great master of this art. Concerning all the illuminati Condorcet had written (*Esquisse*: *Oeuvres*, 1847-49, vol. VI, ch. 12): "They employed all methods, from the humorous to the pathetic, from learned tomes to novel or pamphlet. They veiled the truth from those whose eyes were feeble, while others could delight in piercing the veil. To strike prejudices a mortal blow, they gave them shrewd praise, they never threatened any singly or *en masse*. Sometimes, they quieted the enemies of reason by pretending to favor only partial toleration in religion and only fragmentary liberty in politics. They applauded despotism when it fought sacerdotal nonsense. Yet they kept attacking the fundamentals of both while seeming only to assault their revolting or ridiculous abuses. In other words, seeming to prune a few branches they struck at the roots of the trees. Sometimes they advised the friends of freedom to attack superstition, which covered tyranny like an impenetrable shield; sometimes they denounced superstition to the despots as the latters' true enemy. . . . But always they proclaimed the independence of reason and the freedom of thought as the salvation of mankind." It should be added that the *philosophes* were of Roman Catholic derivation and instruction and subject to Catholic censure and immolation at the hands of an Inquisition that tortured and destroyed Calas, whose champion Voltaire made himself. Immanuel Kant, certainly a man of the Enlightenment, but living under Protestant rule, was able to be more direct. See *Religion Within the Limits of Reason Alone*, Hudson & Greene edition, 1934, pp. 121f.

ways of new doings. They had to discard whatever in the past tethered and strangled; they had to alter and strengthen that from the past which could liberate and sustain. They had to search and seek for alternatives to routine. Survival became everywhere a consequence of readiness to change, of being freed to take thought and of taking it, alone for oneself, and again by choice, together with one's neighbors. Staying alive came to depend, not on keeping ways or works unchanged, but on changing them. Staying alive had to be the same as progress. Where growth was in view, the science and art of making old things over and devising new things became a value paramount. In the humanization of the wilderness, in converting woodland into clearing, clearing into farmstead, sod hut to log cabin, cabin to house, modes of knowing, doing, living, took form which the older values of our Western civilization had to confront and were bound to misprize at every boundary of their trek from the transatlantic rear in Europe to the last new-won frontiers of the Western wild.

In the circumstances, the image of the dynamic relation between individuality and government—all government, not only state rule—which the Declaration signalized, owned an experiential expressiveness it never received elsewhere. Intimate experience underlay the "self-evident truth" that liberty is an unalienable right. Wherever the forms of nature were being transformed to the uses of man, self-help and mutual aid freely interfused; leadership freely accrued to excellence in workmanship, to the knowledge which Bacon revealed is power. Government was experienced as a common instrument conjointly arranged by equal neighbors, each different from each, and all endeavoring together to secure for themselves and one another their diverse yet equal rights to live freely and safely. The "self-evident truth" that government is instituted by men "to secure these rights" and derives its just powers from the consent of the governed thus grew from a spreading root in actual experience. The lonely hazard and the neighborly help, creating new patterns of doing and suffering, infused the abstract ideas of freedom and reason with the concreteness of the day-to-day enterprise. They gained an operational meaning, pregnant of consequences which during long millenia had been treated as vulgarities unworthy of the dessicate, conventional mystique of church and school. The workaday enterprise transvalued freedom and reason from the exalted invariant faculties of dogma, with its revealed certainty and salvation by grace of authority, into earthly hazards of innovation, trial, error, and survival by force of thought taken and work accomplished in forest and in field, in house and in shop. De Tocqueville was struck by the change. Where the traditional hierarchies of European society, he observed, enable men to cultivate "the arrogant and sterile researches of abstract truth . . . the social conditions and institutions of democracy prepare them to seek immediate and useful practical results of the sciences."[3] What wonder then, when at last the social contract now reverenced as the Constitution was offered by its framers to the contracting people for underwriting, they had refused to vote it without the Bill of Rights which secured a moiety of the basic liberties as terms of the contract.

The "arrogant and sterile researches of abstract truth" were deprived by this development of neither prestige nor power. Although they were known to be irrelevant to the actual methods of inquiring and learning, they lost neither eminence nor authority in the churches and the schools. They were long held to be the nobler parts of knowledge, the disciplines of the liberal education, the fruits of culture, and the hallmarks of the gentleman and scholar. This appraisal survived also at the advancing frontier. As the missionary later was said to follow the flag, so culture followed vocation. In settled and stabilized communities imports of the older patterns of authority and hierarchy tended to overlay the new ones of freedom and mobility. The latter impelled every man to seek to be as good as his betters; and since the image of the better was the figure of the born gentleman with his culture and refinement, the religious and educational establishments tended to preserve and repeat what the daily life wore away and cast off. Barrett Wendell

[3] *Democracy in America*, III, p. 89.

remarked that the emergence of the representative American was due in no small degree to the attrition of the manners and morals, spiritual and intellectual as well as social, of his European cultural inheritance; he was disposed to equate attrition with regression. There took place some sort of rebirth of the spontaneity of perception and of the directness and simplicity of judgment that recalls the enlightenment among the Greeks after the Persian wars. In the confrontation of inherited values and new vision, the apparent advantage was with the former. They were elaborately articulate, smooth with age, and on the face of it, complete, final. Preserved as the inalterable deliverances of the fathers, given forth once for all time, they composed the classics of faith and culture. What was there left for any American to do but to take them reverently to his heart, study and follow them, and pass them on intact to his children? To alter them or add to them was beyond his powers. Now and forever, America could be nothing else than a spiritual colony of Europe, dependent upon the mother-continent for all the meanings that dignify man and ennoble his works.

Nevertheless, even the churches and the schools could not remain entirely impervious to the libertarian contagion. Inspirited by newer winds of doctrine from the religious and intellectual establishments of Europe, they employed a metaphysic drawn from Fichte, Schelling and Hegel to reconfirm a theology deriving from Calvin. They thus gave thought a power with things which their more ancestral Scottish realism did not allow; they made of destiny a prospective happiness whose impossibility for the multitudes of men had been Calvinism's foregone conclusion. One can dispute at length whether this conversion of a hard-bitten despair of life, in both this world and the Otherworld, into the optimistic reassurance of what has come to be called "the Genteel Tradition" is a consequence of the new importations from Europe, or whether the employment of these importations resulted from the steady reconstruction of both the old and the new importations by the American experience of freedom and reason. If Ralph Waldo Emerson was a transcendentalist with all the spirit and letters of Europe's culture confluent in the stream of his consciousness, his transcendentalism was but a means to teach and confirm a personal uniqueness, a religion of liberty and self-reliance, which its European counterparts nowhere manifest. And Henry Thoreau undertook to practice what Ralph Emerson preached, bringing the spirit of the frontier into the very center of culture, and on cultural grounds. For him and for Emerson science was still what it had been for Jefferson: the understanding of nature on which is built the growth of man into life ever more abundant, refined, and liberal. Knowledge and know-how, theory and practice were for them but different perspectives of an identical process of our natural lives. Nor was it other for Walt Whitman, who felt that his vocation was to be the poet of this new vision, who proclaimed that "the office of America is to liberate, to abolish kingcraft, priestcraft, caste, monopoly; to pull down the gallows, to burn up the bloody statute book, to take the immigrant, to open the doors of the sea and the fields of the earth. . . . This liberation appears in the power of invention, the freedom of thinking, the readiness for reform."

But in signalizing Whitman, Emerson and Thoreau among spokesmen of the American psyche, we must remember that they were not of the schools and the churches. They had rebelled against those establishments and had been at least in spirit excommunicated from the fane. There the Genteel Tradition wrestled with set-ups which it provided for itself from the "science" of the time. This was not the living science of the frontier of inquiry whose laboratory pioneers were becoming conscious of their own aims and methods and putting into words the operations of their art. This was science in general, envisaged as "natural philosophy," and divided from "moral philosophy." Two ardent faiths gave direction and meaning to the conduct of this science. One asserted, sometimes with deprecation, more frequently with aggression, the dogmas of a supernaturalist Providence of Protestant derivation, such as Newton or Agassiz postulated (the Catholic version was in those days not actively engaged). The other asserted, almost always aggresively, very occasionally with apology, the dogmas of a materialistic determinism such as d'Holbach or Haeckel bespoke. Intolerance and intransigence were attributes of both these faiths. They were equally orthodox religions. Quite other was the frame of mind developed in the separate sciences, each with the problems of its field, its many tentatives of solution, originating first as an idea, an hypothesis, in some man's thinking; taking definite shape in words and other signs, being projected as a program of experimentation, being embodied by means of instruments designed and constructed for the purpose, and being established as valid or discarded by the observed and measured consequences of the experimentation so organized. Somehow, reason as here manifest, with its tentatives, its immersion in perception, its piecemeal empiricism, its open-minded tolerance of alternatives, its shutting out of foregone conclusions, fitted well with the methods and findings of Charles Darwin who, having completed his schooling for a career in the ministry of supernatural religion, lived out his life as a naturalist. The nature he envisaged was postulated on a primal liberty of variation whose new comings survived or perished as they accomplished adaptation with the world they entered. If nature "selected" them, it was not because they were passive matter, molded by the environment to conformation; it was because they had a being and integrity of their own, active in its own preservation; and playing its ineluctable part in the never final process of natural selection. Natural selection was mutual selection, and Darwin found it to account for human no less than for all other living existences. His lifelong studies of change in such existences persuaded Darwin that the conservation of dogma and the pursuit of knowledge could not actively live together.

The findings of Darwinian science, not yet respectable enough to be admitted into the schools and outlawed *ab initio* from the churches, provided a new ground for translating freedom and reason from abstract universals into concrete workings in the specific experiences of living men. Understood in the light of Darwinian theory, scientific discovery is less the uncovering of an *a priori* order everywhere the same, waiting from eternity to be found out, and more invention by man of diverse devices, material, linguistic, symbolic, with which to accomplish the most specific, the simplest, the most economical, the most convenient and elegant solution of the problems his experience presents him with. Seen in their interplay, these arts are the body and soul of reason. Its ways and works are a function of the contingencies of change, of chance, of the trends of action and of the consequential difference such action makes. Ultimately, reason might be envisaged as the self-organization of diverse liberties.

Charles Peirce imagined and worked out articulate hints of such ultimacy. This practicing scientist and mathematician became conscious of what he was doing and how he was doing it; this inventor in logic, this innovator in the interpretation of scientific method, somehow could not or would not shake off the transcendentalism that suffused the intellectual atmosphere in which he came to his maturity. More sympathetic to Lamarck than to Darwin, declaring himself an "objective idealist" with affinities to Schelling, Peirce envisaged the universe as a process of evolution from a chaos of spirit to a cosmos of matter, a process wherein matter is but "effete mind, inveterate habits becoming physical laws." Mind, he argued, was the same as chance, spontaneity; habit or law the same as a growth from "an infinitesimal tendency to habit-taking." Inasmuch as absolute chance alone does not need anything else to account for it, Peirce took absolute chance for his beginning. From any "infinitesimal germ accidentally started" the homogeneous repetition which is "law" can follow, while if the original datum is assumed to be law, variation is necessarily ruled out. Hence our general ideas, our concepts, our universals, wherein we envisage the laws of nature, are habits of belief with which we act. A human habit "is a biological embodiment of a general idea," and the general idea is a system of expectation and plan of action arising out of sensory experience, leading back into it and unable to pass beyond it. Thus, "our idea of anything is our idea of its sensible effects . . . our conceptions of these effects is our whole conception of the object." "Intellectual power is nothing but facility in taking habits and in following them . . . to all kinds of cases like their original." When channelled in the "processes of investigation" which we call sciences, and "only pushed far enough," these habits should "give one certain solution to every question to which they can be applied." This solution is "predestinate," "fated," "sure to come true," "can nohow be avoided." What it discerns is "the real." It is "independent of men's thought, though not necessarily of thought in general." It is final, and its finality pertains to its essence, and is a complete envisagement of its object. Yet what that essence is "does not depend on what anybody thinks."

Nevertheless the emergence of that utter finality is a function of its freedom to emerge. Neither tenacious insistence on this or that solution nor submissive acceptance of a solution on authority can achieve it. At bottom the *sine qua non* is a sort of compounding and orchestration of new habits with old. In this process absolute invariant repetition would put an end to habituation. The uniformities of habit are statistical, not totalitarian. And the diversities with which statistics concerns itself cannot be accounted for by immutability. Also in the pursuit of truth, variety can explain uniformity but uniformity cannot explain variety.

Peirce's philosophy brings together conflicting thinkings about man, nature and destiny. He believed that he had achieved some sort of orchestration of them, but the harmony is one of faith and feeling rather than of logic, even as Peirce recreated logic. Fundamentally, he but designs for the Genteel Tradition a new look, and his present vogue among the philosophically genteel seems to me based on a realization of this achievement. At the time he devised his innovations there was no felt need, such as there is today among the spokesmen of the tradition, for the scientific and mathematical support he gave it. His contributions looked away at first blush from the finalities of safety and certainty which were the traditionalists' deepest care, even as they were Peirce's own. His novelties carried force and meaning only to philosophers repelled by the tradition, and what such philosophers made of them Peirce could not stomach. Nevertheless, that he is remembered at all, and that today's carriers of the Genteel Tradition should find in him the excellences they glorify is due entirely to the appreciation these dissident philosophers first offered Peirce, and the ideas they first credited him with.

The philosophers are, of course, William James and John Dewey. The ideas are those intrinsic to Pragmatism. Peirce, however, never had intended Pragmatism by those ideas and because he undertook to make what he did intend as clear and distinct as he was able, there has been much talk of James's "misunderstanding of Peirce" and a little of Dewey's. This talk is not borne out by the record. James never pretended to be a follower of Peirce's; he but too generously acknowledged a debt to Peirce for a concept whose verbal articulation he accepted from Peirce and which he consciously modified in the working out of his own vision. If James was silent about his differences from Peirce, it can hardly be because he was not aware of them; and it may be because Peirce was vocal enough about them. Dewey, of course, was not silent.

What, then, did James and Dewey receive from Pierce, which Peirce denied he had to give? It was, I think, the new turn that Peirce gave to thinking about Freedom and Reason, which Peirce meant for the support of the ancient finalities and certainties whose human origins Pragmatism uncovers. Peirce's discussion of these values is that of a man concerned about concepts and not about people; it is the expression of a philosophic specialist couched in an idiom personal to himself, with terms like anancasm, agapasm, synechism, tychism, firstness, secondness, thirdness, that are today as tangent to the general language of philosophy as when he invented them. But they possess also a dynamical, in addition to their verbal, relation with the new turns in scientific inquiry into nature animate and inanimate. They helped James in his struggle for his own disenthralment. They confirmed for him, from another, and to his experience unrelated, area of the human enterprise, the new insight that Jefferson, Thoreau, Emerson and Walt Whitman had advanced. Peirce's innovations somehow fell together with these, and hinted a consensus.

In Europe later, other practicing scientists and mathematicians such as Mach, Poincaré, Ostwald, quite without intending it, provided more strengthening for this consensus.

James, however, brought to the new insight an innovation of his own, a transforming innovation, that set the reenvisagement of Freedom and Reason upon the course of development which the Pragmatic Movement signalizes. It derives from the attitudes toward self and destiny which James chose to take in order to resolve the most inward and momentous crisis of his personal history. To formulate, to test, to verify, the beliefs expressing this attitude became for James the creative impulsion of philosophical inquiry. It prompted his last researches no less than his first, and he meant *Some Problems in Philosophy* to bring his findings to a form as complete and precise as they could sustain and he achieve.

Owing to his father's own enduring crisis and the faith which Henry James the Elder was ever modifying in order to resolve it, James can hardly be said to have grown up in any community. The James family was continually on the move, from New York to New England, from New England to Old, to Switzerland, to Germany, to France, and back again. Outside the family there was for James no continuity to speak of, either of school or companionship. The one continuing influence, at once provocation and nurture, was the father, and forty-year-old William so wrote the latter, when he believed him at the point of death, and was not sure that he would ever see him again.[4] The provocation came from Henry James the Elder's philosophic faith, of which he was ever trying to persuade others. A reaction against Calvinism, and a reworking of Swedenborg's system into personal and American terms, this faith could not easily win adherents from the ranks of transcendentalists and scientific determinists to whom its apostle proposed it. Round the family table it generated bright controversy. The nurture came from the spirit in which the controversy was conducted: respect for the variant, rejection of sectarian dogmatism, the practice of a toleration in which vigorous argument was delivered with maximum

[4] "In that mysterious gulf of the past into which the present soon will fall and go back and back, yours is still for me the central figure. All my intellectual life I derive from you; and though we have often seemed at odds in the expression thereof, I'm sure there's a harmony somewhere, and that our strivings will combine. What my debt to you is goes beyond all my power of estimating— so early, so penetrating and so constant has been the influence." *The Letters of William James*, vol. I, pp. 218-220.

force and democratic temper. The spirit was one of generous sportmanship, of scientific fair play.

This spirit qualified William James all his life. Yet there was no sanction for it in any absolutist system of faith, naturalistic or supernaturalistic. Every such system made a man's existence a bondage and his destiny a predestination. Henry James the Elder, in a mood of torture and despair, had found in Swedenborg an instrument of release from that damnation. His son, William, had pulled himself out of suicidal depths by reflection upon Renouvier. Each had undergone an agony, had experienced evil in the most poignant way religion can mean evil. Each had resolved his tragedy by an act of assent to a way of thinking whose validity followed hence from its function as meaning for survival or extinction and not from its structure as a logical system.

It was the logic of the prevailing system of scientific determinism, with its foregone conclusions, that had so impatterned the agony of frustration of William James, that to cease from existing, alone could bring surcease of evil. For a long time, James, as he wrote to his friend Thomas Ward, was "on the continual verge of suicide." He came to believe, indeed, "that no man is educated who has not dallied with the thought of suicide," and he always held a vivid sense of the experiences that prompt it. "The lunatic's visions of horror are all drawn from the material of daily fact. Our civilization is founded on the shambles, and every individual existence goes out in a lonely spasm of helpless agony." When it does not so go out, it is because of an extreme personal effort bringing a sudden insurgence of new force, ineffable reinforcement of the helpless striving already in act. "The huge world that girdles us about puts all sorts of questions to us, and tests us in all sorts of ways. Some of the tests we meet by actions that are easy, and some of the questions we answer in articulately formulated words. But the deepest question that is ever asked admits of no reply but the dumb turning of the will and tightening of our heartstrings as we say, 'Yes, I will even have it so!' When a dreadful object is presented, or when life as a whole turns up its dark abysses to our view, then the worthless ones among us lose their hold on the situation altogether, and either escape from its difficulties by averting their attention, or if they cannot do that, collapse into yielding masses of plaintiveness and fear. The effort required for facing and consenting to such objects is beyond their power to make. But the heroic mind does differently. To it, too, the objects are sinister and dreadful, unwelcome, incompatible with wished-for things. But it can face them if necessary, without for that losing its hold upon the rest of life. The world thus finds in the heroic man its worthy match and mate; and the effort which he is able to put forth to hold himself erect and keep his heart unshaken is the direct measure of his worth and function in the game of human life. He can *stand* this Universe. He can meet it and keep up his faith in it in presence of those same features which lay his weaker brethren low. He can still find a zest in it, not by 'ostrich-like forgetfulness,' but by pure inward willingness to face the world with those deterrent objects there. And hereby he becomes one of the masters and the lords of life. He must be counted with henceforth; he forms a part of human destiny. Neither in the theoretic nor in the practical sphere do we care for, or go for help to, those who have no head for risks, or sense for living on the perilous edge. . . . Thus not only our morality but our religion, so far as the latter is deliberate, depend on the effort which we can make. *'Will you or won't you have it so?'* is the most probing question we are ever asked; we are asked it every hour of the day, and about the largest as well as the smallest, the most theoretical as well as the most practical, things. We answer by *consents or nonconsents* and not by words. What wonder that these dumb responses should seem our deepest organs of communication with the nature of things! What wonder if the effort demanded by them be the measure of our worth as men! What wonder if the amount which we accord of it be the one strictly underived and original contribution which we make to the world!"[5]

The ever-present feel of effort thus realized and appraised became, I believe, the vital gradient of James's thinking. It was the act of lifting himself out of his apparently predestinate suicidal agony, of dissipating his "horrible fear of his own existence." It

[5] *The Philosophy of William James*, pp. 332-334.

occurred as a free choice between opposed alternatives either of which once chosen, could confirm itself consequently. The event was to him a direct experience of freedom, the perception of its ineffable inwardness, the sensible substance from which derived Peirce's mathematical chance and contingency, and Jefferson's liberty, the unalienable right. It provided better than conceptual sanction for spontaneity and change, being of itself power of alteration, redirection and innovation. It was not liberation merely, but liberty; and its consequences, in the perspectives of prevailing purposes, interests or needs, could be as impartially disruption as creation. Being the spontaneity it is, unframed by any purpose, unguaranteed by any providence, it is also risk and the responsibility which pertains to risk.

Whatever its operation when it has occurred, the free event presents the philosopher with one of his major problems. In the philosophic tradition it is always being regulated, conformed or explained away, equated with irrationality and evil. Yet any person in the course of his life may "accumulate grain on grain of wilful choice into a habit," by each act confirming the continuity of the act. For himself James had found that the act of believing "in my individual reality and creative life" sustains and enlarges that which it is belief in. "I will posit life," he decided, "in the self-governing resistance of the ego to the world."

To the orthodoxies, whatever their species, such resistance is the same as the unpardonable sin of pride. All, however, that is fresh and fruitful in James's philosophic faith is the child of that unpardonable sin. It is a humanism born of human nature *in extremis*, and it leads to whatever is most seminal and distinctive in James's thought: his pluralism, temporalism, and functionalism, his radical empiricism, his appraisals of religion, science, society and their action upon one another. In these there is in operation a view of the origin and workings of knowledge and reason about which the major controversies over pragmatism had centered during James's lifetime. He has been charged with being "against intellect," with a "pathological aversion" to logic, with taking "vital lies" for real truth, and so on to no end.

Yet all that the charges in the end come to is, that James, by bringing his unique experience of crisis together with the reports of Darwin, Renouvier, Spencer and others, was able to disenthrall himself from the millenial worship of Consciousness as an immortal, inalterable soul, and of reason as its supreme faculty, absolute, universal and eternal. He became able to understand them as spontaneous variations, within an animal organism, that had become with the ages concrete yet ever-changing functions of adjustment. He was never "against intellect." He was never averse to logic. But one phase of his lifelong research led him to the perception that the idolized identity-logic of the schools and the facts of the enormously greater mass of residual experience could not live together, and he chose to take the facts and let the logic go. He was able to show that the Reason and Soul cherished by the tradition were instruments hypostatized, tools transvalued into idols, and to reveal the actual conditions of their freedom to function. This is the specific innovation of his psychology. "I still must contend," he wrote, apropos of Herbert Spencer's definition of mind, "that the phenomenon of subjective interest, as soon as the animal consciousness realizes the latter, appears upon the scene as an absolutely new factor . . . the knower is not simply a mirror, floating with no foothold anywhere, and passively reflecting an order that he comes upon and finds existing. The knower is an actor and co-efficient of the truth on one side, while on the other he registers the truth he helps create."[6]

The great *Principles of Psychology* develops and varies this observation. It called attention to the continuity of process as against psychological associationism and atomism in the stream of consciousness; it brought out the role of interest in the activities of attention, and the import of all this to the formation of concepts as tools of adjustment in discriminating, comparing, analyzing, abstracting. Such formations, it pointed out, can be unpredicted and unpredictable waves of the stream, spontaneous variations established by their successful operations as "necessary truths." They

---

[6] *Essays and Reviews*, pp. 65, 67. Contrast this with Peirce's idea of "man's glassy essence."

are postulates whose conformation is consequential, not prior. In a plural and diversifying world, futurity is central, and mind would naturally be a selective propensity toward what is not yet. "The pursuance of future ends and the choice of means for their attainment are then the mark and criterion of the presence of mentality in a phenomenon." But the ends are consents or choices; they are postulations of the organic will to believe, and once decided on, the mind's searchings and seekings are a consequential analysis of some given "booming, buzzing confusion," original or created, in a process of give and take wherein ideas emerge. One or another of these we trust and hold for true, or distrust or doubt, and change, modify or discard, thereby appraising them as false.

This, in sum, is what Pragmatism had evolved as, when James came to call it "a new name for old ways of thinking." The ways of thinking were indeed old, but James's thinking about them was as new as the name and newer. It denuded the process of actual thought from the accumulated dialectic of the schools and the rhetoric of the churches, and brought to light its nature as a human enterprise, with all its hazard of faith and contingencies of works upon its head. And it was through these ideas, especially as they came to expression in the *Principles of Psychology*, that both Schiller and Dewey accomplished their own disenthralment and went out to confront their own difficult occasions.

Schiller's were European, and remained so, even after he had settled on the Pacific Coast and had been taken for a somewhat unreassuring oracle by the sect of Personalists who had established a communion there. A skilled dialectician attuned to the prejudices and subtleties of an Oxford steeped in neo-Hegelian ratiocination, Schiller's refined dissection of formal logic and his masterly reconstruction of this logic for use, developed in his lectures at Corpus Christi College during many years, came to print too late for the wider influence they merited. Logical theory had already taken other turns: one in the direction of the symbolic logic which has become the stereotype of a strange scholasticism, the other toward that technical analysis and restatement of James's observations whose present top is Dewey's *Logic: A Theory of Inquiry*. Schiller's own studies have made little impact. Yet the great essay, *Axioms as Postulates*, which he contributed some half century ago to the collection known as *Personal Idealism* is a classic instance of the philosophic imagination building an exciting theory of life and knowledge upon foundations provided by James, and spontaneously used by the most modern of mathematicians. Schiller always preferred to call himself Humanist rather than Pragmatist, and urged the claims of that designation upon James. He loved to refer his Humanism back to the martyred Protagoras, from whose dicta regarding man the measure, and concerning the existence of the gods, he could draw the whole of his humanistic wisdom. Canning Schiller was a bold thinker, and a witty one, with special *aperçus* not less seminal than those of Charles Peirce and susceptible, when the time is ripe, of an analogous repristination. He divides with Bertrand Russell the merit of being one of the simplest, clearest, wittiest writers on philosophy in English. Yet somehow, he figures hardly at all, to students of the Pragmatic Movement, as one of its agonists and a true maker of its spirit.

The reason for this tangency is not, I think, the localism or provincialism of American pragmatists and their opponents. It is that by general philosophic consent, Pragmatism has been identified as the philosophic differentia of the American way, alike by Europeans and others who condemn it and by those who approve it. And truly, as a vital and efficacious variant upon the philosophic tradition, this new way of thinking about old ways of thinking is a growth of the American soil. What other philosopher of his day and age was so sensitive as William James to the difference which is America? "Our nation," he told the multitude who had gathered at the Boston Common to witness the unveiling of the monument to Robert Gould Shaw, the Yankee who had volunteered to command a Negro regiment of the Civil War,[7] "our nation has been founded in what

[7] *Memories and Studies*, p. 93.

we may call our American religion, baptized and reared in the faith that a man requires no master to take care of him, and that common people can work out their salvation well enough if left free to try. But the founders had not dared to touch the great intractable exception: and slavery had wrought until at last the only alternative for the nation was to fight or die. What Shaw and his comrades stand for and show us is that in such an emergency Americans of all complexions and conditions can go forth like brothers, and meet death cheerfully if need be, in order that this religion of our native land shall not become a failure on earth."

That every man shall be left free to choose for himself at his own risk the goal and the gaining of this salvation, was of course the last inwardness of this American religion, and for James, ultimately, the *fons et origo* of all religion. This is what the churchly enterprises—their creeds, their sacraments, and other rituals, their confessionals and testimonies—either confirm or nullify, mostly nullify. "The feelings, acts and experiences of individual men in their solitude so far as they apprehend themselves to stand in relation to whatever they may consider divine"[8]—this for James was the ultimate of religion. That his studies of it led to his much debated hypothesis of "piecemeal supernaturalism," of each man experiencing in his extremity, a saving "more-like-ourselves," is no contradiction of his appraisal of democracy as religion. A philosophy of life for free men freely joined to one another in a free society so ordered that each vindicates his own singularity more surely and abundantly than he could by himself alone *could* signalize an operative ideal generating the consequences usually craved of "God." *What* God specifically turns out to mean was not so important for James as that the meaning should be the specific object of some living individual's living faith, and that his faith should be the projection and upkeep of his integrity in all the darks of life, amid the hazards and hardships in whose overcoming alone "we catch real fact in the making and directly perceive how events happen and how work is actually done."[9]

[8] *Varieties of Religious Experience,* Modern Library Edition, p. 31.
[9] *Ibid.,* p. 492.

No candid friend or foe of democracy can deny that it has been and will continue to be as truly a religion as any for which this status is claimed. In an essay on which he himself laid great emphasis, James gives certain specifications of how this faith came alive in his own experience. The essay is *On a Certain Blindness in Human Beings*. The pluralism and individualism which democracy presumes, he concludes, "absolutely forbid us to be forward in pronouncing on the meaningfulness of forms of existence other than our own; and it commands us to tolerate, respect and indulge those whom we see harmlessly interested and happy in their own ways, however unintelligible these may be to us. *Hands off*: neither the whole of truth nor the whole of good is revealed to any single observer. . . . There is no point of view absolutely public and universal. . . . Private and uncommunicable perceptions always remain ours, and the worst of it is, that those who look for them from the outside never know where. . . . The practical consequence of such a philosophy is the well known democratic respect for the sacredness of individuality—is at any rate the outward tolerance of whatever itself is not intolerant. . . . Religiously and philosophically, our ancient national doctrine may prove to have a far deeper meaning than our people now seem to imagine it to possess."

These words were written in the easy and simple days of moral smugness and general assurance that democracy was invincibly on the march to its manifest destiny. To James himself, however, this deeper meaning was always the most momentous, the most weighted option of his life. It was that thrust of his will during his personal crisis, with all its contingencies and consequences, wherewith he affirmed his own being, and came thus to know the ineffable freedom. It is the burden of his essay *On What Makes A Life Significant* and it keeps coming up in his expression in all sorts of contexts.

He gives it a signal presentment in his exposition of what makes a life significant. "Sweat and effort, human nature strained to its uttermost on the rack, yet getting through alive, and then turning its back on its success to pursue another more arduous still. One may perceive it everywhere, in banks and factories and churches, in colleges and theatres and laboratories as well as on freight trains, on the decks of vessels, in cattleyards and mines, on lumber-rafts, among firemen and policemen . . . wherever a scythe, an axe, a pick or a shovel is wielded." Those who disenthrall themselves of their ancestral blindness can note courage everywhere, "human nature *in extremis* . . . sweating and aching and with its powers of patient endurance racked to the utmost under the length of hours of the strain." Perhaps they note joy as well. But by themselves labor and moods are alike insufficient. To embody meaning they must also be the responsible working out of an ideal, articulately expressed and consciously intended as a program of the active will, generating for the idealist new stuffs and new experiences, ennobling work with vision, and giving direction and meaning to the will. Work without vision is sodden and brutal; vision without work is empty and effete. Although the fighting virtues have a life in them which intellectual breadth never reaches to, that life redeems itself from insignificance only as ideal aspirations compenetrate pluck and will, and culture shapes them to significant form.

The religion of democracy might be called reverence for this diversity of significances peopling the land. True, there is much in America altogether contrary to it: the thinness and barrenness, the shrillness and impatience, the intolerances, the mania for bigness, "the moral flabbiness born of the exclusive worship of the bitch-goddess Success." But the democratic faith redeems us from thraldom to those wizardries. Everywhere the forward thrust of individual life upon a way self-chosen and singular to itself, treading it audaciously through every hazard of sorrow and disaster, act by act reshapes and transvalues those aliencies toward its own ideal. "If a divided universe," James wrote somewhere in his diary, "be a conception possible for his intellect to rest in, and at the same time he have the vigor to look the universal death in the face without blinking, he can have the life of meliorism—the life that is, which betters itself, hour to hour and enterprise to enterprise, without guarantees and without finalities." Success is a democratic pantheon of divinities, the bitch-goddess is not the only divine being called by that name, and often as not the others overrule her, subdue her and harness her to their uses. What they accomplish is the exercise of the creative intelligence. "The thing of deepest . . . significance in life," James summed it up, "does seem to be its character of *progress,* or that strange union of reality with ideal novelty which it continues from one moment to another to present. To recognize ideal novelty is the task of what we call intelligence."

In the tradition, intelligence figures as both a fact and an ideal, an activity and a rule. Its origins, its operations, the relation of the two roles to one another, and their transformations have from the beginning been the dominant interest of the pragmatic spirit. Although James was more concerned to disenthrall our experience as freedom, change and innovation from subservience to intelligence hypostatized into authoritarian Reason, both Schiller and Dewey devoted their most constructive labors to seeking out, defining and demonstrating, as clearly and distinctly as they were able, the *how* and *what* of intelligence as it is actually at work in our diverse experiences. That is, their professional stress was greater upon epistemology and logic than the other varieties of the philosophic enterprise. Dewey's inquiries, of course, have penetrated all the philosophical disciplines—ethics, politics, esthetics, religion, education—wherever philosophic curiosity could reach. But from the *Studies in Logical Theory* of 1903 to *Logic: A Theory of Inquiry* of 1939, decisions as to how we think and know have given the critical turn to Dewey's findings in every field.

In 1910 William James died. He was sixty-eight years old. He left many friends and hardly any disciples. His career had been that of a God-sent Jonah in the philosophic Nineveh, a lone voice crying in the wilderness of rationalisms and rationalizations. The originality of his insights, the seminal power of his ideas precluded perhaps his building a system or founding a school. His effect was rather to engender a spirit, to establish an attitude, to give reasoned utterance to a brave, poignant faith from whose center of initiation all sorts of ideas might spurt into systems yet not lose touch with the vital spring. In 1910 John Dewey had long been the recognized leader of a school, James's admired companion in philosophic arms, one of the first apostles of the pragmatic spirit. He was then fifty-one years old, at the height of powers that have retained their force longer than those of any philosopher known to history. James's junior by almost a generation, he was different from James in temperament, background, education, as any two men of genius could be: Dewey, always shy, deliberate, hesitant in speech and not often graceful in expression; James, outgoing, swift, vivid, with sudden insights and light-creating phrases.

I have already written of James's father and his household. Dewey's was a Yankee grocer in a Vermont town, where everybody was everybody else's neighbor. His son grew up in a community still edging the wilderness. The schooling he received was of the kind prevailing in such places—still in the traditional curriculum assumed to produce the traditional liberal education. Bookish as Dewey was, his education in fact developed from his chores at home, his jobs of work on a farm, in a sawmill, at a limekiln. His great contribution to the theory and practice of education was bringing together what the educational tradition has thus so long successfully kept apart. Save for the months toward the close of the Civil War that Dewey, as a young child, lived in war-devastated northern Virginia, where his mother had gone with her children in order to be near his father, then in the quartermaster service of the Union army, Dewey did not get very far from the home scene until he went away to teach all subjects in a country high school in Pennsylvania. Oil City, however, was still the old Main Street with a somewhat different accent.

Dewey was nineteen years old when he really left home for the first time. At nineteen James had entered the Laurence Scientific School of Harvard, had been to school in France and Switzerland as well as America, had visited England, had tried himself out at painting and was still unsure of his preference and vocation. His life, outside of school, had been spent in considerable urban communities among an "élite" of wealth and culture. His philosopher of a father had been rich enough to provide him with "advantages" that Dewey's parent probably never imagined. William James could be "idle" at no risk, while John Dewey could not even labor with any certainty of earning enough for his needs. For Dewey, thus, the American way of working his way was a habit of life, building itself unconsciously into his character as he grew up, and long taken for granted; the philosophic enterprise was an independent variable, an affair of schools and books, consisting of the impatterned verbal abstraction his teachers had imparted to him. For James, on the other hand, the American way was a momentous discovery curing him of "ancestral blindness," and the philosophic enterprise a struggle for freedom initiated by an act of choice in his life's great crisis, a struggle of whose successes and failures the struggle which is the American way become the great exemplification.

During many years of Dewey's career as a teacher of philosophy his occupation and his life ran separate lines: From the point of view of higher education the courses of study at the pioneer University of Michigan or the University of Minnesota were different in no important respect from that at the University of Vermont. They were all transmitters of the Genteel Tradition. Although his marriage in 1886 to Alice Chapman did turn Dewey's attention "from the commentative and classical to the field of contemporary life," it little affected his occupational concerns. He had experienced a considerable degree of intellectual stirring through reading Hegelians and Hegel and was much taken by the dialectical interdependences and the necessary unity their logic purported to demonstrate. But it was reading James's *Psychology* that awoke him from his Hegelian slumbers, and set his attention on intelligence and freedom as living works in his own personal history and ongoing operations in "the field of contemporary life." In a mild and easy way, reading James gave Dewey's thinking the same sort of new turn that reading Renouvier had so poignantly brought to James. Michigan Alice Chapman's pioneer spirit, her unbookish awareness of how children think and learn, her religious feeling free from churchly stereotypes, must naturally also have been influences toward the readiness which Hamlet says is all.

That the midwestern scene also played its part to turn Dewey from Hegel to James, is hardly to be questioned. It was the time of the Gilded Age. Farming and trade had been first supplemented and then superseded by manufacture and banking as the modes of enterprise. In all fields—food-processing, mining and smelting, oil-refining, railroading, tool-making—great corporations were being formed whose goal seemed to be monopoly and whose means seemed to be varieties of force and fraud. They suborned government to the unlawful purposes of business; they shaped the political boss into the creature, if not the creation, of the highest bidder. Congress had enacted its anti-trust laws, it seemed, to no purpose. Where the oppression of working men and the suppression of their unions were not declared lawful by servile courts, they were imposed by the violence of private armies recruited *ad hoc*. The provision of such armies became a form of enterprise. Also the free press, so integral to the self-maintenance and growth of free society, was brought into subservience to the vested interests. At most points in the national economy corruption so compenetrated creation that it seemed as if the two were equally vital phases of an identical process, that no one could become a captain of industry without at the time becoming a robber-baron. Mark Twain's works span the transition from the frontier of Tom Sawyer and Huck Finn to the frontier of Col. Sellers and his companies. If many of the humorist's works are bitter laughter at the national blasphemy of the national religion, he nevertheless remained convinced of the religion; and in *A Connecticut Yankee in King Arthur's Court* symbolically vindicated its precepts and skills against all ancient fraud and new deception. Remove the greed, the cruelty, the magician's pretenses, and what is left, if not the pioneer's *know-how* reworking things and men and their relations into freer, more humane forms? What is left if not the application of intelligence to the service of freedom? But such employment of intelligence requires that intelligence shall itself be free, and how can it be free requires that inteligence shall itself be free, and how can it be free when its tools and vehicles are under the police rule of monopoly?

This momentous question in all its diverse forms came to exert a directive influence on the trend of Dewey's inquiries. The question was brought to him through his friendship with Franklin Ford, who seems to appear once in the record and then no more. At least, I have been able to find only one reference to him, but that one highly significant. It is in a letter from Dewey to William James,[10] written not long after the appearance of James's *Psychology,* and urging acquaintance with Ford on James. The letter recounts Ford's impact on Dewey's thinking. It but reduces, Dewey wrote, "what was a wonderful personal experience into a crude bit of cataloguing." Ford was an economic journalist; "he was on a paper and he wanted to inquire." His employers, however, wouldn't let him "inquire," so he went about finding out for himself, *Why?* And the answer he found was that "the social structure prevented freedom of inquiry." He discovered that the truth could not be sought, or if sought and found could neither be told for free nor sold for money because interests of class, possessions, prestige hinder the free play of intelligence, and because control of such vehicles of communication as the telegraph, the railroad and the like is the control of freedom of communication. Ford concluded that the business of finding the truth and selling it for money calls for the type of organization in which not only the parts but the whole would need a representative "whose belly interest . . . is identical with its truth interest." From this Dewey drew certain conclusions regarding "the social bearings of science and art," regarding the relations of an idea to the conditions of its objective expression, regarding the need that free inquiry should always be able to challenge, on behalf of free thought and its completely free movement, "the authority of all so-called authorities." The findings, Dewey wrote James, had brought him "freedom of sight and treatment in ethics."

The letter was written from Ann Arbor, June 3, 1891. Students of Dewey will of course recognize in it at least one dominant theme of his philosophy. Here was a disenthralment, a "freedom of sight and treatment" of ethical issues, a fresh confrontation of an occasion whose pile of difficulties has by no means been estopped from pyramiding. If James was led to share Dewey's feelings that Ford

[10] See Perry: *Thought and Character of William James,* vol. II, p. 514.

had achieved a momentous and liberating insight, the currently available record does not say. The inspiration of James and the illumination of Ford do however compenetrate in Dewey's thinking, and cannot today be separated. Dewey even joined in the project of a journal, *Thought-News,* which failed to come off.

But Ford, for whatever reason, passes out of the picture. Dewey and James, until James's death, join together to meet the new occasion, by new thought and new action to disenthrall the human spirit and accomplish the repristination of Freedom. In the nature of things personalities so different with such different histories and backgrounds would differ in their basic preferences and appraisals also. To my mind they did differ and were aware that they did. But so long as the great disputation over Pragmatism was on, their controversial front against the common foe was seamless. Each took pains to assert his unqualified agreement with the other, and each so reinterpreted points of possible differences as to validate his own assent. The alliance began to take form after the publication of the Chicago decennial *Studies in Logical Theory.* Also in those days the University of Chicago was an academic enterprise with oomph and go. Its founder had been ambitious to make it the great midwestern center of the higher learning and had gathered from all the corners of the land a faculty of scholars as marked in their personalities as they were distinguished in their fields. This cost money, and money cost freedom. The interest of the patron and benefactor somehow became a gradient for the interest of the inquirer and a measure of the acceptability of his discoveries. The institution had its servilities, and to Thorstein Veblen "the higer learning" was there, even more than elsewhere, "the hire learning." Nevertheless, the practice of the arts and sciences was not excluded from the teaching of them; originality was not entirely subordinated to correctness; and for a time at least, there was more freedom, not less, than in other places.

Dewey had been among the first of a faculty that came to include William Vaughn Moody and Robert Herrick as well as Thorstein Veblen, W. I. Thomas, Albert Michaelson, Jacques Loeb, and Anton J. Carlson. The philosophers and psychologists counted George Mead and James Tufts and James Angell. Among the neighbors of the spirit were Jane Addams and Ella Young. Education was made a part of Dewey's province. One of his academic functions was to direct the famous laboratory school—the *Dewey School* it came to be called—where at last he was able, with the cooperation of distinguished colleagues, to bring the book to action and action to the book.

With that school the theory and practice of education, not in America only, but in all the world, crossed a momentous frontier of educational freedom. But the President of the university did not favor the great adventure, treated Dewey badly and lost him to Columbia, just one year after his university's decennial celebration. The collection of philosophical essays which signalized Chicago University's tenth birthday was dedicated to William James. "It may be," Dewey wrote the latter in March, 1903, "the continued working of the Hegelian bacillus of reconciliation in me that makes me feel as if the conception of process gives a basis for uniting the truths of pluralism and monism and also of necessity and spontaneity. . . . I cannot help feeling that an adequate analysis of activity would exhibit the world of fact and the world of ideas as two correspondent objective statements of the active process itself —correspondent because each has work to do, in the doing of which it needs to be helped out by the other. The active process itself transcends any possible objective statement (whether in terms of fact or of ideas) simply for the reason that these objective statements are ultimately incidental to its new ongoing—are for the sake of it. It is this transcendence of any objectified form, whether perceptual or conceptual, that seems to me to give the clue to freedom, spontaneity, etc., and to make it unnecessary to have recourse to such a hypostatizing of chance as Peirce seems to me to indulge in."[11]

This letter, some argue, embodies the divergences of Dewey from James and communicates the enduring trends of his thought. James for his part saw in the *Studies in Logical Theory* a fresh

[11] R. B. Perry: *Thought and Character of William James,* vol. II, pp. 522-23.

strengthening of his own faiths, wrote an appreciative review of it, and described it to Schiller as the product of "a flourishing school of radical empiricism of which I for one have been entirely ignorant."[12] He singled out Dewey for special praise. "Dewey is a hero," though his work "needs a great deal of building out and following of his principles into all sorts of questions of detail. But it's noble work and deserves a worthier style than the too dry and abstract one the writers employ."[13] Acknowledging the review, Dewey claimed James's psychology as "the spiritual progenitor" of his own thought, and as already furnishing the instrumentalities for a pragmatic logic, ethics and metaphysics. He disclaimed originality for himself: "None the less so far as I am concerned I have simply been rendering back in logical vocabulary what was already your own."

Of course Dewey was too modest. He was not rendering back, he was selecting, varying and transforming. The more fully he assimilated James's ideas, the more they became different and new. He was aware of divergencies[14] and more reticent than James[15] about how far they agreed. He preferred to denote that which he rendered back by the word *Instrumentalism,* rather than *Pragmatism* or *Humanism.* He intended by Instrumentalism such an expansion of what he had drawn from James as would "establish a precise logical theory of concepts, of judgments and influences in their various forms, by considering primarily how thought functions in the experimental determinism of future consequences." This led him to interpret mind as one adaptive function of an evolving animal organism, with a brain that operates as an instrument of coordination in generating habits of prospective adjust-

[12] *Ibid.*
[13] *Ibid.,* p. 525.
[14] *Ibid.,* p. 525; letter of November 28, 1907. Dewey felt from the first that James made reservations on behalf of the Self as Will which he did not make on behalf of the Self as Thought. Dewey argued that the ego need be no more transcendental in acting than in knowing. See "The Ego as Cause," *Philosophical Review,* III, pp. 337-341. He recurs to the issue almost forty years later in a paper "The Vanishing Subject in the Psychology of James," *Journal of Philosophy,* XXXVIII, pp. 589-599.
[15] "As I understand Dewey and Schiller," James told an inquiring reporter to whom he defended Dewey against the charges of obscurity, "our views absolutely agree."

ment. It led him to recognize that intelligence is no "glassy essence" but is a step-by-step cybernetic integration of a problematical environment and an insecure organism into a "new and harmonious unity." In the unity, logically speaking, hypothesis transforms into "warranted assertion." The process of unification is somehow continuous, the outcome prospective and the form of it not given in advance. To unify is the prime role of intelligence. Its operations are alterative and its consequences are an ongoing enlargement and liberation of men: "All intelligent thinking means an increment of freedom in action, an emancipation from chance and fatality." Such thinking converts past experience into knowledge and projects that knowledge as ideas and purposes which anticipate what may come to be in the future and indicate how the desirable may be realized.

Thus intelligence remakes the old by uniting it with the new. In this continuous remaking, liberty, Dewey writes in *Liberalism and Social Action*, is "always relative to actually felt oppression." It consists in "release from the impact of particular oppressive forces: emancipation from something once taken as a normal part of human life but now taken as bondage." This is the case with the older individualisms. Those, whether rugged or tender, first thought out as instruments to free intelligence and to confirm and enhance individuality, are now devices to mark and rationalize new oppressions. Any new individualism, hence, must realize individual liberty in terms of its relation to social change, and the lasting task of the liberal is to be alert to the process of change and to mediate the indicated adjustments. In all situations liberalism seeks to replace stasis with movement, to abolish boundaries and monopolies, to free communication, to share experience. In the schools, the implementation of such seeking is education: in the sciences it is the winning of truth, in the arts it is consummating experience, in political economy it is democracy, in international relations it is peace, in the personal history it is growth in freedom through reason. Everywhere it is religion. And everywhere the primacy accrues not to the singularities of discontinuous goals, but to the commonalty of the continuous going, to the method of transition whose happiest use occurs in the sciences.

This is, of course, also the inwardness of democracy. The task before democrats, Dewey wrote in the first year of the war, 1939, to the gathering assembled to celebrate his eightieth birthday, is to make and keep democracy creative, to turn what has been historic accident into social purpose, what had been natural luck into deliberate choice. "Realize in thought and action that democracy is a *personal* way of individual life . . . controlled by a working faith in the possibilities of human nature . . . as . . . exhibited in every human being" with his "capacity for intelligent judgment and action. . . . For what is the faith of democracy in the role of consultation, of conference, of persuasion, of discussion, in formation of public opinion, which in the long run is self-corrective, except faith in the intelligence of the common man to respond with common sense to the free play of facts and ideas which are secured by effective guarantees of free enquiry, free assembly, free communication? . . . To take as far as possible every conflict which arises . . . out of the atmosphere and medium of force and violence as a means of settlement, into that of discussion and of intelligence is to treat those who disagree—even profoundly with us, as those from whom we may learn, and in so far as friends."

Underlying this faith is an ultimate religion that is prior to and supervenes upon all denominational diversifications with their claims and pretensions. It is the common faith of freed minds. It is experience as the free interaction of men with one another and with the world around them, creating and sharing the knowledge which this interaction generates. The experience is spontaneously ends and means together. The knowledge is science day by day creating what does not yet exist and sharing what it creates in a process of mutual release and enrichment. Faith in experience as thus creative is the faith solely held by democracy; and until experience is no more it is the task of democracy to incarnate faith in works. If a name were put to this faith, the name would be Humanism.[16] It is, I think, in the spirit of such a Humanism that Dewey wrote:

"Fidelity to the nature to which we belong, as parts however weak, demands that we cherish our desires and ideals till we have converted them into intelligence, revised them in terms of the ways and means which nature makes possible. When we have used our thought to its utmost and have thrown into the moving unbalanced balance of things our puny strength, we know that though the universe slay us still we may trust, for our lot is one with whatever is good in existence. We know that such thought and effort is one condition of the coming into existence of the better. As far as we are concerned, it is the only condition, for it alone is in our power. To ask more than this is childish; but to ask less is a recreance no less egotistic, involving no less a cutting of ourselves from the universe than does the expectation that it meet and satisfy our every wish. To ask in good faith as much as this from ourselves is to stir into motion every capacity of imagination, and to exact from action every skill and bravery."

If this calls for a loyalty to our own being, it does so conditionally, as a function of the nature in which we live and move and have that being. It assigns to that nature a certain providential harmony with the human creature which is one of its own multitudinous diversifications. It accents intelligence as the art of actualizing and amplifying this harmony in the works and ways of sharing experience and thus of transforming multitude into oneness, discord into peace and thereby mutual obstruction into facilitated liberty. So far as I can see, with all Dewey's devotion to James as progenitor and liberator, with all of his sympathetic restatements of James's insights into forms more congenial to the trend of opinion and to the movement of his own philosophy,[17] he never came to share James's feeling for the integrity of the unharmonizable and the irreconcilable, for the invincible spirit whose freedom is to

[16] In 1933 Dewey was one of the signers of a Humanist Manifesto. Among the others were not only philosophers of different philosophic persuasion but physicists, biologists, sociologists, economists, rabbis and Protestant clergymen.
[17] See "The Development of American Pragmatism" in *Philosophy and Civilization*, especially the reinterpretation of "The Will to Believe"; "What Pragmatism Means by Practical" in *Essays in Experimental Logic;* "The Philosophy of William James" in *Problems of Men*.

stand helpless and alone before the omnipotent universe and choose annihilation rather than to yield. He never came to share James's feeling for the freedom which is experienced directly, by acquaintance, which intelligence cannot mediate, but from which, for which and by which the mediating intelligence develops and grows, from next to next. Dewey never came to share James's sense of crisis in which simply not to yield is victory; or to agree that immediate vision can be knowing, that mystical experience is genuinely cognitive, that "supernatural" functions do occur in nature. Perhaps he never wanted to, nor could want to.

And why should he? If Dewey were merely repeating James, what would he have had for James, that James did not already have, what would he have had for the later generations whose light and leading he is these scores of years? To them, James is a scarce-remembered voice, Dewey's forerunner, not his master. Someone has said that Dewey is to the works and vision which distinguish our own time what Aristotle had been to the thought and civilization of his Greek world. There are those who would carry the analogy forward by adding that as Dewey is the twentieth century's Aristotle, so James is its Plato, and that the two supplement one another, the younger man continuing and diversifying the thought of the elder as Aristotle did not Plato's. The analogy has its merits. Both thinkers signalized free acquiescence in vision and reflection as self-correcting processes, supporting the continuity of changing experience; but one signalized the spontaneities and initiations of the process, the other their linkage and unifications. For both, the world is an open world, pregnant with alternatives whose *terminus a quo* and *terminus ad quem* is Freedom, with Reason the way from the initiating to the consequential Freedom. The paramount value in James's philosophic faith was that Freedom for which the word in other contexts is chance, contingency, plurality, novelty, with Reason derivative, operational, a working tool. The paramount value in Dewey's philosophic faith is Reason, whose right name is Intelligence, and whose work is to liberate by unifying, organizing, controlling, the kind of freedom to which James gives primacy. Dewey once called that freedom a nuisance[18] and stated that the task of intelligence is to emancipate the thinker alike from this nuisance and from fatality by working out a desired path through change and chance and necessity.

This diversification of Dewey from James—or for that matter, of thinker from thinker as generation from generation—in a process of give and take that achieves self-correction whenever it results from a free meeting of free minds inquiring into a problem, seems to me to exemplify the spirit of Pragmatism come to its maturity. It postulates, I believe, both those freedoms as intrinsic to the human enterprise, and acknowledges the irreducible diversity of preferences between them. There was more than romantic fantasy in Margaret Fuller's confession that she accepted the inescapable universe. Precisely because it is inescapable, the integrity of man might consist in rejecting it, in setting himself over against it; like Job, refusing to accept survival at the price of integrity.

As for me, I stand here with James. The indefeasible singularity of initiation and decision seems to me primal, and I hold with those who think the world's determinism a consequence of the succession of its ongoing piecemeal determinations, with perhaps every single item of it—certainly every human being—holding fast to its integrity, and every so often crying out to the residual universe *Hands off!* as it goes upon its unique ways from its contingent birth to its unconditional death. But when Freedom does not sustain this separation and division, Reason works as recreator, unifier and reconciler, seeking such an orchestration of the many as will assure the onmoving integrity of each more greatly than it could achieve by working it out alone. Dewey is disposed to belittle or ignore the occasions and necessities of this aloneness; James is disposed to signalize them beyond their power to affect our destinies save, perhaps, unto death. The spirit of Pragmatism seems to me to live in the constant play of these dispositions on one another.

[18] See "Philosophies of Freedom" in *Freedom in the Modern World* edited by H. M. Kallen.

For this spirit the sentiments of Lincoln's poignant call to prayer are descriptions of the course of human life. It observes that in all the institutions of our civilization every Today has its new occasions and new difficulties to which Yesterday's doctrines and disciplines are inadequate. But it does not therefore condemn Today as incurably evil, nor glorify Yesterday as inalterably good. It recognizes simply that every Today calls for some disenthralment from Yesterday, and prompts intelligence to unprecedented ideas and doings that shall today save freedom and liberate growth. It appraises the liberating innovation in faith and works as the differentia of every free society of free men, never final, never absolute, but consequentially adequate to the occasion, to be in its turn freely succeeded by still other innovations apter to the newer difficulties of the newer occasions. In whatever place, on whatever scale, in whatever degree democracy is a going concern and science[19] a successful enterprise, they seem to me to embody this spirit. Pragmatism is the philosophy of their works and ways.

In the perspectives of this philosophy, there are no last terms, no finalities, no ultimacies. In so far as metaphysics is a reasoned envisagement of finalities and ultimacies, always and everywhere one and the same, Pragmatism is a philosophy without a metaphysic. It expresses a posture of the spirit uncommitted to any foregone conclusions, unprejudiced in behalf of any ideal securities which are in fact hazardous postulates by hypostasis exalted into infallible principles. The pragmatic mind is an open mind confronting an open world, where, so long as it lives, it has a chance to *make* destiny and not merely submit to destiny; where the inevitable is contingent. For the pragmatic spirit, there is no conflict between Freedom and Reason; the authority of Reason is consequential, not original and intrinsic. For the pragmatic spirit, that is, Reason is a

[19] See C. H. Waddington: *The Scientific Attitude,* p. 92, Penguin Library, New York, 1942. The ethos of science is "an ethos based on the recognition that one belongs to a community, but a community which requires that one should do one's damnedest to pick holes in its beliefs. I know of no other resolution of the contradiction between freedom and order which is so successful in retaining the full values of both."

mode of relating free energies, a constellation of discursive and operational arts which constitute the use of these energies. It can be neither an absolute, universal and eternal order which the human mind images and conforms to, nor an unaltering and unalterable human faculty conforming things-in-themselves to itself. However it began, Reason is now a patterned activity which alters what it works on and alters in its own being as it works, bringing into existence not foregone conclusions but ends different from their beginnings. Reason is the art of guiding chance by choice, and surmounting fatality by judgment; the art of transition from simpler, more limited liberties to liberties diversified and expanded wherein, to paraphrase Dewey, choices become more conscious, more varied and flexible, and more alert to their own meanings as those meanings change and grow in unexpected as well as expected ways. Reason is thus recognized as creative intelligence. It is what, concretely, Jefferson's "free right to the unbounded exercise of reason and freedom of opinion" has grown to between his time and ours.

There are those in our time, as there were in Jefferson's, who are terrified of this growth. Events, between his day and ours, have more than vindicated his faith that mankind everywhere might burst the chains under which monkish ignorance and superstition had persuaded them to bind themselves, and to work and fight together toward that equal liberty of faith and works which the Declaration of Independence envisioned. The fearful ones are shaken by the feeling that the work and warfare, which so arduously and with always great hazard, embody ideal in fact, principle in practice, program in institution, have been attended with deep tragedy and have cost and are costing too great a tribute of blood, sweat, tears and disillusion. They are enthralled by the alternation of chronic and acute crises which makes up so much history. They cannot forget the horrors of the acute ones such as our own Civil War, the first World War "to make the world safe for democracy," the second World War to vindicate "the four freedoms," nor how each time peace has nullified what war seemed to have won. They cannot forget the constant abortion of the Bill of Rights and of the 13th, 14th and 15th Amendments to our Constitution. They cannot forget the League of Nations and its Charter and how they were nullified and betrayed by sovereign states pledged to their enhancement and growth. The memories aroused by fear, sustain and nourish the fears which aroused them. They set in an atmosphere of anxiety and distrust today's United Nations Organization and the Universal Declaration of Human Rights which its Assembly has adopted, giving concreteness and explicit specific range to what is general and implicit in the Declaration of Independence. They note, not without *Schadenfreude,* how powers that had solemnly pledged themselves to the strengthening and growth of freedom and reason through the union of the nations practice upon both abortion and nullification. They keep reminding themselves and us that for more than a generation, now on a global scale as in Lincoln's day on a national, the case is new, the occasion piled high with unprecedented difficulties. But they insist we need neither think anew nor act anew, that innovation is immolation, and only the eternal dogmas of the past can save us. As they read the sciences on nature and man, and in the light of them interpret the course of history, they appraise scientific determinism as fatality and statistical determination as chance. They look upon both as necessities of reason and feel helpless before both. Their hearts yearn for a security neither provides; which they feel nothing in experience can provide. Existence is for them an anguished weakness to which alone some supernal absolute can bring release and healing.

Their state of mind, with its view of events as uncontrollable expressions of either inexorable lawlessness or inexorable law, its sense of confusion and helplessness, its mood of dumb rebellion alternating with dumb submissiveness, has its historical precedents. It is what Gilbert Murray had designated as "the failure of nerve" in his accounts of the Graeco-Roman mind around the beginning of the Christian era. That mind, when expressed in the Platonic, the Epicurean, or Stoic philosophers, did envisage reason as the savior from fear and insecurity. But it envisaged reason as the one, eternal, universal and necessary order of the universe, and salvation as reconciliation of man to a universe he is helpless to turn or to alter, as therefore submissively making the best of a bad job. When

Kallen—Dewey and Pragmatism

its mood was rebellion rather than submission that mind looked for salvation to being freed from the cosmic necessity which lays upon us the burden of sin and sorrow and suffering coming to its term only in inescapable death. Such a freeing the rites of the esoteric religions guaranteed. They postulated a break in the unbreakable chain of natural necessity, a turn of reason from its foregone conclusions to consequences unimplied. Faith in such breaks and turns invokes Providence to overrule necessity, miracle to break causal law. This faith had to be contrary to reason. It had to be reason's master. Only where it obtained could the fear of death be effectively transposed into assurance of life, and the intrusions of supernatural Providence invoked to nullify the necessities of natural law.

The resulting Otherworldliness, and the concurrent contraction and degradation of the human enterprise and the damnation of human life in this world are of record. So also is the recovery of reason, the renewal of the human enterprise in this world and the restoration of the dignity and worth of actual human life here and now, which have been maintaining their painful, brave advance since the Renaissance.

The critical steps of this advance were the freeing of the individual conscience, the bringing of reason to a new and more living autonomy, the initiation of modern democracy, the creation and multiplication of the sciences, and of the industrial arts which enchannel and apply them. Each forward step has been a new creation by freedom and reason together working on nature and the human scene. And each step has been haunted by past dogma and forbidden on its authority. Interests afraid for their present security and future survival, and ridden by a sense of doom, keep calling it up from the vasty deep. From reason as creative intelligence at work contingently in the here and now they appeal to reason as a universal and eternal Order foreordaining a necessary destiny. From freedom as the experience of initiation, deliberation, choice, decision, innovative action leading to liberation here and now, they appeal to a supernal Providence magically intruding its grace and miracle into the natural sequences of here and now. Since the first World War the totalitarian Providence of their salvation has been called by other names than God—names of communist, fascist, nazi, falangist, as well as ecclesiastical derivation; it has been the power of hierarchical race, state, class, caste as well as the power of hierarchical church. But whatever the name it was called by, believers in the power, compensating their feelings of insecurity and fear with their belief, endow it with the supernatural grace which saves all at once and forever that, in the Genteel Tradition, pertains only to omnipotent God. Afraid of the actualities of freedom and impatient of the laborious piecemeal workings of the creative intelligence, with its calculated risks, its unforeseeable set-backs and unguaranteed advances, they take refuge in the perennial dogmas of an eternal and universal salvation, whose experiential reality consists in this or that church or state, pushing greedily for a global extension of its temporary and local dominion.

Such is the working of the failure of nerve, continued as a habit of life and a ground of culture. In recent years, however, it has developed a mutant expression for which antiquity, so far as I can see, supplies no precedent. This is Existentialism, a philosophic discourse deeply aware that death is ineffably the end and celebrating every man's personal history as a unique agony of transition from birth to death. Everybody is a lonely existence going it alone, with no eternal and universal reason to give him justification or goal, nor any God whose grace may miraculously save him. Everybody is a fissionable nucleus of liberty exhausting itself in a sequence of blind choices which involve him blindly with men and things and impose upon him a responsibility without rationality whose cumulus from birth to death constitutes his fate. Fate is that freedom which has spent itself and come to nothing. Within its conspectus each man lives naked, suffering and sole. The eternity and universality of saving grace is a fear-engendered dream with which he deceives himself. The actual workings of science, democracy and industry which are the stuffs of man's reason, shaping and reshaping himself and his world toward a surer and wider freedom, are but passing anodynes against a permanent doom. Life cannot be lastingly bettered and may be daily worsened. Existence is ineffably freedom and freedom is as ineffably a tale told by an idiot full of sound and fury signifying nothing. Of course, there are mitigations of the existential anguish. Of course, the man living out his agony alone does enter into comradeship, especially when resisting the totalitarian enemy, such comradeships as men have entered into during the Christian inquisitions, in the concentration camps of the nazis and the communists, and in every willed resistance to a totalitarian foe. But the inconsolable end is death nevertheless. Life must be lived in a stark courage, without illusion certainly, but infallibly without hope.[20]

The spirit of Pragmatism overrules both existentialist hopelessness and supernaturalist illusion. It neither regrets life nor fears death. True, we do live in a world which was not made for us, a world where we happen, where life is a struggle for survival and survival a struggle ending in death, and all our powers as men are achievements of our thoughts acting upon this indifferent and often unfriendly world, that we enter as animals and that we may have to leave without yet having become men. True, all our living, all our learning, all our growing, all that we call our personal being does inevitably and utterly cease. Yet each day every increment in knowledge is a gain in our power as men and one more step in the remaking of the world from a jungle to flee from into a home to live in.

Especially since the democratic revolution set reason free and affirmed the equal liberty of different human beings everywhere in the world, has this remaking—whose method is science and whose ends and means are the free cooperation of free men on equal terms —broken through barrier after barrier until it has become the common working faith of the frontiersmen of the human spirit everywhere. It is this faith in the power of the free intelligence to work its way, item by item and day by day, to that union of the different in equality of right which the United Nations Organization purports and the Universal Declaration of Human Rights affirms. Of course, the creative labor is attended by hardship, frustration and

[20] Cf. J. P. Sartre: *L'Etre et le Neant; Existentialism;* and his novels and plays, such as *Nausea, The Reprieve, The Age of Reason, The Flies.* Other existentialist writers, Simone de Beauvoir, Camus, develop variations on the theme, but do not alter its fundamental intent.

defeats. Of course death dogs each and every step and will outpace them all at last. But what of that? To the pragmatic spirit, nor the contingencies of life, nor the hazards of intelligence can enter a veto upon our human affirmations and the values they create. True, the cosmic guarantees of our existence in idea are compensatory illusions. But it is no less true that where we efficaciously transpose our ideal compensations for unalterable existence into programs for actually altering existence, we are able to work in hope without illusion and we do make that world freer and more reasonable; we do progressively enhance the dignity and worth of the human being. Then, let come what doom there may, if we have not yielded these inward values of our humanity, we have won the victory for the human spirit.

As I see it, Pragmatism is the philosophic expression of the sober faith in man and his works which the democratic ideal embodies, and John Dewey is at once the greatest as well as the most venerable and most influential living prophet and teacher of this American faith.

Dewey and Art

by Irwin Edman

THE INFLUENCE of John Dewey was widespread and profound in education and in general philosophy long before it was suspected that his basic conceptions had consequences, subtle and far-reaching, for art and its understanding. There are several reasons for this. Up to his seventieth year Dewey had written nothing directly or specifically on the subject of "aesthetics." Those who had read him with care, however, knew from his essay on "Qualitative Experience," from more than hints in his early "How We Think," from the whole central theme of realized individuality in *Democracy and Education,* that he had been alerted to the aesthetic implications of his leading ideas. Dewey, his readers knew, was concerned with thought as an instrument toward enrichment of life. No one knew better than he that the art actually experienced in creation or enjoyment was a paramount instance of such fulfilment. It was clear from his earliest writings that what interested Dewey about that experience about which he wrote so much was its vital consummation, its sustained freshness, its ordered and dynamic fruition.

It is curious that Dewey's concern for experience vitally and pervasively realized should so long have escaped even attentive students of his writings, not to speak of his unsympathetic and sometimes obtuse critics (the latter often rendered obtuse by blinding traditional preconceptions of their own). But under the circumstances it is less curious than it seems. Much of Dewey's work has been, (and is even to his ninetieth year) devoted to an analysis of the logic of method and the significance of method both in the solution of human problems and as an index to the precarious and problematic character of experience and nature themselves. Dewey, moreover, has been enunciating a theory of logic as scientific method and of nature as experience in the context of an academic tradition in which the dialectics of nineteenth century metaphysical idealism held the field. Dewey, himself an able dialectitian, felt it his obligation not only to state his position as to logic and metaphysics but to argue a case against entrenched idealism and supernaturalism and conventional academic notions of science, knowledge, morals and metaphysics. On the other hand, his always sensitive awareness of the social issues of his own times and of all times led him to accent the more obviously pressing problems of economic and political reconstruction, a consideration of the agencies by which democracy might liberate and nourish individuality.

It is not surprising under these circumstances that Dewey should have neglected to emphasize what was, however, always present by implication, and in overtone, the ordered vitality, the patterned enrichment by which the quality of life is to be realized and by which the success of all methods and institutions is to be measured. Dewey for so long took for granted that texture and vividness of life were what counted that his hasty readers sometimes wrote as if he were either unaware of such values or totally opposed to them. His critics wrote as if he celebrated method for method's sake, instrumentalities for the sake of their own manipulation, as if in these consisted Dewey's conception of the good life. It required the publication of *Art as Experience* to spell out for a good many readers the lesson that, far from neglecting or ignoring the claims of art, art was the illustration *par excellence* for Dewey of the ultimate meaning of intelligence, morals, democracy, education and even ultimately of the nature of things.

There is one additional reason which must in all honesty be mentioned as to why Dewey's philosophy, curiously fertile in suggestion concerning the nature of art, has for long been regarded as with no, or at most destructive, implications for the life of art and the imagination. Dewey's style lacks all the obvious graces of a thinker gifted with the poetry and wit of Santayana. There is a singular absence in most of his works of concrete and vivid illustration, seldom the enchantment of image or cadence. In the interest of speaking always to the point (a point not infrequently quite novel and unprecedented in philosophical thought), Dewey's style is often awkward, lumbering and bleakly abstract. The tone of his prose, his forthrightness, sincerity and sometimes homespun eloquence, do not quite suggest a philosopher who would in *Art as Experience* say that experience is only *completely* realized where it is imaginative and that experience is only purely and thoroughly realized in or as art.

Yet despite these obstacles, the attentive reader might long before Dewey's only explicit work on the subject have realized where Dewey's heart lay and where his mind pointed. On the surface it looks as if Dewey, for all his rebellion against traditional philosophy, had in his philosophic career followed a conventional pattern. Previous thinkers, including those makers of synthetic systems, for whom Dewey has notoriously little use, had rounded out their careers, after writing a logic, an epistemology, a metaphysics, finally late in life, like Shakespeare in the cliché explanation of *The Tempest,* had turned to the presumably calm serene meditations concerning art. But it is a total misconception of Dewey to assume that having finished the "serious" business of the analysis of logic and metaphysics, he, like so many of his predecessors, had turned in a mild afterglow to afterthoughts about art. Something almost the reverse is the case. What Dewey eventually was to say about art was implicit in all he previously had to say about experience. In fact, in the processes of artistic creation and of artistic enjoyment (that latter also as he makes clear is a process) experience of itself becomes most patently what it always incipiently is. A work of art, in any of the arts, is the expressive movement of matter to a formed fulfilment. In art the organization of energies becomes a matter of direct perception. As for Dewey's celebrated notion, often impatiently condemned, that thought is instrumental, critics have neglected to ask "instrumental to what?" Thought, as Dewey has so often pointed out, is instrumental to action. But action itself moves to fulfilment and freedom; art is on a level or in a phase of action where means and ends interpenetrate and fulfil one another and what is done is realized step by step in the doing by immediate qualitative delight, where what is done and what is undergone merge in freshness, freedom and joy. The whole of Dewey's philosophy of art is not so much what is commonly called "aesthetics" as it is a work on experience *in excelsis*, a comment upon, and an analysis of experience as it is when it is what it always is in possibility: rich, rounded, ordered and directly and immediately enjoyable.

It is a matter of entertaining irony that Dewey should so long have been criticized for a sort of methodologic Philistinism, for a vulgar concern with means rather than ends, instruments rather than consummations. For as *Art and Experience* makes clear, as is patent even from earlier works, it is in imagination that experience for Dewey comes to fulfilment. Imaginative activity is by no means, in his judgment, and in fact, confined to the arts; but it is in the arts that Dewey finds the chief locus of that fruition which gives experience an intensity that is more than mere excitation, and meaning that is more than mere sign for action. In so far as ordinary experience, the doings and undergoings of other enterprises share these qualities, they, too, are art.

Dewey's *Art and Experience* illustrates his conception of experience as fulfilment and as initiation. It is the fruition of his own philosophy. For he uses his analysis of experience, previously worked out with care in the fields of logic and moral analysis, toward an understanding of what happens in the enjoyment and creation of art. It is striking that the categories of analysis Dewey has worked out in other fields should have proved fruitful in the study of what happens in aesthetic experience. What aesthetic experience becomes in his hands is not something separate from other kinds of activity but rather all experience as it comes to genuine fulfilment is art. While art as experience rounds out Dewey's philosophy, however, it is also an initiation and an opening up of new ways of exploring, understanding and in a serious sense appreciating the arts. On the relation of matter and form, on the organic unity of a work of art, on the character of expressiveness and on the function of criticism he has said things that have been left unsaid and perhaps unseen by specialists in art history, art criticism and that artificially separate branch of philosophy called aesthetics. On the other hand, Dewey, looking freshly at art without the blinkers of the specialists, has learned much from them that is of significance for a reinterpretation of many hitherto conventionalized and compartmentalized problems of philosophy and of the nature of philosophy itself. For it is clear, Dewey thinks (and convincingly demonstrates) that by examining with care that which constitutes a work of art as actually experienced (not merely talked about), many of the dualisms between subject and object, observer and observed, matter and form, expressive object and theme expressed, break down. These distinctions in reflection are not categories of experience; they are modes of understanding and sometimes of manipulating objects, means of identifying certain strands in the texture of experience for the purpose of practical control. What are defined as order, unity, pattern and coherence in the universe, on the other hand, are projections upon the cosmos of patterns that are experienced chiefly or most clearly in works of art. Again, those rhythms, orders, unities, patterns realized in works of art, both in the creation and the enjoyment of them, are related to those orders, patterns, rhythms and unities experienced in our own organisms and in recurrent phases of the environment in which we are involved. Since Dewey's own point of view is sometimes so much the exploratory, the adventurous, the conjunction of the new and present with the meaningful past in our experience, relations of philosophy to the arts need working out and enlargement. Meanwhile *Art and Experience* offers the suggestions on art and experience and in other volumes, notably *Experience and Nature* and *Philosophy and Civilization* there is a wonderfully fresh group of related hypotheses on the nature of art and its relation to individual experiences and the context of culture in which individual experience is formed.

It is challenging and refreshing to begin with, to come upon a work that starts not with the already separated subject and object, observer and work of art, perceiver and subject of aesthetic perception, but starts analysis with the live creature interacting with focused dynamic factors of his environment. These fused energies are direct qualities for perception. In interaction with them the live creature is *all* alive, his senses alert, his imagination (that is, the funded meanings of his own past) brought into play, his energies brought into active unity. These become for the time being one with the work of art, itself a focusing of energies that serve to clarify, intensify and integrate the liveness of the live creature.

Dewey in a suggestive phrase says that of late art has come to be regarded as the beauty parlor of civilization, instead of being what it has been historically, what it is in essence always, an example of life realized, the measure of the extent to which the human success of civilization is to be gauged. The residual doctrine of Dewey's aesthetic philosophy is that art is a process, that it is something going on, in both the activity of the creator and what, for want of a more adequately dynamic word, we call the observer. The process is enriched as it moves, cumulates and becomes self-fulfilling as it goes on. The movements of artistic creation and of artistic enjoyment are not essentially different from the processes generally thought of as artistic, in the ordinary interactions of the organism and its environment, the individual and society, the worker and his work. The processes of art are not essentially different from other activities of nature and of mind. In all of these there are tendencies coming to fulfilment, energies cumulating or tending toward fruition, and in turn initiating other processes and contributing to their realization. But in art these energies are released, ordered, clarified and transmuted into objects of directly enjoyed quality.

The treatment of art as experience in these dynamic terms is in sharp contrast with traditional treatments of the aesthetic experience and of still persisting contemporary treatments. The phenomenon of aesthetic perception is still often discussed as if it were the passive registration by a mildly concerned sensorium (sometimes, as in Kant, called "disinterested") of sensations derived from a static physical object. Or if beauty is not thus treated in terms of physical sensations noted in calm instantaneousness by a motionless beholder, it is described in other equally static terms. It is thought of as a visitation or a revelation of an essence, supernatural and timeless, disclosed to a mind temporarily liberated from time.

Dewey reminds us that "aesthetic experience," like all other experience, involves *active* response in time on the part of the observer, an energizing which comes to focus in identification with energies themselves brought into focus in the work of art. For the time being that organization of energies, which functionally *is* the work of art, in effect constitutes his whole environment and his whole being for the observer. The observer, it must be repeated, is not a *mere* beholder but an active center of response. His is an enjoyed participation; in a genuine, not merely a rhetorical sense, it is an act of union. Past experience and present perception become one in any aroused and full aesthetic response. Not only are the senses stirred and engaged but also those funded meanings we call mind. Dewey's analysis seems to account more adequately than the usual compartmental theories of aesthetic perception for what actually goes on in the experience of art. What goes on is more than a merely momentary sensuous excitation, it is an energetic involvement in the ordered relationships of lines and masses, volumes, tones, melodies and harmonies, curves or cadences, phrases and episodes. Awareness of these perceived relationships is deepened by their felt context with the whole funded past of the observer. The physical quality of what is present to the eye or ear is suffused with previously experienced meanings. Aesthetic creation produces a unique *new* experience through this union of present perception with past awarenesses. A work of art is "expressive" because of what the participant in it brings to bear of his own psychological background, what of his past is evoked by the acutely present sensuous qualities. What is so arresting in a work of art is the overtone of funded meanings fused into the very qualities of what is there to be seen or heard. It is this fact which Dewey starts with and which his theory makes intelligible. For it is not a problem of how a physical thing becomes the bearer of meanings external to it. If we responded only to physical qualities, the problem of expressiveness in art would be almost insoluble. In Dewey's analysis of art as a fusing of immediate quality and past experience into one, expressiveness comes to seem natural and inevitable. To the living creature a work of art cannot help but be expressive, for not only his eyes but his imagination are aroused.

There is another aspect of experience of and in the arts that Dewey's analysis better, perhaps, then most, makes clear, the singular union, the strange necessity of art, the fusion of calm and excitement, of serenity and intensity, of vitality and order. Here again the notion of the energies involved and realized in both artistic creation and artistic enjoyment is the key to understanding. In Dewey the key to the understanding of anything from animal behavior to the ultimate nature of things is process, energy, activity. But in art energy is realized in a special way. It is rendered more clear, more intense, more free and therefore more delightful than energy as it is crossed and thwarted and distracted in the activities of government, industry, and the daily human relationships of family, friendship and love. In art energies are *more* free, *more* intense, *more* lucid and therefore more directly delightful, but not *completely* free or lucid or clear.

There is in art as in other aspects of life tension and resistance. Yet in art those tensions are cumulatively resolved as in the resolution of a melody, the equilibrium of masses and rhythm in architecture or painting. The tensions establish the intensity, the urgency, the suspense, the drama of art; the achievement of ordered and cumulative solutions provides the sense of rest, calm, serenity and peace. But the quiet and peace are heightened by the residue of previous resistances and tensions merged. The calm has incorporated the storm. What Nietzsche described as the Dionysian and Apollonian aspects of art are both present. Tension and resolution of tension through poised and cumulative rhythms make intelligible both the unique peaceful intensity, the intensified peace of art.

All in art that goes with expectancy and suspense, all that goes with balance and poise and quiet are explained by the twin and supplementary facts of tension and resolution, of tensions which are incorporated into the achieved balance and order of art.

Balance and order in art are usually discussed as if they were the static geometry of objects. But the balance and order acquire their aesthetic and human value by the sense of poised forces, tensions that have been resolved. Energies are felt as fulfilled in the pattern seen or heard. The acuteness of the tensions is felt in their very resolution as the final chord does not simply *end* the music but is a fulfilment of all that has gone before. Art, as Dewey suggests, is perhaps the chief example of experience where it is pure, in the sense of being realized without distraction or distortion, where it is in any complete and direct sense experience at all. Art is what experience in a humanly successful life, in a genuinely free society, would always be. In that sense and in that sense only may art be said to be an escape, a flight, gradual or sudden, to fullness of experience, not a retreat from it.

There are several reasons, social and psychological and historical, why the experience of art has been treated as if it were different in kind from the other contexts and enterprises of life and why it is so often discussed as if it were an anodyne, an opiate or a consolation, as on occasion it is. In most of our experiences, as Dewey makes clear, there is a division of means and ends, of matter and form, of what is said and the manner of our saying it, of present and past, of physical perception and explicit meaning. These dualisms are distinguished intellectually for various theoretical or practical reasons. Some of these dualisms, like that between means and ends, are characteristic of a disordered society where dull work is done for ends beyond the work itself, as unskilled labor is performed for pay. In a work of art the means are cumulative in as well as toward the ends, what is said is inextricably involved in the mode of the saying, what is understood is at the same time perceived qualitatively, what is perceived is also felt imaginatively as resonant of the past and suggestive of the future.

Dewey examines with some care the reasons, social and psychological, why the arts have been treated as if they were necessarily isolated. Since the Renaissance art has been the prestige entertainment of the propertied and privileged classes. Meanwhile since the Industrial Revolution there has been a wide chasm between the class of things of use, manufactured cheaply by standardized techniques for mass production, and luxury items made by individual craftsmanship. It has come to seem normal for useful things like a barracks to be without beauty, routine for beautiful things to be regarded as somehow remote from the world of use. For the production of necessary goods, houses, automobiles, clothes, the assembly line has gradually usurped the craftsman's bench, machine produced furniture has replaced the lovingly made household things now become collector's items. (There have, of course, been survivals of craft arts but these have been exceptions to the general trend.)

The mass of men, as Ruskin was so bitterly to point out in the middle of the nineteenth century, spent their lives amid standardized ugliness, punctuated by sordid escapes into the tawdry and the sensational. Industrial workers passed their working days at tasks repetitive and meaningless, their vacant leisure in houses and in surroundings that aped the regularities and bleaknesses of their working hours. The factory and the factory town were to be the gray epitome of the direction in which the useful was moving.

Meanwhile, partly in rebellion, the "cult of beauty" became a mode of protest against the crudities and dullnesses of an industrial and mechanized world. Self-conscious artists, self-conscious connoisseurs, tried to escape from the dreariness of current standardized mediocrity and from a machine made environment to something dainty and ethereal called beauty. The Pre-Raphaelite solemn breathlessness and exoticism about art, the cult of the Parnassians in French poetry, the art-for-art's-sake movement in the Nineties, simply accented the notion that art and beauty had nothing to do with use but were escapes into some dreamed timeless Heaven, or some artificially revived and irrelevant past, or something exotic in the South Seas, in the East or on the moon. Often the very industrialists whose operations were making the world into the Smokeover of L.P. Jacks and the Five Towns of Arnold Bennett were trying to bring beauty into their homes by pillaging the past, by decorating their homes with expensively bought trophies, paintings and statuary, "glorifying" their cities with whole classic buildings or imitations of classic buildings, like the branch banks made to ape a Greek temple. The art of the past was lifted bodily from the context of the cultures that had produced it. The Elgin marbles, the paintings of the Renaissance, the genre pieces of the French eighteenth century, were used as expensive decorations, as costly ways of escape or consolation from the bleak contours of the present, or as flamboyant ways of showing at once culture and wealth.

Meanwhile artists themselves in all the arts have for a long time tended to regard themselves as a class superior, esoteric, unappreciated, whose interests were far nobler and more exquisite than those of the Philistines of the middle class or the dull sots of the working class. The little reviews indeed still exhibit this tendency. Connoisseurs and critics have encouraged this notion of art by treating the aesthetic experience as if it were the exclusive potentiality of a rare class of gifted and sensitive darlings. The snobbishness of the aesthetes encouraged on the other hand the contempt of the practically or the socially active, who regard the arts and the artists as truants from important human concerns, the preoccupations of the trifling, the irresponsible and the perverse.

Dewey, by way of both history and psychology, reminds us how fantastic is the notion of works of art as isolated objects and artistic creation as a phase of civilization, but one essentially precious and negligible. Not only among the classic Greeks but in many so-called "primitive" cultures, what had to be done was done imaginatively, what was needed was not only made but made beautiful, what served for daily life was so produced as to nourish the imagination. And what was made thus beautifully and imaginatively was organically related to the culture of which, like religion and government and philosophy, it was a mode and an expression. The arts historically have been the embodiments of ways of life, of feeling and thought, in images intrinsically delightful, like the winding stairways of chateaux in France, like the aisles of a Gothic cathedral, like the cupolas of the mosques at Istanbul. The memorable periods of art have been those in which the arts through their special media transmuted and immortalized the interactions of human beings not only with the physical world but with the social and religious, the practical and the domestic aspects of their lives.

The arts have been communications through making freshly clear the phases of experience to which habit had dulled men. The fact of communication, and the significance of what and how art communicates is the burden of much of Dewey's essentially social philosophy of art. For in terms of Dewey's analysis of art as experience the usual separations of levels of the aesthetic response become meaningless. Art as communication and the nature of what it communicates cannot, he correctly points out, be understood in terms of the usual demarcations of sensuous surface, formal designs and meanings externally conveyed by material and form. The relationship of the observer (or better the participant) to the work of art is that of experience, experience with all the implications which that word has for Dewey. The same energies are called forth in the aesthetic as in all other experience, but called out in a fashion at once more direct and more pregnant, more embodied, one might almost say *in*-bodied with meaning.

The study of art as experience is the study of fused energies, but energies and tensions both physical and social. The physical statue or painting cannot be studied apart from the meaningful experience of it for it is only as experienced that it is a work of art, not merely a physical object. But art as experience is a unity and the fact of such a unity makes it impossible to suppose that somehow material, form and meaning originally separated are put together mosaically in a work of art. What is commonly called the material of a work of art is its medium, the medium of an ordered and integrated communication. What is commonly called form is the name for the ordering of energies, which includes the momentum of traditions, symbols, rites, manners, mores in the whole past of the observer.

Form in aesthetics is commonly thought of as a visual pattern, a geometric design. For Dewey form, like everything else in his analysis, is connected with energy; it is his name for the organization of energies. Form is as experienced, not something imposed on matter nor something eternal and bodiless of which matter is the incarnation. It is the name for that organization in which energies function as a work of art. Form is not to be understood as something to be contrasted with matter. Art is the name for *formed* matter, for *patterned* energies. Form is not a geometric pattern, nor is it an explicit intention separate from the work of art. It is a functioning unity, almost one might say the organic unity of a work of art. It functions to organize the energies aroused in perception. It is this organization, this dynamic order, which gives the living clarity to a work of art. Form is the Gestalt, the vital unity of the work, the ordered cumulative movement of experience. Form is the objective name of tensions held in equilibrium, resources both gathered up and resolved.

There have of late been many attempts to explain fusion in the aesthetic experience, unity in the work of art. Dewey's theory is peculiarly happy in accounting for the unity as experienced and for the unique unity in each work of art, for form in each, as realized by the participant. Dewey's own illustrations come most naturally from painting, an art for which he has peculiar sympathy, though as he somewhat sketchily indicates, music might be an even more apposite instance.

What Dewey means by form in general is best illustrated by his analysis of painting where patently form is the totality of tensions held in equilibrium, resistances overcome, by cumulative inclusion and vitalities mutually controlling and fulfilling each other. Form in the predominantly visual arts of painting and sculpture[1] does not consist simply in linear patterns, but in the total internal relationship of masses and color and line and light. What looks at first glance like the purely static relationship of lines, in the total organization of a painting is the poised relationship of several energies, the fusion of a number of processes. The notion of form as the order and equilibrium of energies accounts for what is otherwise difficult to account for in the experiences of art, the tension and expectancy, in the midst of quietude the sense of involvement and concern, as if

[1] Dewey is careful to point out how over-rigid is the conventional separation of spatial and temporal arts.

our very fate were felt in the conjunction of these lines and masses, or in these chords and melodies. Because form thus conserves the tensions it resolves, art is not a marmoreal calm; it is an edged serenity, a heightened peace.

Part of the passion involved in aesthetic experience is relatively "purely" aesthetic, that is, it has to do with the energies aroused by sheer visual or auditory arrangements. But the notion of pure art is a contradiction, as Dewey also makes clear, of the facts of human experience in the arts. Part of the poignancy of art is the overtone of human feeling, the quality as previously noted that the participant brings to his perception. The *whole* of experience of art includes what is conventionally called "expressive values" in the arts. It is usually compartmentally assumed that an object seen or heard is a vehicle for something not seen, not heard but suggested or symbolized, that the visible painting, the audible music, has a subject matter, a theme, a content.

Dewey, holding fast to the notion that experience is a whole, not compartmentalized, throws important light on the question of expressiveness in the arts, not least in his explicit treatment of the relation of substance and form. Substance and form are like sense and meaning, usually separated. There are artists and critics who have written as if each art exploited a pure and isolated sense, as if painting simply aroused and gratified the sense of seeing, as if music were only the fulfilment of a psychologically disconnected sense of hearing. Dewey is no less aware than the most puristic critic of the special quality of the medium in each art, what Pater called "the element of song in the singing," the plastic values in painting, the specifically musical character of music. But Dewey makes explicit theoretical recognition of the fact that the eye with which one sees is the eye of a human being, the ear with which one hears is the ear of a humanly involved being. "The eye, the ear, whatever is only the channel *through* which the total response takes place. A color as seen is always qualified by implicit reactions of many organs, those of the sympathetic system as well as of touch. It is a funnel for the total energy put forth, not its wellspring. Colors are sumptuous and rich just because a total organic resonance is deeply implicated in them." [*Art as Experience*, p. 244]

And not organic resonances only. One of the most suggestive features of Dewey's analysis is the way in which he expounds the part played by prior experience in shaping aesthetic perception, in qualifying the qualities of the sensuously here and now, in rendering objects perceived by the senses truly expressive. We see painting with the eye, hear music with the ear, but it is we, human beings with a past, who see and hear. "The quality of what is seen and heard varies with past experience. The scope of a work of art is measured by the number and variety of elements coming from past experience that are organically absorbed into the perceptions had here and now." The freshness of a work, the excitement, the reverberation of it in awareness is more than a merely sensory seizure; it is fusion of the past with the present. What we humanly bring to bear is sensuously embodied, and gives overtone, resonance and range to color, line, mass, volume, word, cadence, musical motif. Virgil's "tears of things" are our tears, too.

The word imagination is the favorite though vague word in aesthetic discussion. For Dewey the meaning is specific and his use of it throws light not only on art but on philosophy. Imagination operates when there is the fusion of the previously encountered and the currently perceived just noted, through an object rendered acutely and coherently vivid to the senses. This fusion mediated by a work of art, itself a subtle set of internal relations, constitutes a *new* as well as a *whole* experience. Though the poet may, the painter may, give us "the light that never was on sea or land," it is a light related to light on sea or land. But now everything is bathed in a new luminosity, in an unprecedented intensity. These perceptions are ordered into a novel design of, in some sort, familiar materials; the perceptions are fresh and what is also fresh is the quality of the light thrown on already familiar experience, the quality that the past is in this creative act made to confer upon apparently purely present colors and lines and patterns. In so far as there is spontaneity, freedom, novelty possible in experience, it is in this fusion of old and new. It is precisely the imaginative wedding of the present to the past in which creation consists. And in so far as science and philosophy are truly creative, they share this process with art, they, too, are victories of imagination and insofarforth are also art.

There is an ancient quarrel, says Plato, between poetry and philosophy. There is an almost equally ancient quarrel between those who insist that art is pure and those who insist that it is about something, between those who hold that art says only itself and those who claim that it says something about something. But the issue is an artificial one, present to the dialectics of analysis, not to the experience of art itself. The values of sense and form about which purist critics make so much ado come to the live creature in the modulations due to his past history. Lines bound objects, or express time and space relationships, or they express human situations, intensify the familiar common properties of human interaction with the world. Volume, mass and light are seen as features and phases of our general experience. The rhythms of lines or tones are expressive ordered tension, unfolding developments, familiar in life outside of art. Rhythms are the points of emphasis in a developing experience, in art rendered more perspicuous than usual, each stage toward fruition itself perceptually delightful, and yet contributing to the fulfilment of the whole. "Art is fine," Dewey puts it, "when it draws upon the material of other experiences, and expresses their materials in a medium which clarifies and intensifies its energy through the order which supervenes."

If one were to sum up Dewey's philosophy of art, one might, I think, put it thus: The arts are modes of experiencing, in which through the imaginative use of a medium, the organization of color, light, line, sound, all the resources of the arts, the liveness of the live creature is enlivened, and his liveness given a vital order through form. The arts are modes of energy which function as ways of communication. But the communication of art is something far different than conveying practical information or stating general and abstract ideas. Art communicates by celebrating the qualities of human experience. Its celebration is through the delight, at once perspicuous and vivid, of patterned energies, ordered experience. Art communicates because it renders available in clear and heightened unities the qualities of experience that are seen with absorption and heard as direct and as delightful. The special way in which art communicates is through the operation of imagination as Dewey conceives it. The arts present in each genuine (not merely academic and repetitive) instance, a new experience.

But this experience is not quite new, the forces afoot in the world as previously experienced are thrown into a fresh perspective, a novel context, lighted with an intensely strange and yet familiar light. This creation of a new experience, paradoxically enough, unites men. For whatever variations there be in personal history, human beings inhabit the same world, share the same essential human nature. The freshness of works of art helps liberate men from the routines of habit, from the conventional distinctions made for theoretical or practical reasons. It reorients men in the qualitative feel, tang, intensity and order of experience itself, not the commonplace verbal substitutes for it. By way of art men are reborn into the experience from whose vitalities they have been cut off by artificial intellectual distinctions, and by social rigidities and dogmas and by the sheer weight of routine which has caused them to neglect all qualities save those pertinent to the narrow business in hand, in physical materials organized to present perceptions.

Dewey's work is full of suggestions as to the particular arts and has hints that need development as to the ways in which the arts are varied emphases of the same human experience. He has a telling analysis of criticism in which he re-defines the function of criticism as that of enlightened and expertly sensitive discrimination. The hypotheses in science are instruments for control. But though Dewey's reflections on the arts are themselves aids to criticism and to the sharpening of perception in the arts, it may be said, I think not unjustly, that his chief contribution to aesthetics is in an important sense a philosophical one. That is to say, he has provided a fresh, empirical approach to the basic issues involved in understanding the arts, but he has shown, what is of even more importance, the implications of the experience of art for the enterprise of philosophy. Most theories of art are really exercises in epistemology. The arts are made in some degree cognitive and contemplative. Dewey, as I have tried to show, treats art simply as a fully realized experience, and it provides a unique control for the imaginative venture of philosophy.... "The significance of art for experience is unique for the adventure of philosophic thought."

For creative philosophical thinking is for Dewey a genuine adventure, and an authentic exploration. It is an act of imagination. It brings to bear the accumulated experience of the past as a tool for a liberating and fruitful use of the present. In philosophy traditional distinctions of matter and mind, the subject and the object, sense and reason, are made for special purposes in the context of a metaphysics formulated on experience dialectically conceived. Since art as experience shows best what experience is, an adequate empirical philosophy must look at what goes on in response to art, where our interactions with our environment are not broken up and dislocated. In routine daily life, we only on occasion have experience pure, clear, ordered, alive, whole. Practical urgencies, intellectual or social necessities compel us to dissect experience and then come to look upon our post-mortem chart as the colors of life. Ordinary experience is full of dead spots, made dead by routine or habit or inadequacy of technique, of distorted social arrangements or by lack of imagination.

In our ordinary activities experience is marked by distortions and dislocations, made for practical or personal, or sentimental or dialectical reasons. Passion drives us to exalt the senses as the chief quality of experience; on the other hand to the intellectual analyst all experience is essentially cognitive. There are in our society occasional orgies of sense without meaning. Among intellectuals there are orgies of abstraction without the vividness of the senses. In ordinary experience or in experience not quite fulfilled there seems to be conflict between the individual and the universal, between feeling and thought.

Only in art and modes of social life or intellectual work emulating art do we have experience whole. A work of art conveys meaning but it is meaning *embodied*. A painting is at once a moment of direct vision, a delight to the eye and a nourishment to the imagination. What is seen is delighted in, but part of the delight is the unique bodying forth of common features of human experience, the fresh presentation of the public features of the physical and social environment. The work of art is at once sensuous and meaningful, unique and universal.

The problem of the *new* has plagued philosophers. What is it, is it really possible and how? It is possible in art, and the mode of the work is the how of its possibility. In art the new and old are experienced as in a fresh fusion as one and in philosophy, too, a philosophy of experience brings to bear its heritage upon its present. An adequate philosophy of experience is one that like a work of art sees life freshly and sees it whole. Dewey's philosophy began as a revolt against those systems of thought that alleged an intellectual Absolute as the really real. There is an aesthetic Absolute in Dewey, too: experience in its integrity. But mostly in art do we find instances of such integrity, means fused with ends, medium with meaning, part with whole. Art thus becomes a measure of success in civilization and in life and in wisdom. Art offers a myriad examples of what an undistorted experience would and should be. It serves as a model of what society and life might approximate, ordered vitality, patterned energy and immediate delight. Dewey's philosophy of art is, in the deepest sense, the culmination of his moral philosophy. In art human beings achieve that intrinsic freedom which is the meaning, for Dewey, of democracy, a free society in which intelligence functions. Art is intelligibility become an immediate delight and freedom enjoyed.

Instrumentalism and the History of Philosophy

by GEORGE BOAS

IN DEWEY's long bibliography there are about twenty items which might be called historical, in the sense that they deal with the philosophies of his predecessors. There is no book or article, even including *Reconstruction in Philosophy* or *The Quest for Certainty* or the essay on Darwin's influence or the lectures on German philosophy and politics, which is simply the discovery of precisely what happened to an idea or philosophical system over a period of years. And yet his whole orientation is in a sense historical, for like Croce and Bergson, from both of whom he differs on most points, he has integrated thought into the historical processes and, unlike them and many others, he has been willing to accept the consequences of temporalized thinking. He has never, except in his youth, believed in Eternity and as a consequence he has never believed that one should turn to the past for a solution of present problems. Thus both questions and answers have dates and the notion of persistent problems of philosophy would be as foreign to his way of thinking as the notion of persistent structures of society. Perhaps the most eloquent testimony to this side of his writings is the close of his autobiographical sketch in *Contemporary American Philosophy*. "I think," he says there, "it shows a deplorable deadness of imagination to suppose that philosophy will indefinitely revolve within the scope of the problems and systems that two thousand years of European history have bequeathed to us. Seen in the long perspective of the future, the whole of western European history is a provincial episode. . . . A chief task of those who call themselves philosophers is to help get rid of the useless lumber that blocks our highways of thought, and strive to make straight and open the paths that lead to the future. Forty years spent in wandering in a wilderness like that of the present is not a sad fate—unless one attempts to make himself believe that the wilderness is after all itself the promised land."

In other words, philosophical problems like all problems turn out to be relevant to historical situations and become obsolete like instruments of manufacture. The main problem then of the historian of ideas turns into that of first discovering to what situation a man's ideas were relevant, for unless one discovers that, one has not discovered what Dewey would call the meaning of the idea. It is here that he has been most provocative and most unsatisfactory, for he has raised the question and given very little by way of answer. The challenge to the historian remains unless Dewey's theory of knowledge is refuted. But even should it be refuted, he has made it clear that no history of philosophy should be undertaken without first deciding what is the role of ideas in human history. If they are instruments, then one must know their ends, their success or failure in achieving those ends, their strange ability to survive after they have become obsolete as instruments, their charm for people who have no intention of using them, their curious way of pervading a whole society or a large portion of a society, their manner of concealing their instrumental origin, their transmutations into solving problems for which they were not devised. On most of these puzzles we have next to no information to guide us. It would be absurd to maintain that we really know how most of the ideas of the Greek philosophers were developed. Even in the case of Plato and Aristotle, whose works survive so copiously, we do not know why the former constructed his theory of ideas or what the word *Idea* meant; nor why the latter should have made his elementary distinction between matter and form. We can let our imaginations reconstruct these reasons, but whatever we may conclude will be based largely on conjecture. In Aristotle's case our conjectures will be sounder than in Plato's, because the form of his discourse is not dramatic but expository. He sets down the course of his reasoning and we can spot his assumptions as well as his inferences. In Plato's case we are always hard put to it to know when he is being dramatic and when—if ever—he is speaking *in propria persona*. We do not even know why a philosopher should have chosen the dramatic dialogue as a form of exposition. How then answer the question of what was the instrumental value of his theories?

Here Dewey has made a guess which seems plausible but which no one has ever substantiated. Ratner pointed out in his introduction to *Intelligence in the Modern World* that as early as 1897 Dewey had traced the interactions between philosophy and social economic, political and scientific movements.[1] But the tracing was at best somewhat vague and consisted in the demonstration of certain similarities between large sets of ideas. It was most convincingly made in such a work as *The Quest for Certainty* where philosophy became the rationalization of culture. Thus Plato and Aristotle were systematizers "in rational form of the content of Greek religious and artistic beliefs." "They glorified the invariant at the expense of change." They "thus diverted thought from inquiring into the purposes which experience of actual conditions suggests and from concrete means of their actualization."[2] The same theme was developed in *Reconstruction in Philosophy*, where the contrast between philosophies of eternity and those of time was set forth in simpler and less technical language. But it was not until one came to *German Philosophy and Politics*, published in 1915 during the first World War, that any detailed account of the relationship between philosophical and other ideas was given. After quoting Heine (p. 76) to the effect that nations have "an instinctive presentiment of what they require to fulfill their missions," he later lets it appear that by "nations" he really means "social structures," for one finds him saying (p. 127 f.) "If an *a priori* philosophy has worked at all in Germany, it is because it has been based on an *a priori* social constitution—that is to say, on a state whose organization is such as to determine in advance the main activities of classes

---

[1] Ratner is referring (*Op. cit.* p. 11) to Dewey's essay on the significance of the problem of knowledge, later republished in *The Influence of Darwin on Philosophy* (1910).
[2] *The Quest for Certainty*, pp. 16 ff.

of individuals, and to utilize their particular activities by linking them up with one another in definite ways." But such an *a priori* social constitution might seem to exist also in both the United States and in the France of the Third Republic, in neither of which countries has the *a priori* type of philosophy been popular. Here again then, in spite of the greater detail of his argument, the exact relationship between philosophy and society has not been set forth and the program remains unfulfilled.

What Dewey has called the anthropological attitude towards the history of philosophy is one which the present writer, if he understands it, finds to his taste. He is also agreed in general upon the instrumental value of ideas in their origin, that is, that they arise as solutions to specific problems and that problems are by nature observed deviations from the rule. But two problems are to be noticed in this field which have not attracted so much attention as they would appear to deserve. (1) How much deviation is required to create a new problem? (2) Why do old solutions to problems persist?

In regard to the former of these questions, it is to be noted that a temporalist must admit the novelty of each event as it occurs, not merely its novelty as a new individual happening, but also qualitative novelty. Existential novelty would be admitted without argument; qualitative will demand substantiation. Just what substantiation will prove conclusive is questionable, but we submit the following as plausible, though clearly unsatisfactory to those who demand *a priori* apodeictic certainties. If one takes large social events of the type that appear in books of history, wars, revolutions, reigns, and so on, it will be granted that their individual characteristics are fairly well marked and that the common nouns and adjectives which name and describe them are accurate only to a very vague degree. Similarly individual biographies will be granted to have a high degree of specificity, though possibly the grosser chemical constitutions of the individuals concerned will be on the whole identical. Animals and plants seem fairly regular in their behavior to people who have not been intimately associated with them and generalizations about them seem less faulty; though the person who has trained dogs or horses or even raised vegetables on a farm knows that their individualities become almost as marked as those of the farmers who raise them. It has, however, been pretty widely believed that sooner or later one will arrive at qualitative elements, sometimes called sensory data, which will be all alike and which can be accurately named by the usual adjectives, like red, green, and blue. But here again, what will become an individual sensory datum will vary with the observer's powers of discrimination and a little experimentation will, I think, show that qualitative similarities are produced by the deliberate—or unconscious—neglect of qualitative differences. Any painter or decorator discriminates between visual data which seem identical to others; he also knows that a given pigment will vary qualitatively in relation to its background or associated pigments. Qualitative simplicity is as much determined by the observer as by the so-called objective stimulus which is supposedly being observed.[3] Aside from any original endowment of various observers, there is undoubtedly a pragmatic element of interest involved, which orients the observer's eye to qualitative differences which other people do not see. The total epistemological situation then is not simply a two-term relationship between observer and stimulus or object, but a situation in which the pragmatic interest, as well as the medium of observation and the environmental atmosphere are integrated. It has been shown to be possible to purify situations in laboratories to the point where to all intents and purposes two experiences are qualitatively identical. But the fighting words in this context are "to all intents and purposes," and the question remains unanswered of how much difference is a real difference, important enough to create a new problem.

The history of knowledge proves one thing above all in this connection and that is that the most minute deviations from the rule may sometimes give rise to the most startling scientific innovations.

[3] During the second World War it was my good fortune to interrogate a prisoner who had been used by the Nazis to forge Allied currency. He was presumably an expert engraver and thus able to produce bank-notes which most people would think to be perfect imitations. Yet he maintained that if he were shown two or more counterfeit five pound or dollar notes, he could unhesitatingly pick out those made from plates which he had engraved.

One need only cite the case of the perihelion of Mercury, or that of the variations within organic species to demonstrate this. The former had been observed at least as early as 1845 by Leverrier, the latter by Lamarck. Neither case would seem very important to the layman and yet both instigated new theories which have changed the course not only of the relevant sciences but of many related sciences, not to speak of popular thinking. Dewey's comment on all this would be that of his Howison lecture, namely that "experience" is the name usually given to "the least inclusive context."[4] In the context of the kitchen, the variation in the markings of chickens may rightly pass unnoticed and similarly in the context of high school classes in astronomy one may glide over the irregularity in the secular perihelion of Mercury. Similarly the Japanese may have forty-odd words for "rice," and one for "beef." Ambiguity is a phenomenon to be noticed not merely by lexicographers but also by epistemologists, for sometimes, if not always, it indicates a wilful refusal to name differences even where they can be clearly seen. For sometimes, in spite of obvious differences, it becomes desirable to dig out a fundamental unity, as it will be called, out of apparent diversity. The desire in that case usually rises from sentiment. This all boils down to the possibility that elemental qualities common to existential plurality are constructed for a purpose in a certain context and are the elements out of which all experience is compounded.

If this is so, then the rule from which deviations are to be noted is simply the accepted order, the laws or theories inherited from the past which, when true, are true only in the set of relations in which they are formulated. It would then be one of the essential tasks of the historian of philosophy to attempt the discovery of the contexts in which these theories were first elaborated. There is no denying the fact that the social scene as a whole is not to be neglected in the performance of this task, but that amounts to little more than saying that philosophers do not float in the stratosphere but are human beings. For just as there is no such thing as philosophy divorced

[4] *Context and Thought,* University of California Publications in Philosophy, XII, no. 3 (1931), p. 222.

from life—but life includes philosophy—so there is no such thing as society divorced from the people who compose it. Among such people are philosophers. And though some philosophers are still thinking as if they lived in what they believe to be fifth century Athens—which they usually call Greece—most philosophers are aware of the peculiar problems of their time and always have been. If one is to say that something called social conditions determines or even influences to some degree the formulation, to say nothing of the entire meaning, of philosophies, then there must be some definition of "social conditions" which does not include philosophizing, schools, universities, journals, and conversation. But can one imagine Athens without its Sophists, the Academy, the Lyceum, the Stoa, the Areopagus; Alexandria without the Library; thirteenth century Paris without its monastic orders, its churches, its university? These institutions are as much an integral part of the societies in which they are located as are the form of government, the tools of production, the menus of the people, or the architecture. It would seem then to follow that a selected set of social conditions, as orthodox Marxists used to say, determines all the others without receiving in turn a reciprocal set of influences. But orthodox Marxists, including Engels, soon admitted their myopia and the need for granting on occasions—otherwise, alas, undefined—that ideas might change the selected set of social conditions.[5]

One is driven from a literally organismic theory of society to a conception by which social groups are loosely related to one another, to a notion which would probably be called nowadays a pluralistic theory of society. Society from this point of view seems to be a collection of groups which are sometimes in conflict, sometimes in harmony, and whose members indeed are not exclusively of any one group. Thus a professor of philosophy in the United States may be a Roman Catholic and yet teach in a secular institution; he will find that certain of his interests are in conflict with others. No one so far has prohibited the teaching of Thomism in a secular university in spite of the fact that a Thomist would be hard put to it to absorb into his system such theories as statistical

[5] I refer of course to Engels' famous letter to Bloch.

mechanics or evolutionistic biology. (I do not say that he could not absorb them, for I do not know whether he could or not.) Were he convinced both of the desirability of the statistical method in science and of the syllogistic method in logic, he would perforce be in a state of conflict or would elaborate a doctrine of twofold truth. But it is precisely such conflicts which at times have been most fertile in new philosophic theories. It seems likely that among the social conditions which gave rise to Platonism were the existence of Sophistry and the *Dissoi Logoi,* as in 1949 the prevalence of neo-authoritarianism is in part explicable as a reaction against relativistic value-theory. Sophistry, to be sure, was part of the social scene, as relativistic value-theory is now, but it was not the entire social scene. Moreover, though Sophistry responded in all probability to a definite need of Athenians, it was an intellectual discipline and only by metaphor a political and economic discipline. So when historians come to speak of middle twentieth century American philosophies, they may very well attribute their diversity to the various ways in which Americans earn their livings—industry, agriculture, and so on—and they may continue to speak, as some of our contemporaries do, of our intellectual confusion. The confusion lies more in the minds of those who believe that a multiplicity of beliefs is an evil or an anomaly than in the minds of the various people who hold those beliefs. A first year graduate student may be confused when he listens to the lectures of his various professors who disagree about epistemological dualism or the relation of logic to fact. But the individual professors are no more confused than a dog is when he sees a horse grazing. Only a latter-day Xenophanes could adequately summarize the philosophies of such animals, but it is safe to say that the carnivore at most shrugs his shoulders in amused tolerance at the dietary preferences of the horse. Philosophic sects and schools do not differ quite so much as carnivore and herbivore nor do the differences which exist arise from the same causes. But the contempt, despair, or amazement which is variously expressed by our critics at the sight of our diversity of beliefs arises simply from refusing to think of society as a collection of people and instead thinking of it as a single individual.

A pluralistic conception of society would deter one from such popular generalizations as an Industrial Society, an Agricultural Society, an Urban Society, and so on. These terms at most indicate kinds of living which are modal, but not pervasive. The United States, though heavily industrialized, nevertheless has a very powerful agricultural bloc in Congress and in fact there are almost as many people employed in government, federal, state, and municipal, as in agriculture. But the number of people in a given field of work is no index of political or social or intellectual power. The number of people employed in mining and marketing silver must be very small in comparison with those employed in other industries, but the silver bloc nevertheless has succeeded in passing legislation whose effect on world economy has been very great. Again the so-called commission merchant in market cities produces no food and is not a numerous tribe, but he controls to a very great extent nevertheless the price of foodstuffs brought to him for sale by the farmer.[6] Even if one moves to a larger context and maintains that there the pattern of American culture is that of a competitive capitalistic society, the generalization must be tempered by the observation of protective tariffs, federal supervision and control of interstate traffic, the suppression of inventions by the purchase of patents, and covert agreements to maintain prices. Is one then to say that the current state of American philosophy is a reflection of the diversity of American "life"? We simply do not know how complex or simple American philosophy is. All we know of it is what appears in the philosophical journals and books which have the good luck to be published. From personal observation, which is confessedly unreliable, one might imagine that American instruction in philosophy is more standardized than in other countries largely because of the activity of text-book publishers and the desire of professors to increase their inadequate incomes by writing texts. It would be admitted, one guesses, by everyone acquainted with philosophy in France that French philosophy is more diversified than

[6] For instance, at the end of August 1949 when sugar corn was retailing at fifty-one cents a dozen in Baltimore, farmers were told by the commission merchants in that city that there was no market for it and were consequently forced either to throw theirs away or cart it back to their farms and feed it to their hogs.

ours. And yet the French as a whole might be thought of as more standardized in their way of life than we are, being even today largely agricultural, largely Roman Catholic, small property owners, and of a homogeneous cultural tradition. There is no need to push this discussion further, however, for it is fruitless.

It is fruitless because, though philosophy springs up as an answer to vital questions, no answer is simply a reflection of anything. If Descartes invented—or discovered—analytical geometry, that was indeed because he had the leisure to do so, but it was not a reflection of his leisure; it was a reflection of, if anything, his extraordinary intelligence. Even if a problem arises in a social context, such as the problem of free will, that does not mean that everyone faced with the problem will see it. We are too ignorant of why some people see problems and others do not to answer this particular question and until we know more about the processes of the creative intelligence, histories of philosophy will have lacunæ at exactly this point. Neither Dewey nor his predecessors have ever tackled this puzzle, nor do I pretend to say why. But one may guess that it is a problem only if one assumes *a priori* that *The Reason* is homogeneous, completely incorporate in all human beings, and operating through contemplation of eternal essences. But that is scarcely a tenet of the pragmatic schools. It was a problem for Plato, and one which he faced, or at least one which he formulated. But as soon as epistemology and logic became associated with psychology and anthropology, it ceased to be a problem.

This takes us to the second of our questions, the persistence of obsolete solutions. Since a solution is always the solution of a specific question, and since a question is raised in a specific context, or in what Dewey would call a problematic situation, as soon as the situation changes, one might expect that people confronted by it would change their minds to meet its challenge. But the fact is that they do not. There are so many obsolete methods of meeting the most concrete problems of today that one is embarrassed to know which examples to choose. But at the risk of being too obvious, let us illustrate the matter from the field of economics. All along the Atlantic seaboard from Maine to Georgia there are small farmers who are carrying on independent and non-cooperative farming. The cost of farm labor is such that in order to make any profit, they should farm by machinery. But the capital investment required to purchase tractors and tractor ploughs, harrows, manure spreaders, rakes, hay loaders, threshers or combines, is such that no individual farmer can afford them. Consequently he continues to farm as his grandfather did and is at the mercy of every accident that happens, as well as of the length of time it takes him as a single individual to plant, cultivate, and harvest. It would not be impossible—except psychologically—for a group of farmers with adjoining land to buy the needed machinery together and thus to obviate the failures which are a steady recurrence. But the small scale farmer prefers to resign himself to these accidents in the hope that he may have better luck than his neighbors and, one suspects, that he may have the pleasure of gloating over his neighbor's bad luck on some future date, for like Lucretius' man on the shore watching some poor devil struggling for his life in the waves, there is nothing that a peasant enjoys more than the misfortunes of others. That is the compensation for his own bad luck. He continues therefore to employ old methods of agriculture and accepts failures as the rule and success as a God-given reward for his Job-like patience. He has retained from his forbears a notion which is ethical, not agricultural, of self-dependence, a form of that rugged individualism which successful men always preach to others. He is thus in a state of conflict: the conflict between his ethical notions and the economic situation. He has in effect refused to make the necessary abstraction which would separate growing food from building character, and, like a hero in a Greek tragedy, has to make a choice between conflicting ends. (That there might be some ethical value in co-operation does not of course occur to him; whence could it arise?) He is so exhausted at night that he does not read the papers or magazines, and hence has no idea of how large scale farming is carried on; he has no idea of how prices are fixed; and were one to intimate to him that he might solve his economic problem in some new way, one would be looked upon as a dangerous radical. He is in the situation of Fabre's dung-beetle which wore herself out trying to surmount a little obstacle lying in her path rather than walk around it.

This is an illustration of the survival of obsolete solutions where a conflict of values occurs. One sees it in many other contexts. No one denies, for instance, not even the Catholic Church, that too many children are being born. It is very easy to solve the problem by announcing that the way to prevent the birth of too many children is by not begetting so many, and even an imbecile would agree. But the real problem—and by "real" one means "practical"—is that of means, not of ends, and it is at this point that the conflict arises. When the Church preaches continence, it is very easy to denounce it as old-fashioned, obscurantistic, and so on, but that overlooks the actual fact that here again is a strife of doctrine, the strife between certain religious beliefs and certain social beliefs. In such cases, we are maintaining, there is no reconciliation; one must choose. The choice will inevitably lead to the abandonment of one of the alternatives. The Church's argument rests on Scripture and tradition; the argument of the believer in the usual methods of birth control cannot and will not accept these arguments. We no longer know what problem gave rise to the Scriptural doctrine (though anthropology might give one a clue); and the Church to be sure would add to our difficulties by declaring that it was not due to any problem but was a divine command. But if we assume the naturalistic attitude, we should be forced to conclude that it was not a solution to our present problem, which is that of over-population. It survives, however, as a solution to a religious problem which in the long run is that of making human desires conform to God's commands.

But there are times when the choice of solutions lies less within the power of the individual, though I am far from denying the influence of the group on the two solutions already mentioned. One of the problems now troubling Western man is that involved in the existence of national sovereignty. The modern European nation is an outgrowth of feudalism and represents the agglomeration of fiefs under more and more powerful overlords. It arose as the result of military and economic force and served purposes far beyond those for which it was presumably invented. For once the modern nation was stabilized, it gave its citizens security of a sort and all the blessings of security. So much cannot be denied it. But though the King or Emperor brought peace within his lands, he did not maintain peace with other kings or emperors and the tradition of international warfare has continued even after personal sovereigns disappeared. At the present moment, the hundred and fifty years of anti-nationalistic propaganda are beginning to bear fruit and the issue between national sovereignty and international government has been moved outside the walls of the study into the sphere of practical politics. If one may judge from private conversation and some of the public opinion polls, the majority of individuals would prefer peace and the loss of national sovereignty to national sovereignty and warfare. But that is not true of those individuals who have the power of decision and of some individuals who sincerely believe in warfare as a means of developing certain ethical virtues and of keeping the population down—to say nothing of those few who still see in it a chance of increasing their incomes. Here a solution is forced on the individual by his government, which has the power to conscript him and to imprison him if he makes the wrong choice.

This is analogous to the survival of philosophic doctrines which are preserved in schools and sanctified by authority. The initiate does not formulate his own problems, for he is not even aware of them. In the United States he is taught through the medium of a textbook which has the problems all formulated and gives the correct solutions as well. It is similar to instruction in elementary chemistry, where the student performs other people's experiments and seldom, if ever, has to invent an experiment of his own. But one gathers that the same sort of thing has always happened in the history of philosophy. It is next to impossible to discover what instruction was like in the Academy, but in the Lyceum it apparently took the form of lectures in which the teacher both formulated and answered the problem. Judging from the literary structure of the *Enneads,* one would say that the same was true of Plotinus' teaching methods, though it may be that the questions which open the various chapters were submitted to him by his pupils. The answers in any event were his. But beginning with Philo, if Wolfson is right, we have philosophy turning into the exegesis of a sacred text. Here the problem becomes not the solution of a difficulty of action, but of interpretation. For it is clearly quite different to ask, What ought I to do? and to ask, What does this mean? The Philonic tradition, as carried through the Middle Ages, removed answers from the realm of time and put them into the realm of eternity. Philosophy thus became like geometry and the terms it used lost their relevance to history. They became abstract counters which were inter-related by logical consistency and never had to be submitted to the tests of verification. It was small wonder that natural science divagated more and more from metaphysics.

Any obsolete science could still be discussed in this manner, were there any interest in so discussing it. Astrology, which still survives in some culture-areas, alchemy, humoralistic medicine, were not unorganized collections of ideas, but highly systematized theorems. Their weakness was not inconsistency, but inapplicability. Yet, were there any supposed practical benefit to be derived from them, including that of religious conformism or ethical edification, there can be little doubt that we should still be giving courses in our universities which would explain among other things why twins do not always have the same fate though born under the same star, and on the anatomy of melancholy. But many a philosophical theorem is as obsolete and is still seriously discussed. There must be thousands of young people in this country who hear lectures on essence and accidents, substance and attributes, the One and the Many, and, for all I know, on the infinite divisibility of matter. But it will also be noticed that such subjects are treated by philosophers whose main interest is religious and who believe metaphysics to be a kind of religion without sentiment. There is no propulsive force which sends one from the causal law to the problem of free will, but once one has accepted the existence of free will, the existence of the causal law presents a problem. Similarly there was no inevitable logical passage in Descartes's *Discourse* from the proof of his own existence to that of God, but having never doubted the existence of

God, he naturally set out to find reasons for his belief in it. In this type of situation an obsolete problem survives in a factitious manner: one holds a prior belief and then has to reconcile it with beliefs arising from discovery. This kind of philosophizing consists in the main—for nothing is *purely* any one thing—of making diverse ideas originating in various fields consistent. The technique of making them consistent must perforce have recourse to widening the contexts involved until one finally arrives at something which will be called pure being.

It was maintained by Jouffroy and later by James that philosophy consists of the unsolved problems of mankind. It would be fairer to say that it also consists of obsolescent problems. This sounds, to be sure, like a cheap form of satire, but if it be true that problems arise in contexts and are relevant only to those contexts, then when contexts change new problems arise which cannot be solved by old solutions. One way of disregarding change in contexts is by enlarging the scope of one's inquiries, passing, for instance, from the individual to the class and from there to more and more inclusive classes. But that is precisely what happens in philosophy. When a philosopher begins to study the problems of Mankind-as-a-whole, what he can say about them is so vague that it amounts to little more than tautologous statements whose nature is concealed by their verbal form. No one could object to analytic judgments in which the predicate actually informs one's readers about the meaning of the subject-term. But it is one thing to inform one's readers about the meaning of a term and another to talk about the things which the term names. The great weakness of ethical treatises is their dependence on such analytic statements. An individual who is faced with a specific ethical problem can find little help in such formulations as, *Man is a rational animal,* or even, *Man is the vehicle of the collective unconscious.* What he wants to know is whether he should enlist in the Army or wait to be drafted, whether he should resign his job and go to college or stay home and help support his family, whether he should be courteous and lie or tell the truth and hurt someone's feelings. His solutions can, to be sure, be pushed back rationally to certain basic principles, but every

Freshman who has taken Logic I knows that a given proposition can be deduced from a large variety of premises, so that the basic principles in the long run are logically indifferent, however important they may be psychologically. A given ethical conclusion can be deduced from a kind of Neo-Darwinism, from the ethics of self-realization, from simple altruism, from utilitarianism, from quietism, and so on. For a man may decide to enlist in the Army because he believes that men are inherently combative and the weaker will go to the wall, that by fighting he will achieve an integration of his partial self into the larger self of the community, that military service will permit him to sacrifice himself for others, that it is the most pleasant form of life, that he must resign himself to the greater power of the government and do what he is told. The philosophic problem then becomes not that of enlisting or not enlisting but that of finding premises from which he can rationally justify his choice, and that in turn becomes the problem of choosing that set of premises which—for reasons of which he is often, in fact usually, unaware—seems most honorable, decent, noble, or perhaps pleasant. No one could really make a choice of action through deduction from premises, but he could be educated to believe in the sanctity of certain principles and to cite them automatically when he has made his choice. To rationalize one's choices on the basis of Neo-Darwinism aligns one with a group of people with whom one may not wish to be aligned. To rationalize them on the basis of simple patriotism immediately throws one into a group with whom one may feel more at home. But these are psychological, not logical, motivations. It is at best questionable whether the Government cares in time of war whether a man enlists from patriotism or from quietism; it wants soldiers. So long as two philosophies give identical results, the Government will be philosophically neutral. It overlooks the psychological fact that the soldier who enlists from patriotism may act in one way and that his quietist comrade may act in another, once they are in uniform. For no ethical theory was ever exclusively concerned with one simple act or type of act.

Such philosophies serve not only the useful purpose of giving our beliefs some rational structure, but also bind us together into schools and groups. Anthropologists will sympathize with this and accept it as a normal enough phenomenon. The yearning which we have had in the West to associate with others in everything we do—not merely in thinking—is common enough to cause no surprise. It is of course true that even here, as everywhere else, there have been recalcitrant individuals who have fled from association, who have tried to be hermits, as Descartes gave every appearance of doing as he warmed himself by the stove in Neuberg. But Descartes, like the rest of us, was so closely integrated into an intellectual society that he was quite unconscious of his dependence upon it. If an historian of philosophy would really try to understand the progress of thought, he would give particular attention to the texts of such thinkers and see what they actually took for granted. He would then discover a set of notions which seemed so obvious that they required no investigation whatsoever and gave rise to no doubts.[7] Descartes, for instance, could be interpreted as either a continuator of scholasticism or as a great innovator and both interpretations could be justified. Certainly no one in the seventeenth century, not even the Church, thought of him as a traditionalist, regardless of his scholastic assumptions, his three dreams, or his repeated professions of faith in Catholicism. He himself believed that he had discovered a new method of philosophizing and new doctrines of philosophy. Nor can it be denied that his influence was on the side of innovation rather than on that of tradition. What he demonstrated to the instrumentalist historian of philosophy was the obsoleteness of certain scholastic principles as solutions to problems, for on their basis one could arrive either at Cartesianism or Thomism, terms which, we admit, are vague but at least suggestive.

Even the most original and vehemently rebellious of thinkers is associated with his predecessors. Even Whitehead, whose vocabu-

---

[7] A thorough study of what have been called the protophilosophies of the pivotal thinkers of Europe has yet to be made and could be made only by someone with many years of undisturbed work ahead of him. We have tried to indicate what must be done in studies of the presuppositions of Aristotle (*American Journal of Philology*, Vols. LV [1934], pp. 36 ff., LVII [1936], pp. 24 ff., LVIII [1937], pp. 275 ff., LXIV [1943], pp. 172 ff., LXVIII [1947], pp. 404 ff.). See also *Journal of Philosophy*, XLV (1948), pp. 673 ff.

lary is so largely of his own invention, nevertheless has suggested to some readers the influence of Plato, Hegel, Bergson, and others.[8] A man perforce, if he tries to make his ideas intelligible, either to others or to himself, must use words and phrases which convey certain inferences or suggestions to his readers as well as to himself. Moreover, there is always a residue of one's conversations and readings in one's thoughts of which one is not always aware. Whitehead, whom I cite because of his undoubted originality and the peculiarity of his terminology, though he accepted process as real, nevertheless could explain the recurrence of events only on the basis of what he called eternal objects. Granting the words, the idea behind them is clearly Platonistic, as Platonistic as Santayana's essences. A man with Whitehead's great ingenuity did not choose that idea from either perversity or stupidity. It must have seemed reasonable to him as the best solution of his problem. Yet if one is to accept the reality of process sincerely, one need have no recourse to eternity whatsoever. This is not the place to argue with our predecessors, but after all if events have temporal dimensions, then one must make the best of it and nothing can be literally reproduced. If one accepts the subsistence of eternal objects, then one has bifurcated nature—or the cosmos—into the temporal and the eternal and such bifurcation is no better—and no worse—than any other. Moreover, an eternal object enters and leaves the time-stream, undergoes change and ceases to be eternal. But such considerations could not have worried Whitehead to any great extent, since he kept his eternal objects and used them as an explanatory device. One cannot now answer the question of why he did this, except in the sense that one can state the function which they performed in his system. But one can surmise that with neutral entities, subsistent *Annahmen,* sense-data, and essences in the ambient atmosphere, it seemed reasonable enough that eternal objects might join them and one's metaphysics be none the worse.

Here if anywhere is evidence of a perennial philosophy which, like a perennial plant, finally deteriorates and dies. If by perennial

[8] But see Victor Lowe's "The Influence of Bergson, James and Alexander on Whitehead," *Journal of the History of Ideas,* X (1949), pp. 267 ff.

one means everlasting, then no philosophy is perennial. For the perennial philosophy of the Scholastics was only metaphorically in the minds of the ancients and what is common to all Catholic philosophers is their religious faith, not their metaphysical theorems. Yet certain philosophic tenets, both doctrinal and methodological, do last for many years, and it is a fair assumption that some people in 1949 still reason like Milesians about the structure and substance of the universe. Some of these people do this through ignorance of anything else, others through choice. I do not know why the latter situation should prevail, but in thought as in art everything seems to survive somewhere. One can call this the inertia of custom, compulsive as all inertia is. An example of such survival is what might be called the Empedoclean analysis of change, according to which all change is thought of as the action of an agent upon a patient. This seems to imply that nothing would change "of its own accord," and that in every change a cause must be sought which will be external to the event. This analysis is one of the oldest preconceptions of Western thought; and yet it will not work except in cases where one has an easily distinguishable set of phenomena, like the human body, or gross lumps of matter like billiard balls. It becomes absurdly metaphorical where change occurs within a system or when there is purposive action or, for that matter, in any vectorial situation. Yet the survival of the Empedoclean analysis of change is neither to be denied nor to be ridiculed. It survives as an antiquated vocabulary survives, as when we speak of spirited horses or phlegmatic people or the highest values or immortal poems or the deepest insights or improper fractions or chemical affinities or water seeking its own level. These are phrases which are to all intents and purposes self-explanatory, unquestionable, self-evident in their intention. Another example of such survivals is what Theophrastus called the likeness-theory of cognition, according to which the subject and object of knowledge must resemble each other. We find this used as late as Bergson in his *Introduction to Metaphysics,* where he says that it is inconceivable for a static instrument of cognition to know the dynamic. Again, at the risk of vulgar burlesque, let us suggest that one can usually spot such survivals when the philosopher raises the rhetorical question, "Can one conceive. . .?" Most of such impossible conceptions are not logically but psychologically impossible. That a quantum of energy can appear here and there without traversing the intervening space is inconceivable only if one has already accepted the behavior of gross material objects as standard. So too it is inconceivable that changes occur without there being something to undergo the change, only if we make the Galilean object or substance the standard.

I see no way of an Instrumentalist's answering the question of why obsolete ideas survive except anthropologically. We see the same thing happening in social institutions and in the arts, where things which are known to have been invented as instruments towards the attainment of definite ends remain as objects endowed with inherent—or terminal—values, turning into ends themselves. The importance of an idea, which term here covers systems or clusters of ideas loosely associated, is not to be measured by its truth, for there is no way of determining the truth of primitive ideas. It is rather to be measured in terms of its "significance." For even the most abstract of our ideas are invested with an emotional aura, their metaphysical pathos, as Lovejoy has called it, which attracts us to them as objects of love or worship. One scarcely knows the proper domain of such ideas, whether they be scientific, ethical, or religious.[9] The suspicion arises that here the relation between philosophy and the fine arts is particularly close. It has been proposed by some writers to attribute the quality of truth even to pictures and, one is astonished to find, to music. In that sense of the word, one might imagine that a set of metaphysical postulates might also be true and would survive as the Sphinx and the ruins of the Parthenon have survived, not because anyone could possibly verify them, but because they are so moving.

Whatever the answer, the historian of philosophy has to take account of such things. He must perceive with the most delicate attention what ideas persist through history and not merely record the innovations of philosophers. For if he discovers nothing else, he will have seen the background against which innovations have been

---

[9] See W. P. Montague, *The Ways of Knowing*, p. 225.

erected, and will thus understand more precisely why the innovations seemed important. He will also see why it seemed important to the traditionalists to combat them. We know of very few, if any, philosophers who have had only one idea, and yet the histories of philosophy present most of them as if they had never had more than one. Thus Locke becomes something known as an empiricist, Berkeley a subjective idealist, Hume a phenomenalist, and so on. But it is far from certain that either in their own eyes or in those of their contemporaries epistemological views were the most important. The selection of their epistemologies out of their total writings was made originally, in all probability, in order to organize the history of philosophy into certain contrasting schools with sharp antitheses between their basic tenets. The result might be an extraordinary deformation of the total thought of a man, and in Locke's case, as Lovejoy has shown, even a deformation of his epistemology. Such deformation is by no means inevitable and it goes without saying that one cannot discuss at one time—or in one sentence—a man's total philosophy, even when he has one. It is essential, if one wishes to talk sense, to analyze and sort out a person's ideas on the great variety of problems with which he has been concerned. Those which one selects for discussion may not be those by which he was most troubled. The utility of Dewey's attitude towards ideas of the past is in the question which it constantly raises: just what problem of his time was he trying to solve? He has perhaps overemphasized the social relations of ideas, and seems to have emphasized man's preoccupation with problems involved in them to the exclusion of others. Yet there is nothing inherent in instrumentalism which would deny the utility of ideas to other ends. A man may organize his thoughts into a logical system for the sheer aesthetic pleasure of contemplating formal organization. Indeed the *Quest for Certainty* dwells upon such pleasure at great length. But it is also true that Dewey in that book as elsewhere seems to presuppose a correlation between such pleasure and certain social conditions. He writes as if such values were the special prerogatives of the members of a leisure class. If he was arguing that only members of such a class would desire certainty, or that philosophies of certainty were a "reflection" of a society based on the labor of slaves, then he could easily be shown to be wrong. But if he was talking history and pointing out that probability has increasingly taken the place of certainty as the experimental method in science gained ground, and that the experimental method gained ground as men began to replace the ideal of contemplation by that of control over nature, and that finally that substitution took place in the period of explorations and discoveries, which gave the discoverers and their patrons solid financial returns, which returns in time remade society, then he was right. But the quest for certainty has no more died out than the belief in lucky numbers has died out and modern society is as stratified in its beliefs as it is in its methods of production.

These are indeed many words about a few sentences. They are evoked not so much by what Dewey has said as by what he has not said. An Instrumentalistic history of philosophy has yet to be written. It would have to tackle the following problems before any others: (1) the specific end which a philosophic solution was devised to attain; (2) the possibility of a given solution's being used for a variety of ends; (3) the survival of obsolete questions and answers; (4) the rise of the terminal value of obsolescent ideas. Like all genuine histories, and by "genuine" I mean histories which accept the reality of change and do not attempt to explain it away, it would have to detect as far as is possible the causes of the changes which have taken place, only some of which are logical inferences. For even logical inference is guided by non-logical motivation. It would be wiser to frame a broader definition of "social" than is usually proffered, so that society would not be a non-rational animal. Finally it would utilize the tensions and conflicts between men to explain how they think and not merely base its conclusions on periods and ages and times which are supposed to be homogeneous. Whether Dewey would agree to this, I do not know. But that he could agree without doing violence to the general course of his thinking, is probable.

Culture and Personality

The psychocultural approach to a democratic social order

by LAWRENCE K. FRANK

THE MAJOR contribution one can make in any field of endeavor is to prepare the way for his successor. The genesis of all new developments is in the critical, reflective and creative thinking of the gifted individuals who are able to free themselves, in part at least, from their coercive traditions and to make new assumptions and develop new methods and techniques of inquiry. But such gifted individuals in these explorations, in the very act of rejecting traditional beliefs in the area of their concern, are also being guided and encouraged by the tradition of critical thinking and of creative courageous exploration that is the most significant pattern in our Western culture.

John Dewey exemplifies the foregoing as few others have ever done. In his early *Essays in Experimental Logic,* written at or before the turn of the century, he indicated the new ways of thinking which are making possible new and promising approaches to contemporary problems, as sketched in the following pages.

To understand man and his social order we may today utilize the psychocultural approach which operates with a conception of culture (spelled with a small c) and of personality. This conception derives from the findings and interpretations of anthropology, sociology, social psychology and the arts to illuminate our understanding of culture, and from psychiatry, especially psychoanalysis and clinical psychology, to provide insights into personality development and expression.

Combining these new understandings gives a dynamic conception of the circular processes which produce personalities who in turn maintain the culture and perpetuate the traditions which constitute a culture. Like all ongoing circular processes, it is self-regulating and self-perpetuating but cannot be directly observed. The process and the circularity, however, may be inferred from the operation of culture and of personality, as revealed in their varied products.

Not being a "cause and effect" relationship, the culture-personality process cannot be fractionated into antecedent and the consequent or variables that can be isolated for experimental manipulation. The process must be viewed in its circularity and approached at whatever stage in the cycle may offer an advantageous beginning for its study and description.

Looking, then, at the cultural aspect of the process, it is possible to make a number of assertions for which there is cumulative evidence to support these inferences.

Thus, we may say that man is unique among all other organisms in having escaped the coercion of organic differentiation and bodily differentiation through which other organisms adapted to and become dependent upon the life zones of their environment. Early in his career, man undertook to create a human way of living, relying, not upon organic adaptation to the environment, but upon ideas and tools whereby he could develop uniquely human ways of living. With his large brain and capacity for speech and with his skilful hands man could learn to act toward the world *selectively* and purposefully, in terms of ideas and conceptions which he created and imputed to, or imposed upon, nature and man; thereby he could discriminate among the many events and ongoing processes of the environment.

This capacity for developing ideas and symbolic conduct made it possible for man to develop orderly purposive conduct as a response to the meanings and the valuations he put upon situations in accordance with his assumptions about nature and man.

Purposive conduct arises when the individual responds, not by organic impulse or naive reaction to the immediate situation, but acts toward the present, immediate situation as instrumental to a future situation. This involves two learned activities: investing situations with meaning, as signs or symbols of their significance in the sequence of events leading to the future; and responding in the pattern of learned conduct which is addressed to that situation as the antecedent to the goal or purpose he is striving to reach. Needless to say, all such learned conduct is predicated upon all the beliefs and assumptions of the individual's cultural background and is the product of his life experience.

Unless we reflect upon this, we may not grasp the implications of this process, especially since it conflicts with the intellectual and theological traditions that so have so largely guided our thinking.

The cultural situation arises when a human organism, with all his functional needs and capacities derived from his mammalian ancestry, learns to impute meanings to the environment and to his fellows and then transforms his functional processes and naive impulses into purposeful conduct oriented to the meaningful situation which he himself has created by investing it with such meaning.

This apparently is what each group of people did in the early days of their cultural development. No one knows or can ever find out how and when the process started, but seemingly it began with the attempt to meet the persistent problems of life more purposefully and effectively than was possible through impulse and naive reactions to events. These problems have faced man from his earliest days and will confront him as long as he exists.

The human problems of life may be described as involving, among others, these, basic tasks:

(1) Coming to terms with the environment and developing a systematic way of obtaining food, shelter, security, especially for the family, during pregnancy and infancy of the human;

(2) Developing and maintaining some kind of group living in which cooperation and division of labor (especially between the sexes) and security of person could be established.

(3) Regulating human behavior and transforming it into the orderly purposeful conduct necessary for social order and the achievement of these tasks.

To meet these problems without paying the price of organic adaptation, man kept his own organism plastic and undifferentiated, while organizing the environment and patterning his thinking, acting, and feeling for living in the organized environment that he himself created and dealt with by his ideas, his learned conduct and his tools and weapons.

Again, it is clear that we cannot ever know how this process began but it seems clear that early man began the process of culture building and its perpetuation by acting upon certain assumptions. Out of the multitudinous events and bewildering, often hazardous, activities surrounding him, man selectively perceived the environment according to the assumption or conceptions he utilized to organize and interpret his experiences.

In order to meet the persistent problems of life, he had to make some tentative assumptions or propositions; that is, to formulate in action, if not in speech, the conceptions with which he could selectively perceive the environment and act toward what he perceived and interpreted as its meaning for fulfilling his needs and achieving his purposes.

Thus, it appears that in some form, however crude and tentative, early man developed a series of basic assumptions or conceptions of:

(1) The nature of the universe or the kind of world he lived in, how created and operated, by whom or by what powers, as essential to obtaining food, shelter and safety for his organic existence;

(2) His place in that world and his relation to the power which controlled events;

(3) His relation as an individual to his fellows and the group life they carried on, including his privileges and his obligations (who shall be sacrificed for whom?);

(4) Human nature, the image of the self, what impels man to act as he does.

These four assumptions or organizing conceptions provided a framework of beliefs about nature and man in terms of which man could impute meanings to all events, to others' behavior and begin to orient and explain himself and his conduct, not only to others, but to himself.

Every culture is an expression of an *eidos* and an *ethos* which is more or less peculiarly its own. By *eidos* is meant the beliefs and assumptions, the conceptions or preconceptions for organizing and interpreting experience, the criteria of credibility and the logic and ways of reasoning employed by members of each culture in their thinking, action and investigation.

By *ethos* is meant the awareness and sensitivity to experience, especially in interpersonal relations, the accepted, often conventionalized, ways of responding emotionally or with feeling to events such as birth, death, marriage, etc., and all the other episodes and crises or conflicts encountered in life.

Each culture with its *eidos* and *ethos* has its peculiar orientation to the world of nature and of man and looks to the expression of these basic beliefs and feelings in religion, philosophy, law, and the arts, to make life appear reasonable, normal and purposive.[1]

The situation in which man finds himself is of an environmental complex of events, of plant and animal organisms, of ongoing physical, chemical and other processes. Each of these is sending out a variety of messages (stimuli, impacts, threats, promise of fulfillments) which, as Norbert Wiener has suggested, are *To Whom It May Concern* messages. Each organism has developed its specialized concerns and a selective capacity for receiving and interpreting these messages to which it responds with the patterns developed through the prior history of its species.

Man faces the environmental complex with his organic concerns (for food, shelter, security, etc.) but he is not bound by inherited organic patterns of action or of perception. He can and does create his own selective perception of the environment in terms of his basic assumptions and he selectively transforms his organic needs and concerns into goal seeking and purposive conduct and thereby he establishes his human way of life.

This involves selective perceptions, transformed organic needs

[1] For centuries metaphysics has looked critically at every idea and systematic statement of belief or convictions, has attempted to undercut the assumptions and logic of all philosophies which differed from those of the metaphysician. Now we are recognizing that metaphysics is a product of Western European culture, operating with the assumptions, the criteria of credibility, the logic that are peculiar to Western cultures. It is becoming clear that metaphysics, as we have known and practiced it, is "culture bound" and therefore is susceptible to the same kind of approach and evaluation as all cultural traditions, subject to the kind of critical examination that we must now give to the *eidos* of all cultures.

and concerns, imputation of meanings and response thereto in patterned purposeful conduct. These are perpetuated as traditions from generation to generation, as learned lessons: they are not organically fixated but can be changed by developing new ideas, discovering new meanings and learning new patterns of conduct for those new meanings.

Man lives in an *as if* symbolic world, which he has created and maintained by acting and responding to the world in the patterns he has learned to utilize for conducting his life career. But he is reluctant to realize that it is his own *as if* world, a symbolic world he imposes between himself and nature.

Culture, as the traditional pattern of ideas, beliefs, action and feeling and the tools and techniques they foster, may be viewed as an essentially human environment which man has selectively developed from the potentialities of nature and of human nature. Culture is the expression of man's concerns that selectively recognizes the potentialities and dangers of the environment and also of man's way of conducting his life within that humanly created social environment.

Each group of people, living in a specific location or environment of land and water, plants and animals, of mountains or plains, of jungle or desert, of hot or cold or temperate, has been exposed to different organisms and different configurations and life zones. But in all of these diverse environments the underlying physical, chemical and biological processes, including those operating in man himself, are essentially similar.

While the processes of nature and of human nature therefore are essentially similar, regular, almost uniform and unchanging, they have produced in different parts of the world these different geographical environments. Then, man, who is essentially similar in functional processes and organic needs, has, with the same processes of culture building and maintenance, created and perpetuated his diverse ways of life, the many different designs for living of the different cultures, great and small, literate and illiterate, all over the world.

Cultural diversity may be viewed then as the different products of the same underlying processes operating in different environments by different groups of people. Each group has developed its version of the organizing conceptions for making human life secure, orderly and meaningful and for insuring the perpetuation of that way of life. Every culture is an aspiration, "that which is sought," as Ortega y Gasset has said.

Over the centuries specialized practices, rituals, ceremonies, signs and symbols and patterns of relationship have been established to make group living an orderly (more or less) regulated, over-all design which we call social order. Here again we may see the same circular process in operation since each individual learns to approach others according to their meaning, the valuation, the importance, the hierarchical position as defined for him by tradition, law, social convention, etc., and to act toward others as thus defined in the group sanctioned patterns and institutional practices which in turn evoke from the other person the appropriate responses that he has learned to make to such approaches.

This interpersonal action, reaction and interaction should be clearly distinguished from the concept of action-reaction of classical physics. In human living we see one person acting in his idiomatic purposeful fashion to evoke a response from another that is not equal and opposite, like billiard balls, but is idiomatic and purposeful and the ensuing interaction is a unique resolution of either conflicting or congruent strivings. This process is similar to, if not identical with, *the trans-actions* as recently described by Dewey and Bentley and now published in *Knowing and the Known* (Beacon Press, 1949).

Social life is carried on through these interpersonal and intergroup interreactions and trans-actions which are more or less highly organized, that is, they are patterned, sanctioned, or prescribed as *the* only way in which one person can communicate and evoke a desired or counter-response (or rejection) from another. Social orders are maintained by the conformity to these prescribed patterns in which all individuals react and interact according to their learned expectations, utilizing the common group patterns and practices for their individualized private goals and purposes, their idiomatic desires and feelings.

The regularity, the systematic orderliness and predictability of social order arises from this patterning of human conduct exhibited by all members of the group thereby giving rise to statistical regularity and orderliness from individual variations and deviations, as in gas laws.

Social order and these regularities are not the expression of some superhuman or supernatural systems, mechanism, force or law, above and beyond man's reach and control. These essentially defeatist beliefs, cherished by theologians and by many social scientists, are derived from the earlier theological beliefs and from the Newtonian conception of a system operated by large forces acting at a distance to maintain the system in equilibrium. This eighteenth century conceptual apparatus, it may be noted, is no longer the model of scientific thinking but the newer dynamic conceptions have not yet been translated into social science, to supersede these older assumptions of a static system.

If we accept this conception of culture as man's own invention of a dynamic process for making human life meaningful and orderly, we should also realize that the human adventure of culture making and maintaining it is an ongoing, continuing enterprise for which there can be no final form so long as man exists. He must in every generation face the same persistent problems and seek the same enduring values; hence he must continually renew his culture in the light of new understanding of nature and man. He cannot "solve" social problems since they are the persistent tasks of life that each generation must face. The "solutions" of one generation give rise to the problems of the next generation, which can restate them in the light of new knowledge and understanding and keener sensibilities.

The needs, the urges, the aspirations which gave rise in early man to culture building are operating in man today and will continue to operate in his descendants. The human organism while transformed into a personality, a carrier of cultural traditions and a participating member of social order, is still an organism, with all the wisdom of the body, all the needs and functional capacities derived from his mammalian ancestry, necessary for his existence and perpetuation of the species, still plastic and capable of changing its operation through renewal of culture.

The same processes of culture building and perpetuation operate to shape the growing developing child, transforming the infant organism into a personality who grows up to believe what his group believes, to think and act, to speak and feel as his fellows do, but always in his individualized way.

Today as our increasing understanding of human growth and development from conception on is showing, the human organism, above all others, is plastic, flexible, capable of learning, of redirecting and transforming his organic needs and functional capacities into diverse patterns, of developing a capacity for self-directed, purposive conduct, comparable to his mammalian capacity for organic self-regulation (homeostasis).

The major steps or stages (never separate or isolated in operation) through which the human infant passes from birth on, involve a continuous process of learning and relearning, as the infant is progressively socialized and culturized and gradually emerges as a unique personality. Thus we may briefly describe these stages as follows:

First, the organization and regularization of the infant's internal environment, whereby his organic functions are regulated, controlled and patterned. In this process he surrenders some of his organic autonomy of self-regulation and accepts regulation by his parents and by external events.

This process involves the transformation of organic impulses and functions into orderly, purposeful conduct; hunger is transformed into appetite for specific food and all the varied activities of food seeking, eating with rituals, ceremony and etiquette, feasting, fasting, etc.; elimination is transformed into continence, regulated evacuations, sanitation, cleanliness, modesty, shame, etc.; emotional reactions are transformed into varied persistent feelings, some socially approved, some private and concealed or released in disguised fashion; later sex is transformed into love and the many varieties of purposeful conduct and of sex surrogates and vicariates.

Second, the naive reactions and impulsive behavior of the child are regulated so that he transforms his behavior into orderly conduct for social living. Thus, the child learns to inhibit his impulses and thereby to respect private property and the integrity of others and he also learns to perform the prescribed actions of manners—etiquette, rituals, the masculine and feminine roles, etc. In this way the child learns to act toward a world defined by parents in terms of what he must *not* do, may not do, must do and may do. This is a human, social world because he learns these definitions or meanings and these patterns of conduct from other human beings and thereby he becomes a participating member of social order, who exhibits the prescribed conduct in his individualized way, with the feelings as those he developed while learning these patterns.

Third, the use of language and the ideas and beliefs, the assumptions and conceptions of our cultural traditions are inculcated in the child so that he learns to live in a symbolic, cultural world, of meanings, values and purposes, defined for him by parents who interpret, in their individualized way, the religion, philosophy, law, morals, and ethics, the science and folklore they have accepted from their family traditions.

Fourth, the gradual development of the individual's "private world" which arises from the idiomatic version of all these lessons he has learned, warped or often distorted by childish misunderstandings and by the persistent feelings that accompany these living experiences, with the image of the self that he creates from what he has been told about himself and how he has been treated.

Personality emerges as this dynamic, circular process exhibited by each individual in his highly idiomatic way of living, of thinking, of acting, of feeling, of speaking. Therefore, each individual learns to live as if in a "private world" of his own. Personality is the dynamic process which produces these private worlds and maintains and defends them and thereby maintains social order and perpetuates culture. The individual personality responds to every situation and person as friend or foe, as obstructive or instrumental to one's goals and purposes, by trying to impose his idiomatic meanings upon people and all events. Each moment the personality is reacting with feelings to people, often with acute emotional reactions of fear, rage, love or hate, or anxiety, guilt or hostility.

There is nothing subjective, superhuman, esoteric or supernatural in this. There are only organisms and their varied environments which each selectively utilizes for meeting life needs. Only man, however, has been able to create his symbolic environment we call culture and to maintain it by learning to live according to the meanings he himself has created and projected upon that environment and has inculcated in his children. Only man has developed personality which is this dynamic process by which the individual lives as a human being.

So soon as we grasp this circular process which is continually operating dynamically, we may "solve" a host of problems that have perplexed mankind for ages and especially the many philosophical problems which can be solved by showing they arise from assumptions about nature and man no longer valid or useful.

This psychocultural approach offers what eventually may develop into a fruitful, comprehensive formulation for social science research, in dynamic terms as contrasted with the static formulation of the classical social theories derived from the eighteenth and nineteenth centuries and still being used today.

It has great promise for research because it enables us to formulate problems which can be stated in terms of basic assumptions about nature and man that are congruous with, and more or less equivalent to, recently developed conceptions of natural sciences, expressive of the new ways of thinking now being developed.

These new ways of thinking offer a hopeful and constructive approach to the disorder and conflict of our present disorderly social and international world.

We can now repudiate the traditional beliefs about the fixity of human nature since it is clear that human nature is amazingly flexible and plastic, capable, as the study of diverse cultures shows, of being shaped, molded, patterned into a great variety of personalities for different social orders. The potentialities of human nature, only partially recognized by any one culture, and rarely given opportunity to develop harmoniously (that is, without being stunted, warped and distorted in the individual personality or without severe conflicts with society), await future evocation and expression by a revised ethic and program of education from birth on, based on these new insights and understandings.

The many varieties of misconduct, of destructiveness, of antisocial and self-defeating personalities, such as criminals, delinquents, alcoholics, drug addicts, sex offenders and those who, with social sanction and reward, dominate, exploit, domineer and misuse others in social, economic, political affairs, all these are to be viewed, not as expressions of innate evil and human perversity, but as unhappy personalities, products of the process of personality development. They are irresponsible because they are not aware of what they are doing and are unable to change unaided. Both the parental methods of child care, rearing and education (in the larger sense of socialization and culturization) and the traditional beliefs and practices which guide parents are the sources of human misconduct and self-defeat.

Every social problem we face is generated by the beliefs and assumptions, the traditional evaluations we have put upon people and events, and have translated into economic, political, legal, religious and other social institutions and practices by individuals. Thus, we may, with increasing warrant, speak of *Society as the Patient*. (Cf. the writer's *Society as the Patient,* Rutgers University Press, 1948.)

We will contribute to human welfare and advance toward our enduring goals when we cease to dream of utopian solutions and bend our energies to the task of critical examination of our traditions, of all our laws and institutions, our socially sanctioned practices and careers, our legally prescribed conduct and relations, our customary ways of thinking and evaluating, and systematically and continuously revise them in terms of our growing understanding and insights, our increasing sensitivity to human dignity. In this we will be guided by an awareness of the significance of every individual personality for the health and welfare of the whole of society which all individuals maintain. Instead of dreaming of or seeking utopias, we will then accept the persistent tasks of life as the responsibility of each generation; to meet these with increasing understanding and clearer, saner meanings derived from scientific thinking and new insights.

This points to the Promethean task that is becoming increasingly exigent—to assay every culture and every social order in terms of their human consequences—what they are doing to and for the human personality as the living agent and the living product of traditions. This task becomes inevitable as the traditional cultures all over the world and the long established social orders slowly break down or rapidly disintegrate and collapse, making renewal of culture and reconstruction of social order an inescapable necessity for every group of people, as we develop a world community through orchestration of cultural diversities.

We have the clue to a courageous acceptance of this great task in the recently developed conceptions of nature and man, of culture and social order, the insights into personality development and in the new ways of thinking and evaluating whatever we believe and accept and do.

The critical apparatus for examining a culture and a social order is being developed in the conception of cultural relativity. It involves an awareness that every tradition, every belief and expectation as well as every social institution and practice is relative to the whole cultural context and has had a history. They were developed by men like ourselves who, facing the same persistent life tasks and their contemporary difficulties, interpreted them according to the climate of opinion then prevailing and devised "solutions," by creating these institutions and patterns of thinking, of conduct and of feeling.

These were valid then because they served to meet a human, social aspiration and they measured up to the criteria of credibility of those times. But human and social needs and aspirations change and the criteria of credibility alter, as we today so clearly see. With the same aspirations toward meeting human needs and advancing human welfare, it becomes our obligation and our great privilege (and that of our successors) to do for today what the great figures of the past did for their day.

So long as we are clear about our goals and purposes and will evaluate human potentialities and personality according to the criteria of worth and dignity of man and of group or social welfare, we can and must look critically at traditions and endeavor to modify, correct, improve and otherwise devise more effective ways of achieving those goals. That is the only way we can preserve our "values" by continually revising the methods of evaluating them and translating them into human conduct.

The next great ethical advance will come with the acceptance of the doctrine of cultural and social responsibility as an essential supplement to, and extension of, the historic doctrine of individual responsibility. This conception of group responsibility recognizes that we cannot expect individuals to be responsible and capable of autonomy unless we provide the care, rearing and education, which will enable them to become mature, sane, cooperative adults who can bear the burdens of freedom, can act as self-directing personalities, free from the coercion of their childhood and youth and the persistent feelings of anxiety, guilt and hostility that distort their human relations, injure society and drive them to self-defeat. Human personalities are the individual expressions of our culture; our culture and social order are the group expression of individual personalities. Hence we must operate concurrently to modify culture and society and to help individuals to become the kind of personalities who can realize our ethical aspirations by creating a better society.

This is what science, medicine and art have been doing for centuries, recognizing that they can be loyal to their enduring goals and aspirations only by continually revising their assumptions, their methods and their practices in the light of new understanding and of critical thinking.

Our task is to do for social living what has been so clearly established by scientists, physicians and artists, recognizing that it is the striving for human welfare, for a social order addressed to the dignity and worth of personality which is important, indeed, the goal of social life and the basic aim of culture which can never be fully achieved. Indeed, it is because they are unattainable goals which challenge human courage and imagination to strive and keep on striving, that they have any meaning.

Only as we see living as purposeful striving and accept this challenge and this opportunity can we be said to be humanly alive. Only as we face situations as problematic, to be evaluated and met with concern for the human consequences of our decisions and actions, can we live as autonomous personalities, free to make ethical choices and thereby to realize in some measure our human potentialities and carry on the basic aim of culture to create and maintain a human way of life.

The clue to an effective and deliberate approach to these goals is in changing the processes which operate to perpetuate traditions and to maintain social order as it is. These are the processes of education, especially those of personality formation in childhood and youth, of education in schools and particularly of reeducation of adults, whose capacity for relearning we are just recognizing.

Probably never before was the situation more favorable to adult reeducation, since the confusion and disorders are making even the most conservative and insensitive aware of the need to consider new possibilities and the widespread program of subversive propaganda is stimulating discontent with traditional beliefs and things as they are. Thinking and reflection are becoming necessary in the face of doubt and conflict. What is lacking is a systematic program to focus this growing uneasiness and active discontent into more constructive channels than sheer rebelliousness or blind acceptance of authority, however radical it may call itself.

Those who despair of making any headway against the well organized propaganda and seeming "apathy of the masses" are inclined to forget that the most potent appeal is the recognition that as individual personalities each one has beliefs and feelings which will be respected and will be given a hearing by the group.

Against the leadership principle of demanding passive obedience to a leader and acceptance of doctrinaire teachings (which is the common formula of the radical and the reactionary) there is the emerging principle of group decision and group therapies which utilizes the basic circular process of personality formation and expression and relearning.

The method of group decision and group therapy operates to encourage each individual to reveal what he believes, how he thinks and feels about any question or problem. Often for the first time the individual is encouraged to articulate his assumptions and to see them in the light of others' beliefs and ways of thinking. Not being compelled or encouraged to defend his beliefs or to attack others, he may be able, with the active support and example of others, to alter lifelong convictions and habitual patterns. He may then, tentatively at first, begin to impute new meanings to familiar situations and people, to try out new ways of evaluating situations and persons and new patterns addressed to those redefined situations and reevaluated persons. In this way he may discover that they provide a more effective way of thinking and acting, more fulfilling of his desires and goals, less costly to others and less self-defeating.

Every time an individual critically examines his beliefs and his patterns of action, rejects them or modifies them, he is changing culture, altering traditions, especially when he deliberately refrains from indoctrinating his children with the old beliefs and practices now revealed as obstructive to healthy, sane, mature adults.

This gives each individual member of society a new and enlarged significance with possibilities for active participation in group life, replacing the long accepted belief that the single individual is impotent in the face of large scale social forces, a passive spectator of inevitable trends, owing submissive obedience to laws and authority as his major social duty. The defeatism of our traditional social theories may thus be replaced by a courageous acceptance of the individual's ethical responsibility for maintaining and for altering culture and social order, not limited to voting on political issues and pressure group tactics, but actively and critically participating in the renewal of our culture and the reconstruction of our social order through his or her individual daily living and his choices and by his contribution to group decision.

This may be offered as an expression of the democratic aspiration which, to be realized, must go beyond freedom of action, speech and belief within the established traditional patterns, must go beyond voting and representative government and the maintenance of our political, economic freedom, precious as are these hard won rights and privileges. The democratic aspiration looks to the recognition of the individual as both the agent and the goal of social order, as the personality who bears and also renews culture, interpreted as the common aim of mankind, to create and carry on a human way of life.

What John Dewey early realized was that, not facts and knowledge, not Truth (with the capital T) nor any of the fixed ideas and values that have been reified in our intellectual tradition were the significant focus or goals of human inquiry and living. Rather, as he has consistently and persistently labored to make clear, it is the *process* of inquiring, of testing, of knowing and evaluating and of acting that are crucial, both in inquiry and in all human living which are governed by the meanings we impute to all experience.

In his early formulations of instrumental logic, "the logic of experience" as he later called it, we find both explicitly and implicitly stated what has become the core of contemporary science and reflective thinking, the major theme of the emerging climate of opinion. Thus we are learning to recognize that we approach all inquiries and all problematic situations with assumptions or postulates which we must continually scrutinize and validate by testing their meanings in action—in experiment and in living.

Here we see how contemporary theoretical physics has moved from purely empirical generalization to the postulation of assumptions that are self-consciously chosen to guide inquiry and to direct thinking.

By the same process we are learning to recognize in our culture and our social order the traditional, underlying assumptions and beliefs which guide and direct our individual and group living, and which we today can and must critically examine in the light of our growing knowledge of nature and of man, our new understandings of culture and human nature, our new insights into personality.

Thus, we are clarifying and enlarging the logic of experience[2] as the most potent instrument yet devised for meeting the persistent tasks of human living and for carrying on the unending endeavor to make life ever more meaningful and significant through culture and social order, oriented to the realization of human potentialities.

[2] Lack of space makes it impossible to quote the passages from *Essays in Experimental Logic* in which the major points and procedures outlined in this paper are stated or clearly implied.

Social Inquiry and Social Doctrine

by HORACE L. FRIESS

THE PERIOD of John Dewey's philosophizing, from the 1880's to the present, has seen much new emphasis on man's social nature and social relations. Though contenders for monopolistic authority have not been lacking, it has not been possible for them to secure any exclusive possession of this social emphasis. It has permeated into many diverse doctrines and groups. There are the various brands of economic socialism that have appealed to the labor movements particularly. There are the national socialisms with their call for the primacy of a race, folk, or nation. There are the "social gospels" advanced in various Protestant circles, and the modern social doctrines of the Popes since Leo XIII. Even academic philosophers, detached from party lines, have had their own ways of making a social emphasis in many characteristic recent doctrines of moral and metaphysical connectedness, interdependence, and interrelation. The tendency is not confined to the Hegelian idealists. To mention but a few miscellaneous examples from American philosophy, it is found in the "unconscious natural community" of Henry James, Sr., in the "community of mental action" stressed by Peirce, in Howison's "eternal republic," Felix Adler's "infinite society," and Royce's "community of interpretation."

So the recent past has been a time of many doctrines criticizing the classic traditions of modern individualism. John Dewey has had his part in this critique. Mindful of important values in individualism, he has, nevertheless, consistently pointed to the social, rather than the isolated nature of the individual. [Cf. *Individualism Old* and New, 1930; and elsewhere] Dewey has given such great philosophical significance to the category "social," that it is not surprising to find him sometimes criticized for exaggerating its power and range. Discussing "Social as a Category," in 1928, Dewey expressed his position in such statements as the following. They are cited here, not in order to consider whether they represent an overestimation of the "social," but to help in exploring some features of Dewey's special contribution amid the current whirl of social doctrines.

"Associated or conjoint behavior is a universal characteristic of all existences. . . . Qualities of associated things are displayed only in association, since in interactions alone are potentialities released and actualized. The manifestation of potentialities varies with the manner and range of association.

"Social facts are themselves natural facts.

"The social, in its human sense, is the richest, fullest and most delicately subtle of any mode actually experienced.

"Upon the hypothesis of continuity—the social . . . furnishes philosophically the inclusive category.

"I do not say that the social as we know it *is* the whole, but I do emphatically suggest that it is the widest and richest manifestation of the whole accessible to our observation. As such it is at least the proper point of departure for any more imaginative construings of the whole one may wish to undertake. And in any case it furnishes the terms in which any consistent *empirical* philosophy must speak.

"The commitment of Lockean empiricism to a doctrine that ignored the associative property of all things experienced is the source of that particularistic nominalism whose goal is solipsistic scepticism. In consequence, empiricism ceased to be empirical and became a dialectic construction of the implications of absolute particularism."[1]

The stimulus for a proliferation of social doctrines in recent times no doubt lies largely in the unfamiliar changes that social relations and processes are themselves undergoing. So novel and unfinished are many of these changes that it is impossible for any social doctrine—or all of them put together—to take adequate account of

[1] J. Dewey, "Social as a Category," *The Monist*, v. 38:2, pp. 161-77.

all that is going on. The ferment of social excitement and opinion-making is kept seething. Many of the most dynamic factors effecting important changes in social relations are inadequately considered in social doctrines, because their operations are so continuous, rapid, and out of the ordinary, while their consequences at the same time are so many-sided and far-reaching. The impacts of physical science on technology and communications, of medicine and biology on population problems, of modern warfare on impoverishment and economy, the unsettling of norms in the meeting of hitherto distant cultures—these furnish some of the most obvious, though by no means the only examples. Ongoing and in many respects unforeseen changes in social relations will continue to be in the order of the day, as long as such dynamic factors keep on working.

About the time that *Experience and Nature* was published, Professor F. J. E. Woodbridge remarked at a meeting of philosophers that John Dewey had a bias in favor of change. The existence of such a bias in Dewey may or may not be a fact. But, in either case, Dewey's weighty point has been that, under conditions of culture which enforce such extensive changes as are now going on, intelligence is called upon to consider the methods of effecting change in ways as humanly satisfying and constructive as possible. The significance of Dewey's central concern with social inquiry, more than with social doctrine, springs to light in this perspective. Social inquiry always has its pertinence. But its role becomes unusually vital whenever changes in social relations are going on in such ways and at such pace that social doctrines can not possibly do them all justice.

Both social inquiry and social doctrine are always engendered in some actual context of social relations, and are usually tributary, more or less directly, to ongoing or proposed social action. Though they can be, and sometimes are, pursued in a relatively detached contemplative spirit, the practical functions of each in relation to action are persistent and vital enough to predominate in shaping and sustaining them. Social doctrines usually systematize beliefs about the foundations and the organizational structure of social relations, and also about the initiatives, procedures, and values in social processes. That social inquiry is likewise of practical concern must surely be equally clear. The need to secure and extend knowledge of social relations is absolutely vital to every society on a large or small scale. To some extent at least people must reliably know what they are doing to and for each other. Hence social inquiry can never be entirely neglected in any society, even though the need for it may be discounted by social doctrines claiming the accomplished possession of sufficient insight by the community, its leaders, or its experts.

That social inquiry can be more or less unsettling of existing social doctrines or beliefs, while the latter tend in their several ways to channel and to restrict investigation, is a common enough experience, and one much emphasized by John Dewey. He has pretty continually stressed the critical implications of social inquiry for any belief in the fixity of social relations, privileges, and values. But to claim that Dewey sets up a general opposition between social inquiry and social doctrine, or that his attitude toward the latter is essentially negative, would clearly be wrong. He has not failed to connect social inquiry with positive implications for social relations. Indeed, what he has perhaps principally wanted to show is that experimental social inquiry can thrive only in a social process, involving progressively democratic reconstruction of social relations and doctrines.

Dewey's great central contribution is really this far-reaching conception of experimental social inquiry that he clarified and elaborated. It is a conception of inquiry as not only directed upon social subject matter, but as also social in its procedures and in its responsibilities. To understand this conception it is necessary to attend both to Dewey's view of the human behavioral context of method, and therewith to his idea of an experimental method of social inquiry within that context. The behavioral context of method is that of human activity with its changing bio-social-cultural conditions and consequences. Within this context the experimental method of social inquiry operates to give problems arising from change the fullest and most critical social consideration. It is a method asking:
(i) that attention be directed to specific conditions and problems;
(ii) that communication of information and ideas be full and un-

impeded socially; (iii) that general meanings and ideas be freely elaborated, with all relevant resources of the special sciences, but tested and validated as social through their consequences for reconstruction of specific situations; and (iv) that values and aims entertained be submitted to scrutiny and revaluation as intrinsic parts of the social inquiry, and not be regarded as factors determined outside this experimental process.

Social inquiry, so conceived, is clearly not a matter of applying some exact, self-contained technique from above to social subject matter. It is a complex, groping phase of social processes and relations themselves. It can not claim to circumvent the conflicts in those relations, nor to offer a course of plain sailing to their resolution. What it amounts to is an attempt to bring about as full and responsible a working relation as possible in dealing with social problems between scientific resources and everyday life. The terms of such a responsible working relation can never be fully made out in advance; they have to be worked out in the going and will involve many contingencies of particular situations. But obviously the relation always implicates both science and society. Just as there can be no social inquiry which does not draw upon particular resources of knowing, so there can be none which does not bring into action specific social relations. Fact finding boards may proceed more or less impartially, but only as part and parcel of existing social forces can their work make a difference. Dewey's recipe for social inquiry does read in part like a program for democratic action, and this seems to trouble some who feel that philosophy and special pleading are here confused. Through what kind of social relations and processes would they have us find out about "the public and its problems"?

But Dewey has avoided stiffening the social implications of inquiry into any prescribed social doctrine. To social doctrine he has, indeed, made notable contributions, for instance in *The Public and its Problems*. Here he asks us to see "the state" as constituting and defining itself repeatedly according to the ways public problems are handled, and not as an institution defined once for all in some beginning. His conception of other social institutions would similarly be in terms of their part in a process of changing relations. Nor would he expect fact finding boards to be rigid bodies standardized in advance. In the new Introduction to the 1948 edition of *Reconstruction in Philosophy,* Dewey once again places all emphasis on the importance of *discovery* and *invention,* saying:

"The heart of the method is the discovery of the identity of inquiry with discovery.

"It is a familiar fact that the practical correlate of discovery when it is scientific and theoretical is *invention*. . . . In human affairs and in relations that range extensively and penetrate deeply the mere idea of invention awakens fear and horror, being regarded as dangerous and destructive. This fact, which is important but which rarely receives notice, is assumed to belong to the very nature and essence of morals as morals. This fact testifies both to the reconstruction to be undertaken and to the extreme difficulty of every attempt to bring it about."

Impressed by this "extreme difficulty of every attempt" at inventive reconstruction in human and moral affairs, Dewey goes on to say in the same Introduction:

"The genuinely modern has still to be brought into existence. The work of actual production is not the task or responsibility of philosophy. That work can be done only by the resolute, patient, cooperative activities of men and women of good will, drawn from every useful calling, over an indefinitely long period."

But in the present cultural situation, Dewey concludes, "philosophers" might perform "a useful and needed work . . . in forwarding moral inquiry."[2]

One can only rejoice that Dewey has pursued this main idea of carrying experimental inquiry thoroughly into human concerns with such concentrated, single-minded strength from his early to his present days. The way that strength still pursues the theme into such ramified details of technical criticism as fill the recent Dewey-Bentley articles in "search for firm names"! Without overlooking personal disposition and ruggedness, it seems likely that Dewey has been able to sustain this intellectual course in part because he is so right, when he says that philosophy can have no more important

[2] J. Dewey, *Reconstruction in Philosophy,* enlarged edition, The Beacon Press, Boston, 1948, pp. XXX and XXXV.

task in our time than this one he went after: the improvement of social inquiry. Dewey, one feels, would be the less important if he had mingled the pursuit of this great task with other forms of concern for belief and doctrine.

Yet to find it good that Dewey stuck to his philosophical job does not amount to saying that it is philosophy's one and only big task in our time. Perhaps there is another rather close to his. Both jobs start from the very same present situation of many social doctrines clashing confusedly in a world of social relations changing in many unfamiliar ways. Dewey says philosophy's task, in this situation, is to further social inquiry into social processes and relations in order to reconstruct them and the beliefs that go with them. But he sees that reconstruction in human affairs faces "extreme difficulty" and must occupy "an indefinitely long period." During this long period, and probably afterward too, different people—we must assume—will live together and remain more or less attached to more than one system of social doctrines. Does not philosophy in this find a second job: to interpret these different doctrines and their various functions, so as to further healthy relations between people holding different beliefs?

The two tasks might well be regarded as two phases of one and the same job; in fact, ideally they should be. But they are not identical. If the second concern were a matter of opportunistic compromise in the field of belief for the presumed sake of social peace, its right to be regarded as a philosophical concern would not be clear. But it involves the interpretation of social doctrines and their functions, and also the conception of what healthy relations are, and how they can exist, between people disagreeing in such doctrines. A furthering of social inquiry is definitely implied in this task. The functioning of social doctrines can not become known without social inquiry. Moreover, one revealing sign of healthy or unhealthy relations between disagreeing people is the extent to which they will welcome inquiry. But social inquiry, in Dewey's sense, a process for reconstructing social relations and belief, is not the only task demanding philosophical attention. For while reconstruction is going on, those relations and beliefs are in some manner functioning, and for better or worse are associated with all the values people know and cherish. Without prejudice to reconstruction—indeed, in order to secure it more happily—this fact must be recognized. Reconstruction of social relations and doctrines and recognition of what they are meanwhile representing must somehow be kept in fertile conjunction. Recognition is likely to be purely partisan and defensive unless mixed with social inquiry aiming at reconstruction; on the other hand, unless there is recognition, the relations between disagreeing people are apt to deteriorate so as to block and frustrate reconstructive inquiry. Perhaps social inquiry, in Dewey's sense, provides for both phases, but certainly both must be provided for.

On the side of recognition, Professor W. H. Sheldon argues that philosophy could again achieve a common "body of doctrine" by "harmonizing" the substantial elements of truth in each and all of the main types of world-view that have stood the test of time. He maintains that "the perennial types of metaphysics, such as idealism, materialism, Thomism, and so on, are substantially true" in their main affirmations, though wrong in their denials and several claims of complete and exclusive truth.[3] I can not find the harmonizing of the clashing systems of social doctrine in our time so simple a matter. And, in any case, I am not proposing to identify healthy relations among disagreeing people with getting agreement or concord between them. I should rather identify these healthy relations with sufficient self-possession so that it is unnecessary to one's own security to distort the other fellow's qualities either by idealizing or disparaging them; with mutual give and take, and the desire to learn from one another as opposed to self-isolation; with mutual criticism and an intelligibility across lines rather than befuddling polemics; with humor and patience; and with fighting to good purpose when there is fighting. In terms of such criteria, one need hardly look far today for evidence of much prevailing unhealthiness.

A puzzling problem for all followers of Dewey is to judge the limits of possibility in situations. There surely is a kind of *moira* or

[3] *Cf.* his Howison lecture, *Philosophy's Job Today*, Univ. of Cal., 1947.

fate in the sense of a limiting structure to the situations in which we live. Social inquiry must operate with some estimate of it, but the process and results of inquiry may change a situation's limits significantly. And we can not rely on oracles to tell us where we shall come out. We do best in making provisional judgments of our possibilities and our limits under the conditions we know, and in revising these judgments when we know better. Tragedy is neither inevitable nor surely avoidable in human affairs.

Those who stress the importance of experimental social inquiry, in Dewey's sense, obviously can not agree with social doctrines that reserve decisions on the most important social matters to upper hierarchies, politburos, and other high commands. But they may have the candor to recognize: (1) that all the large existing societies, without exception, do this offensive thing in some degree; (2) that other limiting circumstances besides villainy and stupidity play their part at least in many cases where it occurs in great measure; and (3) that chances for more experimental and democratic reconstruction can either improve or deteriorate, as relations between disagreeing parties become more healthy or unhealthy. One current application of the last point seems to call for immediate comment. In the tender matter of qualifications for academic teaching and scholarly research, considerations of personal integrity and competence must come first and should be judged on an individual basis. Then, in addition, the health of group relations is a second important consideration; and the effect on it of segregating and isolating groups classified as "subversive" is not likely to be good.

It is surely absurd to think that Dialectical Materialism and the C.P. have a monopoly on the progressive social organization of modern technology and economy. But every social doctrine that takes important hold must be in some degree employed to push needed social reconstruction and inquiry somewhere, and it is unhealthy not to give that as accurate recognition as possible. To think that existing cultural conditions will permit impoverished and ignorant millions the world over to organize parliamentary-wise for their pressing necessities seems a bit quixotic. Have even the Western nations as yet very fully accepted democratic controls of their too often still predatory economic life?—Again, looking in another quarter for recognition of facts, it may be that too much dust is commonly raised over "supernaturalism" in discussing the social doctrines and relations of Roman Catholicism. The Church is the power it is, not alone through its Mysteries and through God of Whom it sometimes disavows exclusive possession, but also by reason of the ramified thought and superintendence it gives to hundreds and thousands of small and large human relations. These processes, and the functioning of doctrines in them, need to be recognized and studied more thoroughly, if social inquiry is to have any good chance at their reconstruction.

Since John Dewey's concept of experimental social inquiry developed historically in the context of a socialized liberalism, it would be odd if there were no special affinity between it and social doctrines representative of that context. The most definitive traits of liberalism are its positive appreciation of individuals in their variety, of freedom for growth and development and for discussion and inquiry. *Socialized* liberalism, however, added a large awareness of the changing social matrix, and consequently of new social conditions needed to promote the development of individuals and of free inquiry. It also sometimes affirmed the value, as an end, of diversity in groups as well as in individual persons. In his idea of social inquiry Dewey gave this emphasis of socialized liberalism on social conditions the shape of a self-correcting, reconstructive process, such as he found so productively at work in the experimental sciences. It is a contribution that can convert liberalism into a truly dynamic procedure and carry its vitality beyond the expressions of any single period. But to do this the social inquiry process must itself find nourishment in healthy sustaining conditions.

The mutual alliance in much of the liberal movement between ethical idealism and social inquiry points up this interdependence of inquiry and healthy human relations. Where the connection becomes particularly explicit, the point is underlined and highlighted, as, for instance, in "ethical culture" ideas and activities. Here intensive and energetic commitment to examination and reconstruction of one's human relations is interpreted as central to personality and its spiritual values. Felix Adler's thought combined the ideas of individual uniqueness and functional relation with others. (Whenever he and Dewey cooperated, he had to insist on their differences!) The idea of an infinite worth of the individual made good sense to him only as he took each individual to be an irreplaceable member of an infinite society. He saw the major social institutions —family, vocation, school, state, and religious fellowship—as so many stations in which individuals become personalized, that is, distinctly responsive to this worth-in-relation-to-others. Each station has its essential functions, but no complete sovereign authority attaches to any one of them, nor to all of them together. To Adler the ultimate appeared only in the form of a transcendent Ideal of perfect interrelation. He thus combined persistent social effort and criticism with imaginative vision. "The right course," he believed, "must insure vigor of attack, a relish for the struggle of life, an attitude of interest in finite things, and a certain élan of spirit in grappling with the work-a-day world. . . . A truer vision of the ideal can arise only on the basis of persistence and fortitude in grappling with actual circumstances throughout life."

This sort of energetic personal commitment can be of immeasurable importance in forwarding social inquiry. Emphasis on a variety of relations favors it too. Reciprocally, social inquiry is vital if personal energy is to pursue its goals truly in a widely diversified world. In the familiar contention that man's supreme end is personality and its relations, ethical idealism may well be right. But men, defining personality thus and so as an end, can easily play tricks on themselves in development.To make the effort as humanly sound and productive as possible, what personality means must be investigated, rediscovered, and renewed in ongoing social inquiry and reconstruction. John Dewey was quoted earlier as saying:

"Qualities of associated things are displayed only in association, since in interactions alone are potentialities released and actualized. The manifestation of potentialities varies with the manner and range of association."

It is because the release of potentialities "varies with the manner and range of association" that the dynamic process of social discovery and invention is so important. No thought could be better conceived to combine creatively with Adler's idea of ethical relations.

Social relations, to be sure, do not exist for the sake of social inquiry as their end. But the various ends for which they do exist can not be strongly pursued today unless social inquiry be adequately sustained. Social inquiry need not be advertised as the absolute good. But because it is so central a condition and means for increasing the good of human relations, forwarders of social inquiry will be amply justified in maintaining a critical intransigence toward doctrines that would weaken its vital bases and energies. For the same reason they should positively ally themselves with social relations, beliefs, and doctrines that tend to nourish social inquiry, indeed with all actual and ideal resources that favor its productivity.

Dewey's Theories of Legal Reasoning and Valuation

by EDWIN W. PATTERSON

As one looks back from the mid-point of the twentieth century at the striking social, economic, political, and legal changes that have occurred during that century, what basic philosophic pattern or patterns can one find in the turmoil of ideas and events? One was an attack upon the self-sufficiency of the legal order, upon its capacity to yield solutions for every legal problem from its store of traditional axioms and postulates, and, on the positive side, an insistence that the solutions of legal problems depended, in part at least, upon the appraisal of social factors. Another was the belief that social change, the amelioration of living conditions, need not be left to the control of inscrutable "natural" laws of economics, biology and sociology, but could be promoted by well-planned governmental action through law. A third, more esoteric in character, had to do with the judicial process. However courts may decide the controversies brought before them by legal procedure, they are, in many cases at least, not compelled by the inexorable compulsion of established premises to decide the case just one way. Rather the decision involves deliberation and discretion, in which the attitudes and beliefs of the judge or judges have some sway. All three of these generalizations have, on the positive side, been stated above more moderately and cautiously than their most ardent proponents have stated them. As so stated they are compatible with, and have been immeasurably influenced by, John Dewey's philosophy.

Unlike the dozen eminent philosophers whose practical judgments on legal problems Mr. Cairns has ably expounded,[1] Dewey has not put forth a systematic or comprehensive philosophy of law. In two of his short essays he turned his method of inquiry upon legal problems. His article on "Logical Method and Law"[2] set forth compactly, yet rather too abstractly, the application of his instrumental logic to the judicial decision of cases. In the other article he pulverized most of the traditional concepts of corporate legal personality,[3] and left the fragments on the lawyer's doorstep, just as a reminder that legal problems have to be solved in legal contexts with the emphasis on specific consequences rather than such figments as "persona ficta" or "real personality." Since Mr. Cairns's arguments for the enduring value of the specific ideas about legal problems and concepts put forth by his eminent philosophers do not seem persuasive, it seems just as well that John Dewey has not attempted to construct a special philosophy of law. The theme of this essay is the significance of Dewey's ideas about logic and ethics for the jurisprudential theories of the past half century: its influence upon such theories and its implications for the future.[4]

During the summer of 1922 Professor Dewey, on the invitation of Dean Harlan F. Stone, of the Columbia University Law School, gave a course on Logical and Ethical Problems of the Law, which was attended by a considerable number of American law teachers. From 1924 to 1929 Professor Dewey's Seminar in Legal Philosophy[5] at Columbia, annually attracting an able group of graduate students in law and in philosophy, was devoted to the exploration

---

[1] See Cairns, *Legal Philosophy from Plato to Hegel* (1949). I omit Cicero as he was primarily a lawyer. The other ten are: Aristotle, Aquinas, Bacon, Hobbes, Spinoza, Leibniz, Locke, Hume, Kant and Fichte. Some of them had very little to say about specific legal doctrines.

[2] "Logical Method and Law" (1924) 10 *Cornell L. Q.* 17; reprinted, Hall, *Readings in Jurisprudence* (1938), 343.

[3] "The Historic Background of Corporate Legal Personality" (1926) 35 *Yale L. J.* 655.

[4] In an essay contributed to the volume published in honor of Professor Dewey's eightieth birthday, I outlined somewhat more broadly than here the significance of his ideas for legal philosophy. See "Pragmatism as a Philosophy of Law" in *The Philosopher of the Common Man* (1940) 172. As this volume is now out of print, I have not hesitated to repeat some of the statements made there.

[5] The seminar was conducted by Professor Dewey and the present writer until his retirement. It is still being given.

of the nature of concepts, of their use in the judicial process, and of the meanings of such pervasive concepts as legal personality. Primarily through his writings Dewey had a great deal of influence upon three distinguished law teachers, Walter Wheeler Cook, Herman Oliphant, and Underhill Moore, whose contributions were a part of the skein of ideas that eventually became known as American Legal Realism. Each of these men sought, in a somewhat different way, to test and appraise legal norms and legal procedures by determining their consequences, and thus to provide an empirical foundation for legal propositions. In this they had an objective like that of Dewey's theory of inquiry (logic) and theory of valuation. In their zeal to liberate legal thinking from the traditional shackles of logical, moral, economic, and political beliefs of the nineteenth century, some of the Legal Realists took positions that were, as I shall try to show later, not warranted by Dewey's philosophy. The reaction to these extreme positions appeared in the revival of natural law theories, both of the scholastic and the non-scholastic[6] varieties. Dewey's theory of inquiry was exemplified in Judge Cardozo's revelation, rather startling at the time, of the choices made, with respect both to the decisions and the reasons for decisions, in the judicial process of appellate courts;[7] yet Cardozo cited Dewey's work only in the second and third volumes of his trilogy on reasoning and valuation in legal problem-solving.[8] More recently Professor Julius Stone, of the University of Sydney, has exemplified Dewey's theory of logical method in an excellent analysis of the creative element in the reasoning of appellate tribunals.[9] This sketch of Dewey's influence on legal thinking during the past half-century might be greatly extended by including the influence of those who were influenced by him.[10] However, any account of

[6] See Fuller, *The Law in Quest of Itself* (1941).
[7] *The Nature of the Judicial Process* (1921).
[8] References to Dewey's writings are found in *The Growth of the Law* (1924) and *The Paradoxes of Legal Science* (1928). These and the other important writings of Cardozo may be found in his *Selected Writings* (Margaret E. Hall ed., 1947).
[9] Stone, *The Province and Function of Law* (1946), citing Dewey's article on logical method at pp. 50, 205.
[10] To take two widely divergent instances: Lasswell and McDougal ("Legal

Dewey's influence would be misleading without the reservation that two of the most influential American legal philosophers of the present century, Oliver Wendell Holmes and Roscoe Pound, derived their inspiration and initial guidance chiefly from William James, of whom Dewey was a follower. Dewey's influence is only a part of the influence of pragmatism.

Dewey's account of logical method in law made three assumptions about legal reasoning. One was that the problem presented for legal reasoning is how to deal with a concrete situation, how to arrive at a judgment or decision which will eventuate in action. This assumption is true in the work of the counselor advising a client as to what he should do and of the judge deciding a legal controversy. A second assumption was that the legal reasoner begins with "a complicated and confused case, apparently admitting of alternative modes of treatment and solution."[11] This states the hypothesis on which legal problem-solving is necessary: There must be a problem, and it must be felt as a problem, not as an operation in formal demonstration. Yet there are differences between the problems of counselors and judges. The counselor does typically begin with a concrete and rather confused set of facts presented by his client. Judges, on the other hand, have facts selected by lawyers and already charged with legal meanings; in appellate courts they have (usually) not only the selected facts of the trial court record but also the briefs of counsel which present, or should present, the legal issues of the case. Thus the character of the problem presented for legal reasoning varies with the use to be made of it; Professor Dewey's assumption does not adequately account for those variations, as he doubtless realized. The third assumption was that one does not "find" the law and then apply it to the facts, nor find the facts and apply the law to them; rather the search for law and fact goes on in several stages, and the one influences and guides the

---

Education and Public Policy" [1943] 52 *Yale L. J.* 203) rely heavily on Oliphant's *Summary of Studies in Legal Education* (Columbia University Faculty of Law, 1928); and Cheatham ("American Theories of Conflict of Laws" [1945] 58 *Harv. L. Rev.* 361) pays tribute to Cook, *The Logical and Legal Bases of the Conflict of Laws* (1942). See also Patterson, "Logic in the Law" (1942) 90 *U. of Pa. L. Rev.* 875, especially 889-898.

[11] 10 *Corn. L. Q.* 17, 235; Hall, p. 349.

other. This assumption is warranted, I believe, in so far as the work of the counselor and that of the judge are concerned. The method of reasoning, then, is "to *find* statements, of general principle and particular fact, which are worthy to serve as premises."[12] Once the premises are found, the formal demonstration of the conclusion is automatic. While Dewey's sketchy description of legal reasoning was, as he said, neither novel nor original,[13] it fitted that description of the mental process into the context of logical theory and thus explained how, without the explicit use of logical forms such as the syllogism, it *could* be a rational process. Dewey also asserted that, to attain the best results in the long run, the process of legal adaptation and change *should* be a rational ("reasoning") process.

Any "material" logic, that is, any theory of reasoning that purports to describe (and then to prescribe) the process of reasoning, incurs the risk that it may provide an inadequate description of the varieties of uses of reasoning. Dewey's brief description of legal reasoning was, as has been indicated in the last paragraph, substantially adequate for the work of the legal counselor and the judge. These two uses of legal reasoning held the spotlight of public and professional discussion during the first half of the present century. Holmes's prediction theory of law[14] had signalized the former, and Cardozo's analysis of the judicial process[15] emphasized the latter. However, Dewey seems to have confused the work of the counselor, who is called upon to advise his client what action he should take to avoid litigation, with the work of the advocate, who has to present the merits of his client's claims in litigation on facts already determined, by the most favorable arguments possible within the rather uncertain limits of professional ethics and professional prudence.[16] The uses of law by laymen and by non-adjudicative officials

[12] *Ibid.*
[13] *Ibid.*, 26; Hall, p. 353. The description was, I believe, novel and original, but the idea had been substantially stated by Holmes, Pound and Cardozo.
[14] "The Path of the Law" (1897) 10 *Harv. L. Rev.* 457, 460; "The prophecies of what the courts will do in fact, and nothing more pretentious, are what I mean by the law."
[15] *Op. cit., supra,* Notes 7, 8.
[16] Dewey, *op. cit., supra,* No. 2, 12 *Corn. L. Q.* at p. 23. Hall, p. 350. After describing the advocate's search for one-sided arguments, Dewey remarked that this was not "a model of scientific procedure."

in their daily affairs were not included in Dewey's description, presumably because they are normally routine and habitual, therefore not creative. The same cannot be said of the uses of legal reasoning in the framing of legislation, whether it be an ordinary statute or an administrative regulation. Here the end-product of reasoning is not a concrete and singular decision but a generalization, a universal proposition. Yet this type of reasoning is included in his general statement about the logic of judicial decisions:

". . . logic must be abandoned or it must be a logic *relative to consequences rather than to antecedents,* a logic of prediction of probabilities rather than of deduction of certainties."[17]

The legislator should appraise the consequences of proposed legislation, and those consequences can only be estimated as more or less probable.[18]

Before raising some further questions about Dewey's theory of legal reasoning, it seems necessary to point out that it did not imply two positions that were sometimes suggested by Legal Realists, and have sometimes been ascribed to Dewey by his critics: The "hunch" theory of judicial decisions, and the view that the judicial opinion is a mere rationalization giving the "good" reasons but not the "real" reasons for the decision. While the two are interrelated, they call for separate discussion.

In its moderate version the "hunch" theory merely asserted that judicial decisions (including here judicial rulings and orders) are arrived at by intuitive "hunches" rather than by a conscious search for legal and factual premises. That that kind of deciding occurs in the judicial process can scarcely be doubted. For instance, a Federal judge once told me that in sustaining or overruling objections to the admissibility of evidence made during the course of a jury trial

---

[17] *Ibid.*, 25; Hall, 353.
[18] *Cf.*, in general, Llewellyn, "The Normative, the Legal and the Law Jobs: The Problem of Juristic Method" (1940) 49 *Yale L. J.* 1355, 1373-83.

he ordinarily had no time to consult a law book or even to formulate in his own mind any generalizations to guide his conclusion; he acted on his "hunches." Dewey recognized that unreflective judging occurred and that it often produced praiseworthy results, yet it is a second-best method; while it may be "reasonable," it is not "reasoned."[19] He also recognized that lawyers and judges have developed a trained intuition which enables them to use previously learned generalizations without explicitly formulating them. Such generalizations

". . . are no less a means of constructing judgments because they are not always operative in the existential work of reconstituting existential material. . . . A map is no less a means of directing journeys because it is not constantly in use."[20]

Yet even this use of the trained intuition is not quite a first-rate type of legal reasoning as appears from Dewey's later statement in the same volume:

"An operation not formulated in a proposition is logically uncontrolled, no matter how useful it may be in habitual practice."[21]

The context of this quotation makes it clear that "operation" is a logical step in reasoning and that he does not mean to say that the reasons for a judicial determination of a complex litigation can or should be compressed into a single formula. The judge who explores the reasons for his hunches and formulates them has no certain guaranty against error, but he is more likely to detect his error or to enable others to detect it.

The "hunch" theory was borrowed from psychiatry, psychoanalysis, and social psychology, and thus became the rationalization theory. Now every judicial decision must have at least one intuition, and commonly they have a good many, since no matter how explicitly the reasons are formulated, the process must end somewhere: The "reasons" for some reason must be unexpressed and

---

[19] 10 *Corn. L. Q.* 17, 18; Hall, pp. 343-4.
[20] Dewey, *Logic: The Theory of Inquiry* (1938), 136.
[21] *Ibid.*, 274.

intuitive. An extreme version of the "hunch" theory assumed that some inner secret non-rational psyche, the "real" man, was pulling the puppet strings of overt or explicit reasoning and was therefore running the show.[22] Dewey never accepted such a view. Commenting upon Westermarck's monumental work showing the connection between customs and morals[23] Dewey remarks that Westermarck, in his anxiety to displace an unreal rational source of morals, sets up an equally unreal emotional basis, and adds:

"In truth, feeling as well as reason springs up with action."[24]

In other words, feelings or emotions are no more the ultimate grounds of action than is reason. The late Sir Frederick Pollock wrote to O. W. Holmes on May 2, 1929:

"I have formed a sort of notion that Dewey holds reason not to be something outside the order of nature, but the order itself: to which I need no persuasion."[25]

That Dewey conceived "reason" to be "the order of nature itself" is questionable; but he did conceive reason to be a part of *human* nature.

The term, "rationalization," has become so common in the discourse of law students and their teachers that it is hard to realize that it was first popularized, if not invented,[26] less than thirty years ago, in James Harvey Robinson's non-fiction best-seller, *The Mind in the Making*.[27] Robinson's basic purpose was to promote creative thinking about social and political changes by releasing the mind from its routine and unexamined prejudices.[28] One kind of think-

[22] See Schroeder, "The Psychologic Study of Judicial Opinions" (1918) 6 *Calif. L. Rev.* 1128. For a careful analysis of the influence of the "unconscious," see Robinson, *Law and the Lawyers* (1935), Ch. VII.
[23] Westermarck, *Origin and Development of the Moral Ideas* (1912).
[24] *Human Nature and Conduct* (1922), 76. See also 314.
[25] 2 *Holmes-Pollock Letters* (Howe ed., 1941) 242.
[26] The word "rationalization" was used in a somewhat similar sense in the nineteenth century. See Murray's English Dictionary.
[27] (1921).
[28] *Ibid.*, 3.

ing about social problems he called "rationalizing," the giving of "good" reasons for our cherished beliefs when they are challenged.[29] He derived the idea partly from abnormal psychology. When an insane person does something that upsets the routine of his asylum and is questioned by his supervisors, he invents "good" reasons which he believes will be acceptable to them but which are obviously not the "real" reasons.[30] Transferred by others to the realm of judicial decisions, this theory was used to support the view that the opinion of a court is a mere rationalization of the decision, a statement of the "good" reasons rather than the "real" reasons. Oliphant combined this theory with the behaviorist conception of the conditioned response to propose a new way of determining the legal significance of a judicial precedent: The judgment is the court's response to the stimulus of the facts; judicial opinions are "vague and shifting rationalizations" and are unworthy of "scientific study."[31] Dewey did not accept this view. He distinguished between the "logic of exposition," the process of formulating the reasons for a conclusion, and the logic "of search and inquiry," by which a reasoned conclusion is arrived at. The purpose of the judge in writing an opinion is to set forth the grounds for the decision, "so that it will not appear as an arbitrary dictum and so that it will indicate a rule for dealing with similar cases in the future."[32] The opinion of the court has a public function to fulfill but it is not a mere public ceremonial.

Two questions about Dewey's theory of legal reasoning may properly be raised: What part should antecedent legal rules and principles have in a "logic relative to consequences rather than to antecedents"? What value, if any, does formal logic have for legal

[29] *Ibid.*, 40-48.
[30] Dewey inserted in our seminar readings, as explaining rationalization, excerpts from Hart, *The Psychology of Insanity* (1916) 66 and Tansley, *The New Psychology* (1920), 159, 160, 168. Robinson referred to "modern psychologists" (p. 44) but based his arguments chiefly on social psychologists.
[31] Oliphant, "A Return to *Stare Decisis*" (1928) 14 *A.B.A.J.* 71, 159, N. 5; 1928 *Proc. Assn. of Amer. Law Schools* 76.
[32] 10 *Corn. L. Q.* 17, 24; Hall, p. 350.

reasoning? The first was partly answered in a previous essay.[33] The legal norms and precedents which have been shaped by successive generations of judges have a *prima facie* claim to be taken as expressing the best ways which experience has shown of dealing with with such cases. A court cannot re-examine afresh every proposition of law involved in every case. There is in Dewey's writings a substratum of Hegelianism, of belief that when ideas clash the best will survive if only the reasons for each are adequately exposed and intelligently appraised.[34] His view that the logical systematization of law is a useful tool (though only a tool and not an end)[35] would have no meaning unless there were something, antecedently given, to be systematized and worth systematizing. Indeed, the prediction of probable consequences is necessarily based upon antecedent experience. In his zeal to show that antecedent legal formulas, whether those of the reign of Henry IV or those of the most recent legislation aimed at "social justice,"[36] *could* not yield absolute legal certainty and *should* not be applied formally without attention to the facts of social life, he minimized, somewhat unduly, the interest of the community in "the maximum possible of stability and regularity of expectation in determining courses of conduct."[37] He also failed to mention (probably because he deemed it a professional rather than a philosophic problem) the limited scope of the judicial function, as compared with that of the legislature, in adapting law to the changing facts of social life.

Dewey's deprecation of the usefulness of formal logic for legal reasoning was also, I believe, an argumentative over-emphasis. To be sure, judges and lawyers do not frame their opinions and their arguments in the forms of the syllogism; yet with very rare exceptions their arguments are enthymemes, or partial syllogisms, that satisfy the formal requirements of validity. Since Dewey believes

---

[33] *Op. cit., supra*, N. 4, at p. 190.
[34] In his autobiographical sketch, originally published twenty years ago and recently re-published, he acknowledged the influence of Hegel upon his thinking. See "The Philosopher-in-the-Making" in *The Saturday Review of Literature* (Oct. 22, 1949), 9, 40-41.
[35] 10 *Corn. L. Q.* 19; Hall, p. 345.
[36] *Ibid.*, 27; Hall, p. 354.
[37] *Ibid.*, 25; Hall, p. 351.

that "symbolization is a necessary condition of all inquiry and of all knowledge,"[38] he can scarcely fail to recognize that the explicit formulation of premises, both legal and factual, will aid the legal reasoner in determining whether his conclusion is well grounded. In choosing judicial procedure as a literal instance of his theory of the construction of judgments, he recognizes that the final "judgment" (in a legal sense) is the result of a series of intermediate judgments (in a logical sense) which are governed by the "correspondence" between the "proved" facts and the legal meanings that give them significance.[39] Such "correspondence" can be better judged if legal and factual propositions are arranged in a formal pattern, even though this is only a temporary scaffolding of legal reasoning. One of Dewey's former pupils has well shown the relation between instrumental and formal logic in legal reasoning.[40]

Dewey's contextual theory of meaning has pervasive significance for legal reasoning. The meaning of a legal term is to be determined from the meaning of the proposition in which it occurs; and the meaning of this proposition is to be determined from the larger context in which it occurs. Legal language is "scientific language" in the sense that each meaning "is expressly determined by its relation to the other members of the language system."[41] A few instances of the implication of this theory may be noted. O. W. Holmes pointed out that words used in common speech, such as "malice," "intent," "right," "duty" have meanings, when used in legal contexts, which are different from their popular meanings.[42] The late Wesley N. Hohfeld, and after him Professor Arthur L. Corbin, clarified the meanings of such legal terms as "right" and "duty" by defining them in terms of legal consequences,[43] that is, actions for redress and defenses. Morever, the same symbol frequently has different meanings in different legal contexts. "Conver-

[38] *Logic*, 263.
[39] *Ibid.*, 120-122.
[40] Morris (Clarence), *How Lawyers Think* (1937).
[41] *Logic*, 50.
[42] *Op. cit., supra*, N. 14, 10 *Harv. L. Rev.* 459-462.
[43] See Hohfeld, "Fundamental Legal Conceptions as Applied in Judicial Reasoning" (1913) 23 *Yale L. J.* 16; Corbin, "Legal Analysis and Terminology" (1919) 29 *Yale L. J.* 163; Hall, *Readings in Jurisprudence* (1938) 471-484.

sion" has one meaning in the law of torts and another in the term, "equitable conversion." A more interesting example is the word "employee," which has been held to include women doing piecework at home, for compensation paid by a company which supplied the materials and received the finished product, under the Fair Labor Standards Act[44] but not under the Social Security Act.[45] Such examples do not show any contradiction between legal propositions, nor any inconsistency in legal reasoning. On the other hand, the contextual theory of meaning does not signify that judges are, like Humpty-Dumpty, at liberty to give a word any meaning that they please. As Dewey says, "the quality of the problematic situation (*i.e*, the proved facts) determines which rules of the total (legal) system are selected."[46]

However, the contextual theory of meaning does raise, for legal terminology, two important problems. How far does the relevant context extend? By narrowing contexts one could limit the meaning of a legal term to the context of a particular sentence of a statute, or to the context of a particular litigation, so that it would have no meaning for any other context. This *reductio ad absurdum* does not show that the contextual theory of meaning is absurd; it merely shows that sagacity in interpretation must be used by the legal reasoner to determine what legal meaning is the appropriate one in a given legal context. Every legal term falls in the larger context of the ends of the law, of the state, of society. The other problem is, how can legal terms have professional and exact meanings in legal contexts and yet be translatable, as they often must be, into terms of popular terminology? The lay witnesses whose testimony proves facts, the jurors who determine issues of fact with the aid of legal criteria, and the lay legislators who vote upon proposed laws, are examples of the need for such translation. This question raises recurrent problems of judicial administration.

Dewey's prescription that legal reasoning should employ a logic of consequences rather than antecedents is itself a part of a theory

[44] *Walling v. American Needle Crafts, Inc.*, 139 F. 2d 60 (C.C.A. 6, 1934).
[45] *Glenn, Collector v. Beard*, 141 F. 2d 376 (C.C.A. 6, 1944).
[46] *Logic*, 121.

of valuation. In a long essay contributed to an encyclopedia[47] he presents, in rather abstract language and with but few illustrations, an analysis of the traditional meanings of value, of his own conception of valuation-propositions, and of the process of valuation. While the discussion makes only a few references to legal valuations and its implications are not clear, it has significance in several ways for jurisprudence and for an empirical science of law.

Dewey distinguishes between valuation-propositions and propositions *about* valuations.[48] The latter are statements about matters-of-fact, namely, that a certain valuation *has* (or *has not*) been made. The former are generalizations about the way or ways in which certain operations *should* or *shall* be performed in the future. A legal proposition, as a rule for the judicial decision of controversies in which certain factual situations are proved, is a valuation-proposition. A statement that such a rule has been enacted or judicially established in a certain jurisdiction is a proposition about a valuation. In the ordinary legal discourse of judicial opinion and legal treatise, these two types of propositions are commonly combined. Thus the statement, "the legislature of New York has enacted that a written promise, signed by the promisor, to pay the promisor's debt, previously discharged in bankruptcy, is legally enforceable"[49] combines a valuation-proposition ("is legally enforceable") and a proposition about a valuation ("has enacted"). Dewey insists upon the importance of propositions about valuations: Without them, valuation propositions in a *"distinctive"* sense cannot "exist."[50] The reason for this view is that valuations are acts of prizing or appraisal by human beings, and it is always important to know by whom and under what conditions the valuation has been made. For legal propositions as valuation-propositions this means that one needs to inquire as to the authority of the valuer. Dewey would agree with Holmes that law "is not a brooding omnipresence in the

---

[47] Dewey, "Theory of Valuation" (1939) II *International Encyclopedia of Unified Science*, No. 4. The page references are to the pamphlet edition.
[48] *Ibid.*, 19-20.
[49] See N. Y. Personal Property Law § 31. The statement in the text is not a mere paraphrase of the statutory language, which states, in effect, that any such promise shall be void *unless in writing* and signed by the promisor.
[50] *Op. cit., supra*, N. 47, 20.

sky"; whether he would also agree that it is "the voice of an articulate sovereign" is not so clear in this context, though he would agree that the authority and competence of the valuer would constitute a part of the conditions for the evaluation of the valuation. That the Constitution of the United States or the Supreme Court of the United States has made a certain valuation is a cogent reason why a Federal judge should follow it, but it is ordinarily no reason why a French judge should follow it.

Dewey's conception of valuation includes but is not confined to "activities to which the name moral is applied."[51] He rejects the role of "feelings" (including moral feelings) in valuation, as inner states of mind which are "wholly private, accessible only to private inspection."[52] His purpose here is to release valuations from "unexamined traditions, conventions and institutionalized customs"[53] (in which moral feelings have their secret origin) and to relieve the present tension in society between the emotional and the intellectual by "the establishment of cultural conditions that will support the kinds of behavior in which emotions and ideas, desires and appraisals, are integrated."[54] Dewey does not explicitly reject the view that there is a distinctive moral sense or moral intuition that tends to govern many human valuations, but he would have it controlled by the intellectual process of valuation, that is, the appraisal of ends and means. In this sense he seeks a theory of valuation which is common to all practical disciplines: morals, engineering, medicine, law, etc. For legal valuations this has the immeasurable advantage, I think, of discarding the notion that they must be governed at some higher level by a body of valuation-propositions known as "ethics."[55] A good many, perhaps all, legal valuations are governed to a considerable extent by considerations of administrative expediency, or political principle. Recently, for example, several American courts have differed on the legal right of a minor child to recover

[51] *Ibid.*, 21.
[52] *Ibid.*, 10.
[53] *Ibid.*, 64.
[54] *Ibid.*, 65.
[55] See Cairns, *The Theory of Legal Science* (1941) 9, where "a rational theory of ethics" is regarded as a necessary component of "jurisprudence as a social science."

damages from a defendant who alienated the affections of his parent. One court recognized such a right on grounds that were primarily "moral,"[56] while another rejected the claim on the ground, among others, that actions for alienation of affections had been used for purposes of extortion.[57] Again, the political principle that officials shall not have power arbitrarily to deny a citizen freedom to speak his beliefs, however bizarre or unpalatable to the majority, does not mean that the majority are under an ethical duty to go and listen to him. While I agree thus far with Dewey, I do not agree if he means to say that legal valuations do not have distinctive characters which set them off from those of, say, medicine and engineering.

A third position of Dewey is that standardized ends provide "more or less blank frame-works where the nominal 'end' sets limits within which definite ends will fall, the latter being determined by appraisal of things as means."[58] The ends of the law as set forth by some legal philosophers are thus of no value unless they serve to indicate means of attaining them. Here one may compare Bentham's four ends of the civil code (security, equality, subsistence, abundance) with Stammler's ideal of a community of free-willing men.

A fourth position is that valuation-propositions must be grounded in physical generalizations,[59] that is, upon temporal and "causal" relations. By this is meant that valuation-propositions must have empirical bases. This position has, of course, been urged before. The Legal Realists proposed to investigate the consequences of legal rules and doctrines, as a basis ultimately for legal change. However, in their zeal to assimilate legal valuations to scientific procedures, they tended to blur or to obliterate the important difference between factual and normative (or prescriptive) generalizations. Hence the proposed plan to divorce the "Is" and the "Ought" temporarily for the purpose of investigation[60] and study, seems

[56] *Daily v. Parker*, 152 F. 2d 174 (C.C.A. Ill., 1945).
[57] *Taylor v. Keefe*, 134 Conn. 156, 163 (1947).
[58] *Op. cit., supra*, N. 47, 45.
[59] *Ibid.*, 53, 57.
[60] This was set forth with moderation and caution, as one of the beliefs held in common by the Legal Realists, in Llewellyn, "Some Realism About Realism—Responding to Dean Pound" (1931) 44 *Harv. L. Rev.* 1222, 1236. However, some Legal Realists apparently went further.

basically unsound and impracticable. Dewey's theory of valuation seems to indicate his view that the facts—of things as means and consequences as ends and their relations—to be used in arriving at valuations are to be selected and tested with a view to a definite valuation or set of alternative valuations. While legislative committee hearings are not models for empirical valuation, in so far as they conduct their investigations as genuine inquiries into facts selected with a certain proposed statute or statutes before them, they conform to the theory of valuation. It is, therefore, futile to believe that "social scientists," working with "facts" alone and with no valuations in view, will provide the ready-made empirical basis for new legal valuations. On the other hand, the propositions-about-valuations of present legal systems (legislation and case law) provide empirical bases for generalized valuations, as is shown by Pound's theory of Social Interests.[61] The current conception of "public policy" or "policy" as a kind of criterion for judging is based upon an interpretation of legal valuations in relation to consequences. When used in the process of judging, social interests or policies compete and conflict with each other. At this point Dewey's theory of legal reasoning complements his theory of valuation. Taken together they serve to explain the most important aspects of the changes in legal method and in legal substance of the last fifty years.

[61] See Patterson, "Pound's Theory of Social Interests" in *Interpretations of Modern Legal Philosophies* (1947) 558.

Dewey's Contribution to Historical Theory

by SIDNEY RATNER

HISTORY AND philosophy should be mutually enriching disciplines. They represent complementary elements in thought and require constant interplay if the first is to gain light and guidance from theory, and the second substance and testing from past human experience. Unfortunately, some make a virtue out of their intellectual impotence in any field outside their specialty and depreciate the value to be derived from the cross-fertilization of different disciplines. With some wit, but little wisdom, they attack such activity as "cross-sterilization." Others who profess respect for fields other than their own fail to utilize the insights and techniques of the other disciplines.

This failing has been true of more historians and philosophers in England and the United States than a friend of both groups would like to admit. Anglo-American philosophers since the turn of the century have centered their attention on our knowledge of the external world as derived from natural science and commonsense perception. The status and special problems of historical knowledge have until recently been so ignored or slighted as to provoke the charge of "a conspiracy of silence" on the subject among philosophers.[1] On the other hand, research historians in America since the 1880's have been primarily concerned with proving that history is as rigorously scientific in its methods and as productive in its discovery and publication of facts as other longer established university studies. The preponderant majority of such

---

[1] R. G. Collingwood, *The Idea of History* (Oxford, 1946), 142.

historical scholars have had little interest in the theoretical presuppositions of their work. To them Ranke had set the standards of their craft once and for all time to come when he had declared in 1824 that the function of history was not to judge the past or to draw lessons of wisdom for the present and future, but "merely to show what actually occurred."[2] These positivistic historians were repelled by the errors or excesses of the earlier theological, racial, or economic interpretations of American development as well as by other striking theories advanced by Buckle, Herbert Spencer, Spengler, Pareto, and Toynbee. These storm-centers of controversy, no matter what truth eventually emerged from them through the sifting of critical analysis, confirmed the rank and file of American historians in their Baconian fear of speculative hypotheses.[3] They agreed fundamentally with John Bach McMaster's feeling that "It is not the business of a historian to be a philosopher."[4] They wished to avoid the dangers of generalization and the pains of critical reflection on the logic of historical interpretation.

Fortunately, some bold spirits in both disciplines have had the strength and courage to break through the academic wire-fences and have succeeded in promoting an advancement in understanding. Carl Becker once said, "I would not willingly charge a reputable historian with harboring a Philosophy of History. Yet I recall that one day [Frederick Jackson] Turner . . . said: 'The question is not whether you have a Philosophy of History, but whether the philosophy you have is good for anything.' "[5]

" 'Whether the philosophy you have is good for anything'—that question is one that historians and other scientists cannot escape, no matter how desperately they may seek to avoid it. Henry Adams

[2] G. P. Gooch, *History and Historians in the Nineteenth Century* (London, 1928), 76-102.
[3] Cf. Michael Kraus, *A History of American History* (New York, 1937), esp. 291ff.; J. H. Randall, Jr. and George Haines, IV, "Controlling Assumptions in the Practice of American Historians," in Social Science Research Council, Committee on Historiography, *Theory and Practice in History* (New York, 1946), 17-52.
[4] Eric F. Goldman, *John Bach McMaster* (Philadelphia, 1943), 107.
[5] Carl L. Becker, *Everyman His Own Historian* (New York, 1935), 207.

has fascinated American historians by the questions he raised on the meaning of human history. Though they have tended to be skeptical of his 'Dynamic Theory of History,' they all too often have not known how to refute it. To many, Henry Adams, like his brother, Brooks, is important because he attempted to deal with the whole sweep and direction of Western history in the 'spirit of modern science.' "[6]

Unknown to most historians and philosophers is the fact that Henry Adams in 1910 had submitted his privately printed volume, *A Letter to American Teachers,* later reprinted as *The Degradation of the Democratic Dogma,* to William James for the latter's comment and judgment. James, with the knowledge of a scientist and the acumen of a logician, saw through the imposing "scientific" structure Adams had so laboriously built up for his pessimistic theory of history; James gave a definitive evaluation and appraisal that deserves far wider currency that it has ever received. Adams' key to the laws of history had wit and erudition in its favor, but no scientific validity. James pointed out that the second law of thermodynamics, upon which Adams based his theory, is wholly irrelevant to "history," except for setting a terminus to the latter. History is the course of events before that limit is reached. All that the second law says is that, whatever history occurs, must take place between the initial maximum and the terminal minimum of difference in energy-level. The value of human actions and institutions has nothing whatever to do with their energy-budget. Certain arrangements of matter on the same energy-level, are, from the human point of view, superior, while others are inferior. Finally, though the ultimate state of the universe may result in the extinction of all life and mind, "there is nothing in physics to interfere with the hypothesis that the penultimate state might be the millenium—in other words a state in which a minimum of difference of energy-level might have its exchanges so skillfully *canalisés* that a maxi-

[6] Charles Beard, "Introduction" in Brooks Adams, *The Law of Civilization and Decay* (New York, 1943), 3-53.

mum of happy and virtuous consciousness would be the only result."[7]

This interchange between the most noted figures in American history and philosophy at the time is an important illustration of the contribution that philosophy made in testing the soundness of a theory of history that has become a modern classic. Unfortunately, the literary qualities of Henry Adams' philosophic writings on this theme outweighed his scientific and logical errors for most of his readers. Gradually the tide of opinion will turn, as the wisdom of James's verdict becomes more widely appreciated.

John Dewey's philosophy has much to offer historians concerned about the logic or theory of historical inquiry and interpretation. Some of his central ideas, especially in their early form, have influenced notable historians like James Harvey Robinson, Carl Becker, Charles Beard, and Wesley C. Mitchell (in his important but usually slighted role as economic historian). Through them the "New History" in its various forms has affected the main currents of American life and thought. Yet Dewey himself has nowhere brought all his reflections on the nature of history into one single treatise. This is regrettable because few historians have had the time or philosophic training to sift out from his numerous writings insights of the greatest potential value and pertinence to them. No future Henry Adams, if he knows Dewey's philosophy, will be likely to write what Adams wrote in 1896: "As History stands, it is a sort of Chinese Play, without end and without lesson."[8]

It is worth noting, if merely to make philosophers realize that historians contributed something to the education of a great philosopher, that Dewey took a "minor" in history and political science at Johns Hopkins in the early 1880's with Herbert Baxter Adams,

---

[7] Letter to Henry Adams, June 17, 1910; Henry James, *The Letters of William James* (2 v., Boston, 1920), 2: 344-47. Adams' illness from the spring of 1912 to his death in March 1918 prevented his revising his theory in the light of James's criticisms.

[8] Letter from Adams to Dr. J. Franklin Jameson, Nov. 17, 1896, cited in Roy F. Nichols, "The Dynamic Interpretation of History," *New England Quarterly* (June 1935), 8:164.

one of the pioneers in the teaching of scientific history in America. In H. B. Adams' seminar he met, studied and debated various political and historical questions with fellow-students of ability, one of whom was Woodrow Wilson.[9] Dewey also learnt much about intellectual history and method from George Sylvester Morris, his main professor of philosophy, who had translated Ueberweg's *History of Philosophy* into English and who drew upon a rich historical background in all his teaching. Dewey, moreover, gained insight into the problems of historical research and interpretation very early in his career from his work in teaching courses in the history of philosophy at Johns Hopkins and elsewhere, and in writing critical studies in the history of ideas. The latter range from essays on Spinoza, Kant, and Leibniz in the 1880's to later studies of Darwin, Herbert Spencer, Hobbes, Locke, Plato, and such recent or contemporary thinkers as James, Peirce, Bergson, and Whitehead. Many of these essays and numerous contributions on different doctrines, schools, and phases of the history of philosophy to authoritative publications like Baldwin's *Dictionary of Philosophy and Psychology* and the *Encyclopaedia of the Social Sciences* refute the charge that Dewey has never set down a record "of objective and impartial knowledge of the past."

Nor should we overlook Dewey's keen interest in and writings on the historical background of crucial modern political, economic, educational, and social problems. Concerned as Dewey has been with solving issues of importance for the present and the future, he has always appreciated the wisdom of studying how the problems emerged. *Vide* his *Public and Its Problems, German Philosophy and Politics, Liberalism and Social Action,* and *Freedom and Culture.* The challenge the historian has to meet in evaluating historic figures and social changes Dewey has met in an impressive series of articles, embodied in part in his book, *Characters and Events.* Most of the judgments set forth in that work have stood the test of time and have proved his capacity for making as sound

---

[9] William Diamond, *The Economic Thought of Woodrow Wilson* (Baltimore, 1943), 22 n. 26. Neither Dewey nor Wilson has referred to their association at John Hopkins in print, so far as I know.

evaluation of trends and issues, as any historian of note.[10] Finally, Dewey has demonstrated his skill as a master in the analysis of evidence, the heart of historical inquiry, in such controversial cases as that of Sacco-Vanzetti.[11] Here he has practiced the theory of sound reflective thinking which he advanced as far back as the 1890's. His *Studies in Logical Theory* and related writings have been commended by such authorities on historical, economic, and sociological methodology as Allen Johnson, Wesley C. Mitchell, William F. Ogburn, and Frederick J. Teggart.[12]

History to Dewey, as to historians generally, is a double-barrelled word. It "is that which happened in the past and it is the intellectual reconstruction of these happenings at a subsequent date."[13] This characterization accords in part with accepted usage in distinguishing between history as the record of events and history as the events themselves.[14] But Dewey's account differs from the stereotyped one or Carl Becker's: "History is the memory of things said and done"[15] in that Dewey stresses at the outset the role of scientific inquiry in establishing the evidence for the belief or warranted assertion that certain events have occurred. To him historical statements or judgments form one phase or part of all empirical science, that which deals with "spatial-temporal determination" or "narration-description." That is why Chapter XII of his *magnum opus, Logic: The Theory of Inquiry*,[16] contains the

[10] See Jane M. Dewey, ed., "Biography of John Dewey," in P. A. Schilpp, *The Philosophy of John Dewey* (Evanston and Chicago, 1939), 3ff., esp. 15-19, 38-45; and "Bibliography of . . . Dewey," *loc. cit.,* 611-76.
[11] Cf. Morris R. Cohen and Ernest Nagel, *An Introduction to Logic and Scientific Method* (New York, 1934), 350.
[12] Allen Johnson, *The Historian and Historical Evidence* (New York, 1926), 37-8, 167-9; Stuart A. Rice, ed., *Methods in Social Science* (Chicago, 1931), 211, 676 f.; Frederick J. Teggart, *Theory of History* (New Haven, 1925), 155, 189.
[13] John Dewey, *Logic: The Theory of Inquiry* (New York, 1938), 236.
[14] James T. Shotwell, *The History of History: Volume I* (New York, 1939), 4 f.
[15] Carl Becker, *op. cit.,* 235.
[16] Dewey, *Logic,* 220-44. Though the whole *Logic* should be read by every historian, the other chapters that would be of maximum help to him would be Chapters XXII-XXV. They deal with causation, scientific method and subject-matter, social inquiry, the logic of inquiry and philosophies of knowledge.

most extended analysis of historical knowledge to be found in his writings, or in any modern Anglo-American treatise on logic since F. H. Bradley's *Principles* appeared in 1883.

A second point of difference is that Dewey purposely makes the term "history" cover the "human" and the "non-human." Most historians follow James Harvey Robinson in his restrictive assertion:

"In its amplest meaning History includes every trace and vestige of everything that man has done or thought since first he appeared on the earth."[17]

Dewey's theory of history may be most conveniently presented as a series of leading ideas, with accompanying comments in explication or qualification.

(1) Any and every historical inquiry about the course of past events arises out of the need or desire to solve a problem or set of problems.[18] For Dewey, as for Frederick Jackson Turner, historiography consists of the *Frage,* of putting questions to oneself and others about doubtful or indeterminate situations and seeking the answers thereto. Living history is like a Platonic dialogue: an interchange of questions and answers about problems in the light of discoverable evidence and explanatory hypotheses.[19]

(2) These explanatory ideas or hunches inspire or lead to a quest for relevant data through controlled observations—extensive and intensive, the formation and use of criteria for selecting and rejecting proposed data, the ordering and arranging of the authenticated evidence on the basis of the systematic conceptions employed by the historian.[20] Here Dewey has set forth four crucial phases of

[17] James Harvey Robinson, *The New History* (New York, 1922), 1.
[18] Dewey, *Logic,* 35, 107ff., 232.
[19] Dewey acknowledges that Plato "still provides my favorite philosophic reading . . . the dramatic, restless, cooperatively inquiring Plato of the Dialogues . . . the Plato whose highest flight of metaphysics always terminated with a social and practical turn." "From Absolutism to Experimentalism," G. P. Adams and W. P. Montague, eds., *Contemporary American Philosophy* (New York, 1939), 2:21. Cf. his "The 'Socratic Dialogues' of Plato," in Columbia University, *Studies in the History of Ideas,* Volume II (New York, 1925), 1-24. On Turner, see Carl Becker, *op. cit.,* 207-8.
[20] Dewey, *Logic,* 232.

every historian's task: a) the necessity for hypotheses in order that *facts* as well as *laws* and *patterns* may be discovered; b) the need for *activity*: obtaining, studying, and experimenting with different source-materials in order to get the data required for establishing historical propositions; c) the use of accepted canons of what constitutes reliable evidence, or the creation or extension of such criteria (the hallmark of the scientific historian is his awareness of and articulateness in stating his methodological presuppositions or guiding principles); d) the creative element inherent in every historical presentation, since no story can be told or problem solved without the historian choosing or discovering what seems to him the best (logical or rhetorical) order of arrangement of his data and conclusions.

(3) Continuity, for Dewey, distinguishes history from annals, the records of isolated episodes. Absolute origins and absolute closes or termini of the world are mythical. History involves the use of temporal propositions based on rhythms in physical nature and human life, cycles of events marked by periodicities, intervals, and limits. But in Dewey's, as in customary and honorific, usage, the word "history" is differentiated from cosmic mythology and almanac or diary recordings by focusing upon "continuity of change from beginnings to endings,"[21] a "cumulative continuity of movement in a given direction toward stated outcomes."[22] Here Dewey is in agreement with the classical thesis that every history displays an action, in the dramatic sense, with a beginning, middle, and end.[23]

The basis for continuity in historical narrative lies in the continuities that scientific inquiry discloses in physical nature and human life. Dewey is conscious of the fact that continuity and discontinuity are polar categories. He has explained the occurrence of problematic and unsettled situations as "due to the *characteristic union of the discrete or individual and the continuous or relational.*"[24] But

[21] Dewey, *Experience and Nature* (New York, 1929), v.
[22] Dewey, *Logic*, 234.
[23] Frederick J. Teggart, *Theory of History*, 17.
[24] Dewey, *The Quest for Certainty* (New York, 1929), 234. Italics in the original text.

like Darwin he emphasizes continuity both as a methodological postulate for future inquiries and as a verified relation or a warranted assertion about past and present knowings-knowns.[25]

What Dewey has written about continuity as a primary postulate of a naturalistic theory of logic holds equally well for a naturalistic theory of history:

> "The idea of continuity . . . excludes complete rupture on one side and mere repetition on the other; it precludes reduction of the "higher" to the "lower" just as it precludes complete breaks and gaps. The growth and development of any living organism from seed to maturity illustrates the meaning of continuity. The method by which development takes place is something to be determined by a study of what actually occurs. It is not to be determined by prior conceptual constructions, even though such constructions may be helpful as hypotheses when they are used to direct observation and experimentation."[26]

This means that the direction or course of events in any history under investigation may take or follow any one of a number of possible historical patterns, *e.g.*, linearly progressive, spiral, cyclical, retrogressive. In the last analysis, all natural existences or things in space-time, as well as human beings, have careers: are born, undergo qualitative changes, and finally die, giving place to other individuals.[27] It is the responsibility of natural and human history to determine the specific pattern of development and change taken by different individuals or groups, whether stellar constellations, biologic species, tribes, states, churches, corporations, or scientific societies.

(4) The sensitivity of Dewey to change and interrelations has been balanced by an awareness and appreciation of qualitatively unique individuals and relatively discrete, distinct, or isolated ob-

---

[25] Dewey, *Experience and Nature*, 275. Speaking of human growth from infancy to maturity, he said, "The reality is the growth-process itself. . . . The real existence is the history in its entirety, the history as just what it is."

[26] Dewey, *Logic*, 23-4.

[27] Dewey, *Experience and Nature*, 78-120, 163f., 273ff.; and "Time and Individuality," in New York University, James Arthur Foundation, *Time and Its Mysteries: Series II* (New York, 1940), 85-109.

jects and systems. In various writings, notably *Art As Experience,* he has celebrated "situations in which self-enclosed, discrete, individualized characters dominate."[28] But he has sought to stress the need for doing justice to conjoined qualitative and "relational" analysis. "In other words, all experienced objects have a double status. They are individualized, consummatory.... They are also involved in a continuity of inter-actions and changes, and hence are causes and potential means of later experiences."[29] This double sensitivity has led Dewey to warn historians against trying to justify continuity by resorting to "a falsely named 'genetic' method, wherein there is no genuine genesis, because everything is resolved into what went before."[30] To him Egyptian civilization and art were not just a preparation for the ancient Greek, nor were Greek thought and art simply reedited versions of the other and older civilizations from which they borrowed so freely. Anticipating Ruth Benedict's *Patterns of Culture,* he wrote: "Each culture has its own individuality and has a pattern that binds its parts together."[31]

Here is a point which many historians fail to keep constantly in mind. The nineteenth century's exaltation of history and evolution had made explanation of a phenomenon exclusively or mainly in terms of its origin into a fashion that still prevails in certain quarters. Dewey has avoided the excesses of historicism and of antihistorical rationalism in what he has come to call the "genetic-functional method."[32] An adequate exploration of that method requires another essay. For historians, however, the essential idea is that each culture and period needs to be studied both in terms of the particular qualities, elements, and patterns that characterize it at any given time of observation, and in terms of the processes whereby they came into being, and continue to function or operate.

(5) Dewey recognizes pluralism, as well as continuity, in history as a logical correlate of his perception and judgment that individuals are basic elements, aspects, or phases of physical nature

[28] Dewey, *The Quest for Certainty,* 235.
[29] *Ibid.,* 236.
[30] Dewey, *Art As Experience* (New York, 1934), 335.
[31] *Ibid.,* 336.
[32] John Dewey, *Problems of Men* (New York, 1946), 416.

and human society. With William James he rejects both extreme "atomism which logically involves a denial of connections" and "an absolutistic block monism which, in behalf of the reality of relations, leaves no room for the discrete, for plurality, and for individuals."[33] Dewey has developed a viable and verifiable alternative to these theories in a pluralism or concatenism, which does justice to the connections between things and the manifold ensembles, *Gestalten,* fields or situations of which they are part.[34]

The diversity of things and of directions of change makes it impossible for a cosmically comprehensive history to be written. The totality of events and objects cannot be done justice to at any one time or in any one treatment. Hence, there are as many histories as there are types of subjects, events, or methods of approach, for study. Only the economics of research costs and consumer demand sets limits to an infinite series of histories. "Strains of change have to be selected and material sequentially ordered according to the direction of change defining the strain which is selected. History is of peoples, of dynasties; is political, ecclesiastical, economic; is of art, science, religion and philosophy."[35] History also embraces solar systems, planets, plants, and animals. Each thing or organism, each type, class, or species, has a history than can be or has been written. Nature or the cosmos "is an affair *of* affairs, wherein each one, no matter how linked up it may be with others, has its *own* quality."[36] Each history has its own value and excellence. Though Dewey has been labeled "anthropocentric," he fully recognizes the infinite variety of things and other species that constitute "Nature *as* background" for man, and the special frames of reference that may be built up around non-human things, inanimate or animate, and that would put man in the background and some non-human

[33] Dewey, "Experience, Knowledge and Value," in P. A. Schilpp, *op. cit.,* 544.
[34] *Ibid.,* 545. It is important to realize that Dewey does not regard the "individual" or the "social" as something *given* or fixed. See Dewey, *Reconstruction in Philosophy* (New York, 1920), 193ff. On the meaning of "situation," see Dewey, *Logic,* 66ff., John Dewey and Arthur F. Bentley, *Knowing and the Known* (Boston, 1949), 294, 302, 304.
[35] Dewey, *Logic,* 234.
[36] Dewey, *Experience and Nature,* 97.

object or being, *e.g.*, star, flower, quadruped, in the foreground.[37] Similarly, while critics have objected to Dewey's stress on the need for social unity through cooperative inquiry and action, Dewey himself has warned repeatedly against exaltation of the state and the search for "*the* final good, and for *the* single moral force." Hence, he recognizes the claims of histories written about the voluntary associations that men form in order to achieve the diversity of goods life offers, as well as of those histories centered on national and world states or institutions.[38] His historical approach is in harmony with the social and natural pluralism on which it is based.

Owing to its crucial importance, special treatment must be given to Dewey's judgment: "*All historical construction is necessarily selective.*"[39] This truth has been recognized and proclaimed by others; in our day, notably by Charles Beard and Carl Becker.[40] Their challenging assertions, however, have provoked more heat than light. Orthodox historians and philosophers fear that the foundations of scientific history have been undermined.[41] Dewey's writings, if carefully correlated and interpreted, provide a theory that avoids arbitrary impressionism, special pleading, and chronological parochialism in history. Dewey also enables the critical reader to work out the principles of an "objective relativism" or "relativistically objective history" that will embrace all the valid points of the Historical Relativists without taking on their theo-

[37] Dewey, *Problems of Men*, 195ff., and "Experience, Knowledge and Value," *op. cit.*, 533f. Cf. Frederick J. E. Woodbridge, *The Purpose of History* (New York, 1916), 37-58.
[38] Dewey, *The Influence of Darwin on Philosophy* (New York, 1910), 48, and *Reconstruction in Philosophy*, 203f.
[39] Dewey, *Logic*, 235. Italics in original text.
[40] Charles A. Beard, "Written History as an Act of Faith," *American Historical Review* (Jan. 1934), 39:219-31; "That Noble Dream," *loc. cit.*, 41:74-87; and (with Alfred Vagts), "Currents in Historiography," *loc. cit.*, 42:460-83; Carl L. Becker, *Everyman His Own Historian*, 233-55.
[41] R. L. Schuyler, "The Usefulness of Useless History," *Political Science Quarterly* (March, 1941), 51:23-37; Theodore C. Smith, "The Writing of American History . . . 1884 to 1934," *American Historical Review* (April, 1935), 40:439-49; Maurice Mandelbaum, *The Problem of Historical Knowledge* (New York, 1938); Arthur O. Lovejoy, "Present Standpoints and Past History," *Journal of Philosophy* (August 31, 1939), 36:477-89.

retical errors. Occasionally Dewey, in his zeal for correcting established practices and prejudices, overstresses a point and lays himself open to misinterpretation. That is why the whole range of Dewey's works must be considered in order to do justice to his intent and the richness of his thought.

(1) To Dewey the basis of every historical enterprise is the fact that each historian *elects* or *chooses* the problem or subject he investigates and writes about, be it "the history of a dynasty, of an enduring struggle, of the formation and growth of a science, an art or a religion, or the technology of production."[42] This element of personal choice Dewey recognizes as an arbitrary or contingent fact, but he realizes that history, like all science, starts from the insight and will, genius and character, of the investigator, and achieves rationality as the result of the interaction between the historian and his subject matter. The latter exercises a control over speculation, a check upon hypothesis.

(2) In the process of inquiring and writing, each historian "*postulates* a career, a course and cycle of change."[43] Here the individual makes a personal contribution of what ideas or hypotheses he has about the nature of the thing he is studying. Alternative assumptions are possible. Again the *choice* or *selection* of a certain theory or set of ideas has to be made by each individual, either as "something taken for granted as the true basis for reasoning or belief" or as a "condition required for further operations" of inquiry.[44] In other words, historians may be dogmatic or consciously tentative and experimental. "Glorification of empirical research has gone so far that many historians believe that to be open-minded means being empty-headed; free of infection by hypotheses and theories."[45] The only available option is between having inarticulate major premises or articulate ones which one realizes may need revision in part or whole. American historians of the last few decades, like their European colleagues, pride themselves upon being hard-

[42] Dewey, *Logic*, 236.
[43] *Ibid*. Italics inserted.
[44] John Dewey and Arthur F. Bentley, *Knowing and the Known*, 80.
[45] Sidney Ratner, "Presupposition and Objectivity in History," *Philosophy of Science* (Oct. 1940), 7:503.

headed empiricists. Nevertheless, the vogue, over successive periods, of Turner's frontier theory of American history, Beard's economic interpretation of the Constitution and Parrington's ideological explanation of the main currents in American thought indicates how seductive oversimplified theories may be even to historians desiring to be scientific. Though each of these great figures was acutely conscious of many of his assumptions, each ignored or failed to develop some important assumptions. Yet each of these men rendered a service by formulating a fruitful hypothesis that helped to illuminate part of the complex development of American civilization.[46]

(3) The selection of a subject and the formulation of a theory about its course of development or change lead the historian to decide on the appropriate *context* or *framework* for his central theme. No event "is *merely* dynastic, merely scientific or merely technological. As soon as the event takes its place as an incident in a particular history, an act of judgment (by the historian) has loosened it from the total complex of which it was a part, and has given it a place in a new context, the context and the place both being determinations made in inquiry, not native properties of original existence."[47] Here Dewey takes issue with the notion stemming from Ranke that historical inquiry simply reinstates the events that once happened "as they actually happened." Dewey would agree with William James's statement:

"The real world as it is given objectively at this moment is the sum total of all its beings and events now . . . While I talk and the flies buzz, a sea-gull catches a fish at the mouth of the Amazon, a tree falls in the Adirondack wilderness, a man sneezes in Germany, a horse dies in Tartary, and twins are born in France . . . Does the contemporaneity of these events with one another and with a million others as disjointed, form a rational bond between

---

[46] Sidney Ratner, "The Historian's Approach to Psychology," *Journal of the History of Ideas* (Jan. 1941), 2:95-109. *Cf.* Wassily Leontif, "Note on the Pluralistic Interpretation of History . . . ," *Journal of Philosophy* (Nov. 4, 1948), 45:617-24.

[47] Dewey, *Logic*, 236. Italics in original text.

them, and unite them into anything that means for us a world? Yet just such a collateral contemporaneity, and nothing else, is the real order of the world.

"We have to break that order altogether,—and by picking out from it the items which concern us, and connecting them with others far away, which we say 'belong' with them, we are able to make out definite threads of sequence and tendency; to foresee particular liabilities and get ready for them; and to enjoy simplicity and harmony in place of what was chaos."[48]

Relatively few historians have attained Dewey's appreciation of the necessity for each historian's consciously formulating the frame of reference for each specific inquiry. They would acknowledge that "Selective emphasis, with accompanying omission and rejection, is the heart-beat of mental life."[49] But, once having taken over traditional criteria of what the relevant or strategic variables in the situation are, or staked their reputation on some hypothesis, they tend to trust unwarrantedly their set of presuppositions. The fashions in historical explanations rival those in other disciplines, and have ranged from the geographic, biologic, political, and economic to the psychoanalytic and psycho-somatic. "The law of fashion is a law of life," Justice Holmes has remarked. But that is no reason for historians not trying to moderate, if not avoid, their pendulum-swings in theory. One aid to such intellectual sobriety is the construction of alternative postulate-sets. "For ultimately the only logical alternative to open and aboveboard formulation of conceptual alternatives (as many as possible) is formation of controlling ideas on the ground of either custom and tradition or some special interest. The result is dichotomization of a social field into conservatives and progressives, 'reactionaries' and 'radicals,' &c."[50]

(4) Dewey's contextualism, his emphasis upon the historian's preparing the most adequate frame of reference for his subject, induces him to war against "the fallacy of selective emphasis" as embodied in the "existing division of social phenomena into a num-

---

[48] William James, *The Will to Believe and Other Essays in Popular Philosophy* (New York, 1897, 1931), 118-19. Paragraph 2 in quotation precedes paragraph 1 in original text.
[49] Dewey, *Experience and Nature*, 25.
[50] Dewey, *Logic*, 508.

ber of compartmentalized and supposedly independent noninteracting fields."[51] The injurious effects of scientific overspecialization, concentration on too narrow a range of elements and relations, makes him suggest the urgent need for breaking down conceptual barriers "so as to promote cross-fertilization of ideas, and greater scope, variety and flexibility of hypotheses."[52] Among the best illustrations and confirmations of Dewey's point are Charles and Mary Beard's *Rise of American Civilization,* Carl Becker's *Heavenly City of the Eighteenth Century Philosophers,* Arthur F. Bentley's *Process of Government,* Wesley C. Mitchell's *Business Cycles* (1913), and Gunnar Myrdal's *An American Dilemma.*

The most striking testimony of Dewey's influence upon a major pioneer in such cross-fertilization is to be found in the late Wesley Mitchell's recollection of his student days at Chicago in the late 1890's:

"There I began studying philosophy and economics about the same time. The similarity of the two disciplines struck me at once . . . . Give me premises and I could spin speculations by the yard. Also I knew that my deductions were futile. . . .

"Meanwhile I was finding something really interesting in philosophy and economics. John Dewey was giving courses under all sorts of titles and every one of them dealt with the same problem—how we think. I was fascinated by his view of the place which logic holds in human behavior. It explained the economic theorists. The thing to do was to find out how they came to tackle certain problems; why they took certain premises as a matter of course; why they did not consider all the permutations and variants of those problems which were logically possible; why their contemporaries thought their conclusions were significant. And, if one wanted to try his own hand at constructive theorizing, Dewey's notion pointed the way. It is a mistake to suppose that consumers guide their course by ratiocination—they don't think except under stress. There is no way of deducing from certain premises what they will do, just because their behavior is not itself rational. One has to find out what they do. That is a matter of observation, which the economic theo-

[51] *Ibid.* On the fallacy of selective emphasis, see Dewey, *Experience and Nature,* 27, 32.
[52] Dewey, *Logic,* 508.

rists had taken all too lightly. Economic theory became a fascinating subject—the orthodox types particularly—when one began to take the mental operations of the theorists as the problem, instead of taking their theories seriously."[53]

Another exemplification of Dewey's idea of cross-fertilization is Charles and Mary Beard's *apologia* for writing *The Rise of American Civilization*:

"The history of a civilization, if intelligently conceived, may be an instrument of civilization. Surveying life as a whole, as distinguished from microscopic analysis by departments, it ought to come nearer than any partial history to the requirements of illumination. As long as the various divisions of history are kept separate, each must be incomplete and distorted; for, as Buckle says, the philosophy of any subject (that is, the truth of it) is not at its center but on the periphery where it impinges on all other sciences. . . .

"If the history of a people is a philosophy of the whole social organism in process of becoming, then it ought to furnish material with which discernment can be whetted. . . .

"The author of such a work must at the outset accept the theorem that history is philosophy open at both ends and in selection and construction must wrestle continually with that baffling proposition."[54]

(5) Appreciation of the need for intellectual cross-fertilization and critically formulated frames of reference has been derived in part from Dewey's acute awareness of the tremendous extent to which historical inquiry "is controlled by the dominant problems and conceptions of the culture of the period in which it is written."[55] Most historians and scientists believe themselves sophisticated and think present-day methods make them more objective than their predecessors. Dewey is equally concerned about objectivity: the discounting and eliminating of merely "personal factors in the operations by which a conclusion is reached."[56] But be-

[53] Letter from Wesley C. Mitchell to John M. Clark, August 9, 1928, in Stuart A. Rice, ed., *Methods in Social Science*, 676-77.
[54] Charles A. and Mary R. Beard, *The Rise of American Civilization* (New York, 1930), vii, ix, xiv.
[55] Dewey, *Logic*, 236.
[56] *Ibid.*, 44.

yond this he has striven to drive home a set of insights which he calls *cultural naturalism*.[57] This position stresses the fact that every inquiry grows out of and proceeds in a cultural matrix—a "complex whole of knowledge, belief, art, morals, law, custom, and any other capabilities and habits acquired by man as a member of society."[58] The intellectual assets with which every historian works include the guiding ideas and tested data given through the medium of the language or languages he has acquired as a bio-cultural being. His intellectual liabilities include the prejudices, biases, and other limitations of insight, interest, and knowledge he has absorbed from the society in which he was born, lives, and has his being.

History, like philosophy, art, and science, is a phenomenon of human culture. Historians in every culture and period, Indian, Chinese, Athenian, the Europe of the twelfth or the twentieth century "find certain preoccupying interests that appear hypnotic in their rigid hold upon imagination and . . . also find certain resistances, certain dawning rebellions, struggles to escape and to express some fresh value of life."[59] From the time of Herodotus and Thucydides to that of Charles Beard and Elie Halévy, historians have written, as Herodotus did, "in order that the things which have been done might not in time be forgotten." Personal preferences and tastes have helped to determine the historian's selection of things which should not be forgotten. But the success or failure of each history has depended in large measure upon the historian's sensitivity to the things that the people for whom he wrote "judged worthy of commemoration in their own lives and achievements,"[60] or in the lives and achievements of their predecessors, friends, or enemies. Of course, in every culture and in every historic epoch there are diverse currents and drives reflecting or expressing differences of varying social groups, each with its economic, regional, and cultural idiosyncrasy. Hence, different types of history reflect not only

[57] *Ibid.*, 20, 42-59, 487ff.
[58] Edward B. Tylor, *Primitive Culture* (6th ed.; London, 1920), I, 1.
[59] John Dewey, *Philosophy and Civilization* (New York, 1931), 6. What Dewey writes about philosophy applies on this point to history.
[60] Dewey, *Logic*, 235.

the patterns, but also the sub-patterns of culture.[61] Any critical study of the history of history will demonstrate this point.[62]

The upshot of Dewey's analysis of the prevailing practice of historians over the ages parallels that of Huizinga, the great European historian and a pragmatic theorist of history: *"History is the intellectual form in which a civilization renders account to itself of its past."*[63] Dewey, however, uses his recognition of *cultural relativity* as a tool for furthering greater objectivity in history and the social sciences. Once one becomes aware of the presuppositions of one's pattern or sub-pattern of culture, one can consciously work out techniques for correcting the biases thereof. Perfect or absolute objectivity like other scientific criteria "is a logical ideal which points the direction in which inquiry must move but which cannot be completely attained."[64] Dewey has been a pioneer in the sociology of knowledge without becoming a victim of extreme cultural or historical relativism. He has anticipated most of the insights that Karl Mannheim and other sociologists have exalted into a new discipline. But Dewey has put most of his energies into developing the conditions for sound social inquiry that will correct class, racial, and other biases.

Historians are now in a position to develop a multicultural approach that will do greater justice to the richness of their subject matter. Cultural naturalism and pluralism unite in Dewey's work to outlaw provincialism and to make possible a history that approaches greater objectivity and universality. The historian, like the philosopher, is a part of society and history; a creature of the past he studies; yet a creator of the future in some measure. To the extent that he and the rest of society are able to perceive and appreciate the plurality of forms history and culture can take, mankind will have advanced to a new and higher level of civilization.

[61] *Cf.* Sidney Ratner, "Patterns of Culture in History," *Philosophy of Science* (Jan. 1939), 6:88-97.
[62] Collingwood, *The Idea of History;* Karl Löwith, *Meaning in History* (Chicago, 1949); Shotwell, *The History of History.*
[63] *Cf.* Johan Huizinga, "A Definition of the Concept of History," in Raymond Klibansky and H. J. Paton, eds., *Philosophy and History* (Oxford, 1936), 1-10, esp., 9.
[64] Dewey, *Logic,* 320.

John Dewey and Education

by JOHN L. CHILDS

IN THE field of education, Dewey is a practitioner as well as a theorist. During his years at the University of Chicago, he founded and directed an experimental school. He organized this University Elementary School because he wanted to put some of his leading philosophical and psychological ideas to the test of practice. It was his conviction that a program for the nurture of the young would provide the most meaningful test of his theories. He believed that the program of the conventional school of that period—the decade of the nineties—was in deep conflict with his conception of the nature of mind and the process by which it develops, as well as with his interpretation of the values and the procedures of a democratic society.

In *School and Society,* Dewey reports an experience which reveals the essence of his objection to the traditional school.

"Some few years ago I was looking about the school supply stores in the city, trying to find desks and chairs which seemed thoroughly suitable from all points of view—artistic, hygienic, and educational—to the needs of children. We had a great deal of difficulty in finding what we needed, and finally one dealer, more intelligent than the rest, made this remark: 'I am afraid we have not what you want. You want something at which the children may work; these are all for listening.'

"That tells the story of traditional education. It is all made 'for listening'—because simply studying lessons out of a book is only another kind of listening; it marks the dependency of one mind upon another. The attitude of listening means, comparatively speaking, passivity, absorption; that there are certain ready-made materials which are there, which have been prepared by the school superintendent, the board, the teacher, and of which the child is to take in as much as possible in the least possible time.

"There is very little place in the traditional schoolroom for the child to work. The workshop, the laboratory, the materials, the tools with which the child may construct, create, and actively inquire, and even the requisite space, have been for the most part lacking. The things that have to do with these processes have not even a definitely recognized place in education."

One wing of the new education movement has made the above principles the foundation of its program for educational reconstruction. It has sought to re-organize the curriculum so as to give a primary place to those values which it believed the traditional school either ignored or suppressed. This group of progressive educators has labored to develop a school in which children would learn from their own first-hand experiences rather than from texts and teachers; in which skills and knowledge would be acquired in a purposeful effort to develop means for the achievement of ends that have direct and vital appeal rather than by a process of drill and rote learning; in which emphasis would be upon significant and rich living in the present rather than upon preparation for a remote and indefinite future; in which a curriculum composed of purposeful projects undertaken in order to meet felt personal and group needs would supplant a fixed curriculum composed of predetermined subjects set-out-to-be learned and re-cited; and in which recognition of the uniqueness of each child and the importance of spontaneous expression would substitute for imposition, regimentation and discipline from above by adults.

An interpretation of the meaning of democracy has been associated with this effort to develop a school program that would be grounded in the interests, the needs, and the purposeful activities of the child. According to this body of progressive educators, the deepest meaning of democracy is found in its emphasis on the dignity and the worth of each human being, and in its moral demand that each person be treated as an end in himself. To treat a child as an end, these educators hold, means to have regard for his unique characteristics, and above all to have regard for his capacity to develop a mind of his own. An immature human being achieves mind as he engages in purposeful activities in which he is given freedom to project ends, and to experiment with the construction and the ordering of means for the attainment of the ends he has in view.

The schools of a democracy, therefore, should be concerned to give each child opportunity to express himself in that kind of purposeful functioning which is mind. It is in and through these purposeful activities that the immature human being acquires the knowledge and the techniques that give him control over his physical and social surroundings. Mind is not inborn, it does not unfold from within according to a predetermined pattern, nor can adults bestow mind upon a child. Mind is acquired through a continuous process of interaction with physical and social affairs—a process in which old meanings are reconstructed and expanded, and new powers of control are developed and matured. Hence mind is something that each child must achieve for himself. The most that adults can do through their schools is to provide the conditions that will stimulate and encourage the young to engage in the kind of purposeful functioning that results in the growth of mind.

In *Democracy and Education,* Dewey gave a classic formulation to this conception of education as a process of growth through the continuous reconstruction of experience. In a democratic society, Dewey contends, education should not be conceived as a process which strives to habituate the young to a fixed system of social, economic, and political institutions. On the contrary, a democratic society aims at its own social improvement, not the preservation of the status quo, and it has no good other than the good of its individual members. The growth of these individuals constitutes the supreme moral purpose of a democracy. And just as there is nothing to which this process of growth is relative save more growth, so there is nothing to which education is subordinate save more education. Viewed from the standpoint of the morality of a democratic society, "the educational process has no end beyond itself; it is its own end."

But when an attempt was made to embody these significant democratic and educational principles in a school program, serious problems began to arise. The view that the curriculum should be grounded in the needs and the interests of children and that children should be made partners in the development of the program for their own education, clearly has elements of great psychological and moral worth in it, but experience has shown that the conception is not free of ambiguity. For example, does this conception assume that the educational needs of the immature define themselves? Will all important needs be met, if the curriculum is restricted to those activities that can be directly derived from the present interests and felt needs of the immature? Are children competent to define their own patterns of development—if not, just what is the role of adult guidance in the construction and the conduct of an educational program?

So also for the principle that the school should have regard for the uniqueness of each child. Obviously, there is something authentic in the demand that the growth of each child be made the controlling educational aim, but how is this process of growth to be conceived? If we hold that the growth of the individual is its own end, does this imply that we do not have to take account of the society in which the individual is to live and to work out his career? And if we recognize that the school is justified in employing common standards and materials in the education of the young, by what process are these standards and materials to be selected and organized into an adequate program of education? Must they be developed on the spot by each teacher working with his own group of children? If so, is there not danger that the individual teacher will have his own "enthusiasms," as well as his own "blind-spots," and that the resulting projects will be conditioned by these biases of the teacher? Morover, how are balance and sequence to be given to the program of the school as a whole, if each teacher in cooperation with his own group of children is expected to determine the projects with which they are to be occupied?

From time to time, Dewey himself has protested against the opportunism and the lack of "continuity" and "integration" in a school program that is centered in the "felt needs" and the initiative of the children. He has emphasized that what are often asserted to be the present needs and interests of the children are superficially derived from what may have been suggested to them by the radio, the movies, the billboards, the newspapers, or current developments in the life of the family and neighborhood. In *Experience and Education,* he denounced the "either-or logic" which assumes that since the predetermined and fixed curriculum of the traditional school is defective, systematic adult planning for the nurture of the young is necessarily evil. Child psychologists increasingly emphasize that the verbal formulations by children of their own interests and needs may only be symptoms of what their actual desires and interests really are. They insist that teachers must be trained to see beneath these surface manifestations to the more significant personal needs that underlie them. But once the process of interpretations begins—and begin it must, unless adults are prepared to accept the dogma that those who have had the least experience are best qualified to define what is important, possible, and desirable in the education of the young—then adults must accept public responsibility for the judgments and choices that they make.

But even deeper difficulties are involved in this child-centered school emphasis. Professor Boyd H. Bode, an outstanding leader of the American movement of progressive education, has defined some of these difficulties in his book, *Progressive Education at the Crossroads.* Progressive education, Bode declares, is in the "doldrums" because "it has not completely emancipated itself from the individualism and absolutism of Rousseau." It has nurtured the pathetic hope that we could find out how to educate by study of the newborn child, and "by relying on such notions as interests, needs, growth and freedom." Actually it is just as impossible to find educational objectives "by inspecting the individual child as it is by looking for them in a transcendental realm."

This reliance on the felt needs of the child has led to an indefensible classroom procedure. "The insistence that we must stick uncompromisingly at all times to the 'needs' of childhood has bred a spirit of anti-intellectualism which is reflected in the reliance on improvising instead of long-range organization, in the over-emphasis on the here and now, in the indiscriminate tirades against 'subjects,' in the absurdities of pupil-planning, and in the lack of continuity in the educational program."

Bode points to the root weakness in the child-centered approach to education. He declares that "the only way to discover a need is in terms of a pattern or scheme of values or an inclusive philosophy of some kind." This inclusive educational philosophy must be, in the last analysis, a social philosophy, because an "educational theory inevitably becomes a theory of social relationships." It is precisely "the lack of an adequate social idea that has burdened the progressive movement with a heavy load of trivialities and errors."

In America, Bode emphasizes, we have no official creed to which everyone is expected to submit. But we do have a tradition of democracy and that tradition, in spite of all its inadequacies, is an affair of genuine moral significance, and it "is deeply imbedded in the life of the American people." Progressive education is today "confronted with the choice of becoming an avowed exponent of democracy or else of becoming a set of ingenious devices for tempering the wind to the shorn lamb."

According to Bode, American democracy has been associated with the rise of the common man, and the heart of the democratic procedure is its respect for the experience of ordinary people and "its quarrel with absolutes." It "stands for the application of 'operational' procedures in the construction of ideals and purposes, as well as in the determination of means for achieving predetermined goals." The great obstacle to democracy, down to the present day, is the Platonic philosophizing which takes purposes or values out of the realm of everyday living and places them where operational procedures cannot reach them. The heart of any "educational program that professes to be democratic must be the irreconcilable conflict between democracy and absolutism."

A democratic society, therefore, must have its own distinctive educational system. This educational system must center "on the cultivation of intelligence rather than submission to authority." It should be grounded "in a theory of values which has as its center the continuous improvement of human living through voluntary reciprocity or the constant widening of common interests and common concerns." The primary obligation of the citizen of a democracy is "the moral obligation to be intelligent." The moment we pull in the boundaries of the moral obligation so as to make them coextensive with the economic situation, we shut out in advance the possibility of becoming intelligent. In order to be intelligent we must come to grips with the basic issue of the conflicts among standards in many different aspects of our experience.

A genuine democracy recognizes this conflict of standards and gives the democratic standards the right of way. This principle of procedure defines the function of education in a democratic society. It can rescue education from the opportunism and the extreme individualism of the effort to base our program on the felt needs of individual children. From the standpoint of the individual, the principle of maximum "growth" requires that he be given the opportunity to discover the nature of the conflicts or cleavages in our cultural heritage, in order that he may unify his own experience. This gives a concrete meaning to the principle of "growth" and the "reconstruction of experience" by suggesting that the reconstruction be directed toward those focal points where it will do some good. From the standpoint of society, the school becomes the agency which provides for this never ending reinterpretation of democracy.

In this conception of democratic education, it is not the teacher's function to predetermine the nature of the future social order, nor need he as teacher be concerned with the development of programs for social improvment. This, however, does not imply a role of cold neutrality. The loyalties of the teacher are indicated by the way in which he formulates the meaning of democracy and translates this meaning into educational procedures. No authoritarian in education can consistently bring to light this conflict of standards and leave the reintegration to each student. The democratic educator can do this for two reasons. First, the growth of the student is of more consequence to him than getting the student to share in any particular social analysis or program. Secondly, his belief in democracy commits him to the faith that the democratic ideal will prevail in the long run if it can be given a decent chance to be heard.

A third group of progressive educators—often termed social reconstructionists—have difficulty with each of the foregoing interpretations of the function of education in a democratic society. These educators are in accord with those who emphasize that the growth of the child is the supreme purpose of democratic education, and they share the conviction that this growth is best provided in a school in which children acquire as they are engaged in purposeful projects of construction and inquiry. They believe, however, that the patterns of child growth are not to be found primarily in the drives, the felt needs, and the interests of the immature human being. They recognize that the native endowment of the child can be patterned in a wide variety of ways depending upon the kind of cultural environment in which it lives and learns. They unite with Bode in the affirmation that any formulation of the educational needs of the child always involves reference to some pattern of human relationships, and that the organization of the curriculm inescapably involves a selective reaction on the part of adults to the existing patterns of thought and life of their society. This group of educators, therefore, believes that child study is only one phase of the educational task, and that understanding of the cultural heritage along with the characteristics and trends of contemporary society is also basic in the preparation of the teacher for his educational responsibilities. In spite of the many important contributions of the child-centered educational group, it has failed to develop an adequate social conception of the meaning of education, and this lack of guiding social principles has indeed burdened the new education with a "heavy load of trivialities and errors."

But the "social reconstructionists" also have difficulty with Bode's conception of the educational function. They share his conviction that a fundamental characteristic of democratic education— a characteristic that distinguishes it from all authoritarian systems of education—is the central place that it gives to the cultivation and the liberation of the intelligence of the individual. They recognize, with Bode, that in a democratic program of education the development of the understanding of the individual must never be subordinated to a desire to commit him to a particular program of social change or reconstruction. The interest of the democratic educator in any specific pattern of belief, of group living, or of social improvement would never justify an effort on his part to inculcate that pattern by a process that suppressed relevant evidence and knowledge of alternatives. Hence the social reconstructionists are in agreement with those educators who make the method of experimental inquiry foundational in their program of education. But they reject the notion that inquiry is all that is involved in the nurture of the immature members of a democratic society.

In particular do they reject the view that all efforts to commit the child to definite patterns of life and thought are in irreconcilable conflict with the morality of democracy. The "social reconstructionists" hold that as each child matures he will inevitably form basic intellectual and emotional dispositions, and that it is a proper responsibility of the school to do what it can to make these developing dispositions as adequate as possible. They find no support in psychology for the notion that a child can use the experimental method of inquiry for a period of years without at the same time developing habits of thought and methods of analysis and verification that are consonant with the procedures of science. One might as well assume that the nurture of a child can be carried on through his formative years in the English language and that at the end of this period he can freely decide what language should be his mother tongue. The "social reconstructionists" find much in the conceptions of democracy and science that would preclude any attempt to breed attitudes and points of view in the young by an educational procedure that curbs free inquiry. They find nothing, however, in science or democracy that opposes the deliberate nurture of the young in those attitudes and allegiances that are implicit in the process of inquiry and deliberation. Nor is this all. The democratic way of living is more than a process of intellectual inquiry, and education in and for democracy involves the introduction of the young to many additional values. A democratic society, for example, believes in the equal treatment of all human beings irrespective of factors of race, color, creed, sex, or the national origin of their parents. The schools of a democracy are expected to nurture the young in the attitudes that are the correlative of this affirmation of the moral worth of all human beings. A democratic society is also committed to the effort to achieve its institutional changes through a peaceful process in which heads are counted, not smashed, and it therefore desires that its young be nurtured in all of the political and civil procedures, techniques, and attitudes by which this effort to institutionalize the process of social reconstruction has been progressively made a social reality. Again, a democratic society believes in the principle of religious freedom and in the principle of the separation of church and state. It expects its schools to develop the young in the attitudes and the allegiances that are the foundation of these elemental liberties. In sum, democracy is a definite form of associated human living, it is continued only as each new generation learns afresh the modes of life and thought that make its life of peace, equality, fraternity, and freedom possible. A democratic society has every right to require its schools to cultivate its young in those common appreciations and behaviors that are the ultimate ground of its health and security.

Today, we live in a period of profound change. In order to preserve our historic democratic values many new modes of group life and allegiance must be developed. We need, for example, to create a coordinated and planning economy that can make a stable and continuous use of our new powers of production. We need to develop a social order which will be grounded in the right of every person to an opportunity to work and to essential security in his job.

We need to develop some form of world organization that will give an alternative to the historic system of nationalism and war. The foregoing are simply illustrations of great needs that now confront the American people. In order to meet these needs new patterns of American life and relationship have to be developd. These new patterns of living call for the nurture of human beings with altered values, and with changed conceptions of what is necessary, possible and desirable. No amount of study of the child, and no amount of devotion to the method of experimental inquiry—indispensable as both of these emphases are in a program of democratic education—should be permitted to keep educators from the analysis of the implications of these momentous social developments for the education of our young.

Apparently Dewey finds something of value in each of the three foregoing conceptions of the role of education. He believes that they are supplementary, not mutually antagonistic. During the days of the deep depression he emphasized in *The Educational Frontier* that "general ideas like transmission and critical remaking of social values, reconstruction of experience, receive acceptance in words, but are often merely plastered on to existing practices, being used to provide a new vocabulary for old practices and a new means for justifying them. Any social conception remains formal and abstract which is not applied to some particular society existing at a definite time and place. If we are not to be content with formal generalities (which are of value only as an introduction of a new point of view) our educational formulations must be translated into descriptions and interpretations of the life which actually goes on in the United States today for the purpose of dealing with the forces which influence and shape it."

In other words, Dewey realizes that if democratic education is to survive, democratic civilization must survive. And if democratic civilization is to be preserved, new patterns of democratic living must be developed. Education has its important part in this struggle to defend and extend democratic values. It should seek to equip the young to live in the context of these emerging life conditions.

Dewey's Revision of Jefferson

by MILTON R. KONVITZ

"NATURE INTENDED me for the tranquil pursuits of science by rendering them my supreme delight," wrote Thomas Jefferson. "But," he continued, "the enormities of the times in which I have lived have forced me to take part in resisting them."[1] This statement John Dewey could have written about himself; for though his greatest delights are in the tranquil pursuits of science, the enormities of the times in which he has lived have forced him to take part in resisting them. He has resisted those enormities in various ways —by heading the commission of inquiry that afforded Trotsky an opportunity to be heard on the subject of the tyranny of Stalin and his government; by playing a leading role in the founding of organizations that led the way to the establishment of the Liberal Party, and in the founding of the Liberal Party as well; by lending his efforts to the establishment of organs of liberal opinion; by leading the movement to make our public schools institutions which will make it possible for our children to grow into freedom and intelligence, institutions built and operated on an invincible faith in the potentialities of human nature; by participating as a founder of the New School for Social Research, which has become a model for progressive schools of adult education throughout the country; in short, by leading or identifying himself with every significant cause that stood for the release and fruition of human effort for the creation of conditions and forms of living that enhance the values of

[1] *The Living Thoughts of Thomas Jefferson*, Presented by John Dewey (1940) 2.

science, art, morals, religion, industry and commerce, and education. John Dewey has spoken of Thomas Jefferson as "our first great democrat."[2] We may speak of Dewey as one who stands in a direct line of descent from Thomas Jefferson, with Madison, Emerson and William James and John Dewey, Woodrow Wilson and Franklin D. Roosevelt as the strongest links.

To gain an insight into John Dewey's mind and achievement it might be well to see what it is that Dewey has taken from Jefferson and how Dewey has revised Jefferson.

Apparently Jefferson's view on freedom took two different lines of direction. At times he seemed to say that, given political freedom, freedom of culture—science, art, religion, industry, and all other social institutions—would follow. He believed that human nature is exclusively and inherently individualist; and the flowering of the individual requires only the abolition of governmental oppression —it requires, that is, only political freedom.

There is, Jefferson believed, a natural equality of men, and man's love of freedom is inherent in him. He will produce free institutions in which the natural equality of men will be manifested if only he can free himself from governmental oppressions. Government is the great enemy, but not an invincible enemy, as the Revolution of 1776 proved. From being the master, government can be made the servant. But government must become and remain a servant that possesses only specified delegated duties and rights (but the rights of government are only duties). Government does not have the duty to create and maintain conditions which will make a free culture possible; on the contrary, men, acting as individuals, will make a free culture if only government does not interfere with their desires and actions.

Man has inherent and inalienable rights, which are unchangeable. This belief of Jefferson's was based on a moral and religious (deist) faith. Nature's God stands in an equal moral relation to all human beings; the inherent and inalienable rights are unchange-

[2] *Ibid.*, pp. 2-3.

able because they express God's will as embodied in the very structure of man's conscience and in the nature of society. If political freedom is not possible, said Jefferson, then there is no God or He is a malevolent being.

But Jefferson's thought took another direction as well. He was worried lest a large increase in industrialization and urbanization would alter human nature and the social institutions congenial to human nature—obviously a fear that love of freedom is not so deeply inherent in man that the culture in which he lives may not extinguish it; obviously a fear that the inherent and inalienable rights may not be embodied so deeply in man's conscience and in the equal moral relations in which God stands to every human being that they will be unchangeable for all time.

There may be, then, intimate and significant connections between free political institutions and the economic and other aspects of culture. So Jefferson insisted on the necessity of general schooling supplied by government, on a free press, and on democracy at the grass-roots level—local (wards, school districts) neighborhood groups managing their own affairs, and citizen participation in self-government, not only on election days but every day. The Industrial Revolution was making changes in the lives of Englishmen, but Jefferson hoped that the looms and spindles, the workshop and factories would not emigrate from the Mother Country, to plague Americans. It was as both a political scientist and a moralist that he kept his eyes on farming as a way of life. Generally speaking, he said,

". . . the proportion which the aggregate of the other classes of citizens bears in any state to that of its husbandmen, is the proportion of its unsound to its healthy parts, and is a good enough barometer whereby to measure its degree of corruption. While we have land to labour then, let us never wish to see our citizens occupied at a work-bench, or twirling a distaff. Carpenters, masons, smiths, are wanting in husbandry: but, for the general operations of manufacture, let our work-shops remain in Europe. . . . The mobs of great cities add just so much to the support of pure government, as sores do to the strength of the human body. It is the manners and spirit of a people which preserve a republic in vigour. A degeneracy in these is a canker which soon eats to the heart of its laws and constitution."[3]

This ambiguity in the thought of Jefferson—faith in the potentialities of human nature if government does not make its hand of oppression felt, and the conviction that the economic and some other aspects of culture generate free or slave institutions—was one of which he was himself unaware. The ambiguity is left unresolved in the mind of Jefferson.

And this unresolved ambiguity is found today in the thinking of many Americans, who maintain that if government were to limit itself to purely police power matters, the work of each individual on his own behalf would result in a cumulative good that would far surpass in merit anything in social living that the world has yet seen; but the same persons support tariff walls, farm price supports, subsidies to airlines and railroads, subsidies to shipping lines, federal aid to education, social security measures, federal bank deposit insurance, government financing of rural telephone service—to cite some of the more obvious instances of government in business or the exercise of governmental power on behalf of the general welfare; that is, government action in the economic and other spheres to help create or maintain a culture in which the citizen will have more of an opportunity, than would otherwise be the case, to enjoy freedom—freedom in politics and in industry and commerce.

This ambiguity in the thought of Jefferson finds itself resolved in the thought of Dewey. The resolution of the ambiguity has in it lessons, on the learning of which may depend the future of our democracy.

[3] *Writings of Thomas Jefferson*, ed. by P. L. Ford, III. 268-269; cf. Dumas Malone, *Jefferson the Virginian* (1948) 384. That Jefferson never changed the essence of his agrarianism, though he did not permit theoretical considerations to stand in the way of practical policies, see Griswold, "The Agrarian Democracy of Thomas Jefferson," 40 *Amer. Pol. Sc. Rev.* (1946) 657. "What is practical must often control what is pure theory," Jefferson wrote Du Pont on January 18, 1802.

First of all Dewey does away with the conflict between individual and society. If we split the individual and the social from one another, inevitably we shall find that they oppose one another. Individual and social stand for traits of unitary human beings; and these traits are so integral that they are aspects of man in his actual existence. It is incorrect to say that "social" ties inhere in "individuals"; they inhere integrally in human beings in their very humanity. We should substitute "human being" for "individual," and avoid using "the individual" and "the social" as nouns or as referring to entities; we should use the terms as adjectives. We should consider human beings in their full human capacity; we should think of a human being in the concrete: a creature born so helpless that he is dependent upon others for his very existence. Without language, for example, no intellectual growth is possible; yet a child is born with language facility but without possession of a language. When one considers an adult, one sees him in many social aspects, as a parent, citizen, wage-earner, employer, farmer, merchant, teacher, etc. If we were to stop speaking of Society or of the Individual, it would become evident that "social" stands for properties that are intrinsic to every human being.

The separation of the individual and social aspects of the human being and the placing them in opposition one to the other has been due, in part, to religious teachings that man is to be viewed as an individual soul who has intrinsic connections only with God. Even Jefferson, though a deist, probably took his line of thought in part because of his religious views.

In our day we see that policies justified by individualism created evils that called for measures (we have mentioned some) to ensure the protection of threatened values and interests. The social measures have been, and are being, undertaken in a piecemeal fashion; each danger is seen as if it stood alone, and each measure undertaken to meet the danger is seen as if it stood alone. And every measure is offered and accepted with apology and a bad conscience; for "individualism" is seen giving way to "collectivism," or "socialism," or the "welfare state," or "statism." We feel the need to protect "the individual" from oppression by "society."

The crisis in our individual and social lives has led to the crisis in our thinking, and in part the crisis in our thinking is an inheritance from Jefferson's belief that the person has an intrinsic, moral connection only with God—not with other human beings but only with God.

But to swing from the pole of "individualism" to the pole of "socialism" is only to perpetuate the old separation and opposition. The habit of using "social" as a monistic term is as harmful as the habit of using "individual" as a monistic term.

In brief, the separation of individual and social is artificial and leads to great mischief. As Whitehead expressed the same idea:

"The whole concept of absolute individuals with absolute rights, and with a contractual power of forming fully defined external relations, has broken down. The human being is inseparable from its environment in each occasion of its existence. The environment which the occasion inherits is immanent in it, and conversely it is immanent in the environment which it helps to transmit."[4]

One line of Jefferson's thought, we have seen, took the direction of making political freedom primary—given political freedom, freedom of culture would follow. Dewey rejects this view; for, he says, today we see that while political institutions affect the relations of industry, science, art, religion, etc., we see even more clearly that political institutions are an effect, not a cause. The problem today is "to know what kind of culture is so free in itself that it conceives and begets political freedom as its accompaniment and consequence."[5] Unlike Jefferson, Dewey starts from the character of our culture rather than from any view of an original human nature. To Jefferson it was enough to keep the idea of liberty alive and to watch the actions of government officials in order to achieve a society in which there would be ample opportunity for the pursuit of happiness by each citizen; to Dewey this program is pathetically inadequate. We can put no trust in man's inherent love of liberty,

[4] *Adventure of Ideas* (1933) 50.
[5] *Freedom and Culture* (1939) 6.

for "men may be brought by long habit to hug their chains."[6] It is not the native constituents of human nature that determine culture and the degree and nature of freedom found therein; on the contrary, the culture of a period or group is the determining influence in the arrangement of the native constituents of human nature.

Jefferson's belief in the primacy of political freedom and in rights which are inherent, inalienable and unchanging, and his consideration of these matters often in isolation from economic and other cultural aspects of life, led to a subordination of cooperativeness to liberty and equality. Many factors interact to create a state of culture; the isolation of any one factor can be fatal to understanding and to action directed by intelligence.

Freedom, then, does not inhere in persons; there is no conflict between "the individual" and "society." Despite Hobbes's eloquence, individuals do not need to be tamed or socialized. "If we want individuals to be free we must see to it that suitable conditions exist. . . ."[7] We must be concerned with cultural conditions—conditions of science, art, morals, education, industry, religion, etc.—which will maintain freedom. The problem of freedom cannot be isolated from the cultural conditions which nourish or starve freedom. In our concern with freedom we must do more than worry over the negative aspects, the removal of governmental obstructions. Our forefathers were right in emphasizing a free press and common public schools to provide conditions favorable to democracy, but

". . . to them the enemy of freedom of the press was official government censorship and control; they did not foresee the nonpolitical causes that might restrict its freedom, nor the economic factors that would put a heavy premium on centralization. And they failed to see how education in literacy could become a weapon in the hands of an oppressive government, nor that the chief cause for promotion of elementary education in Europe would be increase of military power."[8]

[6] *Ibid.*, p. 8.
[7] *Ibid.*, p. 34.
[8] *Ibid.*, p. 42.

Literacy and universal suffrage, as we see today when we look at the U.S.S.R., may undermine, rather than be the strength of democracy. Democracy cannot be expressed in terms of political institutions only; democracy is "expressed in the attitudes of human beings and is measured by consequences produced in their lives."[9] Its impact is to be looked for in all aspects of culture. The problem of freedom or democracy is, then, the problem of social organization,

". . . extending in all the areas and ways of living, in which the powers of individuals shall not be merely released from mechanical external restraint but shall be fed, sustained and directed. Such an organization demands much more of education than general schooling, which without a removal of the springs of purpose and desire becomes a new mode of mechanization and formalization, as hostile to liberty as ever was governmental restraint. It demands of science much more than external technical application—which again leads to mechanization of life and results in a new kind of enslavement. It demands that the method of inquiry, of discrimination, of test by verifiable consequences, be naturalized in all the matters, of large and of detailed scope, that arise for judgment."[10]

Although political conditions are not, according to Dewey, of a primary character in the determination of freedom in a culture, for all kinds of conditions interact, yet political conditions, in a sense, do play a pre-eminent role; for democratic political institutions are "indispensable to effecting economic change in the interest of freedom."[11] Conditions in totalitarian countries have brought home the fact that democratic political institutions encourage freedom of discussion, criticism and free association. Dewey speaks of the task of liberalism as that of "mediator of social transitions."[12] The same may be said of political democracy. It has the same work as that of the intelligence; that is, the remaking of the old through union—peaceful union—with the new. Furthermore, our political freedoms are congenial to the scientific method, for

". . . freedom of inquiry, toleration of diverse views, freedom of

[9] *Ibid.*, p. 125.
[10] *Liberalism and Social Action* (1935) 31.
[11] *Freedom and Culture*, 93.
[12] *Liberalism and Social Action*, 48.

communication, the distribution of what is found out to every individual as the ultimate intellectual consumer, are involved in the democratic as in the scientific method."[13]

Thus Dewey, by giving to the "individual" and to the "social" meanings that are adjectival instead of substantive, and by approaching the human being through a study of his culture and its components, avoids the opposition between "the individual" and "society" that is inherent in Jefferson's thought, and resolves the ambiguity in Jefferson's thought regarding the relations between political conditions and other aspects of culture. In the end, however, political freedom does come out with a major role or status of primacy. In Jefferson, however, political freedom is given primacy because through it the citizen will be able to confine the actions of government, leaving to the citizen scope for full expression of his inherent, inalienable and unchanging rights; while in Dewey political freedom is given primacy because through it citizens can act cooperatively to bring about economic changes peacefully, and, furthermore, because through it freedom of inquiry or the free use of the scientific method becomes possible. Without freedom of speech, press and assembly and freedom of suffrage—that is, true freedom of suffrage, and not merely the freedom to vote for the candidates of the only legal party, in which the state's sovereignty is vested—freedom of science or inquiry is impossible. The existence of "Soviet genetics" and "Soviet astronomy" bring home to us the truth of this point.

And freedom of science stands in a much more intimate relation to freedom of culture than was seen by Jefferson. "And I am for encouraging the progress of science in all its branches," he wrote to Elbridge Gerry in 1799. Science, he wrote to Adams in 1813, "has liberated the ideas of those who read and reflect," and science is progressive and one day will lead in America to a successful insurrection "against rank and birth." He thought it to be a much greater thing to be a Newton than to be a ruler.

But science that can provide the conditions for a successful in-

[13] *Freedom and Culture,* 102.

surrection "against rank and birth" is a science that explores the recesses of nature and releases the energies of human beings at the same time that it liberates their minds and spirits. Apparently, however, Jefferson labored under the notion that science may be confined to one aspect of culture; namely, agriculture.

Agriculture, he wrote to David Williams in 1803, is

". . . . a science of the very first order. It counts among its handmaids the most respectable sciences, such as Chemistry, Natural Philosophy, Mechanics, Mathematics, Natural History, Botany. In every College and University, a professorship of agriculture, and the class of its students, might be honored as the first. Young men closing their academical education with this, as the crown of all other sciences . . . , instead of crowding the other classes, would return to the farms of their fathers. . . ."

What a rude awakening from his pastoral dream Jefferson would suffer could he see our giant mechanized farms, our factories in the fields, some of them employing many thousands of wage-earners, whose problems are the same as those of workers in commerce or industry. Jefferson did not see how radically science would change the face of the farm and the face of the farmer. And he did not see how science would change the face of the nation and of the world. He disliked and feared looms and spindles, but he did not say how he proposed to keep science out of the workshops and factories. He loved science but hated the urbanization and industrialization which science made inevitable; and he believed that freedom is possible only if the American people remain an agricultural folk.

If Jefferson were right, our human condition would be desperate, indeed. Dewey—to paraphrase John Bright—stands upon the shoulders of Jefferson, and sees farther. The quality and quantity of freedom we want or have depend upon culture, which includes a great deal more than farming or the agricultural way of life. Just as freedom means more than the absence of governmental restraints, so it means more than the absence of industrialization and urbanization. Just as a farming culture can be free or slave, so, too, an urban and industrial culture can be free or slave. Jefferson's mistake was to link freedom inextricably and only with an agricultural community. Had he seen the expansive and explosive role of science in its true dimensions, his thought would have taken a different turn and would not have needed Dewey's revision.

The problem of freedom, to both Jefferson and Dewey, is the problem of the form of social organization or culture; and both Jefferson and Dewey see "free intelligence in inquiry, discussion and expression"[14] as playing a central role in making freedom possible. But the "free intelligence" enjoys much more freedom in Dewey's philosophy than it does in Jefferson's. It is not confined to the countryman's home, farm and nation. It bloweth where it listeth. It may be integrated with all social movements and may be a chief factor in giving them direction. It may not only characterize individual human beings; it may also become a "method of cooperative experimental intelligence."[15] Science cannot commit itself to an agricultural or any other system of society, any more than it can commit itself to a Nazi Germany or a Communist Russia: "Because science starts with questions and inquiries it is fatal to all social system-making and programs of fixed ends."[16] Jefferson sought freedom for the expression of the static human nature of the independent American farmer. But Dewey reminds us that "We are free not because of what we statically are, but in so far as we are becoming different from what we have been."[17] Jefferson's plan of an agricultural America was in fact a vision of a closed society, despite the fact that science, opener of doors and windows, was his supreme delight. "In its reality," says Dewey, "freedom is a resolute will operating in a world in some respects indeterminate, because open and moving toward a new future."[18]

To both Jefferson and Dewey the intelligence is anchored in freedom. What is the anchor that provides the security of the link

[14] *Liberalism and Social Action*, 32.
[15] *Ibid.*, p. 47.
[16] *Individualism Old and New* (1930) 164.
[17] *Philosophy and Civilization* (1931) 291.
[18] *Ibid.*, p. 298.

between intelligence and freedom? We shall see that on this point, too, Dewey revises Jefferson; but as in all other instances, the revision is carried out in the spirit of the original text.

As we have seen, Jefferson's belief in freedom, in inherent and inalienable rights, was based on his belief in the existence of a righteous Creator who stands inseparably connected with and in equal relation to each of His creatures. This connection and relation are essentially moral; they create an "equality of moral claims and of moral responsibilities."[19] Dewey shares the spirit of this faith but would naturally express it differently. "Other days," he says,

". . . bring other words and other opinions behind words that are used. The terms in which Jefferson expressed his belief in the moral criterion for judging all political arrangements . . . are not now current. It is doubtful, however, whether defense of democracy against the attacks to which it is subjected does not depend upon taking once more the position Jefferson took about its moral basis and purpose, even though we have to find another set of words in which to formulate the moral ideal served by democracy. A renewal of faith in common human nature, in its potentialities in general and in its power in particular to respond to reason and truth, is a surer bulwark against totalitarianism than is demonstration of material success or devout worship of special legal and political forms."[20]

The American democratic tradition founded on Jefferson's views, is, says Dewey, a moral one, and attack on that tradition involves moral issues and can be settled only upon moral grounds. "Anything that obscures the fundamentally moral nature of the social problem," says Dewey, "is harmful. . . ."[21]

This moral basis of and attitude toward democratic values are a union of the ideal and the actual, which operates both in thought and action. To this union, Dewey, like Jefferson, gives the name God; for whatever introduces genuine perspective is religious, making possible a working union of the ideal and the actual in human

[19] *The Living Thoughts of Thomas Jefferson*, p. 24.
[20] *Ibid.*, p. 25.
[21] *Freedom and Culture*, 172.

existence. The values of art, knowledge, education, fellowship, love, and growth of body and mind are relatively embryonic.

"Many persons are shut out from generous participation in them; there are forces at work that threaten and sap existent goods as well as prevent their expansion. A clear and intense conception of a union of ideal ends with actual conditions is capable of arousing steady emotions. It may be fed by every experience, no matter what its material. In a distracted age, the need for such an idea is urgent. It can unify interests and energies now dispersed; it can direct action and generate the heat of emotion and the light of intelligence."[22]

Every effort of Thomas Jefferson's and of John Dewey's has been in the direction of ways that release the creative energies of men, deepen experiences, make for "that complete unification of the self which is called a whole," and bring men together in a fellowship that means a broader freedom and a fuller life. If Dewey sees farther than did Jefferson, it is only because the child stands upon the shoulders of his father.

[22] *A Common Faith* (1934) 50.

Laity and Prelacy in American Democracy

by HERBERT SCHNEIDER

RELIGIOUS DIVERSITY is one of the oldest and most persistent traits of American culture. Though there were early establishments in the Colonies, there was a diversity of establishments. The circumstances which created this diversification of faith and rite were neither temporary nor superficial; religious differences were symptomatic of moral conflicts, class struggles, national rivalries, and all the other deep-seated sources of European strife and chaos. America could easily have become the hottest hot-bed of holy wars and the bloodiest arena of Europe's madness, for in this new world the enemies were thrown together into the same communities and were armed with greater resources and opportunities for carrying on the traditional battles and for creating new ones. Even the Calvinists and Catholics, who were least prepared spiritually to separate religious and political issues, were driven by this menace to sanction disestablishment and to regard themselves as "free" churches. And even Roger Williams, who is hailed as the apostle of American religious liberty, had to be driven to the realization that religious diversity and civil unity must be compatible in practice, whatever be the theoretical grounds for holding such compatibility impossible. The separation of church and state in America was, therefore, no accident, but a deliberate compromise reached after bitter experience. The recent revival of the doctrine of cooperation between state and church has called our attention once more to a basic predicament in American culture, namely, "How can a single state, even with the best of will, cooperate with so many conflicting churches?"

With few exceptions, the American churches have learned to view this religious diversity and conflict as a blessing. Uniformity and conformity have ceased to be ideals, except in small and proud circles where the conformist faith serves to make would-be Europeans a conspicuous and "peculiar people" among Americans. In America "catholic" and "ecumenical" are fighting slogans for rival church politicians. But they are more than that. The overwhelming majority of religious Americans are monotheists and profess, even in their conflicts, to be worshiping the one, true and only God. In theory, at least, God has no proper name, so that Christians, Jews, and philosophers are all able to sanctify their disagreements as diverse revelations of an Infinite Glory. Such diversity-in-unity is appropriate in American religion and expresses the basic *in pluribus unum* pattern which pervades American life despite the official *e pluribus unum* motto. But at the same time it is more difficult to make such a paradoxical faith plausible theologically than politically, so that American theologians have both a great problem and a unique opportunity.

A central difficulty in the construction of any theology appropriate to American pluralistic democracy is the theory of the priesthood. Traditionally the priestly caste or class, both in East and West, has enjoyed certain prerogatives over laymen, not only religiously but politically and socially. Fortunately for American democracy the various types and orders of clergymen who here perform priestly offices have been so disdainful toward each other and so unwilling to recognize their various orders as truly "holy orders," that there has been little danger of an American "Lords Spiritual" to lay the foundations of a class-society. Nevertheless, the problem of the relation of spiritual to temporal authority is no mere academic problem, and the current theological debate on the subject has practical implications and clerical overtones. The lurking menace to democracy is not lessened by the fact that even among the so-called "secularists," there is a tendency to conceive spirituality as a class possession and to make common cause with the clergy against the worldly masses and temporal authorities. It is conceivable that there may emerge among American intellectuals, lay and clerical, an idea analogous to that propounded a century ago for English nationalists by Thomas Arnold and Samuel Taylor Coleridge, the idea that the nations should cultivate a "clerisy," a special enlightened, spiritual class ("educators") to act as a redeeming power on the mass of sinners. Though hailed as a radical, collectivist idea, this theory certainly fitted into the class structure of British society better than it would fit into American democracy. It may, therefore, not be entirely fantastic to consider seriously and radically what a truly democratic theory of the relation between priest and layman would be, and to raise the question whether the American state should, in the European sense, be a *lay* state.

The theory that appears to be most radically democratic is Luther's doctrine of the priesthood of all believers, which amounts in practice to: "Be ye priests one to another!" For no one would be a priest unto himself. Being essentially a social function, the priestly ministry, if not professionalized, would have to be reciprocal service. Such an idea naturally struck the professional priests of Luther's time as an insult, blasphemy, and folly combined. And the Lutherans themselves, once established, used the convenient subterfuge of calling their professional priests "pastors" or shepherds and allowing them to administer the sacraments and in other ways to function very much as a professional priest does. Anyone who knows what a priest is and does could see at once that he is by the nature of his duties not merely "confessional" and not merely following a "vocation," but in the fullest sense a professional. To interpret Luther's theory as sanctioning an amateur priesthood and to believe that any professional priesthood is a violation of "Christian liberty" and lay democracy is to be impractical, not radical. There are, to be sure, small denominations in which the priestly office is successfully performed by amateurs because all their religious institutions and expressions are of and by amateurs. I have witnessed a thoroughly democratic administration of the Lord's Supper among New England congregations, which is not only extremely simple, beautiful and impressive, but eloquently symbolical of the democracy of a small New England town. Luther's theory is thus applicable quite literally to certain types of communities and communions, but it is obviously not so applicable to the more typical and institutionalized American churches. There is no reason why the professional priest should not find his respectable and respected place among the professions as they exist in American society, and even professional clerical organizations functioning as pressure groups and lobbies would be appropriate forces in American democracy as it exists today.

It is not as a profession, therefore, that the priesthood is incompatible with religious and political democracy. Professions we know and confessions we know, but who is this "spiritual authority"? The difficulty is less with the priestly office than with priestly pretensions. Luther was less a critic of the idea of priesthood than he was an enemy of priestcraft and his famous formulations of Christian liberty are less valuable as a philosophy of religious democracy than as slogans against the prerogatives and pretensions of a priestly class. In this sense the conflict between laymen and priests is but an instance of the more general conflict among professions. Calvin, the lawyer, apparently appreciated this fact and asserted in a more civic spirit the *rights* of laymen against priests. Lawyers, teachers, physicians, scientists, bankers have their respective types of craftiness, as well as priests do, and the continual rivalry of professional groups for political plums is an old story in both the Old and the New Worlds. It is necessary, therefore, in democratic politics that these various professional vested interests compete and occasionally combine to prevent any one profession from becoming politically dominant. The "lay" professions thus are on their guard against priestcraft as priests are on their guard against the craftiness of Luthers, Calvins, Voltaires, Jeffersons and Deweys. All this is democracy in action, and though it gives rise to protests and counter-reformations, there underlies it a commonly respected, but ill-conceived ethics of competition or fair play. In the vulgar idiom we can say that "We chalk it all up to collective bargaining." In other words, the lay professions naturally expect the priestly profession to assume its place as an equal and to recognize its own interests as private and its political influence as a lobby. There is no justification for identifying the clerical interests with the religious interests of the people or public, nor religious interests with "spirituality" in general. Laymen who refuse obedience to priests are not on that account "secularists" and the assertion of lay "spirituality" and conscience is not "secularist dogmatism" but ordinary democratic morality.

But we are still not down to "brass tacks" as regards the intellectual issue, an issue which must be faced in terms of the theory of "mediation." Here Christian theology and Dewey's philosophy of democracy both face a difficult problem, as well as facing each other. Dewey's theory amounts to: "Be ye mediators one to another!" Christian priestly theory amounts to: "Ye laymen need the mediating power of the sacraments which God has charged us to administer unto you!" This appears to be in essence Luther *vs.* Rome once again. But there is an important difference. The two theses are not necessarily incompatible as were those of Luther and Rome. A democratic theory of the mediatorial function can make its peace with a professional priestly office, provided the priestly "channels of grace" are interpreted not as peculiarly "divine" but as forms of "common grace." Here the Christian humanists, if they really mean what they say, can render a service to democratic theory and practice, for they can explain to their theologically unsophisticated brethren how the Holy Spirit, the Apostolic Succession, the sacraments, and all the other elements of divine mediation can be reinterpreted in the light of a democratic ethics, though their nomenclature, origins and history are anything but democratic. A priest can be a good priest and a faithful one, without making claims to being endowed with supernatural grace, or even with a monopoly of revealed truth.

There is an ironical instance of the central moral issue in connection with the "insubordination" of Father Feeney and St. Benedict's Center at Boston. That Father Feeney should be disciplined for insubordination is a matter of church discipline and not strictly relevant to the issue of democracy outside the church, which is the issue now before us. That he should be disciplined for promoting

"tendencies to bigotry," and that the literal and obvious meaning of the notorious Bull, *Unam Sanctam,* should thus be officially recognized as a bigoted interpretation, are facts highly gratifying to all who still hope for some reconciliation of religious liberalism and Roman Catholicism. But the serious issue for democratic morality in this "heresy" case is that Father Feeney and his associates are expected not to "attack the catechetical teaching proposed by legitimate authorities." To refuse the elementary academic freedom of thought and teaching to an academic group because they are "members of a religious society" and as such obligated not to disturb the peace of the church, is a good illustration of that feature of clerical morality which must be obnoxious to a member of a democratic society. If church discipline implies such slavish acceptance of the opinions of "legitimate authorities" as a normal obligation of *religious* discipline, it is certainly impossible to reconcile such discipline with the elements of democratic morality and intellectual liberty. To be disciplined for bigotry seems reasonable, to be disciplined for disagreeing with superiors is not reasonable if the person disciplined is supposed to be a member not only of a religious order but also of an academic profession in a democratic society, and if the subject of disagreement is a recognized matter of dispute and doubt concerning which a self-respecting scholar is supposed to make up his own mind. A teacher whose ecclesiastical obligations are thus incompatible with his intellectual obligations to the community of scholarly research is put in a serious moral predicament. A bigot is, to be sure, precisely a man who is not living up to his obligations to the community of scholarship, but in this community there are no "legitimate authorities."

A priest is, of course and by definition, a "servant of God" or even God's slave. But he is also, in the same sense that a physician or teacher is, a servant of laymen. *Servus servorum* has served both as a proud title for the papacy and as an expression of the essence of Christian humility. The "minister of ministers" may be minister plenipotentiary and not merely menial of menials! Is the Pope merely the servant of the servants of God, that is, High

Priest or Primate? Or is he together with all other priests, also at the service of laymen?

Spiritual power, if it means anything compatible with democracy, means the power to serve others, the ability to be of real help. Temporal power governs; spiritual power aids. The same person may wield forms of power, but he ought not to confuse them. Spiritual power is not a form of authority, but of ability—an ability to render a difficult, skilled, competent service. A priest, accordingly, like any other genuine "servant" of his fellow men functions for the sake of laymen, and the sacraments and religious institutions which he administers should be not only "service to God" which they are technically, but help to laymen, which they are or are not empirically. A teacher or physician or scientist betrays his "spiritual" power when he falls back on his professional office or authority in lieu of practical service; similarly a priest who conceives himself as a member of a mediatorial class by *right* and not by *service,* is not truly spiritual. Most priests have learned to pay lip service to this democratic conception of their "spirituality," but the "secular clergy" among them are well named! They assume subconsciously, and occasionally even teach openly, that laymen exist for the church, and not the church for laymen. Let the *Servus servorum* live up to his title, and let those who serve God professionally serve their lay brethren actually, and then we may approach something that can more appropriately be called religious democracy. Or, to put the issue in the language of political democracy: the layman has a *right* to insist that clergymen do not insist upon their *clerical rights* except as they are the correlatives of their services to laymen, recognized by laymen as such.

Organized Labor and the Dewey Philosophy

by MARK STARR

DEWEY'S PHILOSOPHY in education has an obvious importance for organized labor. Because the trade unions originated out of deep social needs and are themselves a collective effort to meet those basic economic needs by a major section of the community, the implications of Dewey's theories to the ideals and actions of the unions should be examined. Then, too, insofar as Dewey's seminal ideas have changed the grade and high schools and colleges, they must have seriously influenced the educational procedures which affect the formative years of the sons and daughters of over 15 million trade unionists, not to mention the workers of hand and brain who comprise the total 42 millions of wage-earners of the United States. But here also an attempt will be made to see what changes in attitude might be expected if the philosophy of Dewey were applied to trade union practices. What might we expect as the students leave school and participate in community life and in their trade unions and professional associations?

His native background in Vermont would not have given Dewey much contact with organized labor in his early years, but his common sense soon made him brush aside all professional snobbery which would divide the teacher from the ranks of organized labor. His record of activity in the formation of what is now the Teachers Guild in New York, with Henry R. Linville and others, has been continued down to a message to the most recent Convention of the American Federation of Teachers (AFL).[1]

[1] To the 1949 Convention of the AFT, in his 90th year Dewey wrote in part:

It would, of course, be a mistake to think that there has been a reciprocal interest and a wide conscious study of the philosophy of John Dewey in the ranks of American organized labor, or even in the workers' education section of its activities. However, there is something in common between the economic pragmatism of Samuel Gompers and the philosophic pragmatism of John Dewey. The approach of the American Federation of Labor in working out its theories in the light of daily practice is surely experimentalism. As a matter of fact, just as Dewey has been accused of having no organized body of thought, so the AFL has been accused of emphasizing rule-of-thumb methods to the exclusion of any understanding of ultimate goals. Deeper consideration, however, shows that in both instances the assumption is not well based, although usually the long term aims are implicit rather than fully stated.

It is important to recognize what there is in common between the practices of organized labor in the United States and the educational practices arising from Dewey's theories. There are many touching points and, indeed, there may be an increasing mutual influence between the two.

In the general approach to education, there have been three main attitudes clear and distinct from the position taken by Dewey. There is the educator who believes that he can be "above the battle" and that education is somehow an intrinsic good in itself, remaining

---

"I do not believe that any educational organization is more ready or better prepared to take such a courageous view of the present situation than is the American Federation of Teachers. It has never been a body to take the cheap and easy way; it has never cultivated illusions about the seriousness of the work to be done. It has recognized that together with its larger organization, the American Federation of Labor, it has a cause that demands, and that has obtained, and will continue to obtain alertness of observation and planning, and solidarity in action. It knows, from experience, that these things bring their own reward with them. Confidence and courage grow with exercise. There are many fields of labor within the American Federation of Labor. There is none in which the need, the opportunity, and the reward are surer than in that of teaching.

"I count it one of the satisfactions of my own teaching career that I have had from the first, the opportunity to be a member of a Local of the American Federation of Teachers. Today I prize this special opportunity to join in rejoicing in its past, and in looking forward with confidence to its future.

"May it continue to be steadfast in the great work in behalf of the schools of America, and thereby throughout our common America, in a world that must grow in common understanding, if it is not to perish."

unsoiled from partisan interests and from the sectional struggles which are present in all communities.

Then there is the second position which believes that education should serve the status quo and be a mental buttress for all existing institutions. In the early stages of education in the United States and elsewhere, there were unintelligent Tories who even did not recognize the usefulness of education in this respect. The Tories prophesied that if workers were given education, then they would no longer be content to remain in "that station of life into which it had pleased God to call them." There is, for example, the much quoted denunciation made by Governer Berkeley of Virginia:

"I thank God there are no free schools nor printing, and I hope we shall not have these hundred years; for learning has brought disobedience and heresy and sects into the world, and printing has divulged them, and libels against the best government. God keep us from both." [*Report to the Committee for the Colonies,* 1671]

When public education was grudgingly adopted, it was surrounded by many safeguards. For example, Hannah More (1745-1835) only wanted that "the poor be able to read their Bibles and qualify for domestic duties, but not to write or to be enabled to read Tom Paine or be encouraged to rise above their position." Both in Britain and in the United States men like William Cobbett and Thomas Hodgskin respectively denounced such ducation as "the indoctrination of the poor with the principles of submission to authority" and "training for the yoke."

As a natural reaction from this educational support for the status quo were early developments of workers' education which tried definitely to undermine the status quo. This third attitude was Marxian in its economics and in its interpretation of history, although it was modified in the United States. Later the trade unions in Britain gave some support to this, although the Marxist ideas were revised and adapted and are distinguished clearly from their later Stalinist applications.

In this view, education was a reflex of the economic interests of the ruling group, and the group rising from below would necessarily oppose and replace the educational theories of their masters. In *Democracy and Education* (1916) Dewey criticizes both Plato and Marx for the divisive effects of their ideas of education— Plato for elevating a literary ruling caste and Marx for splitting the community into rival classes.[2]

Probably the trade unions in the United States, where class mobility was present, were influenced by their cooperation with Horace Mann to win support for the tax-supported public school. Mann thought of education as a balance wheel to keep opposing economic forces in equilibrium. Education was to destroy the tendency of capital to dominate and of labor to cringe. If all had opportunity and well-being, than envy would have no base.[3]

Dewey implicitly rejected all the three positions and insisted upon education as an instrument whereby communication among the various groups in the community can be achieved. Education was a problem-solving process. In every instance the problems did not stand still but were themselves in a continued process of change. This dialectic view, of course, applied to all social ideas and institutions which were perforce constantly changing. Its acceptance would remove fear of change, including the fear based on mutual ignorance between management and labor. The trade unionist has the same basic needs as other members of the community— beyond individual technical skills and competency, he needs to know his civic rights and responsibilities.

Dewey, over the years, has never hesitated to express his belief

[2] Cf. Jim Cork's valuable essay "Karl Marx and John Dewey," pp. 331-350.

[3] "Surely nothing but universal education can counterwork this tendency to the domination of capital and the servility of labor. If one class possesses all the wealth and the education, while the residue of society is ignorant and poor, it matters not by what name the relation between them may be called: the latter, in fact and in truth, will be the servile dependants and subjects of the former. But, if education be equably diffused, it will draw property after it by the strongest of all attractions; for such a thing never did happen and never can happen, as that an intelligent and practical body of men should be permanently poor. . . .

"Education, then, beyond all other devices of human origin is the great equalizer of the conditions of men—the balance-wheel of the social machinery. . . . It gives each man the independence and the means by which he can resist the selfishness of other men. It does better than to disarm the poor of their hostility towards the rich: It prevents being poor." [*Annual Report on Education* (1848), pages 668-669] in fundamental social reforms. The reader might well consult the essay, "The Economic Basis of the New Society," written especially for *Intelligence in the Modern World,* edited by Joseph Ratner (Modern Library, 1938). Here Dewey reprints his views expressed 20 years earlier, and regrets that he still has to insist upon the necessity of the right to work, the intelligent administration of our industries and also on the right of workers to participate in the administration of industry. His paragraph on this third point is worth quoting (p. 422):

> "The third phase that I mention is the need of securing greater industrial autonomy, that is to say, greater ability on the part of the workers in any particular trade or occupation to control that industry, instead of working under these conditions of external control where they have no interest, no insight into what they are doing, and no social outlook upon the consequences and meaning of what they are doing. This means an increasing share given to the laborer, to the wage earner, in controlling the conditions of his own activity. It is so common to point out the absurdity of conducting a war for political democracy which leaves industrial and economic autocracy practically untouched, that I think we are absolutely bound to see, after the war, either a period of very great unrest, disorder, drifting, strife—I would not say actual civil war, but all kinds of irregular strife and disorder, or a movement to install the principle of self-government within industries."

Dewey indignantly describes the disastrous failure to provide job security and the waste of precious human material created by unemployment. He shows how low our standards are for the majority of the workers and insists that we could produce and distribute more efficiently. As an educator, he protests against the waste of the precious capacities of human beings.

For more than thirty years Dewey has asked for a full and extensive program of social security, even before some of the trade unions recognized this need and long before their successful current requests for pensions and other forms of welfare work.

Writing in 1938, he saw clearly that one of the first indications of Fascism was the suppression of the trade unions. The trade unions insist, and so does Dewey, that industry must be run for men and not men for industry. In education the schools exist for the pupils. Not subjects but children are taught. His idea of planning was not the blueprint imposed from above but the society which was continuously planning by the participation of its own intelligent members. He repeated the Emersonian idea that "Ends preexist in the means" and stressed that we can get a democratic society only by the democratic participation of the people who are making it.

The extensive writings of Dewey have no blueprint plan, no attractive slogans for organized labor. When Dewey writes about "How to Anchor Liberalism" (*Labor and Nation,* Nov.-Dec. 1948), he advises labor technicians to recognize "the need of a thorough examination of what freedom demands under present conditions if it is to be a reality and not just a cover of this and that scheme." He wants Labor to know "the specific means and agencies by which organized planning and intervention will result in promotion of freedom. . . ." Instead of abstract talk about "the individual," Dewey advocates "more study of specific social conditions to try to discover what kind of organization . . . will bring about a wider and hence more equitable distribution of the uses and enjoyments that our present technical resources make possible." Surely the trade unions with their increasing research and educational facilities represent not only a partner in such a study but an important potential aid to apply the findings of such a study.

Sidney Hook (*European Ideologies,* pp. 1059-1063) has shown that organized labor is consciously and, in part, unconsciously humanist because it places the welfare of human beings above output as the aim of industry. Logically this is parallel to the Dewey view that the growth of the child is much more important than the adherence to the rules of any educational system. And the end product of education (if it is not a contradiction to speak of a terminal point to a never-ending process) should be an alert, useful citizen shouldering his civic responsibilities. Obviously such responsibilities include the citizen organized where he *works* as well as where he *lives.* The participating student in the classroom engaged in group activity will prepare himself to be the participating voter and trade unionist. For our modern society is composed of a complex of groups, interacting one upon the other. Paternalism in industrial relations has become outmoded and furnishes no permanent base for the relations of adults, for both teacher and parent must consider themselves to be expendable. Unchallenged dictatorship is alien and indeed inefficient and wasteful in the modern factory. Collective bargaining between representatives of Management and Labor seems the best proven method for industrial relations and fully in accord with democratic ideals with its respect for majority opinion and also for the value and integrity of the individual worker.

Dewey as a fervent advocate of "continuing education" would certainly welcome the activity of trade unions in the field of adult education particularly when it emphasizes "adequate instruction for a new type of citizenship in which political questions will be seen in their economic background and bearings." In his essay "Education and the Social Order" there is also suggested that both subject matter and study methods need reorganization upon a "directly social basis and with a social aim." Obviously the unions would benefit both directly and indirectly from such a move which would avoid the danger of planning by dictatorship. Here also is the real antidote to the dangers of "bureaucracy" and "statism" and the fear that individuals would look to the state for handouts in exchange for their freedom.

Instead of the onetime conception of trade union education as a weapon in the class struggle of ideas, it can become the means whereby the union can understand itself better. But communication will not stop there because (if the employers' corporation no longer practices unrestrained exploitation and no longer refuses even to recognize the union) the educational activity of the union can be used to remove blocks in the communications between the union and management by studying the industry itself and discovering opportunities for mutual cooperation. Instead of putting a sharp emphasis upon differences both in immediate and ultimate aims, trade union education may also serve as a liaison with modern management and public opinion. Naturally, when the labor unions endeavor to obtain over-all social security, they must appeal to the community as a whole. They do not build old-fashioned barricades in the street but must try to engineer social consent for their reforms. Education becomes an instrument for making social change; it functions to solve problems and to remain critically alert to examine the faults and weakness of trade unions and other social institutions. Constantly new problems, new solutions and new shapes and forms of democracy will be emerging.

Some suggestions are in order upon the practical applications and results of the Dewey philosophy in the current operation of modern trade unions. How should we think, write and act in labor unions in line with Dewey's influence? Obviously the unions should be conscious of the oncoming generation and be prepared to cooperate with the lively students as they come into industry from the modern schools. Indeed the unions should not wait for graduation exercises to make contacts. At least in one high school in Newark, N. J., a Labor History Week has been instituted, with the local union leaders brought in to serve as supplementary teachers and to give information about local union activity. Dewey repeatedly attacked the false division between the liberal and mechanical arts and the resulting snobbish disdain for manual skills. Unions conscious of change should be able to plan ahead in cooperation with the school to meet the labor needs of industry by training plans.

With or without the benefit of earlier preparation, the young union members particularly should be fully informed about their union rights and duties. If we believe that "whoever is affected by any decision or policy should have some part in shaping it," then we should see that the new members are assisted to understand the structure and functioning of their union as well as its history and problems. But that knowledge is best acquired by its exercise. "The creative quality of life is to be found in communication-participation." You learn responsibility by being made responsible. Unions should be at pains to activize their members by allocating duties and responsibility to them with, naturally, competent supervision in the early stages.

Unions, in too many instances, suffer more from apathy than from outside attack. The member who never attends meetings, who thinks of the union merely as a penny-in-the-slot machine to deliver shorter hours and higher wages, is a source of weakness. Democracy too easily dies by default in labor organizations as elsewhere. The absence of member participation results in an arrogation of authority by the officers, even among those leaders who initially try to plan it otherwise. Unchecked power corrupts in unions as elsewhere. The training, development and encouragement of the younger members despite all difficulties—the brashness of youth and the rigidity of old age—should be given support.

The attitude of the officers would also be improved by better training and preparation. They too would be conscious of "participating planning" with their colleagues and members. Neither officers nor rank and file members would be a yes-man chorus for the higher echelons of power. Authoritarian methods in industry were challenged by the unions as they were in the school by the ideas of Dewey. Union leaders should not be a new type of boss, repeating the mistakes of the dictatorial employer.

The great parliaments of organized labor in its union conventions will be not only parades of union strength with long speeches from public figures to patient delegates. Rather they will be a sober stock-taking and a preparation for future contingencies, with local delegates doing most of the talking. Weak spots, such as the discrimination exercised by a few unions against Negroes, would be acknowledged and remedies sought. Dangers of ossification and corruption are possible in unions as in other human organizations. (Organized religion, politics, education and even bridge clubs share the danger of control by a few.) Internal democracy in the union would prevent the trend to dictatorship by permanent leaders. The possible rotation of office, the evils of factionalism and how to overcome them, the combining of efficiency with democratic controls are all dependent upon an alert and active participating membership. Some unions suffer from the curse of bigness and personal domination as do some corporations. Democratic procedures, if preserved, can take care of their own mistakes.

If unions accept the Dewey conception of unending change, then they will flexible and adaptable to industrial and social changes. The larger view would surely rule out the jurisdictional disputes and anti-social practices which on occasion discredit organized labor. In addition to developing internal understanding, unions will better recognize their role in industry and in the community, and thus integrate themselves into community life. Many progressive elements in the community are ready and willing to cooperate with responsible labor organizations.

With such applications of Dewey's philosophy to secure a better informed and active membership, an improved and imaginative personnel and leadership, a more farsighted policy and closer cooperation with other sections of the community, organized labor can better "understand and rectify specific social ills" and participate in planning for real freedom and a better world when our social understanding will equal our technical powers.

The Desirable and Emotive in Dewey's Ethics

by SIDNEY HOOK

> *"In morals there are immediate goods, the desired, and reasonable goods, the desirable."*—DEWEY

THE STERILITY of most discussions of the nature of value has long been a source of complaint. One of the causes of this sterility, it seems to me, is that the approach to human values has not been sufficiently empirical, even on the part of some theories that regard themselves as empirical. Another reason is that too much emphasis has been placed upon preliminary *definitions* of value. As distinct from attempted definitions of qualities and relations in other fields, such discussions have usually turned into an analysis of the nature of definitions—sometimes into an analysis of analysis—as if this were a necessary preliminary both to a definition of value and to subsequent investigation of the relationships between values and the conditions of their discovery.

Most philosophers are ready enough to admit that in other fields definitions should be laid down at the conclusion of investigations, or, when a subject matter has been sufficiently organized to permit some control over the adequacy of the definition. But this procedure has rarely been followed by philosophers in the field of value. Among the things that a definition of value must be adequate to is, of course, common usage. But common usage, it seems clear, is not the only control over adequacy, if only because common usage is inconsistent and may change overnight because of other changes, for example a dictator's decree, which all investigators into the nature of values agree are irrelevant to what they are trying to understand. The problem then becomes what kinds and occasions of common usage are relevant. Unless it is assumed that there is some natural language sense, universal in extent, which can be disclosed by peeling away different layers of conventional usage, we cannot justifiably ignore the possible relevance of such questions as: *why do people speak as they do? what events in their experience account for this one or that particular usage? what* observational tests enable us to determine what they mean? This takes us outside of verbal usage to other human behavioral facts. Otherwise we remain in the predicament of trying to get insight into the nature of ethical behavior, merely by examining what are allegedly the rules of good linguistic usage and, indeed, of *English* usage. Imagine what would happen if at the United Nations someone were to attempt to criticize the ethical pronouncements of representatives of other countries on the ground that they were illegitimate or prohibited by the standards of good English usage!

This situation would hardly arise in other fields of study in which questions of conflicting usage arise. There is a clear sense, for example, in common usage in which *both* "position" and "velocity" can be attributed at the same time to anything that moves. When the physicists declare that under certain conditions it is illegitimate to attribute both of these predicates at the same time to a given particle, they are apparently running counter to common usage. Nothing would seem to be more futile than to dispute their statement, as some seem inclined to do, on the ground that it violates common usage. The question which should concern us is: What in the experimental situation leads them to say what they do?

Corresponding in ethical discussion to the attempt to get back of the question of correct usage in other fields, is reference to the empirical facts of moral behavior, including the facts of conflict and disagreement as well as those of agreement. Any credible theory of value must do justice not only to how people talk but to how they behave in other ways. It is not necessary to begin with a precise definition of the meaning of value any more than an investigation of color theory begins with a definition of color or biological investigation of the nature of frogs begins with a definition of frogs. It is enough to begin with an assorted selection of colored things or frogs or value facts and then to formulate some conception of the quality or thing in question, which will enable us to organize more effectively our other knowledge about it and facilitate the subsequent process of inquiry and systematization. Ultimately the test of a good definition—and all definitions are in some sense analytic—is whether it makes it easier to relate in a significant and fruitful way our existing knowledge without establishing semantic or other blockages to the discovery or recognition of new knowledge. Definitions are adequate or inadequate, not true or false like the primary statements of observation with which knowledge begins and always ends. But the fact that they are justified or controlled by the consequences of their use gives them a cognitive status that purely arbitrary nominal definitions do not have.

The most obvious empirical fact often disregarded in current discussion is that questions about specific values in human experience arise out of problematic situations. Such questions arise when habitual responses are insufficient to sustain the free flow of experience or when these responses are challenged by others and we grope for a guide or justification. This is a commonplace, but if it is *dismissed* as a commonplace, as if it had no further bearing upon judgment of value, subsequent discussion has removed itself from the most important element of *control*.

The fact that questions of evaluation arise out of problematic situations is not a discovery of John Dewey. It is recognized in the classic formulation of the fundamental problem of ethics: What should we do? When we ask such a question we are implying that the answer will be a proposed decision, a decision to do not something in general but something specific from a number of alternative modes of action all relevant to the problem that evoked the question, and that a satisfactory answer will indicate *why* one proposed decision is to be selected rather than others. The good of that situation will be the realized object of the decision.

In making such a judgment of value are we making empirical

cognitions that are certifiable by the methods of scientific or rational inquiry? Or are such judgments merely judgments of feeling, true or false, depending upon whether we have them or not? Or are they no judgments at all, but merely or primarily expressions of attitude or commands?

Before answering these questions a number of observations must be made about what such a situation involves. First of all, whenever we are mature enough to make a decision or even begin to be puzzled, we never start *de novo* or from scratch. We carry with us a heavily funded memory of things previously discovered to be valuable, ends or goods to which we feel committed as prima facie validities. The list will not be the same for everybody or for any one all the time, but it will contain values like health, friendship, security, knowledge, art, amusement in their plural forms. It will also include certain general rules like thoughtfulness, honesty and truthfulness, which are the conditions of any social life in which human values are systematically pursued and sufficiently enjoyed to make social peace preferable to civil war.

Secondly, the situation is one that demands a choice between incompatible alternatives, not the application of a fixed universal rule to a concrete case, which could be done perhaps by a complex calculating machine.

Third, the choice involved in moral deliberation is between conflicting ends of a kind that will determine or redetermine the character or disposition of the agent. That is why there is no sharp decision between knowledge relevant to moral situations and other types of knowledge. Any problem of choice may become a moral problem when our own relatively permanent dispositions of character are involved, because they bear on relationships which involve other human beings. Any act acquires a moral character as soon as it has consequences for others that could have been foreseen.

Fourth, the resolution of any concrete problem is a conclusion about what is most worth while doing here and now, in this place and this time. We *assume* that certain ends of action are valid in the course of our deliberation and that certain consequences of the means used in removing the conflicts between ends are satisfactory.

Now we can go through the verbal motions of challenging these consequences as themselves satisfactory. If we justify *them* by reference to further consequences, we can raise the same question over and over again. So long as the discussion remains on the plane of a purely theoretical possibility, there seems to be a danger of an infinite regress. But the point cannot be too strongly emphasized that ethical discussions are forced upon us by life situations and their concrete problems. They do not grow out of talk. We do not in *fact* ask why? why? why? unless there is some genuine perplexity, some genuine need or difficulty which seems to coerce us into making a choice. It simply is *not* the case, and the adequacy of the whole empirical approach to ethics depends upon recognizing it, that before we can justify to ourselves a decision in the light of consequences, we must justify these consequences, and the consequences of these consequences, and go on until we reach some consequence or other which in fact serves as an anchor ledge for the whole, and which itself is forever beyond possibility of being challenged. In human experience there are no beginnings and there are no final endings to the succession of moral problems. We always find ourselves, and this is recognized not only by Dewey but by other writers, like Stevenson, "in the middle course."

Fifth, every envisagement of a possible decision in relation to a problem is an incipient first step in the formation of a favorable or unfavorable attitude to the objects involved. In one sense all statements of fact in relation to problems put our body in a state of motor readiness, but a statement about what should be done in a problematic moral situation, because it expresses a special concern or urgency, has a quasi-imperative force. It is a preeminent judgment of practice designed to move us and others to action. There is not only a quasi-imperative force in the meaning of the proposed ethical judgment, but an emotive influence as well. As Dewey puts it: "A moral judgment, however intellectual it may be, must at least be colored with feeling if it is to influence behavior." [*Ethics*, 2nd Edition, p. 296]

These verifiable characteristics of the problematic ethical situation will have a bearing upon the analysis of the meaning and validity of value judgments. If they are true, then it will be clear why immediate enjoyments as experiences which are merely had, generate no problems even when different people have them. They do not need to be warranted because their existence cannot be challenged, but only indicated either by a word or by a sound. There may be a problem as to whether the proper word is being used to indicate them, for example, when someone is using a foreign tongue, or whether the sign of the enjoyment or suffering has not been masked for purposes of social amenity. But no problem of *valuation* attaches to them. It is in this particular sense that it is true to say: "Concerning tastes there is no disputing." Coffee tastes pleasant to me, it does not taste pleasant to you. No argument can alter the facts. Never is there a *conflict* of attitudes towards coffee as an experienced taste here and now. The difference in attitudes might become a conflict in attitudes when some such question is asked as: Should we order coffee again? Is coffee a more enjoyable drink than tea? If all a person means to assert by "coffee is good" is that at the moment he finds the coffee pleasant-tasting—and he knows that this is his meaning—it is an observable fact that he will never dispute with someone else who says: "Coffee is not good," if he understands this expression to mean that at the moment the other person finds it unpleasant-tasting.

But there is another sense in which we can, according to Dewey, very well dispute about tastes. This is the sense in which we ask: is this *truly* or *really* or *objectively* a good thing? and we find that our judgment of value is significantly denied or that it can be mistaken. Dewey uses the expressions, italicized in the previous sentence, interchangeably with what is genuinely "valuable" or "desirable." And he believes that whenever something enjoyed or desired is questioned, it becomes necessary to give adequate or relevant grounds for regarding what is desired as desirable or what is enjoyed as enjoyable.

In the first sense "the Good is that which satisfies want, craving, which fulfills or makes complete the need which stirs to action." [*Ethics*, 2nd Edition, p. 205] In the second sense, the good as something to be justified by thought "imposes upon those about to act the necessity for rational insight, or moral *wisdom*." Dewey goes on to add, "For experience shows that not every satisfaction of appetite and craving turns out to be a good; many ends *seem* good while we are under the influence of strong passion, which in actual experience and in such thought as might have occurred in a cool moment are actually bad." [*loc. cit.*]

This position has been the occasion of acute criticism by Professors Stevenson and White which I propose to examine. Since Professor Stevenson's view is much closer to Dewey's than is Professor White's, I shall discuss the latter first.[1]

The nub of Professor White's criticism is that whereas "x is desired" is an empirical statement, "x is desirable," on Dewey's analysis, is not an empirical statement in the sense in which "x is desirable" and "x ought to be desired" are synonymous terms. Professor White argues that Dewey, like Mill, has been misled by the suffix ending of "desirable," *able*, except that Mill made the error in a cruder form by thinking that "desirable" is like "soluble," whereas Dewey makes the more subtle one of thinking it ("desirable") is a disposition-predicate like "objectively red" (1, p. 325) or objectively hot, fluid or heavy. The difference between "soluble" and "objectively red" is that to say "x" is soluble" is to say that it is capable of being dissolved. And if there are *any* conditions under which x dissolves, we can say it is soluble. One dissolution, so to speak, is as good as a million. For objectively red (or the other qualities) this is not true. Something may appear to be red without being objectively red, although everything which is objectively red will under determinate conditions appear red. "X is objectively red" is synonymous with "x looks red under normal conditions" (1, 324) to normal people, but the fact that something appears blood red in the light of a garish sunset, is not sufficient for us to call it objectively red.

[1] *Cf.* his (1) "Value and Obligation in Dewey and Lewis," *Philosophical Review*, Vol. LVIII, No. 4, July 1949, pp. 321-329; and (2) Chapter XIII of his *Social Thought in America* (N.Y. 1949). I shall refer to these as 1 and 2.

Dewey grants that "x is desired" does *not* mean "x is desirable." Indeed, he insists on this. Otherwise there would be no problem for evaluation. But his mistake, according to Professor White, is to assume that "x is desirable" is equivalent to "x is desired under normal conditions." But "x is desired under normal conditions" is no more *normative* than "x looks red under normal conditions." On this analysis there is as much sense in saying "x ought to be desired" as "x ought to appear red." [1, 326] Dewey would assert the first, but certainly not the second. But he should assert the second, so the criticism runs, if his analysis of the first were sound. Since neither he nor anyone else would do so, his analysis of "desirable" is unsound.

The relevant passages are from Dewey's *The Quest for Certainty*:

"The formal statement may be given concrete content by pointing to the difference between the enjoyed and the enjoyable, the desired and the desirable, the satisfying and the satisfactory. To say that something is enjoyed is to make a statement about a fact, something already in existence; it is not to judge the value of that fact. There is no difference between such a proposition and one which says that something is sweet or sour, red or black. It is just correct or incorrect *and that is the end of the matter*. But to call an object a value is to assert that it satisfies or fulfills certain conditions." [p. 260]

"If one likes a thing he likes it; that *is* a point about which there can be no dispute:—although it is not easy to state just *what* is liked as is frequently assumed. A judgment about what is *to be* desired and enjoyed is, on the other hand, a claim on future action; it possesses *de jure* and not merely *de facto* quality. It is a matter of frequent experience that likings and enjoyments are of all kinds, and that many are such as reflective judgments condemn. [p. 262-3]

"To assume that anything can be known in isolation from its connections with other things is to identify knowing with merely having some object before perception or in feeling, and is thus to lose the key to the traits that distinguish an object as known. It is futile, even silly, to suppose that some quality that is directly present constitutes the whole of the thing presenting the quality. It does not do so when the quality is that of being hot or fluid or heavy, and it does not when the quality is that of giving pleasure, or being enjoyed. Such qualities are, once more, effects, ends in the sense of closing termini of processes involving causal connections. They are something to be investigated, challenges to inquiry and judgment. The more connections and interactions we ascertain, the more we *know* the object in question. Thinking is search for these connections. Heat experienced as a consequence of directed operations has a meaning quite different from the heat that is casually experienced without knowledge of how it came about. The same is true of enjoyments. Enjoyments that issue from conduct directed by insight into relations have a meaning and validity due to the way in which they are experienced. Such enjoyments are not repented of; they generate no after-taste of bitterness. Even in the midst of direct enjoyment, there is a sense of validity, of authorization, which intensifies the enjoyment. There is solicitude for perpetuation of the *object* having value which is radically different from mere anxiety to perpetuate the *feeling* of enjoyment." [p. 267]

The difficulty in Dewey's position, according to Professor White, is that whereas statements like "x is desired," "x appears red," "x is objectively red" are all *de facto,* statements like "x is desirable," which are analogous to "x is objectively red," suddenly take on *de jure* status, too. By a kind of transsubstantiation the factual becomes normative. "Here we have generated a normative or *de jure* proposition by performing a suitable operation on merely *de facto* propositions" (2, p. 214), the complaint runs.

To begin with, it should be pointed out that Dewey is drawing what he calls a "formal analogy" between the two kinds of qualities. He nowhere actually says that "x is desirable" is synonymous with "x is desired under normal conditions." What formally corresponds to "normal conditions" where values are concerned is "understood in the light of its causes and consequences." Where what is desired, say a craving for a certain food, is understood in the light of its cause, say a pathological state of the organism, it will have a bearing on the desirability of the desired. Where what is desired is understood in the light of its consequences, on health, fortune, etc., that, too, will have a bearing on desirability. Consequences are usually the most important; but the desirable is that which is desired *after reflection* upon relevant causes and consequences. What gives the desired desirability is that it is reaffirmed in the light of its actual and possible connections. This means that it takes on a *new* character, desirability, without losing the old one, being desired. That this is possible is evident from the fact that in many other situations, things take on new qualities in new relations —corn becomes a food, gold money, etc.

The crucial difference, however, overlooked in Professor White's analysis of "desirable" and "objectively red" is that the problematic situation in which we seek to find what is really good or desirable is one that requires a "genuine practical judgment" in answer to the question: what should I do or choose? whereas the analysis of "seeming red" and "objective red" has been conducted without reference to any practical problem of choice. Complete the analogy and introduce a situation in which it becomes *important* to distinguish between apparent and real color, and *"objectively red"* acquires a normative status that "apparently red" does not have. *Apparently* red is not good enough in matching draperies or in any other situation in which we want to know what color we are really choosing. Only the "objectively red" will do. Professor White believes that this is a *reductio ad absurdum*, because it would follow that *all* true scientific statements would have a *de jure* quality (2, p. 215). Not at all, unless he maintains that as scientific they all bear *per se* upon immediate practical problems of what should be done. But the propositions of science are theoretical until they are applied in some practical situation—a tautology which in this connection has significance because it marks a definite distinction in function. Dewey's contention is that every true proposition *in use* in a concrete situation provoking choice does have a normative status, because wherever relevant it determines in some degree what we should choose. But the great body of scientific propositions at any time are not in use.

This view seems very paradoxical to Professor White. "Take, for example, the statement that the table upon which I am working now is actually brown. In what sense is this normative?" he asks (1). The answer is: in no sense, because he has uttered a detached statement in the blue unrelated to any problem of choice. This example is trivial, but it is easy to think of situations in which a man's life may depend upon knowing (in medicine and other practical disciplines), what the real or objective property of a substance is. But let him ask: What color of cloth or ornament should I choose for this table? And at once the actual color of the table, if he wishes to choose wisely, becomes a normative element for his action. (The analogy between the analysis of the normative scientific statement and the normative ethical statement is formal. It does not mean that the normative scientific statement is an ethical statement, since not all problems of practical choice are ethical.)

What Professor White has established is that in any *theoretical* argument we cannot reach a conclusion with an "ought" term unless one of the premises contains an "ought" term (1). If this is the decisively relevant point, then any naturalistic account of "ought to be desired" would have to be ruled out—a position which he leaves open—and not only the specific one Professor White rejects. But a "phenomenological" account of the nature of the problematic ethical situation will show that "theoretical" propositions when relevantly introduced, do acquire from their context a directive and practical status on our decision which they do not have in isolation.

A disregard of the living context of the practical judgment—and all evaluative decisions are practical judgments—leaves us with the truism that from any set of matter of fact propositions, no conclusions about what should be done follow. If there is no "ought" or "should" in the premises of the "detached" argument, no "ought" or "should" is entailed in the conclusion. But within a context in which something must be *done,* the "ought" of the decision or conclusion is, so to speak, ultimately derivative from the urgencies of the problem, and supported or justified by the factual statements about the probable consequences of doing one thing or another to meet the situation. The normative element in the conclusion is in a sense provided by that which distinguishes the situation as a practical one from one that is purely logical or theoretical. The underlying premise is: that should be done which appropriately meets the needs and requirements of the situation, broadly conceived to include the demands and expectations of the community or traditions in which we find ourselves. Then, by ordinary scientific means, we discover that the probable consequences of *this* act, meet these needs and requirements and conclude it should be done. The underlying premise of the argument is not an explicit statement at all, but the situation itself.

Charles Beard, the late American historian, was fond of saying that no aggregation of facts by themselves determined any policy. Of course, literally construed, this is quite true. Statements of facts by *themselves* without reference to the problem-situation and its conflict of ends, on which the facts bear, determine nothing. Certainly, they do not *logically* determine anything. But if by policy we mean not a course of action to realize an *already decided upon end* (which would mean that the moral problem had been settled), but a course of conduct that defines what the end should be, and some proximate means of achieving it, (as when we say that the U. S. needs a foreign policy); and if "determine" means providing evidential grounds, it is hard to see what else could determine policy except the aggregation of relevant facts from different fields. What we ought to do in any particular situation is that which we choose to do *after* reflection upon the relevant consequences of proposals framed to meet the needs of the situation.

The underlying criticism of Dewey's theory of value by Professor White, it seems to me, does not depend upon the latter's rejection of the parity of analysis between the disposition-predicates "desirable" and "objectively red." What he really believes is that Dewey's theory of value has nothing to do with ethics, because the ethical "ought-to-be" imposes a kind of obligation foreign to all empirical statements. It is this antecedent acceptance of the separation of natural good and moral good, of the entire realm of empirical findings in anthropology, economics, law, psychology, politics, etc., from what is binding in a special moral sense which is challenged by Dewey's theory according to which, without reducing the *concept* of right to good, morals are as wide as the area of everything which affects the values of human living (*Ethics*, p. 349). This separation is challenged not only by Dewey's theory but by the historical record which shows that judgments of morally right and wrong, despite theoretical pronouncements to the contrary, do, in fact, change with wider understanding of biological and social phenomena.

There is another variant of Professor White's criticism of Dewey's theory which should be briefly considered. According to this criticism, knowledge of the causes and consequences of our desire, and of what is desired, does not make the desired desirable unless among the consequences there are some other desirables. Unless we can get back to some rock-bottom desirable in itself, the position is circular (2, p. 217). Again the failure appears to me to result from disregarding the facts of actual moral situations. Of course, there are other desirables that have to be taken into account in assessing the consequences of proposed modes of conduct in a problematic situation. These desirables are assumed or *postulated* as valid because they summarize previous experience. That is what it means to say that we no more start from scratch in ethical inquiry than in any other kind of inquiry. The knowledge that the desired has consequences, which we have reasons to believe desirable, when added to relevant knowledge of the causes of our desire, makes what is desired desirable. The important point here is that the knowledge which makes the difference is knowledge of fact, of the non-value facts (usually causes) and of the value-facts (usually consequences), won by ordinary scientific methods and investigation. The value-facts which are introduced as data can, of course, be challenged, but that is another problem. "Should I take a vacation or continue this piece of work?" someone asks. Among the consequences is the discovery that if a vacation is not taken, he will probably have a nervous breakdown. This is assumed undesirable. But why is this undesirable? This is another problem entirely, and to be a genuine one, must be taken very concretely. In the course of settling it, he may discover other value-facts. Unless he preserves his health, his children will suffer. This is bad. Why is it bad? Another problem, in the course of the solution of which he discovers that his children are so much a part of his life that it would be sadly altered if anything serious happened to them. One can keep on asking questions until the inevitable one is reached: "Is life itself worth living?" But must we really answer that question, too, and an indeterminate number of others, in order to be able to answer the question we started from? No one can seriously maintain this. Whether life is worth living *may* arise as a specific question and is answerable one way or the other. But it is not relevant to most of our ethical problems.

Professor Stevenson's position is much closer to Dewey's than that of the previous critic. Not only does he believe that ethics "must draw from the *whole* of a man's knowledge," denying the separation between empirical evaluations and moral obligations; he forswears any attempt to find "ultimate principles" or "otherworldly norms." Some chapters of his brilliant *Ethics and Language*, especially the chapter on "Intrinsic and Extrinsic Value," are substantially along the same lines as Dewey's ethical theory. His main difference from Dewey is on the place and significance of emotive elements in ethical language and behavior. And here it becomes hard to determine how important the differences are, since Professor Stevenson professes to be interested only in the analysis of ethical language and asserts that the theoretical differences between Dewey's position and his own reflect Dewey's concern as a moralist.

There is one general criticism, however, which Professor Stevenson makes of Dewey's theory as a piece of analysis, which is central. This is that Dewey, although less so than most critics, neglects the role of emotive meaning as a factor in the determination of ethical issues. And by words possessing emotive meaning are intended those non-descriptive words which by expressing attitudes have a persuasive function on conduct. Stevenson's view is that descriptive meanings—roughly the reasons we give for an ethical position—may influence beliefs, but beliefs do not by themselves always determine attitudes, even if they are beliefs *about* attitudes. Where they seem to do so, it is always because they are wedded to some emotive meaning, whose presence is just as relevant for the understanding of ethical judgment as the cognitive meaning of the supporting reasons. For Dewey, anything "worthy" of being done—which is the meaning of "should be done"—depends for its justification completely upon the cognitive reasons or "factual evidence available." These, and these alone, make the normative or practical judgments valid. Every ethical judgment for Dewey is a "recommendation," a proposal, a prescription. Therefore, their function is quasi-imperative. For Stevenson, if this is true, it cannot follow only from its cognitive support and the emotively laden meanings of the cognitive terms in the problematic situation, but from some relatively independent factor of irreducible emotive meaning. It therefore becomes necessary to examine Stevenson's theory a little more closely.

In some ways it is curiously difficult to assess the precise difference between Dewey and Stevenson. But concerning two of these differences, it is possible to speak with some assurance. First, for Dewey a term that functions in a typical context of human communication can only influence conduct if it has some cognitive meaning. Whatever its emotive effects, they are dependent upon direct, peripheral, or suggested cognitive meaning. Stevenson seems to believe that some terms possess independent emotive meaning, although he asserts that what is distinctive about his position does not really depend upon this particular thesis. So far, however, he has not been able to present any indisputable illustration of terms that have persuasive, emotional force that do not depend upon the hearer or reader taking them as descriptive signs, too. The nearest he has come to establishing the existence of independent emotive meaning is in the use of expletives like "Damn!" or "Hell!" and the more strongly expressive four-letter words.

It is one thing to use such terms as abstract illustrations: it is quite another to observe how they function in a living context. In the latter case, these terms are read in the light of the whole situation. A man who misses his train or who, instead of hitting a nail square on the head, hits his thumb square on the nail, conveys a rather definite meaning, no matter what kind of language he uses. Even syntactically nonsensical expressions are taken as signs designating certain states of affairs if they are not considered as detached from, but as related to, their actual uses. In this connection one is reminded of De Man's story of the date vendor of Constantinople who did a brisk trade hawking his wares with repeated cries of "Hassan's dates are larger than they are!" to the impotent envy of his fellows. It is safe to say that either Hassan's dates were *in fact* larger than those of his competitors, or that his hearers thought they had heard him say something very much like it. What is meaningful in ethical discourse cannot be determined merely by the form of a linguistic expression alone. It is necessary to observe the wider context of interest, situation, and activity in which the expression is used. When this is done, there seems little evidence for the belief in the existence of independent emotive meaning.

Although Dewey insists that the purpose of an ethical judgment is to influence conduct, he refuses to regard this purpose as a constituent element of the meaning of the ethical judgment, or to give to the emotive elements of discourse an equivalent function in the legitimate determination of ethical issues. Dewey does not deny that emotive means are employed to resolve conflicts any more than he denies that brass bands, hypnotic suggestions, and physical coercion are effectively employed for the same purpose. But he denies that all modes of effecting agreement are ethically relevant. Mere agreement on attitude does not settle an ethical issue independently of how the agreement is achieved any more than mere agreement settles a scientific issue. Only when someone is persuaded by argument, when the grounds or reasons of an action have become one of the psychologically efficient causes of the action, do we feel that persuasion on an ethical issue has been appropriately effected. That is why, according to Dewey, we disallow the relevance of emotive elements in ethical situations, even if they do influence or redirect attitudes, when we are considering the truth or falsity of judgments of value.

According to Dewey, evaluative decisions are made not only in ethics but in all fields of human activity, including science. Although the subject matter of the natural scientist differs from that of the moralist, when he is trying to make up his mind about what hypothesis to approve of, he is seeking, like the moralist, to find grounds for a decision which also will express his attitudes. A scientist who is making an evaluative decision about whether he should commit himself in the way of belief—with its corollary of experimentation—to one or another theory of light or disease may be emotively concerned or affected by the things he is investigating. But he would not regard these emotive elements as in any way relevant to the weight of evidence which determines his appraisal.

In any situation where an evaluative decision is to be made, "x is valuable," for Dewey, may roughly be analyzed as "I will choose or approve of x after reflection on the relevant consequences of my choice. The relevance of the consequences is determined by their bearing on the situation which has provoked my indecision and on the interests which constitute the relatively permanent core of my self." Professor Stevenson asserts that such an analysis is incomplete because it leaves us with an indeterminate number of unrelated predictive judgments. The result is that we can never specify what ethical sentences mean; nor can we account for the distinctively quasi-imperative meaning of ethical terms.

I submit that Professor Stevenson has overlooked the continuous control of the problematic situation itself upon the number and kind of predictive judgments which are ethically relevant. We don't predict for the sake of predicting, or about everything, but in order to meet the particular challenge set by the particular problem. The predictions are the foreseeings and forewarnings that constitute wisdom. They will vary with the kind of problem. They will be different if I am trying to determine whether to support a strike or report an act of cruelty to the SPCA. But they will not be unlimited. We do not need reference to emotive meaning to help unify all cognitive elements involved. The problematic situation serves as the unifying reference. Many things that may be causally relevant to our emotive attitudes may be logically irrelevant to the ethical judgment. Indeed, although in Dewey's theory we cannot tell in advance the precise amount of knowledge we need in order to justify our making a well grounded evaluative decision, on Stevenson's theory it is hard to see how anything can be ruled out as irrelevant as a reason for an ethical judgment. "Any statement," he says, "about *any* matter of fact which *any* speaker considers likely to alter attitudes may be adduced as a reason for or against an ethical judgment" (*Ethics and Language,* p. 114).

The judgment of what should be done has all the intellectual weight of its supporting reasons. At the same time, it derives its quasi-imperative function not so much from any dependent emotive meaning as from the fact that it is formulated in a situation of stress to resolve a perplexity. We feel caught in a problem that has to be met, and every ethical judgment has the force of a proposed resolution.

When we go from a situation of personal decision to one of conflict between two individuals or classes, the emotive theory of ethics seems to rest on the strongest grounds. For in such cases, the relative distinction between disagreement in attitude and disagreement in belief seems justified even though we recognize that an attitude toward an object expresses an implicit belief about it and a belief about an object involves an implicit attitude toward it. But I agree with Professor Stevenson that this does not make beliefs and attitudes identical. The question is how they vary with each other. In so far as disagreement in attitude is rooted in disagreement in belief, the scientific methods by which we reach agreement in belief are sufficient to effect ethical resolution. In so far as disagreements in attitudes are not rooted in differences in belief, then all agreement in belief will be unavailing to settle an ethical issue. Agreement in practice in such cases, Professor Stevenson holds, can be reached, if at all, by use of emotive meanings if not by stronger methods.

Now there are a number of observations about attitudes and beliefs which seem to me to be true, and which suggest that the role of belief in ethical affairs is perhaps more important than we are at first inclined to think in face of the manifest ethical disagreements of social life. First, in any concrete situation of ethical disagreement, if one knows what an individual's empirical beliefs are about that situation, one can almost always in fact tell what his attitudes will be. Indeed, some social psychologists measure a person's attitudes by his indication of beliefs—although this is very rough since the reliability of statement about beliefs must be checked. Personally, I have never known a case of ethical disagreement which did not seem to turn on differences in belief that were admitted by all parties to be relevant. Second, in cases of ethical disagreement, to assert that an individual's beliefs depend *only* upon his personal attitude or interest, is usually construed as a charge of prejudice which everyone seems concerned to deny by pointing to the evidence on which his judgment rests. It is assumed that his interests are always involved, but it is expected that the *evidence* will be disinterested, and that what it will show is that the judgment is not being made *exclusively* in behalf of the individual interest. Third, in cases where disagreement in attitudes seems to persist where there is agreement in belief, it will almost always be found that the beliefs on which there seems to be agreement are not held with the same degree of assent. They may vary from highly tentative surmise to absolute conviction. Consequently, the weight they have in determining attitudes differs—so that in effect we have disagreement in belief. Fourth, where disagreements in attitudes are not resolvable by agreement through beliefs, if they are compromised—the compromise can be shown to rest on agreement on another set of beliefs, viz., that the consequences of compromise are better in specifiable respects than those of conflict.

I mention these things because they suggest to me the possibility of accepting everything Professor Stevenson says about agreement and disagreement between two or more persons or classes without accepting his entire emotive theory of ethical terms. What he seems to assume is that any normative ethics on a naturalistic basis, which believes that ethical sentences have descriptive meanings, must give conclusions that are not only objectively true, but *universally* true, and since no one can establish *in advance* that an objective universal morality can be established holding for all interests, he believes that the descriptive theory of meaning is untenable. Once we surrender this assumption, however, and recognize the possibility of a relativism, which is, nonetheless, genuinely objective, then I see little pragmatic difference between saying—irrespective of all their other not inconsiderable differences—what Dewey, Perry, Santayana, possibly Lewis, and other naturalists in ethics are saying, and what Professor Stevenson seems to be saying. If the good is defined in relation to human need or interest (or preference, desire, satisfaction)—if, in other words, the nature of morals is conceived as having any relation to human nature—then every statement about the good or better in any situation has a descriptive meaning, and in principle is decidable in reference to the needs and interests involved. The nature of human nature, and most particularly the presence of shared interests in a shared experience, or the possibility of such shared interest, becomes relevant at every point. Whether, as Dewey claims, there exists "a psychological uniformity of human nature with respect to basic *needs* . . . and of certain conditions which must be met in order that any form of human association must be maintained" ("Anthropology and Ethics," *Social Sciences,* p. 34, ed. by Ogburn and Goldenweiser) is an empirical question to which the answer is difficult but not inaccessible to study. Since we know that men are not always aware of what their interests are, and that their interests (or attitudes) often change in the light of the knowledge of their causes and consequences, and since intelligence is also natural to man, in situations of conflict we use the method of intelligence to negotiate differences by seeking a more inclusive interest to enable us either to live with our differences, to mitigate them or to transcend them, and thus convert value conflicts into compatible value differences. This is the constructive moral function of intelligence, which to be effective must be given institutional form—educational, economic, political.

No one who soberly looks at history would wish to assert that all disagreements among human beings must yield to negotiation through intelligence, that we can be certain that men *are* sufficiently alike to work out ways of becoming more alike, or sufficiently alike to agree about the permissible limits of being different. The unwillingness to use intelligence where there is a possibility of using it, does not gainsay the fact that if it had been used, certain shared interests might have been—sometimes we can say *would* have been—discovered.

It is important to point out, however, that it is easy to exaggerate the non-negotiable differences among men, and to convert by theoretical fiat the occasions of disagreement into irresolvable ultimate differences of value attitudes. Most disagreements among men, Professor Stevenson has shown in a remarkable chapter of his book, are about focal aims, major or lesser, and not about allegedly ultimate values concerning which in Western culture, at any rate, most human beings *profess* to agree, to a point where Franco speaks of the "brotherhood of man under God" and Stalin speaks of "freedom."

We must recognize the possibility of a situation arising in which a man has been convinced by reasoning that "x is good" in a descriptive sense, and thereupon shows a greater desire to destroy it. He may have other interests, however, including an interest in peace and survival, which may lead him to restrain his desire to destroy x. And if he is intelligent enough to see that x is really good, his intelligence may suggest the *possibility* of finding an x which furthers a wider, common good. But even if this is not so, I do not see that it impugns the objectivity or truth of the original statement that "x is good" any more than Galileo's statement as to what could be seen about Jupiter's satellites through his telescope was less true because some Aristotelians refused to look through it.

There are two generic alternatives. One of them is illustrated by the Grand Inquisitor in Dostoyevsky's *Brothers Karamazov* who justifies his totalitarian society to Christ returned on earth by arguing that it is the only system that will bring happiness to the poor benighted creatures whom God has created. "There are three powers," he says, "three powers alone able to conquer and to hold captive for ever the conscience of these impotent rebels for their happiness—these forces are miracle, mystery, and authority." I believe it is possible to prove him mistaken about the nature of man, the nature of human happiness, and the methods of achieving it. But his willingness to give grounds for his position, to examine consequences, already sets up a hope for agreement. Contrast this with a situation somewhat nearer the hypothetical case described in the previous paragraph—the apologia of the Inner Party Leader in George Orwell's novel, *1984*, in which the leader differentiates himself from all other totalitarian groups past and present, declaring: "Power is not a means, it is an end. The object of persecution is persecution. The object of torture is torture. The object of power is power." Here there is no attempt to relate needs and consequences, no presence of rational intent. To the extent that the Grand Inquisitor offers reasons on which his attitudes are presumably based, he belongs to the moral community; the Inner Party Leader does not. If he is a man, he is a sick man. If he is not a sick man, then he must be contained or fought.

Granted, then, that there is an element of the *arbitrary* in the source of our moral judgment—a view which, if I am not mistaken, is one of the animating insights of the emotive conception of ethics—I do not see the necessity of carrying what is arbitrary into the moral judgment itself under the flag of the emotive theory. What is arbitrary or non-rational about man is his nature—a statement that would be just as true if he had the nature of an angel or a tiger. But what follows from his nature is not arbitrary in the same sense, particularly not his judgments of evaluation about what is *good* for that nature. Such judgments are empirical cognitions, and rational or irrational because tested and controlled by the outcome of experience.

That man has intelligence is as much a fact about his nature as that he has needs and desires which he seeks to satisfy. And since the successful satisfaction of these needs depends upon the knowledge of all sorts of conditions and consequences, there is no problem about justifying the use of intelligence to the extent that any man has it. He has a natural interest in intelligence because the prospering of all his other interests depends upon it.

Reflection on the social nature of the self, the success of experimental methods in the natural sciences, the costs and ineffectiveness of other methods in human affairs carries us a long way in justifying the use of intelligence in settling *conflicts* between groups and classes. But the *advocacy* of the use of such methods in situations where others may prefer to use different methods, the *proposal*, in the face of differences, to sit down and reason together, can be interpreted as a *decision* not to give ethical status to non-rational persuasive methods of effecting agreement like "emotive meaning, rhetorical cadence . . . stentorian, stimulating tones of voice, dramatic gestures . . . the use of material rewards and punishments" (*Ethics and Language,* pp. 139-140), unless preceded or accompanied by rational grounds.

In other words, we seem to have been implicitly defining "ethical agreement" as one reached through agreement on beliefs by rational means.

This looks very much like a *"persuasive definition"* in Professor Stevenson's sense—perhaps a "persuasive definition" in reverse. Instead of giving a new conceptual meaning to a familiar word, it reinforces an old meaning in current use, and is tantamount to a recommendation to use and continue using rational methods to resolve conflicts until evidence of bad faith or the *actions* of others make it impossible. And so long as this does not commit us to "the emotive theory of meaning," we should not be very concerned to deny it, for almost every critic of the emotive conception of ethics seems to be committed to some such persuasive definition. This is clear in Dewey's case when he tells us that "as far as non-cognitive, extra-cognitive factors enter into the subject-matter or content of sentences purporting to be *legitimately* ethical, those sentences are by just that much deprived of the properties sentences *should have* in order to be *genuinely* ethical." [*Jour. of Phil.,* Dec. 20, 1945, my italics] I believe that it can be shown that almost all writers on ethics have said something similar although they have differed on the precise analysis of what rational method consists in.

From this I conclude that the use of the definition, persuasive or not, is innocent because it expresses what is normally meant by *ethical* agreement when conflicts arise, and that to the extent that it has an influence on conduct, it would make for "an attitude of rationality" in the face of value conflicts.

John Dewey's Theory of Inquiry

by FELIX KAUFMANN

JOHN DEWEY'S *Logic, the Theory of Inquiry* appeared eleven years ago. The last sentence of its preface epitomizes the chief objective of the book: "My best wishes as well as my hopes are with those who engage in the profoundly important work of bringing logical theory into accord with scientific practice, no matter how much their conclusions may differ in detail from those presented in this book."[1]

Considering that scientific inquiry has to comply with the canons of logic, one might ask the question: How can the task of bringing logical theory into accord with scientific practice represent a serious problem? But this question is answered as soon as we realize that Dewey is concerned with what he calls "the ultimate subject matter of logic," that is with the philosophical interpretations of logical forms and canons. Conflicting interpretations of the nature of logic offered by the different philosophical schools are integral parts of their respective theories of knowledge. Dewey's point in criticizing these interpretations is that they are based on inadequate conceptions of knowledge and of inquiry. By establishing the meanings of these terms, and of other terms related to them, in conformity with their uses in science, we succeed in bringing logical theory into accord with scientific practice. This, then, is the enterprise on which Dewey embarks in his *Logic*.

One of the fundamental philosophical issues with which he finds himself confronted, is the problem of the relation between

[1] Henry Holt, New York 1938.

"knowledge" and "truth." Does it make sense to speak of a truth that is not only unknown, but in principle unknowable to man? Is the meaning of "truth" independent of and prior to that of "knowledge"? This problem has divided philosophers as soon as they engaged in systematic epistemological analysis. There is a long and winding road that connects Plato's *Theaetetus* with Dewey's *Logic*. The first milestone on this road is Aristotle's treatment of the problem. His definition of truth and falsity reads: "To say of what is that it is not, or of what is not that it is, is false; while to say of what is that it is, or of what is not that it is not, is true."[2] This conception of truth has been endorsed by those philosophers who are classified as realists. Aristotle traces back the meaning of "truth" to the all-comprehensive concept of being and derives the canons of logic from ontological principles.

The realists' interpretation of "truth" was contested on the ground that it makes the nature of truth unintelligible. This holds particularly for the truth of statements about the physical world. Philosophers of the various idealist schools declared that we must not take it for granted that our experiences of physical things resemble the things as they are in themselves. To state that a perception of blue must be caused by something that is blue in itself is no more reasonable than it would be to maintain that the pain which we experience in being pricked by a needle is inherent in the needle. It is even illegitimate to apply the category of causality, or any other category, to things-in-themselves. We must not trespass the boundaries of experience in using the categories. The conception of truth as conformity (correspondence) of propositions with things-in-themselves is therefore of no avail in an attempt to clarify the meaning of "scientific inquiry." All attempts to establish an ontological foundation of science are foredoomed to failure.

By recognizing Dewey's endorsement of this conclusion we have made a first step toward determining the place of his theory of inquiry in the history of philosophy. We cannot understand his methodological teachings unless we bear constantly in mind that

[2] *Met.* IV, 6, 1011.

he rejects the correspondence theories of truth proposed by the realist schools of philosophy.

Dewey is likewise opposed to the rationalists' claim that empirical knowledge, which they contrast as merely probable with absolutely certain rational knowledge, must have an immutable basis which is provided by logic. This view is indeed one of the chief targets of his criticism. He never tires of driving home the point that the quest for certainty, for the immutable and indubitable, is incompatible with the acknowledgement of the autonomy of the self-corrective process of scientific inquiry.

The rationalist position had been attacked by British empiricists, by David Hume, John Stuart Mill, Bertrand Russell. But Dewey makes it clear that their criticism does not penetrate to the core of the issue. They do not reject the demand for an indubitable foundation of science, but maintain that such a foundation is provided by the data of immediate experience. Sense data or introspective data, or both, are taken to yield the allegedly required absolute certainty. Dewey points out that this view is wrong, because it disregards the fact that knowledge is essentially contextual. Isolated sense data or introspective data are not objects of knowledge; they acquire cognitive functions only when they are employed as signs of something beyond themselves.[3] The conception of passively received data of experience leads to untenable dualistic doctrines which pretend that there is a cleavage between mind and matter. For the assumption of pure passivity requires an assumption of pure activity as its counterpart if we are to account for the organization of the data.

Dewey's contextualism is in some respects congenial with Hegel's teachings. Recognition of this fact makes it all the more important to determine the substantial differences between the two doctrines. But this should not be done by misinterpreting Dewey's naturalism as a monistic *materialism* which may be contrasted with Hegel's monistic *idealism*. Dewey does not hold that the process of inquiry can be *completely* described in physical or biological terms; he only maintains that such terms enter into the description

[3] *Logic,* p. 149.

of this process, and that the general laws of physics and biology apply to the explanation of inquiry as well as to the explanation of any other human activity. He repudiates the doctrines of materialists who would reduce human behavior to the "behavior of apes, amoebæ or electrons and protons," and declares that "man is *naturally* a being that lives in association with others in communities possessing language, and therefore enjoying a transmitted culture."[4]

The preceding remarks were meant to convey a broad idea of some major epistemological problems which had to be explored by Dewey, and had been explored before by the great philosophers of the past, most thoroughly perhaps by Kant. Dewey's references to Kant are frequently polemical, but the gulf that separates his *Logic* from Kant's *Critique of Pure Reason* is not so wide and deep as it is usually supposed to be. Dewey's objective of bringing logical theory into accord with scientific practice is in tune with Kant's aim to show how science, recognized as an established fact, is possible. Both philosophers are engaged in a clarification of the principles of scientific method and both reject the rationalist as well as the sensationalist interpretations of this method. They agree, moreover, in their finitism, which excludes the definition of "human knowledge" in terms of infinite knowledge, and they agree also in the reinterpretation of metaphysical tenets as regulative principles of inquiry. Kant's *Critique of Pure Reason* had, in fact, a strong impact on the thought of Charles Peirce, who laid the cornerstones of Dewey's theory of inquiry.

But Dewey's analysis of science might seem to be diametrically opposed to Kant's analysis in applying a genetic method, whereas Kant rejects any genetic approach to the theory of knowledge.[5] In considering this point we are confronted with the question whether the formulation of Dewey's argument in genetic terms is essential for the attainment of his chief methodological conclusions. An affirmative answer is usually taken for granted, but I do not concur

[4] *Logic*, p. 19.
[5] Kant was, however, not quite consistent in this respect.

in this opinion, and shall presently develop my reasons for holding an opposite view. A brief outline of Dewey's conception of inquiry will bring the issue into sharp focus.

Traditional epistemologies draw a dividing line between theory and practice, between inquiry, conceived as a purely mental phenomenon, and overt action which involves movements of the body and brings about changes in the external world. This division is, in Dewey's view, untenable because it fails to take account of the fact that every inquiry consists of operations, either with existential objects in the strict sense, as in experiments, or with symbols, as in mathematics.

An inquiry is, like any other action, the transformation of a given situation. It is therefore appropriate for a theory of inquiry to establish first the general properties of human actions, and to determine then, within this general frame, the specific traits of inquiry. Human actions are instigated by the desire to attain a state of greater satisfaction. The end of an action is, accordingly, the transformation of a less satisfactory situation into one that is more satisfactory. The plan of action is an anticipation of the means to be employed in the promotion of this end. Each part of the action is united with the other parts in a concerted contribution to the given end; no single operation can be fully understood, if we fail to determine its place and function in the whole series of operations.

Operations that were found successful, *i.e.* productive of the desired effects, are repeated in similar situations. It comes to the formation of habits, and these habits may be explicitly formulated and instituted as prescriptions. One speaks in such cases of established methods in a certain sphere of activity, for instance, of methods of farming. Any method is liable to be altered when different ways of acting turn out to be more successful.

These general observations may now be applied to inquiry. The undesirable quality of a situation which inquiry seeks to eliminate, is its doubtfulness, or indeterminateness. Recognition of the indeterminateness of a given situation with respect to a specific issue is therefore the starting point of any inquiry. The situation must be adjudged to be problematic, and the nature of the problem must be clearly grasped.

By instituting a problem we outline a plan of action. This plan is then carried out by actually creating the conditions that are required for the solution of the problem. Like any other plan of action, the initial plan of inquiry may have to be substantially modified in the course of this process. The inquiry comes to a successful close when the problem is solved by transforming the indeterminate situation into a determinate situation, that is, into a situation where there is no longer need for doubt. In solving a problem we add to our knowledge. "That which satisfactorily terminates inquiry is, by definition, knowledge; it is knowledge because it *is* the appropriate close of inquiry."[6] Considering the ambiguity of the word "knowledge," Dewey prefers to use instead the words "warranted assertibility."

The canons of inquiry with which logic is concerned, emerge from successful habits of inquiry, when these habits are formulated. Rules of inquiry are not ultimately established, but are continually on probation. Like technological rules, they are changed if they fall short of the expected success. This holds for the rules of deductive logic as well as for those of inductive logic, and of methodology in general.

It is one of Dewey's cardinal points that deductive logic must not be severed from methodology. The larger part of his great work is indeed an analysis of the operational significance of *deductive* logic in factual inquiry. But our attention will be focused upon Dewey's analysis of empirical procedure in the strict sense.

The *Leitmotif* of Dewey's theory of inquiry is the vindication of his thesis that scientific procedure is autonomous, that the forms and canons of logic need not and cannot be justified by *a priori* principles fixed antecedently to inquiry. "The theory, in summary form, is that all logical forms (with their characteristic properties)

[6] *Logic*, p. 8.

arise *within* the operation of inquiry and are concerned with control of inquiry so that it may yield warranted assertions. This conception implies much more than that logical forms are disclosed or come to light when we reflect upon processes of inquiry that are in use. Of course it means that; but it also means that the forms *originate* in operations of inquiry. To convey a convenient expression, it means that while inquiry into inquiry is the *causa cognoscendi* of logical forms, primary inquiry is itself *causa essendi* of the forms which inquiry into inquiry discloses."[7]

Dewey's point is, accordingly, that logical theory is established by scientific practice. He associates the idea of scientific practice with the idea of progress, and emphasizes the function of logical canons as guiding principles in the ongoing process of inquiry. But he is, of course, fully aware of the fact that the canons are also standards (norms) of scientific criticism. Any norm may be viewed either from the angle of an agent to whom it is addressed, or from the angle of a critic who has to judge whether or not the norm has been complied with in a particular case.

This observation leads up to the core of our argument. Scientific criticism is an integral part of scientific inquiry. In stipulating the objectivity of scientific knowledge, and in repudiating arbitrariness and bias in the conduct of research, we imply that every step in inquiry, every change in the body of knowledge or in established methods, is subject to scientific criticism. In Dewey's own words: "Inquiry in order to be inquiry in the complete sense has to satisfy certain conditions that are capable of formal statement. . . . To engage in an inquiry is like entering into a contract. It commits the inquirer to observance of certain conditions. A stipulation is a statement of conditions that are agreed to in the conduct of some affair. The stipulations involved are first implicit in the undertaking of inquiry. As they are formally acknowledged (formulated) they become logical forms of various degrees of generality. They make definite what is involved in a demand. Every demand is a request, but not every request is a postulate. For a postulate involves the

[7] *Logic*, p. 3, 4.

assumption of responsibilities. The responsibilities that are assumed are stated in stipulations. They involve readiness to act in certain specified ways."[8]

What Dewey calls "inquiry in the complete sense" is, in my view, the ideal of inquiry as implied in the fundamental postulate of scientific objectivity. It would be inconsistent to emphasize the objectivity of science, and to state at the same time that the establishment of unambiguous standards of warranted assertibility is impossible in any given instance.

Consider the following example: The biologist A declares that the outcome of his experiments warrants the assertion that acquired skills are transmitted to the offspring. The biologist B contests this statement. He does not question the correctness of A's experimental findings, but he denies that the just mentioned general assertion can be inferred from it. This controversy is a logical issue; the question is whether A's inference from his experimental findings conforms with presupposed rules of induction. Now it may well be the case that our two scientists disagree about the rules of induction, and that this is the reason why they are unable to settle their issue. But one cannot state that the issue is *in principle* undecidable without compromising the claim of scientific objectivity. We cannot dispose of the ideal of clear thinking by pointing to the fact of confused thinking. People do think inconsistently, but this does not affect the principle of non-contradiction. An apparently unanswerable question of scientific criticism represents a challenge to make explicit the implicitly presupposed standards of scientific criticism.

But a process of explication (clarification) is not adequately characterized by calling it a formulation of habits of inquiry. To be logically implied in an ideal, or a postulate, is one thing; to be included in habits of observable behavior is something different. Even the habits of the most eminent scientist are bound to fall short of the ideal of perfect clarity in inquiry. But every scientist acknowledges this ideal by submitting his methods of inquiry and his results to the critical judgments of his fellow scientists.

[8] *Logic,* pp. 16f.

The interpretations of methodological and ethical principles as habits of thinking or acting which we find in empiricist doctrines are a sort of counterpart to the rationalist doctrines of innate ideas. They treat ideals as biological or psychological facts. David Hume did not work upon a virgin soil when he accorded these interpretations a central place in his philosophy, but his view dominated pertinent discussions, until Darwin's work permitted the integration of the theory of habits into a general theory of evolution.

The crucial defect of Hume's procedure is that he does not carry the logical analysis of cognitive experience far enough before he turns to an explanation of habits of belief. He fails to realize, for instance—what Leibniz before him and Kant after him did realize—that reference to causality is implied in the establishment of an objective temporal order.

Dewey penetrates much deeper than Hume, but the full import of his methodological analysis is beclouded by the connection of this analysis with a biological theory of habits. We sever this connection by re-interpreting the methodological conclusions at which Dewey arrives through his description of the pattern of inquiry, as postulates of scientific criticism. I shall confine myself to a very brief outline of this attempt.

Let us first consider Dewey's distinction between indeterminate situations and determinate situations. We have an indeterminate situation with respect to a given question if the established state of knowledge does not provide a warranted answer to this question; in the opposite case we have a determinate situation. This is the methodologically relevant sense of the two terms; indeterminate situations represent unsolved problems. A strict division between questions which can, and questions which cannot, be settled on the basis of existing knowledge, is postulated in scientific criticism. This postulate implies the ideal of a precisely determined state of science at any given time. The actual knowledge of any particular person is not referred to in methodological analysis.

The transformation of an indeterminate situation into a determinate situation is accomplished by a chain of steps which are supposed to be in conformity with given rules of procedure. This is to say that rules are postulated which permit critical appraisals of each step. The logician is not concerned with the temporal sequence of the steps, *qua* temporal, but only with the formal structure of the sequence. The "dependence" of subsequent steps upon preceding steps is from his point of view not causal dependence, but logical dependence. The changes in the body of knowledge brought about by earlier steps are taken for granted in judging the correctness of subsequent steps. An analogy with the process of counting in its relation to arithmetic will elucidate this point. In describing this process we may say that the assignment of the number 5 to an object occurs later than the assignment of the number 2, or that the previous assignment of the number 2 is a necessary condition for the assignment of the number 5. But the corresponding mathematical proposition "5 implies 2" does not contain any reference to time or causality.

Teleological terms are, therefore, excluded as well; for the relation between means and ends is a causal relation. In the description of inquiry as a purposive human activity we may properly speak of the contribution of a certain step in inquiry to the solution of the given problem; and of the functional, or operational, interdependence of the different steps. But such terms have no place in an analysis of the formal structure of inquiry, with which logic is concerned.

Changes in the rules (methods) of procedure are likewise subject to scientific criticism. This implies the postulation of rules of a second order by which we may judge the correctness of changes in rules of the first order. Dewey states that the rules of inquiry originate within inquiry and that their retention depends upon their success. But here again we must bear in mind that the logician is not concerned with the process of inquiry *qua* temporal, but only with its formal structure; that is, with the different types of methodological terms and canons and their interrelations. The criteria for the distinction between successful methods and unsuccessful methods of inquiry must be established *within* the system of rules of inquiry. Otherwise we should not have an autonomous scientific procedure. Success in inquiry is largely determined by observational tests. The rules pertaining to these tests are therefore particularly important.

I have tried to make it clear that the aim of bringing logical theory into accord with scientific practice implies the objective of making explicit the standards (rules) of scientific criticism. These standards need not be identical in different fields of inquiry, and in each field they are liable to be altered at different stages of scientific progress. But the various systems of rules have a common formal structure. Such terms as "knowledge," "method," "problem," "explanation," "probability," "induction" are supposed to be significant for any domain and any stage of inquiry; and they have to be clearly defined. This involves a formulation of the principles which are essential for scientific inquiry as such, for instance, the principle of the reversibility of every scientific result. Dewey has made great strides in this direction by excluding from his theory any reference to transcendent truth, to immediate experience as a source of indubitable knowledge, and to an infinite totality of knowledge. This is a remarkable philosophical achievement.

The last-mentioned point is particularly important in comparing Dewey's theory of inquiry with the epistemological doctrines of absolute idealism as developed by Hegel and Bradley. Dewey's interpretation of knowledge is, in contrast with their interpretations, strictly finitistic. The potentially endless self-corrective procedure of science—the "continuum of inquiry"—is composed of well-determined specific inquiries, each of which has to be treated by the logician as a self-contained unit. There is a definite *terminus a quo* for each inquiry—the instituted problem—and there is a definite *terminus ad quem*, the solution of the problem represented by a warranted assertion. This definiteness is not impaired by the fact that any assertion may have to be eliminated from the body of knowledge if it fails to pass subsequent tests. To state that no scientific result is *indubitably* established is not to declare that scientific problems cannot be solved.

Should Dewey's insistence upon the reversibility of every scientific result be taken to imply that he does not believe in truth? People who make statements to this effect reveal thereby that they have not come to grips with the philosophical problem of clarifying the meaning of "truth." We have to ask: "What is it that we believe in when we believe in the truth of an assertion?"

When Peter expresses his belief in Paul's integrity, he means to say that Paul's integrity would prove itself in all temptations to which he may be exposed. Similarly when we express our beliefs in the truth of any assertion, we mean that this assertion would be confirmed by all tests to which it might be subjected. And to believe in truth in general is to believe that there are assertions that would stand up under all conceivable tests. This is to say that "truth" has to be defined in terms of possible knowledge, but it is not to say that knowledge makes truth, as Dewey has been frequently supposed to maintain. As a matter of fact he endorses Charles Peirce's conception of truth. I shall quote the pertinent footnote in Dewey's *Logic* (p. 345).

"The best definition of *truth* from the logical standpoint which is known to me is that of Peirce: 'The opinion which is fated to be ultimately agreed to by all who investigate is what we mean by the truth, and the object represented by this opinion is the real.' A more complicated (and more suggestive) statement is the following: 'Truth is that concordance of an abstract statement with the ideal limit towards which endless investigation would tend to bring scientific belief, which concordance the abstract statement may possess by virtue of the confession of its inaccuracy and one-sidedness, and this confession is an essential ingredient of truth.' "[9]

The conception of truth as an ideal of inquiry need not be associated with the belief in a pre-established perfectly rational world. Dewey rejects the claim that scientific inquiry must be based upon this belief. "The working scientific faith," he writes, "is the belief that concern for objective continual inquiry with assiduity

* *Logic.* The two quotations are from Peirce: *Collected Papers* Vol. V, p. 268, and pp. 394f.

and courage in its performance, is capable of becoming habitual with an ever-increasing number of human beings. The idea that the faith of science is a belief that the world is already in itself completely rational is not so much inspiration to work as it is a justification for acquiescence."[10]

But now you may ask: Are not the questions concerning the meanings of knowledge and truth, and the persistent doctrinal controversies between realists and idealists, rationalists and empiricists, between monists, dualists, and pluralists, merely verbal issues that are devoid of major significance for anybody except a few ivory tower philosophers? And if this be the case, how can it be explained that one of the foremost educators of our time, that a man who is so passionately concerned with the social and political conditions of mankind should take such pains in dealing with these issues?

It seems to me that the first question has to be answered in the negative, which would eliminate the second one. While I cannot here develop my reasons for rejecting the attractive view that philosophy is but the systematic misuse of a terminology invented for this very purpose, I may refer to what has been said before about different degrees of clarity, and the ideal of perfect clarity postulated in scientific criticism.

It goes without saying that Dewey is very far from endorsing Aristotle's claim that the pursuit of clarity for its own sake is the highest form of human activity, but he is also far from minimizing the significance of clear thinking for social and political progress.

In studying his works on ethics, politics, and education, one is impressed by the strength of his conviction that a society in which freedom and order are happily blended, cannot be established and sustained unless discussion of all important public issues is constantly kept alive. This involves the recognition of common standards for the appraisal of beliefs and actions. To clarify these standards is to promote mutual understanding and cooperation among men.

[10] *Logic*, p. 532.

I have dealt here primarily with one aspect of Dewey's *Logic;* other philosophers have approached the work from different angles. It is like a witch's mirror in which every man may see his sweetheart—or the devil. The book will be studied, re-interpreted and criticized by many generations of philosophers. In our own days this task has been facilitated by Dr. Dewey's active cooperation. No scholar has accepted criticism more graciously and examined it more thoroughly. During the past decade he has further developed and elucidated his theory.[11] May he continue his work for many years to come!

[11] *Cf.* particularly "Experience, Knowledge and Value. A Rejoinder" in *The Philosophy of John Dewey,* Vol. I, The Library of Living Philosophers, ed. by P. A. Schilpp, and *Knowing and the Known* by Dewey and Bentley, Beacon Press, Boston, 1949.

Dewey's Theory of Natural Science

by ERNEST NAGEL

THERE IS a curious and distressing paradox associated with the growth of modern natural science. No one doubts that the expansion of experimental techniques in conjunction with the development of mathematically formulated theory has given us unprecedented intellectual and practical mastery over many sectors of nature. Indeed, the maxim that knowledge is power, is widely acknowledged as a truth that has become an almost painful platitude. Nevertheless, scientific theory is frequently so construed that instead of rendering the universe more intelligible and making men feel more at home in it, both the constitution of nature and man's place in it have become more puzzling and mysterious.

Two interpretations of modern science have had an especially wide currency. According to one, the discoveries of natural science, especially of physics, make it impossible to suppose that the familiar aspects of things encountered in everyday experience have a genuine place in the objective order of nature, or that the qualities manifested in our ordinary commerce with the world are anything but illusory appearances. According to the other, the conceptions of theoretical science are mere fictions, and at best only convenient practical devices; they do not express matters of intimate human concern. On either view, incoherent answers await questions concerning the obvious efficacy of scientific knowledge in controlling the course of familiar events, or concerning the relation of the human scene to the rest of nature. On either view, fixed limits are imputed to the scope of scientific method, and in consequence large areas of human experience are held to be inherently incapable of fruitful exploration by responsible scientific inquiry. In short, instead of being recognized as an agent for liberating and redirecting human energies, modern science is viewed in many quarters with anxious dread or complacent indifference.

The factors responsible for this paradoxical state of affairs are to be found partly in the historical circumstances under which modern science has developed, and partly in the inherent character of modern natural science. Natural as well as social sciences have been cultivated in an environment in which powerful vested interests have been hostile to the pursuit of free inquiry. For many centuries, prevalent conceptions of social and political organization, no less than entrenched beliefs on moral and religious subjects, have been coupled with traditional assumptions concerning the mechanisms of physical nature. Accordingly, the intellectual progress that successfully challenged the latter also became a constant threat to hallowed social ideals and deeply laid religious convictions. To be sure, established churches and other institutions eventually learned how to square their theological, social and moral creeds with the latest findings of physical and even biological science. And what more effective means for doing just this could have been devised than that of so construing scientific findings that they are merely convenient formulations of techniques of control, incapable of ever rendering some assumed "inner nature" of things? Even so, a strong emotional and overt resistance still persists to what is widely felt to be the intrusion of scientific methods into the discussion of human affairs.

But there are other reasons, more intrinsic to the nature of modern theoretical science, for the paradoxical philosophies that have trailed its development. Modern science is not primarily concerned with the uses which things have in specifically human contexts, but rather with the invariant conditions under which events occur and with the mutual interrelations of things. In consequence, theoretical physics operates with distinctions that are both highly abstract and apparently incongruous with notions employed in habitual experience. In point of fact, the objects postulated in modern physics, such as atoms and electrons, possess by their very definition few if any of the qualities that identify and mark off the familiar things of human life. For example, neither colors, nor sounds, nor odors, nor even determinate positions and shapes are attributed to the fundamental particles of current sub-atomic theories. However, if physics is assumed to disclose the ultimate and exclusive characters of things, there is an obvious discrepancy between what the sciences apparently teach and what is found in gross experience. How tempting and seemingly cogent, therefore, is the explanation of this discrepancy which views the distinctions and principles in terms of which we order our daily lives as belonging merely to a realm of subjective appearance!

This conclusion, moreover, is often supported by another line of argument. The physics and physiology of perception show that the qualities commonly attributed to things are in fact manifested only under special conditions, among which must be counted the presence of biological organisms. It seems plain, therefore, that the directly apprehended qualities are not traits which things possess absolutely and independently of their interaction with organic bodies. And since such qualities do not belong to the "world of physics," it is concluded that they do not form part of the objective order of nature. In brief, contrary to the naive realistic view, things are not what they seem. On the other hand, every actual inquiry into the causal patterns of nature takes its point of departure from immediately experienced qualitative events, and it also terminates in such an experience. For it is in the precarious existence of qualitative events that the sciences find their problems; and it is in the agreement of their occurrences with assumed laws that evidence for the latter is obtained. But if the qualities encountered in common experience are held to belong exclusively to a realm of subjective appearance, while the mechanisms discovered by physics are taken to constitute the true reality, then science is indeed at war with itself. As one typical contemporary reading of the import of natural sciences states the general outcome, naive realism leads to physics, but if physics is true then naive realism is false. On this analysis, therefore, one is left with the choice of either accepting natural science but rejecting as basically illusory the things that constitute men's most familiar and valued experiences, or accepting the objective character of the common-sense view of things but denying the validity and relevance of modern science for matters of prime human concern.

It is this alleged impasse of modern science, so paradoxical in its formulation and so devastating in its practical consequences, which has been at the focus of Dewey's attention during his long philosophical career. He has consistently maintained that this impasse is generated by misconceptions concerning the relation of the objects and distinctions of physical science to the things of ordinary experience. And he has in fact identified as one of the outstanding issues of modern philosophy the clarification of just this problem.

Dewey has been intensely concerned with the problem, because he recognized early in his career that mistaken notions about the status of physical objects stand in the way of successfully exploiting the potentialities of modern science for the enrichment of human life. In particular, he has noted repeatedly and with untiring zeal the fatal import of the traditional dualistic interpretation of science for the other paramount issue of modern philosophy—the integration of men's beliefs about the world as derived from natural science, with the principles in terms of which men direct and evaluate their private and public conduct. An interpretation of the nature of scientific objects which requires either the wholesale rejection of ordinary experience as illusory, or the condemnation of theoretical science as mere convenient fiction, makes impertinent the findings of natural science to the problems of human society. Such an interpretation effectively deprives the tried logic of scientific method of any authority in the treatment of morality, and kills in the bud the promise implicit in the scientific enterprise of freeing men from the bondage of frustrating custom.

Dewey's ultimate concern with the technical problems of the theory of knowledge is thus moral in intent. However, he has not been content with simply identifying the crucial issues of modern philosophy; and he has never discussed them in merely moralistic terms. A long lifetime of sustained effort has gone into his attempt to solve these problems, and to solve them in a technically competent manner. His analysis of the status of scientific objects is indeed not written for the man who reads as he runs, and is inextricably linked with details in his often difficult account of the nature of knowledge. Moreover, much of his discussion is carried on in the midst of a far-flung polemic against what he believes are outmoded views on the subject. For in his attempt to resolve the alleged impasse of modern science, an essential feature of Dewey's strategy consists in showing that the problem vanishes and becomes unintelligible, when once the traditional preconceptions which generate it are successfully challenged.

Dewey's analysis of the relation of scientific objects to matters of direct experience is rooted in one firm assumption which he does not always make fully explicit. The premise from which he operates is that distinctions must be understood in terms of the concrete uses for which they are devised, and that in particular scientific ideas must be construed in terms of their identifiable functions in the context of inquiry. This assumption is unavoidable in any responsible analysis, and is in any case decisive. Unless scientific conceptions are construed in agreement with it, any proposed interpretation of scientific discourse will be arbitrary; it will be based on preconceptions derived from some tacit philosophical commitments, rather than on the actual operative meaning of the language of science.

It was Einstein who advised students of the methods of theoretical physics to concern themselves, not with accounts scientists happen to give of what they do, but with their actual procedures and achievements. Long before this advice was given, and long before it became fashionable to preach the virtues of functionalist or contextualist analysis, Dewey was practicing it with energy and a considerable measure of consistency. It is from this standpoint that he has conducted intellectual war into the camps of traditional philosophies of science; and by adopting that approach he has saved himself from much futility and avoided some serious errors. It has prevented him from regarding scientific theory as merely a condensed transcript of the immediate content of experience, as well as from attempting the impossible task of translating theoretical statements into statements about directly apprehended sensory qualities. It has led him to emphasize the continuity of refined scientific procedures with modes of solving problems on more primitive levels of behavior, and to recognize in consequence that the conception of scientific theory as a system of mere fiction makes incomprehensible the whole practical life of man. It has enabled him to see that the adequacy or validity of ideas is not warranted by their supposed derivation from materials of sense, but rather by the consequences of their use. And above all, it has served him as the means for showing that science is not a disclosure of a reality superior to and incompatible with the things of ordinary experience.

The central thesis of Dewey's theory of science is that it does not disclose realms of being antithetical to the familiar things of life, simply because scientific objects are formulations of complex relations of dependence between things in gross experience. More specifically, the constructions of theoretical physics are viewed by him as intellectual means for organizing the discontinuous occurrences of directly experienced qualities, as ways of thinking about matters in gross experience in order to obtain some measure of control over their histories.

It follows directly from this thesis that scientific discoveries concerning the conditions of occurrences of things in ordinary experience cannot possibly impugn the objective reality of the latter. Why should the fact, for example, that the occurrence of heat and cold is contingent upon certain distributions of molecular energies, constitute ground for denying that the sun is hot or that snow is cold? And why should the further fact that in the absence of definite physiological conditions these qualities are not manifested, count as a reason for denying that heat and cold are objective features of those existential situations in which both the physical and physiological conditions are realized?

To be sure, physics is not concerned with the physiological conditions for the occurrence of various qualities; for physics seeks to find relational orders of dependence that are invariant for all percipient organisms, and that are independent of the latter's presence or absence. But what is canonical for physics is not therefore a measure of objective existence; and only an arbitrary preference, rooted in an influential intellectual tradition, will assign exclusive reality to invariant relational orders. In point of fact, even the properties which physics ascribes to its objects, such as mass, are manifested only under certain contingent if pervasive conditions. Were every property which is relational in this sense denied a place in the objective order of nature, physics too should be regarded as dealing only with what is subjective. The crux of the matter is that if only absolutely invariant universal patterns of relations are assumed to be genuinely objective, nothing that is individual, specific, and limited can have any place in objective nature. But those who adopt this criterion are then faced with the outrageous paradox of having relations without terms to be related as the sole furniture of genuine reality. Is the notion of a cat with a grin but no body a more fantastic conception of the way of things?

Dewey's account of scientific objects is thus accompanied by a reaffirmation of the claims of gross experience. But the naive realism he defends is free from the dogmatic naiveté so frequently associated with philosophies of common sense. He emphatically includes the various qualities of ordinary experience among the ultimate furniture of the world. But he does not assume that the immediate apprehension of qualities constitutes knowledge of them. Knowledge for Dewey is always the terminus of *inquiry,* and involves the establishment of relations of dependence between what is thus directly experienced and what is not. What these relations are, however, is not to be settled by intuition or authority whether the problem under consideration involves issues of physics, private morality or public policy. It is pre-eminently a matter requiring reflective thought or experimental inquiry.

Indeed, it is precisely in this context that the objects of science manifest their distinctive functions. It is in situations where one seeks to discover the conditions upon which the occurrence of immediate qualities depends, that scientific objects serve as general schema for analyzing things of ordinary experience in terms of their systematic relations to other events and potentialities in nature. Accordingly, the postulated objects of theoretical physics are not things which in turn require to be sensed or directly experienced. When viewed in terms of their status identifiable in inquiry, they represent ways of conceiving and ordering what is capable of being sensed and experienced. No legitimate puzzle resides in the fact that the objects of physical theory do not possess the qualitative differentia of things of everyday experience. A mystifying puzzle does arise only if the former are converted by some dialectical prestidigitation into another set of individuals which require to be directly encountered if they are to be adequately known.

An impressive quantity of concrete evidence confirms Dewey's account of the status of scientific objects, but there are also difficulties which confront it. Both supporting evidence and difficulties must now be briefly examined.

It is beyond reasonable dispute that at least one function of any scientific theory is that of a generalized directive for treading the complex maze of events with which men are directly confronted in gross experience. For as has already been noted, every inquiry into empirical subject matter is initiated and controlled by problems concerning matters that are encountered in such experience. And every proposed resolution of such problems, every theory which aims to specify the conditions upon which the occurrences generating these problems are contingent, must satisfy the minimal requirement of indicating factors to be found in gross experience through which those conditions can be identified. For otherwise problems are not solved, and theories are speculative fancies which cannot be checked by observational data. Accordingly, even when a theory postulates the existence of particles and processes which are quite unlike the materials of ordinary experience, the *raison d'être* of the postulation is the enlarged and clarified understanding of the mutual relations between these latter that the postulation may help to achieve.

It would be superfluous to cite examples in which theoretical constructions do serve as guides for mastering men's environment —the full basis for this claim must be sought in the detailed history of the theoretical sciences and the technologies nourished by them. But apart from examples and history, the claim will be reinforced if attention is directed to some familiar features of physical theory and to certain circumstances of the use of such theory in inquiry.

A striking trait of theories in the natural sciences, and especially of mathematical physics, is the absence of any mention in them of specific places and dates or of individual objects and events. In consequence, these theories do not describe anything actually existing in any specified sector of nature. How then does such a theory acquire a specific import for specific problems dealing with specific spatio-temporal events, for example for a problem concerning the occurrence of a solar eclipse at some place on the earth's surface? The answer is well known. A theory can help resolve a problem concerning definite spatio-temporal occurrences, only if it is supplemented by special information about local configurations of events and objects *which the theory itself indicates as being relevant*. For solving the problem about the occurrence of an eclipse, for example, the special information needed includes the relative positions and diameters of the sun, moon, and the earth at a certain time. But the need for such supplementary information makes plain that a theory is a generalized formula for resolving a broad class of problems, and that one important function of the formula is to indicate *just what* specific data must be secured about an actual situation if a concrete instance of the class of problems is to be solved. Accordingly, although a theory is not itself a description of what happens to exist, it is at the very least a generalized plan for guiding the direction of overt observation and experiment on what does exist.

There is another feature of physical theory that deserves notice. The fundamental assumptions of many comprehensive theories are usually stated for so-called "pure" or "ideal" cases, and more generally theoretical statements are frequently formulated in terms of "limiting" or "ideal" concepts. Such pure cases are rarely if ever encountered in experience; and limiting concepts, sometimes as a consequence of their mode of definition, cannot be taken as descriptive characterizations of anything that is experimentally identifiable. For example, no completely isolated physical systems occur in nature, though at least one of Newton's axioms of motion is stated for just such a system; and notions such as that of instantaneous velocity or perfect elasticity are widely employed in mechanics even though no actual bodies can be directly subsumed under them. Nevertheless, pure cases and ideal concepts have significant uses in inquiry: through their use it is possible to state with maximum economy and comprehensive generality what are the relevant factors in qualitatively diverse materials upon which the course of events depends, and thereby to state the mutual interrelations of apparently independent processes. However, and this is the essential point, the systematic analysis that is achieved through the use of ideal concepts can be carried through only if these concepts are associated with explicit or tacit rules of overt procedure for handling materials of gross experience. For since ideal concepts are not directly applicable to the objects of ordinary experience, these latter must be "cooked" and worked over if they are to be subsumed as "instances" under such concepts. A theory which uses the notion of perfect elasticity, for example, must be coupled with a set of directions that specify, even if only vaguely, how bodies are to be classified and ordered with respect to their elastic properties; otherwise the theory swims in a void, and cannot serve to illumine anything actual. But if such rules are inevitable supplements to viable theories employing ideal concepts, those theories will always contain as an essential component directives for discriminating relevant features in concrete subject matters. It is in part because these associated rules of procedure are frequently not formulated explicitly, that theories often seem so utterly remote from and even incompatible with what is encountered in direct experience. And it is in part because scientific theories are frequently interpreted simply on the basis of their *formal* structure, and in disregard of the tacit rules essential for their use in dealing with specific existential problems, that the function of theories as guiding principles for overt observation and experiment is often ignored.

It has been customary in the analysis and interpretation of science to distinguish between two types of theory. One type, variously labelled as "macroscopic," "phenomenological," and "abstractive," is said to "abstract" determinate relations between macroscopic, directly identifiable objects, and to eschew all hypotheses which assume "hidden" and "unobservable" mechanisms that operate "behind" the manifest phenomena. Newton's theory of gravitation, Fourier's theory of heat conduction, and classical thermodynamics, are the commonly cited examples of this type of physical theory; and Newton's famous dictum *"Hypotheses non fingo"* is generally understood to mean that he declined to entertain theories of any other type. The second type of theory, variously called "microscopic," "hypothetical" and "physical," does by contrast explicitly postulate unobservable particles, sub-microscopic processes, and mechanisms not open to direct observation, in terms of which the complex phenomena of gross experience are to be explained and understood. Familiar examples of this type of theory are the numerous atomic and electric theories of matter.

It is by no means a closed issue whether the distinction between these two types of theory is either important or even well-founded, though this question will not be pursued here any further. The relevance of this distinction for the present discussion is that it helps to make explicit the chief objection usually raised against the conception of scientific theory as being primarily an instrument for the conduct of inquiry. This conception is frequently acknowledged as illuminating and sound when it is stated for macroscopic theories. For in such theories no domain of events and individuals is postulated which is distinct from the events and objects encountered in ordinary experience; and accordingly, the scientific objects assumed by such theories are easily construed as structures of relations between the materials of gross experience. But the situation seems to be quite different in the case of microscopic theories. The impressive successes of atomic and electronic theories of matter in predicting and bringing into systematic order a wide variety of phenomena, have convinced a good fraction of contemporary scientists that the scientific objects postulated by theories of this type are more than systems of relations between familiar objects, and that on the contrary these scientific objects are concrete individuals, possessing spatio-temporal locations and participating in dynamic transactions with each other. Although it is generally admitted that these scientific objects lack most of the qualitative traits which mark off the familiar objects of experience, they are nevertheless believed to be physical constituents and parts of these latter. In brief, the scientific objects postulated by microscopic theories cannot, so the objection runs, be adequately regarded *simply* as conceptual means for organizing and analyzing the objects and events of gross experience.

It must be acknowledged that on this point Dewey is not free from ambiguity. On the one hand, he repeatedly asserts that scientific objects are general *modes* of activity, that they are discursively elaborated *formulations* of connections noted in experience, that they are *correlations* between changes, or that they are *generalizations* of existential conditions founded on a statistical basis. Careful readers of Dewey do not find it overly difficult to see the congruence among these various characterizations. But on the other hand he must cause discomfort even to a sympathetic reader when he writes of swarms of atoms and electrons moving rapidly, or of atoms giving rise to qualities of bitter and sweet. For surely, modes of activity, formulations, correlations, and the rest, cannot intelligibly be said to engage in motions rapid or otherwise, or to give birth in time to sensory qualities.

It is perhaps doubtful whether these apparent inconsistencies in Dewey's statements can be reconciled; and the task will not even be attempted here. But something does need to be said in defense of his account of scientific objects against the critique which draws its ammunition from the prevalence of microscopic theories in modern physics.

It must be noted, in the first place, that the interpretation of scientific objects as systems of relations between things encountered in ordinary experience and as generalized directives for analyzing empirical materials, is intended *primarily* if not exclusively to be an account of the status and function of scientific objects in the *context of inquiry*. And as has already been indicated, whatever else may be validly said about theories that postulate sub-microscopic particles and processes, this much at least can be asserted with warrant—their role in *inquiry* is that of directives for handling observational materials and of formulations which express systems of relationships between such materials. For unless it were possible to connect such theories with things and events that are open to direct observation, the theories would contribute nothing to the resolution of the specific existential problems which generate them. The "hidden" particles and processes postulated by theories of this type thus serve as intermediary and auxiliary termini in the formulation of a system of relationships whose *ultimate* termini are features of things identifiable in gross experience. Accordingly, the cognitive function in inquiry of the postulated elements in microscope theories is that of links in a system of conceptual means for treating effectively objects in familiar experience.

In the second place, there is good reason to believe that at least in some cases the postulated elements of microscopic theories are best conceived as complexes of relationships, rather than as concrete individuals comparable with the substantial things of gross experience. This is not the occasion for arguing this point in detail or with reference to specific microscopic theories. However, it is at least worth noting that in the history of mathematics a similar conclusion has been repeatedly reached; for example, instead of construing complex numbers or the "imaginary" points of intersection of curves as a distinctive and self-subsisting type of number or point, it has been found possible to view these postulated "entities" as relational structures between the more familiar integers or "real" points. A *literal* reading of the formulations of pure mathematics may therefore be a naive and misleading one, for such a reading may overlook the operative significance of what is being said. Similarly, a literal reading of the language of the modern quantum theory may also be misleading, especially since this theory often uses familiar modes of speech (for example, the expressions "particle" and "momentum") in senses that are explicitly recognized to be analogical and metaphorical. There is indeed an influential if not thoroughly consistent tendency among physicists today to dispense with interpretations of even microscopic theories in terms of pictorial models, and to see in the relations expressed by the pictorially neutral mathematical formalism the essential operative content of such theories. An example of this tendency is supplied by a recent commentator, himself a mathematical physicist, on the perplexities generated by the pictorial representation of light as both wave-like and corpuscular: "The picture of what is happening in an optical experiment can be construed in more than one way, and ... different pictures, although they require different methods of mathematical treatment, yield the same end-result for comparison with observational measures" (Sir Edmund Whittaker, *From Euclid to Eddington*, p. 138). Accordingly, there is much in the actual practice of modern physics to support the view that the postulated scientific objects of even microscopic theory should be taken to be patterns of relations rather than concrete individuals and processes. The conception of scientific objects as conceptual means for analyzing and comprehending the things encountered in experience in terms of their mutual relations is thus not without a sound foundation.

Nonetheless, the possibility cannot be excluded, certainly not in a wholesale fashion or on *a priori* grounds, that the postulated elements of microscopic theories *may* be concrete individuals, and that the detailed empirical evidence *may* warrant the conclusion that these elements are more than patterns of relations. Dewey's concern with natural science has focused primarily on issues of logic and method, and he has paid relatively little attention to this possibility. His theory of scientific objects as simply conceptual means for the conduct of inquiry, can therefore not unjustly be charged with being an incomplete account of the nature and function of such objects. At the same time, it is worth noting that there is no incompatibility between maintaining that scientific objects function as conceptual tools in inquiry, and holding that in addition they play a role as elements in the executive order of nature. An incompatibility would be generated only if the former function of scientific objects were claimed to be their exclusive one.

Dewey's preoccupation with the instrumental role of scientific objects in inquiry is in part a consequence of his identification of knowledge as the outcome of inquiry into specific, individual existential situations. When knowledge is so identified then, as he himself notes, "The full and eventual reality of knowledge is carried in the individual case, not in general laws isolated from use in giving an individual case its meaning" (*Quest for Certainty*, p. 208). Indeed, though he recognizes that the word "knowledge" has many meanings, he maintains that in the sense he deliberately assigns to it, it has an especially liberal and humane meaning:

"It signifies events understood, events so discriminately penetrated by thought that mind is literally at home in them. It means comprehension, or inclusive reasonable agreement. What is sometimes termed "applied" science, may then be more truly science than is what is conventionally called pure science. For it is directly concerned with not just instrumentalities, but instrumentalities at work in effecting modifications of existence in behalf of conclusions that are reflectively preferred. Thus conceived the characteristic subject-matter of knowledge consists of fulfilling objects, which as fulfillments are connected with a history to which they give character. Thus conceived, knowledge exists in engineering, medicine and the social arts more adequately than it does in mathematics and physics. Thus conceived, history and anthropology are scientific in a sense in which bodies of information that stop short with general formulæ are not." [*Experience and Nature*, pp. 161-162]

Once this standpoint is taken, almost everything Dewey has to say about scientific objects is a direct consequence from it. But though the sense he selects for the word "knowledge" is not the expression of a personal whim or preference, and though his manner of identifying knowledge is supported by the long history of men's efforts to master their environment, it is also evident that from other standpoints other things may require to be said about scientific objects.

For in the enterprise of science the word "knowledge" is frequently employed, as Dewey quite readily acknowledges, to refer not only to the outcome of inquiry into concrete individual affairs, but also to the theoretical vision of pervasive orders in nature which inquiry makes possible. An account of scientific objects which ascribes to them an instrumental role for achieving knowledge in *one* of the several senses of this word, clearly does not constitute a fully adequate contextualist analysis of their function and nature.

There are other philosophies than Dewey's which seek to defend the objective reality of common-sense objects. But unlike most of them, Dewey does not achieve his aim by viewing the whole of nature in terms of distinctions that are known to be relevant only for the human scene. He does not offer a resolution of the standing problems of modern philosophy by clothing all of nature with anthropomorphic traits, or interpreting the course of cosmic events in terms of values that are of paramount concern only to men. The continuity between man and nature which modern theories of knowledge have helped to undermine and which Dewey wishes to establish, does not obliterate fundamental differences between features that clearly characterize only human actions and those which are presumed to be common to all things without exception. Whatever else it may or may not achieve, Dewey's philosophy of science does not offer a view of things that is more obfuscating than the one it wishes to replace. It is a genuine contribution to the clarification of a basic human enterprise.

However, in spite of the brilliant dialectical skill with which Dewey develops his interpretation of science, and notwithstanding the substantial evidence that the history of science provides for it, it cannot be claimed that his views on this subject have won general assent. The difficulties of his literary style are notorious, and have handicapped even first-rate minds in their attempt to penetrate to the essentials of his philosophy. Moreover, his theory of logic is in effect and by implication a serious intellectual threat to social views whose chief support is tradition and authority; and it would be utopian to suppose that antecedent ideological commitments on the part of his readers have not played a role in their evaluation of his conception of science.

But there are also less external reasons for the hesitations which even those in full sympathy with Dewey's aims and over-all conclusions have experienced with his account of natural science. The great William Harvey is reported to have said of Francis Bacon that he wrote about science like a Lord Chancellor. Of Dewey it can be said with equal justice that he writes about natural science like a philosopher, whose understanding of it, however informed, is derived from second-hand sources. With rare exceptions, the illustrations he supplies for his major theses on the nature of physical science and its methods come from everyday inquiries of a fairly elementary kind, or from popularized versions of the achievements of theoretical physics. It is indeed curious that a thinker who has devoted so much effort to clarifying the import of science as has Dewey, should exhibit such a singular unconcern for the detailed articulation of physical theory. His writings often give the impression that however sound his views on the status of scientific objects may be, they have been arrived at by *a priori* reasoning from general assumptions concerning the nature of knowledge which he takes to be warranted on other grounds. He does not use the language customary in discussions of scientific objects, possibly because he believes this language to be so burdened with traditional associations that in employing it one becomes hopelessly entangled in the preconceptions of dubious epistemologies. But however this may be, the general absence from his writings of detailed analyses of specific theoretical constructions, as well as his tendency to introduce distinctions that are not fully explained, have contributed to the feeling of inconclusiveness which many of his readers share.

There is a disparaging sense, moreover, in which Dewey has been a lone wolf in the formulation of his ideas on science. His central views are in close agreement with conceptions that have been developed during the past half-century by eminent physicists concerned with the methodology of their discipline. Nevertheless, though he is obviously familiar with many of these analyses, he does not appear to have been strongly influenced by them, and he cites them only rarely. But what is more to the point, he does not use these specialized and expert studies to the best advantage in his own discussions; and he employs home-grown arguments and formulations even where more convincing ones are readily available. This tendency no doubt contributes to the freshness of what Dewey has to say; but it also serves to isolate him from important and allied contemporary streams in the philosophy of science.

It is not easy to escape the conclusion—a judgment which is perhaps true of all philosophic ventures—that Dewey's discussion of the relation of physics to ordinary experience constitutes a program of work to be done rather than a systematically complete analysis; and Dewey is probable the last man on earth to suppose that nothing further remains to be said on the subject. But it is a program which is accompanied by a refreshingly sane and wise perspective on things, a clarifying conception of the significance of science, and a wealth of brilliant *aperçus*. In stating it, he has succeeded in showing beyond reasonable doubt that the traditional and fatal antithesis between science and ordinary experience is gratuitous, and he has thereby helped to remove some of the intellectual obstacles to the expansion of science and to the consequent enhancement of human life. In stating it, he has also entrusted to those who must succeed him in the endless task of criticism which is philosophy, an objective for whose realization the best energies of thinking men would not be misspent.

Concerning a Certain Deweyan Conception of Metaphysics

by ALBERT HOFSTADTER

IN THE remarks that follow I shall try to indicate a problem—that of developing a general theory of the "involvements of things"—which may be appropriately conceived as the chief problem of metaphysics, if metaphysics itself be conceived as an empirical discipline. This problem is suggested by a sequence of thoughts to be found in Dewey's writings, particularly his *Logic*. I shall not discuss the actual metaphysics which Dewey has written in *Experience and Nature* and which he has employed in so many other investigations; nor shall I discuss the question whether and how far that system is is in accord with or fulfills the task to be outlined. The line of argument will be this: Inquiry aims at settling the significances of things: the significances of things rest upon the involvements of things; a general theory of involvement is needed to guide inquiry and to serve as background for criticism; this general theory is the theory of the nature of existence, or metaphysics.

In the *Logic* Dewey introduces the notion of a "sign." He does not explicitly give a formal definition, but he says some things that suggest the possibility of a definition. The most important of these is the remark that

". . . existent things, as signs, are *evidence* of the existence of something else, this something being at the time *inferred* rather than observed." [*Logic*, 52]

It is not immediately apparent whether Dewey means that what a sign signifies *must* not be observed or whether he means that it is its being inferred *rather than* its being observed that counts in making the sign a sign. (a) The phrase "at the time" seems intended to suggest that the thing signified is not at the time observed but only inferred. This would fit in with the idea that prediction of what is not yet observed is a function essentially involved in the use of signs. Also we frequently abandon the use of certain things as signs when we are able to observe the thing signified more directly. *E.g.,* before a patient's temperature is taken, the feeling of his head to the touch may act as a sign that he has a high temperature. But when his temperature is taken and discovered to be, say, 103°, we do not generally refer back to the feeling as evidence that he has a high temperature. I believe we do this because the thermometer reading is better evidence than the feeling; although if for some reason we suspected that the thermometer had a defect, we would return to the feeling as evidence, or look for something else. What is suggested, then, is that when we can make observations which are fairly direct, other more indirect procedures are abandoned, and the entities which were used as signs cease to be used. But (b) since observation of a thing often involves the functioning of parts or aspects of it as signs of it, it would seem that making non-observation of the thing signified a definitory condition would make the definition too narrow. *E.g.* suppose I *observe* a cow. I *see,* let us say, something which, if I *am* observing a cow, is its left side—for I cannot see all sides of a cow simultaneously. Since there can be cases in which I am duped by the left side of a skilfully prepared hide of a cow or a papier-mâché prop, it can only be that what I *see* functions as evidence of the existence of a cow; and it seems unobjectionable to say that it is a *sign* of the existence of the cow. Still, in such circumstances, if there *is* a cow, I am said to *observe* a cow. Hence in observation something seen or otherwise sensed or observed may function as a sign of what is being observed.

On the basis of these considerations I believe it preferable to assume that what is signified may also be observed; and I shall make this assumption in interpreting Dewey's remark. But whichever interpretation is made, the general trend of what follows will not be changed in any essentials.

It seems also, however, that Dewey does not intend to use the concept of *inference* to define that of sign; for he says the converse, that the sign-significance relation defines inference (*Logic*, 54). It therefore appears that he wishes to use the concept of *evidence* for this purpose, in the sense in which one may speak of something existent being evidence for the existence of something else. Perhaps, therefore, this comes close:

A is a sign of B in S if and only if
  (1) A exists, and
  (2) A functions in S as evidence for the existence of B.

Here "S" designates a situation. Reference to a situation (or some person, organism or observer) seems required in accordance with things Dewey says and also with his general position. E.g. he says that smoke is a sign of fire "only when the thing exists and is observed" (*Logic*, 52) and that clouds "may signify to us the probability of rain" (*ib.*, 53). Also as a general matter "the signifying property is not inherent but accrues to natural qualities in virtue of the special function they perform in inquiry" (*ib.*, 528).

Two points are of interest here:

(1) An existent, A, may function as a sign in what we may call an *oblique* capacity. (Dewey does not use this word.) This occurs because of "error" with respect to A. What I mean will be clear from an example. Suppose there is a puff of water vapor hanging over a house. Let A be this puff of vapor. Suppose that someone believes A to be smoke, not vapor; and suppose he takes it to be evidence of the existence of a fire in the house. Then A, the puff of vapor, functions as a sign of the existence of fire; but it is not as vapor or as known or believed to be vapor, but as believed to be something else, smoke, that this happens. This shows that although, on the definition, a sign is always something existent, it functions as a sign not *directly* because it is what it is, but because of what it is "taken to be" in a given situation.

(2) That whose existence is signified, B, need not in fact exist in order that A should function as a sign of its existence. This may

happen through (a) error with respect to A and correct inference to B starting from that error, (b) no error with respect to A but incorrect inference from A to B, (c) error in both respects. The above instance is a case of (a), namely, although A functioned as a sign of the existence of a fire in the house, B, no such fire existed; error occurred with respect to A, and the inference was correct but failed to reach an existent because it started from an error. Still, A was a sign of fire.

Both these points indicate that the signifying relation is not a direct existential relation between two existences, but is mediated by virtue of the need for a situation in which A is to function as a sign. The signifying relation starts with something existent, A (though not necessarily with that existent "as it is"), and is mediated through A's being "taken to be" something and also through A's being further taken as evidencing the existence of B. It is true that Dewey says "existences are 'related' to one another in the evidential sign-signified function" and speaks of "significance-connections in existence" (*Logic*, 55). But this is not the same as saying that the sign-signified relation is a direct, unmediated relation between actual existents.

The above two points also indicate that there is a distinction to be made between valid or warranted and invalid or unwarranted signifying (or, perhaps better, that there are degrees of validity of signifying). Valid signifying would then occur when A is correctly taken and when A's evidential force is correctly estimated. Or, at least, one would want to be able to formulate the conditions determining how "good" the interpretation of A and A's evidential capacity is. Valid signifying *could* start from something existent and terminate in something existent, without "obliqueness" at either end. Thus if I see something which I judge to be smoke and I am right and if I infer that there is a fire below it and I am right, then some actual smoke signifies some actual fire. But even here, it seems clear, the signifying relation is mediative, occurring only because there is a situation including me as well as the smoke and fire. The smoke is *produced* by the fire regardless of me; but it *signifies* the fire *via* a function determined by a situation including me.

All this is not new, since it has long been recognized on all sides that the sign-function requires essential reference to a sign-user or a sign-situation. I have mentioned it to emphasize the point that Dewey understands the sign-signified relation to be *existential* and that it is existential in a very special way. There is always something existent, A, which functions as a sign, regardless of whether it does so obliquely, *i.e.* regardless of whether the trait which it is taken to have and in virtue of which it is employed as evidence (hence used as a sign) is correctly or erroneously ascribed to it. There need not always be an existent, B, which is in fact signified; but the *intent* of the sign-user is nevertheless to reach an actual existent; and signification fails of its function if we do not reach or come close to an actual existent as the entity signified. Thus while the relation is "existential" rather than "logical" in the sense in which a meaning-relation is "logical" (although it *is* "logical" in the sense in which any functional relation intrinsic to the procedure of inquiry is "logical"), it is the actual existence of the entity that serves as a *sign* and the *intent* to reach a signified existent, rather than the actual existence of the thing signified, that makes the relation "existential."

Further, an actually existent entity functions as a sign only within an encompassing and actually existing situation. This situation need not be one of inquiry, since signification pervades experience in all its forms. But whatever the form of the experiential situation may be, the occurrence within it of entities functioning as signs is an existential fact; and the kinds of entities functioning as signs and the ways in which they do this are factors in making that existent situation what it is.

In the special case of inquiry as a form of experience, this consideration becomes important for the following reason. Inquiry is an actually existent process in the world. It is a process of transformation, in which the transformation occurs purposefully by means of the application of a technique to a medium, *i.e.* it is a case of "art" in the generic sense of that term. In this process many changes take place: physical, chemical, vital, psychological, cultural. All these changes are changes in existent things (which is tautological). Among these changes are changes in the ways in which existent things function as signs. Changes in the functioning of things as signs are existential, like all changes. There can be changes in the functioning of existent things as signs because the sign-function is a function served by existent things. Now (as I shall argue below) it is Dewey's view that whatever other existential changes are connected with inquiry, either as coordinate or subordinate processes or as processes within which inquiry is subordinated, the process of transformation of the signifying function of actual things is the chief business of inquiry as a logical process. Thus inquiry is characteristically a certain kind of process of transforming actual things so that, as a result, they possess a certain characteristic mode of signifying. When and if this task has been well done, other forms of experience (or also other inquiries) are able to take over and use the product of inquiry. It is, then, because the signifying function is existential, and because inquiry is chiefly a certain kind of process of making and transforming signs, that inquiry is a process of actual, existential production, *i.e.* that the "object" of inquiry is something existentially made and not something existing antecedently to inquiry (just as a glass of orange juice does not exist antecedently to squeezing oranges).

For instance, before Freud a slip of the tongue did not signify a repressed wish. There were slips of the tongue and repressed wishes, and the repressed wishes (we shall suppose) tended to produce the slips of the tongue; but the slips did not signify the wishes. That is, they did not *function* as signs, and hence *were* not signs. Freud made them into signs. He made them into entities which are used as evidence for the existence of repressed wishes. Freud did not make the fact that repressed wishes tend to produce slips of the tongue; he did not make the repressed wishes or the slips of the tongue. He changed us and our culture (hence our situations) in such a way that, under certain conditions, when a slip of the tongue occurs, we respond to it differently from how we did before Freud. This means that slips of the tongue now act in our situations as they did not earlier. A new "power" has accrued to them, so that they have been "changed" too, not by being distorted or rearranged but by being enabled to operate in a context in which they did not earlier enter. They have received the existential status of being signs of repressed wishes.

This, I think, is an appropriate example of what Dewey means by saying that logical forms accrue to existents as the result of inquiry and that the object of inquiry is made by and in inquiry and does not exist as such antecedently to inquiry.

I wish now to argue that the above does represent Dewey's view of the nature of inquiry, *i.e.* that on his view the characteristic function of inquiry as a logical process is the transformation of a situation which is problematic or *indeterminate in significance* into one which is coherent and *determinate in significance*. I do not maintain that this is the only important feature of inquiry. For instance, I do not maintain that according to Dewey it is not the function of inquiry to settle (or aid in settling) more than features of significance in problematic situations. But it seems to me that according to Dewey's ideas what is specifically "logical" about inquiry refers primarily and characteristically to the business of settling matters pertaining to *significance*.

Consider some direct statements by Dewey on this matter:

"The heart of the experimental method is determination of the significance of observed things by means of deliberate institution of modes of interaction." [*Logic*, 511]

"The criterion for the validity of . . . hypotheses is the capacity of the new data they produce to combine with earlier data (describing the problem) so that they institute a whole of unified significance." [*ib.*, 427]

"Operations of experimental observation (1) narrow the field of relevant existential material and (2) effect intersections that converge towards a unified signifying force and hence to a unified conclusion." [*ib.*, 318]

"Inquiry is progressive and cumulative. Propositions are the instruments by which provisional conclusions of preparatory inquiries are summed up, recorded and retained for subsequent uses. In this way they function as effective means, material and procedural, in the conduct of inquiry, till the latter institutes subject-matter so unified in significance as to be warrantably assertible." [*ib.*, 311]

"It is true that problematic situations are such because of the existence of conditions which conflict as to their significance, thus constituting a disordered situation. Hence, a universal property of any inquiry is transformation into a situation unified or continuous in significance." [*ib.*, 531]

These statements clearly indicate that on Dewey's view inquiry reaches its end, as a logical process, when it successfully achieves a whole of unified *significance;* the task of inquiry as a logical process is to reach such a whole. This does not mean that inquiry has no further consequences or that it is not instituted for achieving *more* than unification of significance. On Dewey's view, it seems clear, inquiry in general does have further consequences and is instituted for further achievement.

For instance in a law trial the question may be whether or not a man has committed a crime and should be jailed. Beforehand it is uncertain and indeterminate whether or not he is to be jailed. Hence the trial, which is a process of inquiry, is instituted to decide the issue. The trial ends when the judge pronounces sentence (supposing the man is found guilty). But the situation which evoked and led into the trial does not cease there; the jailer takes over and the man is jailed. The situation of a man sitting in jail is not the end of inquiry as a logical process; it is a consequence of the inquiry, however, since the inquiry was instituted to make clear what should be done with the man. The appropriate end of inquiry as a logical process is the judgment of the judge. This judgment is "a settlement of an *issue* because it decides existential conditions in their bearing upon further activities: the essence of the significance of any state of facts" (*Logic*, 120 f.). Thus it functions on the one hand as the outcome of inquiry and on the other as a directive of future actions. In the former function it is logical, *i.e.* a product of inquiry; in the latter function it is practical, *i.e.* a guide for conduct. And (as I believe Dewey means) it is precisely because in its logical function it is a valid settlement of significances that it is able to be effectively practical as a directive for the achievement of the consequences. There is "continuity" between the process and outcome of inquiry and action beyond inquiry just because inquiry is concerned with the significances of existential items.

The same result appears when inquiry is approached from its problematic initiation. When is a situation problematic? Not simply when there is need, tension or conflict. The indeterminate situation from which inquiry starts is in itself "precognitive." The first step of inquiry as such is "to see that a situation requires inquiry," *i.e.* to adjudge it to be problematic (*Logic,* 107). But how is this done? We would have at least to recognize that the original situation *is* indeterminate, namely, that it is confused, obscure, conflicting. Such traits as these are constitutive of the indeterminacy that characterizes situations tending to evoke inquiry. And each of them makes essential reference to significance. According to Dewey's definitions (*Logic,* 106) a situation is (1) confused when its outcome cannot be anticipated, (2) obscure when its course of movement permits of final consequences that cannot be clearly made out, (3) conflicting when it tends to evoke discordant responses.

(1) If we say that the outcome of a situation cannot be anticipated, do we mean that *no one* could possibly anticipate it? This is hardly the appropriate meaning. What we mean is that the organism in the situation cannot, as the situation then stands, anticipate the outcome. The organism would still be in the kind of situation which would evoke inquiry on his part even though someone outside that situation could predict with unerring accuracy the entire future course of that situation. That is, the organism would still be in an *indeterminate* situation (which indicates that the indeterminacy need not be *causal* indeterminacy). And its confusedness would consist in the fact that its existential items do not function together in a coherent way so as to *signify* a determinate outcome to that

organism in that situation, but not necessarily to any observer in any more inclusive situation.

(2) The obscurity of a situation is to be interpreted in a similar way. The final consequences that cannot be clearly made out cannot be clearly made out in that situation by that organism, although it remains possible that they could be made out by an observer in a more inclusive situation in which the former situation is subject matter. And not being able to be clearly made out consists in not being clearly *signified* by existential items in the given situation.

(3) Why is there a tendency in a situation to evoke discordant responses? Because some aspects or items signify one thing whereas some (even partly or wholly the same) signify something else to the organism in the situation.

In all three cases the traits that constitute the indeterminacy of the situation and in virtue of which the situation can become problematic have essential reference to significance. This, I believe, is what Dewey tells us when he says:

> "Even were existential conditions unqualifiedly determinate in and of themselves, they are indeterminate in *significance*: that is, in what they import and portend in their interaction with the organism." [*Logic,* 106-7]

Thus from the point of view both of initiation and aim of inquiry, inquiry is, as a logical process, one of transformation in significance of evidential function, in which a situation which is incoherent in this respect is made over into one that is coherently unified in this respect. And I believe that examination of Dewey's treatment of any of the intermediate phases or subsidiary processes of inquiry would show that, on his view, they are to be understood as contributing each in its own way to the determination of valid signification.

There is not space here for such a detailed examination; but it may be worth while to refer briefly to the case of the inductive and deductive phases of inquiry. The inductive phase "surrounds" (so to speak) the deductive phase; the latter has only an intermediary function. Induction, first, is a process by which antecedently existing conditions are modified so as to obtain data which *indicate or suggest* possible solutions or hypotheses. Second, it is also a process by which data are obtained which *test* proposed hypotheses. In between the suggesting and the testing of hypotheses there is the process of deductive development of them. The function of deductive development is to obtain from the hypotheses such *if-then* propositions as will direct experimental observations to yield new testing data. When the two processes of induction and deduction work hand in hand they combine to constitute inquiry as a logical process. The aim is to "institute a whole of unified significance" (*Logic,* 427). And the interrelation of the two processes is so articulated as to work toward this outcome:

"The propositions which formulate data must, to satisfy the conditions of inquiry, be such as to determine a problem in the form that indicates a possible solution, while the hypothesis in which the latter is formulated must be such as operationally to provide the new data that fill out and order those previously obtained. There is a continued to-and-fro movement between the set of existential propositions about data and the non-existential propositions about related conceptions." [*ibid.*]

We may conclude, then, that in Dewey's theory of inquiry the signifying function plays a predominant role and that the aim of inquiry, as a logical process, is institution of a situation in which the phase of significance is unified and coherent.

Dewey introduces the words "connection" and "involvement" (as synonymous) in order to designate "that kind of relation sustained by *things* to one another in virtue of which *inference* is possible" (*Logic,* 55). It is clear that by "things" he intends to refer to entities of various sorts, not only substantial individuals, *e.g.* changes, conditions, traits (*cf. Logic,* 278).

The way in which he introduces "involvement" seems at first sight to suggest that he means to identify it with the sign-significance relation; for he distinguishes three *senses* of "relation"—

(1) relations of symbol-meanings to one another, (2) relations of symbol-meanings to existence, (3) relations of existences to one another in the evidential sign-signified function—and he then introduces three *terms* for relations—(1) "relation," (2) "reference," (3) "involvement" or "connection"—with the apparent intent that they correspond to the three *senses* of "relation."

However, upon closer scrutiny, it appears that while "relation" and "reference" are meant to correspond exactly to the first two senses, "involvment" is not meant to correspond *exactly* but only to be closely connected with the third sense, that of the sign-signified relation. That is, as I read Dewey, "involvement" is not intended to designate the sign-significance relation but a relation which is closely connected with the latter.

Although in the above definition Dewey speaks of involvement as a relation in virtue of which *inference* is possible (so that one might be led to think that he means to designate by "involvement" the sign-signified or evidential relation, since inference is said to be defined in terms of this), he also speaks a little further on (55, bottom) of "the connections in things in virtue of which some things are *evidential* of other things" (my italics). (I believe that he means here to refer to connections in virtue of which some things are *validly* evidential of the existence of other things, just as I believe he means in the definition to refer to the possibility of *valid* inference.) Now to speak of connections *in virtue of which* things are evidential is not to identify those connections with the evidential relation but to distinguish them from it. Such connections, if they exist, would be *conditions* of the existence of (valid) signification, but not *instances* of it. (*Cf.* for example: "Inference is conditioned upon an existential connection which may be called *involvement*. The problems of inference have to do with discovery of *what* conditions are involved with another and *how* they are involved. . . . The essential consideration is that the relation is a strictly existential one, ultimately a matter of the brute structure of things" (*Logic*, 278).

And if we consider an instance of involvement we see that it is not, as such, an instance of the signifying relation, but is rather such that, if discovered, it can be employed to institute a valid signifying relation. For example:

"The sudden and excessive rise of the customary level of a river is involved *in* heavy rain storms and involves *with* its occurrence perils to life and property, impassable roads, etc." [*Logic*, 278]

It is clear that to say that a sudden and excessive rise of the customary level of a river is involved in a heavy rain storm is *not* to say that the latter signifies the former, if by "sign" we mean an existent something which functions in an organism-environment situation as evidence of the existence of something else. For there need not be an organism-environment situation in which the heavy rain storm figures as evidence at all. It *implies, together with* our knowledge of the general characteristics of man-environment situations, that a heavy rain storm *can be* a valid sign of rise in river level. But of course that is a different matter. If we assert that heavy rain storms and rises in river levels are items in a relation of environment, then we are speaking about an existential connection different from that of sign and thing signified; though it remains true that if a heavy rain storm *does* involve a rise in river level, then a heavy rain storm *can become* a valid sign of such a rise.

I take it, then, that Dewey does not mean to identify the relations of involvement and of sign-signified, but to relate them very closely, so that involvements are conditions of the possibility of valid sign-signified relations, both involvement and sign-signified being existential relations.

If this is correct, then certain consequences follow. *First,* whereas an existent functions as a sign only within an organism-environment situation, existents are related by involvement generally, both outside and inside organism-environment situations. For instance, the contact of an acid and a base may, in a given inquiry, be taken as a *sign* of the occurrence of a process of neutralization; but acids and bases may also interact so as to neutralize each other even if this process does not occur in an inquiry; they are *involved* in a chemical interaction "outside" (in causal independence of) inquiry.

Second, whereas the signifying functions of things are *characteristic products* of inquiry, the involvements of things are not. Thus the contact of acid and base is *made* into a sign of a process of neutralization by inquiry; but the fact that acids and bases combine to neutralize is not made by inquiry. In an inquiry we can make an acid come into contact with a base, but after that it is the acid and base that do the interacting, and would do so, if in proximity, even if there were no inquiry in progress.

Third, it is only because there are involvements of things which are causally independent of their occurring within inquiries that inquiry can do what it aims to do, make reliable signs. Unless acid and base reacted in a characteristic way, we would not be able to use the conjunction of acid and base as a valid sign of a process of neutralization. This, I believe, is what Dewey means when he says that involvement is a relation *in virtue of which* the evidential relation (or, I think we should say, valid signification) is possible. I think he means that we should have no good reason for believing that the contact of acid and base validly signifies the occurrence of neutralization unless we had reason to believe that it was a characteristic trait of the interaction of acid and base that it issues in neutralization. (The converse also holds.) It cannot, of course, be true that the reason why acids and bases neutralize is that we have simply *decided* to make the conjunction of acid and base a sign of neutralization. Existence is malleable, but only because there are existential involvements which can be exploited for the purpose. In transforming existences we do not transform the basic involvement relations in virtue of which the transformation is possible.

There is no contradiction between Dewey's view that the *object* of inquiry is produced or constructed in the course of inquiry and the view that the purpose of inquiry is to ascertain those involvements by virtue of which the problematic situation may be settled in its significances. Dewey does not abandon his "connective realism" (the theory that existence as such is characterized by involvements) when he asserts that inquiry is not concerned with ascertaining fixed traits of antecedent existence but with ordering and settling problematic situations. At least he doesn't if one understands (or misunderstands?) him, as I have, to mean that what inquiry does is to settle the significative functions of items with regard to the problematic situation. For in order to achieve this settlement—which is the *objective* of inquiry, such that existences when they get their appropriate significative functions are achieved objects (*Logic,* 118-9)—one has, as well as possible, to discover just those independently existential involvements by virtue of which significative functions can be validly assigned. On this interpretation, which seems to me to make good sense of what Dewey says, connective realism is the counterpart to logical instrumentalism, for it is only in terms of connective realism, or something like it, that logical instrumentalism has a ground to stand on. Give up connective realism, and logical instrumentalism becomes what critics of Dewey have often maintained it to be, a neo-Hegelianism in which existence independently of inquiry is a kind of formless matter, almost nothing, and in which knowing makes not only its logical form or significative function but *all* its form or definite character, including its forms of connection. Knowing then becomes no longer the art of existentially fixing the significances of things validly, but the art of making the world.

Now to be sure, the art of fixing the significances of things validly involves testing. Otherwise both data and theories remain in the stage of mere suggestion. And in actual experimental operation, where solution of the problem requires decisions to be made and acted upon, the process of testing is a process of doing and making. Here solving the problem in fact entails the making of a specific thing, the doing of a particular act, etc. In this action the ideas and "facts" are tested as to whether significances have been rightly ascribed. But, of course, this does not mean that in making a thing or doing an act we make the characters of existence in virtue of which things can be made or acts done. I cannot find a passage in Dewey which suggests this. That may be due to oversight on my part, although the general tenor of his thought, together with considerations of consistency and intelligibility, would seem to prohibit any such theory.

The above consequences of the distinction between signification and involvement begin to indicate the importance of the latter idea for (1) theory of knowledge and (2) metaphysics.

(1) If there are involvement relations, as Dewey suggests, such that it is in virtue of them that evidence and inference are possible, then there is suggested also a possible approach to the so-called problem of induction. In the first place, an involvement relation would be an *explanatory reason* for the possibility of a valid evidential relation. Thus if we were to ask, "Why can A be a valid sign of B?" the answer might be, "Because A is a condition (or consequence) in an interaction involving B as consequence (or condition)." (This is obviously too simplified, but it will serve to indicate what is meant.) And similarly, in general, the existence of involvements would constitute an explanatory reason for the possibility of evidential relations: "Why can there be A's which validly signify B's? Because there are A's and B's which are involved in interactions." Thus there is suggested a general existential theory in terms of which the nature and possibility of the functioning of existent things as evidence could be accounted for.

Furthermore, if we had a general theory of the involvements of things, in the sense of a theory of the general kinds and connections of involvments or the general structure of involvement relations, this would serve as a hypothesis which might guide inquiry in the selection and ordering of data, hypotheses, etc. A remark of Russell's is very suggestive in this context:

"Owing to the world being such as it is, certain occurrences are sometimes, in fact, evidence for certain others; and owing to animals being adapted to their environment, occurrences which are, in fact, evidence of others tend to arouse expectation of these others. By reflecting on this process and refining it, we arrive at the canons of inductive inference. These canons are valid if the world has certain characteristics which we all believe it to have. The inferences made in accordance with these canons are self-confirmatory and are not found to contradict experience. Moreover they lead us to think that we shall have mental habits such as these canons will on the whole justify, since such mental habits will be biologically advantageous." [*Human Knowledge*, p. 496]

With a few changes these comments would seem to apply to our situation. Because the world is as it is (because it is such as to have a particular structure of involvement relations) certain occurrences are sometimes, in fact, capable of being used validly as evidence for certain others. To the extent to which we are well-adapted to our environment, entities which are in fact related by involvement to others tend to be employed by us as signs of them; and inquiry is the process by which we try to achieve such well-adaptedness. By reflecting on the process of inquiry when it is efficiently practiced, we arrive at the canons of scientific method. These canons are valid to the extent to which they make it possible to make successful inferences, *i. e.* to construct good signs. And since it is in virtue of involvements that good signs are possible, the canons are valid to the extent to which they reflect the generic features of the involvement structure of the world. Inferences made in accordance with such canons will tend on the whole to be more successful than inferences made in any other way.

But with these changes, there would still remain a major difference between Russell's approach and the one here suggested. For on Russell's view such canons of inductive inference (or as we should rather say, inquiry) are themselves immune from test, being virtually a *synthetic a priori* condition for the very possibility of an evidential relation; whereas on the view here suggested the canons would be formulated on the basis of a conception of the involvement structure of the world which is itself an outcome of previous inquiries and is subject to considerations of adequacy or inadequacy, like any scientific theory, on the basis of how well it works in aiding us to achieve the goal of inquiry.

Nor does it seem that there is a *petitio principii* committed. We make the *hypothesis,* suggested by the results of previous inquiries, that there is a certain world structure. On the basis of this hypothesis we formulate some canons of inquiry. We try to use these canons to make signs, or inferences, and we decide whether or not to retain the canons by considering their effectiveness for the purpose. No *specific* world-hypothesis is then *logically* necessitated as a presupposition of inquiry. Rather the suggestion is that *some* world-hypothesis could and should function to order inference, and that the one that does this best is the one entitled to be used. Unless we believed that there was *some* structure of involvement in existence, we would have no reason which could *explain* why there could be anything of the nature of a valid, determinate and specific evidential relation; although we might simply operate blindly and make inferences by pure chance or arbitrary dictum. Thus a theory of a particular involvement structure of existence would act as a device fulfilling a basic function in inquiry, that of selecting in advance the *general* features of hypotheses to be advanced, data and samples to be selected, methods of inferring from data and samples to hypotheses, so helping to order and regulate the process of inference. Without such a theory (since there is always an infinite number of hypotheses which might be advanced) the choice of which general types to consider for further testing would be unregulated and a matter of blind choice; and similarly for data, samples and methods of inference.

In order to avoid misunderstanding, it is necessary to re-emphasize here that such a theory of involvement structure would not be *a priori synthetic* but would develop out of inquiry in its progressive and cumulative growth.

The above remarks are plainly only vague and preliminary. But it seems to me that they point to a significant alternative in contemporary theory of knowledge, one that deserves to be considered and its consequences realized before our minds are made up on the answer to the problem of induction.

Also it is interesting to note that on such an approach, the theory of knowledge would depend on a metaphysical base which would itself be developed empirically in the course of inquiry.

(2) A general theory of the involvements of things would not only serve as a basis for formulating general canons of inference, but would do this because it would constitute a theory of the structure of existence. And in this latter aspect it would be nothing other than an empirical metaphysics in the sense in which Dewey speaks of metaphysics in *Experience and Nature*. I do not mean that it would be the particular metaphysics which Dewey himself

develops in that book, but rather that it would answer to the idea of metaphysics which he outlines chiefly in the final chapter, "Existence and Value." The question how far the metaphysics of *Experience and Nature* corresponds to and fulfils the task outlined in that chapter is itself a special problem and would need special consideration which cannot be given here.

According to the task as outlined there, metaphysics (as an empirical discipline) is to function as a "ground-map of the province of criticism, establishing base lines to be employed in more intricate triangulations" (*Experience and Nature*, 2 ed., 413). It is enabled to do this because its specific aim is to discover and formulate "the generic traits manifested by existences of all kinds without regard to their differentiation into physical and mental" (*ib.*, 412). Thus Dewey argues that there is a *specific function* which metaphysics is to serve, and that there is a *specific aim* which it has as a form of inquiry and theory, and that there is a *connection between the two*, namely, that metaphysics is able to fulfil its specific function because its specific aim, if achieved, would be what was needed for that function.

This matter may be expressed more generally. There is first the over-all function of philosophy, which, as love of wisdom, seeks to achieve that world-orientation or *Weltanschauung* in the light of which life can be guided both individually and socially toward its best fulfilment. As such, philosophy is more than a theory of the nature of the existential world because it involves commitment to values, their pursuit and ordering. As a general theory of existence, however, metaphysics is an important part of philosophy. And the reason is clear:

"The more sure one is that the world which encompasses human life is of such and such a character (no matter what his definition) the more one is committed to try to direct the conduct of life, that of others as well as himself, upon the basis of the character assigned to the world. And if he finds that he cannot succeed, that the attempt lands him in confusion, inconsistency and darkness, plunging others into discord and shutting them out from participation, rudimentary precepts instruct him to surrender his assurance as a delusion; and to revise his notions of the nature of nature till he makes them more adequate to the concrete facts in which nature is embodied. Man needs the earth in order to walk, the sea to swim or sail, the air to fly. Of necessity he acts within the world, and in order to be, he must in some measure adapt himself as one part of nature to other parts." [*ib.*, 414]

Thus metaphysics receives its function of being a ground-map of criticism because it is to be employed as a part and organ of philosophy in the enterprise of the wise conduct of life; and it is able to serve this function because its specific aim is the discovery of the "nature of nature" or the general nature of the world of actual existence.

Let us ask, then, what it means to speak of an empirical discipline whose aim it is to discover the nature of nature or the constituent structure of nature (*ib.*, 422).

According to Dewey, as I have argued, all inquiry aims at rendering determinate the significances of existential things. This affords one way of describing the difference between ignorance and knowledge. In a state of ignorance, existential items appear isolated to us. They are disconnected with respect to their significances. They do not "portend." We simply *have* them in experience, as immediacies. But when reflective thought or inquiry gets to work, this situation is changed. Reflection introduces "secondary" objects, the objects of refined and scientific experience, whose role is to *explain* the objects of "primary," crude experience, to enable us to grasp them with *understanding*:

" . . . they lay out a path by which return to experienced things is of such a sort that the meaning, the significant content, of what is experienced gains an enriched and expanded force because of the path or method by which it was reached. Directly, in immediate contact it may be just what it was before—hard, colored, odorous, etc. But when the secondary objects, the refined objects, are employed as a method or road for coming at them, these qualities cease to be isolated details; they get the meaning contained in a whole system of related objects; they are rendered continuous with the rest of nature and take on the import of the things they are now seen to be continuous with." [*ib.*,5]

It is hardly necessary to quote from *The Quest for Certainty* on the relational character of scientific objects, since this point is so central in Dewey's thought that anyone who has even thumbed leaves in that book will have noted it. The entire function of scientific inquiry is to reach those relations in virtue of which we may travel in thought from one existential item to another, and hence in virtue of which given items are capable of signifying other items.

Also, it is clear that if the aim of reflective thought is to make this institution and development of the signifying function possible, it can do so (on Dewey's view) only in so far as it aims at the discovery of involvement relations. Indeed it is precisely the problem of *inference* (which uses *discourse* as a necessary but intermediary instrument) to discover "*what* conditions are involved with one another and *how* they are involved" (quoted above, from *Logic,* 278). And if we remember that on Dewey's view the function of discourse *is* intermediary (being that of developing implications on the basis of relations of symbol-meanings, with an ultimate view toward the fulfilment of the inferential function), it also becomes clear that the aim of inference on the whole is not to be distinguished from that of inquiry as such. Inquiry aims at making full and rich inference possible, and inference, aided by the intermediary function of discourse, is the procedure by which inquiry advances. And this means that inquiry or reflective thinking is able to do what it does only because it aims at discovery of involvement structures. *To know is to grasp validly existences in their relations, i. e. in their involvement structures.* (But since to put items together according to their involvement structures requires that items which do not belong together be eliminated, knowing also includes determination of the absence as well as the presence of involvements.)

From this it immediately follows that the aim of metaphysics, as a general theory of existence, is the discovery of the basic types of involvements and their relationships. That is, metaphysics as an existential discipline would seek to discover what ultimate kinds of contexts there are in which items are connected by involvements, and how these contexts are related among themselves.

And from this it becomes clear why metaphysics can be a ground-map of criticism. If understanding consists in grasping existential items in those involvement contexts by virtue of which the items can be significant, then metaphysics would provide a general understanding of things. It would lay out the general ground of significance, the field of involvements of existences, leaving the particular features to be inserted in accordance with the particularities of the situation. And if, as Dewey thinks, criticism of values means viewing values in the context of their conditions and consequences, the general theory of involvement structures would, by describing the basic types of involvement structures in virtue of which there are any such things as conditions and consequences, provide the existential background for estimating values.

If what has been said above is correct, then the notion of involvement stands at the center of both theory of knowledge and metaphysics and also provides the background for the search for wisdom. It accordingly becomes an important problem to identify cases of involvement and to give an analysis of the meaning of the term. Unless this is done it is hard to see how one could begin to work systematically at a general theory of the involvements of things. I have not attempted such an analysis here, my purpose being rather to suggest the need for it. But if I am right, it should be next on the agenda.

Dewey's Theory of Language and Meaning

by PAUL WIENPAHL

"THE TOPIC of meaning is certainly one of the most important in contemporary philosophical discussion . . ." [M&E., p. 353][1] "Just what the meaning of an expression is—what kind of object —is not yet clear; . . . a definition [of meaning] would be a fundamental contribution at once to philology and philosophy." [N. on E&N., p. 120]

Dewey's analysis of human behavior in the contexts of aesthetics and inquiry has resulted in a well-developed theory of language. Because of certain characteristics of Dewey's work this theory is not stated in one place in a specific volume or essay. It is spread through numerous books and papers. Since analysis of language is found increasingly useful in various philosophic problems, it is important on this occasion to consider Dewey's theory explicitly as a theory of language. In the spirit of Dewey's work it is of further importance to consider possible applications of the theory to problems which he himself has not made.[2]

[1] All references to Dewey's and other works will be given by abbreviations in brackets. The key to the abbreviations occurs in the bibliography at the end of the article.
[2] The writer is aware of the responsibility he assumes, particularly in taking results of Dewey's work out of their contexts. ForABewey's theory of language is spread throughout his writings because of that characteristic of his approach to philosophy which regards every problem and its solution as occurring in a context. Therefore, full reference to Dewey's works is given. Further check on the accuracy of the presentation of Dewey's theory may be had by consulting the indexes to Dewey's books under the following heads: meaning, symbols, language, communication, formulation, proposition, media, terms, idea, essence, universal and general.

This paper summarizes certain basic features of Dewey's theory and applies them to the general problem of nominalism vs. realism. In particular, I wish: a) to set forth some of the basic results of Dewey's analysis of language, especially those concerned with scientific or cognitive language; and b) to apply these results to an explanation of the traditional pair of concepts denotation-extension and connotation-intension-meaning. The discussion will show that an important confusion in the analysis of the concepts is clarified by these features of Dewey's views. The confusion concerns the explication of 'meaning' and has resulted in rendering difficult a thoroughgoing nominalistic approach to language analysis by involving us in references to subsistent or abstract entities such as the null-class and propositions which are nonlinguistic, objective entities even when they are false.

The fundamental principle of Dewey's theory of language is that language is a tool used in transforming some phase of the raw material of experience into new objects according to some purpose. If the purpose is prediction and control, the language is scientific. If the purpose is the enhancement of direct experience, the language is aesthetic. The material of both art and science is the interaction of the living organism with its environment. Art and science differ in the media (means) by which they deal with this interaction. The differences in media are due to the differences in function of art and science. [A. as E., pp 319-20]

These media, the languages of art and science, can be understood only in terms of the functions they fulfil. Thus scientific language can be understood only in the context of inquiry. Its function is to make possible prediction and control. Artistic language, which includes dancing, ritual, painting, music, etc., can be understood only in terms of the acts of expression and experiencing for its own sake (feeling and doing, without reference to something to be brought about outside of the present experience).

Linguistic media (symbols, words, gestures and art objects) have two essential characteristics. In the first place, they objectify an idea if their function is scientific, or an emotion if their function is aesthetic. That is to say, they make the idea or emotion capable of being experienced by more than one organism.³ In the second place, linguistic media make possible ideas and emotions or what Dewey also calls meanings. The media make ideas possible because, by being attached to overt responses (sensory and motor), they permit the later occurrence of so-called implicit responses; that is, responses in the absence of the existential stimulus which originally produced the overt responses. Dewey sometimes calls implicit responses vicarious experiences. In one sense of the term "mental," mental life consists in these implicit responses. The media make emotions possible because they work together with ideas in the transformation of a mere impulsion into an ordered release of organic energy. Particularly in the case of what are usually called linguistic media (words and gestures), the media exercise their peculiar function by being attached to organic processes, responses, (formulating the responses, Dewey says in the *Logic*) *and* by being manipulable. We sometimes describe this character of being manipulable by saying symbols are conventional. Both types of linguistic media communicate because they can be experienced by more than one organism.

Another essential feature of Dewey's theory of language is that it explains language as a continuation of biological activities, not as something ready-made man invented to communicate thoughts and ideas he already had. It is apparent that Dewey's method of analysis includes as a requirement of successful explanation the condition that that which is to be explained be examined not only logi-

---

³ It is important to note terminologically that whenever Dewey writes about language he uses the words 'conceptual,' 'ideal,' 'ideational,' 'intellectual,' 'non-existential,' 'an essence,' 'a form,' 'a meaning,' 'a notion,' 'property,' 'a term,' 'a species,' and 'a universal' to refer to elements of events or situations in such a way that it is a necessary though not sufficient condition that the event or situation contain biological activity. When he uses 'existential,' 'existences,' 'fact,' 'factual,' 'a kind,' 'thing' and 'traits' to refer to elements of events or situations, biological activity is not necessarily understood to be a component of the event or situation. In less Deweyan terms, Dewey uses the first set of words to refer to an occurrence in an organism and the latter set for occurrences outside of an organism. The less Deweyan way of making this point is dangerous because, in violating the essential requirement of Dewey's view that the organism not be separated from the environment, it leaves the way open for supposing that certain occurrences in an organism are 'intrinsically' non-existential as distinguished from occurrences 'outside' an organism. [L.,p.33]

I am indebted on this and other points to the critical help which Dr. Herbert Fingarette rendered in various discussions we had concerning Dewey's views.

cally but genetically and empirically. Originally language functioned to coordinate the behavior of one organism with that of another; *i. e.*, for com-munication. Only later was it given what we today call scientific and artistic functions. For Dewey the existence of man's mental life, the having of ideas, making predictions, inferring, etc., are dependent upon, indeed are, linguistic behavior.

Other tenets of Dewey's theory result from analysis of the way in which linguistic media make prediction and control, and expression possible. We are concerned here to develop mainly those parts of the theory which explain prediction. For this purpose we shall suppose that the remainder of Dewey's work on language consists in explications of the explicandum 'meaning.'[4]

Dewey has given a number of explications because the term has a number of uses both technically and in everyday language. 'Meaning' has been and unfortunately still is variously used where 'denotation,' 'connotation,' 'intention,' 'intension,' 'designation,' 'signification,' etc., may be used Dewey's explications have always been clear, but his use of 'meaning' has seemed ambiguous because he has relied on context rather than explicit mention to indicate which of the various senses he is using when the term occurs in his writing without explication. Therefore, I have invented names to separate the several meanings of 'meaning.' These names are inserted in parentheses following any occurrence of 'meaning' wherever it is necessary to distinguish the usage of that occurrence from other usages.[5]

[4] Whether Dewey consciously employed this device is unimportant. I make the supposition because it is a convenient way both of stating important parts of Dewey's theory and of understanding that theory.

[5] By 'explicate' and 'explicandum' I have in mind roughly what Carnap does [M & N., pp. 8-9]. More precisely, explication consists in translating an ambiguous or puzzling term into a term or terms which in the context of the process of explication are not ambiguous or puzzling. Such terms may themselves *subsequently* require explication. This does not impair their uses as explicata when they occur as such. *E.g.,* an explication of "meaning" as it occurs in 'what does he mean to say' is given roughly by 'what does he want to say.'

Early positivists thought explication required "translation" into the terms of physics. Explication has also been interpreted as requiring "translation" of all terms into sensationalistic terms. The view of explication employed in the paper is no less nominalistic in intent than earlier versions, but takes the "translation" of puzzling terms into terms about the use of which there is no question as sufficient to make an explication. 'Table,' for example, is ordinarily used without difficulty, 'proposition' is not. The former does not require explication, the lat-

The consequences which a thing or an event has or produces either in us or on other things are sometimes called the *meaning* (*existential*) of a thing or event. Dewey also refers to the connection between a thing and its consequences as a fact relation. In this sense the meaning of striking a match is a flame. It is this sense of "meaning" we sometimes have in mind when we ask "What does this thing mean?" [M&E., p. 348; A. as E., p. 342; E&N., p. 192; EinExL., p. 246] Dewey also distinguishes proximate and ulterior meanings (existential).

Proximate meanings (existential) are immediate consequences, ulterior meaning (existential) the long-run consequences, which are usually changes in human behavior. [E&N., p. 200ff]

The relation between thing-signifying and thing-signified is sometimes named by 'meaning.' Dewey calls this relation *signification*. [M&E., p. 342; L., p. 55] In this sense of 'meaning' we say "smoke means (signifies) fire." This relation of meaning (signification) occurs between things or events only in a context of biological activity. Things mean (signify) only for an organism, *i. e.*, for a creature capable of having ideas.

The individual existential thing or event for which a word stands is its *denotative meaning*. Thus, this utterance of 'smoke' stands for this smoke. [L. chp. 13] *Concrete* terms have denotative meaning. Denotative meaning must not be confused with symbol meaning (see below). 'Smoke' denotes smoke but it means (symbol meaning) 'fire.' Mathematical terms have no meaning (denotation). [L., chp. 20]

Extensional meaning is the group of existential things or events for which a word stands. For example, the extensional meaning of 'cow' is the group comprising all existing cows. Words which have extensional meaning are called *generic* words by Dewey. Thus, 'concrete' and 'generic' are better considered as referring to different uses which certain words have; namely, of standing for individual things or events (meaning denotatively) or for groups of

---

ter does. If that explication results in terms which are usable without question, we say 'proposition' has been explicated. In the context of Dewey's view, "usable without question" would be equivalent to "usable successfully in inquiry."

things or events (meaning extensionally). Some words have either use in different contexts (*e.g.,* 'cow'), some have only one use (*e.g.,* 'Paul'). [L., chp., 13]

The *connotative meaning* is the habit of operation on existential things or events for which certain words stand. Dewey calls such habits universals. [WAU., p. 268; L. chp. 13] *Abstract* words, *e.g.,* 'whiteness,' connote or have connotative meaning. They do not have denotative or extensional meaning. Although Dewey does not explicitly mention this, it must be observed that many words are used sometimes denotatively, sometimes connotatively. For example, 'length' is sometimes used to denote the length of an object. However, when we are speaking of length as a property or universal, 'length' is being used connotatively to stand for the operation (now habitual) which we perform to get what we denotatively mean as the length of this object.

A type of meaning only abstract terms have is comprehension. The *comprehension* of a word is the group of operational habits for which it stands. Thus, 'triangularity' stands for the group of habits for which 'right-angle triangularity,' 'scalene triangularity," etc., individually stand. Connotation and comprehension are the analogues for abstract words of denotation and extension for concrete words. [L., chp. 13][6]

[6] Words are used concretely to stand for individual things or events, or their traits (*e.g.,* a table, or *its* color). Words are used abstractly to stand for operational habits or what Dewey also calls properties (*e.g.,* portability, the habitual response of carrying). Dewey apparently believes there are individual things or events in the world; but not that the things which are members of kinds have anything *in common* such as existential properties, except in the sense of 'common' according to which we respond in a similar (common) fashion to many things. What is *common,* therefore is the habit of response, the unity of which is no more mysterious than the unity of an arm or leg. People have habits as organic entities in the same way they have arms and legs as organic entities. It is these habits which produce the similar responses, not some "similarity" in the things responded to. And each instance of a habit, of course, has no more in common with other instances than one horse has with another. What instances of habits have in common is the habit, just as movements of an arm have the arm in common. [WAU.; L., p. 252ff.]

Compare with Wittgenstein's rope example: in what sense do a ship and a dock have anything *in common* when a rope is connecting them, since no part or strand of the rope runs all the way from the ship to the dock?

The use of the concept of habit may suggest difficulties. For example, what exactly is a habit? It seems, howeves, that in ordinary use the term "habit" is no more questionable than 'arm' or 'leg.' We recognize that a person has a habit by a process similar to that by which we recognize that he has legs. Questions as

The *intensional meaning* of a word is the set of traits a group of objects have which form a kind. The intension of 'man,' *e.g.*, is all the cases of thinking, eating, etc., which individual men perform. [L. chp. 13]

Designation is either denotation or connotation; that is, whatever a symbol stands for. This includes existential things and events and organic habits. All terms designate, some denote and some connote. [L., chp. 13]

We come now to the central explication of 'meaning' in Dewey's theory: *meaning as idea*. Meaning in this sense is the non-overt or implicit response an organism makes to any other response, overt or implicit, which acts as stimulus. For example, when we say, "What does this mean for this organism?" we might as well say, "What implicit responses is the organism making as a result of this stimulus?"

The existence of implicit responses depends upon linguistic media or symbols. That is, a response can only become and becomes implicit, or has an implicit occurrence, when the behavior of using a symbol has been attached to it by conditioning. The implicit response is the behavior which consists in using the symbol. Thus we have an implicit response for smoke because we can utter aloud or to ourselves 'smoke.' A characteristic feature of an implicit response is its manipulable character; that is, it can occur when the original stimulus which produced the overt response which has been replaced by the implicit response is no longer present. The new stimulus is another implicit response (uttering a symbol). The implicit response which constitutes the response to the other implicit response which acts as stimulus is the meaning of the response acting as stimulus (see *symbol meaning* below). Implicit responses are ideas. In closer keeping with everyday language, an idea is an implicit response which consists in uttering a symbol to oneself. Producing symbols "out loud" is speaking or writing.

A given implicit response or idea stimulates another implicit response because the overt responses in connection with which the

---

to the nature of habits, therefore, appear to be questions for the physiologist and anatomist rather than the philosopher.

implicit responses were developed by conditioning had frequently formed a sequence in the organism's experience. For example, having frequently experienced smoke followed by fire (having an experience of smoke followed by an experience of fire), and having been conditioned to the implicit response of uttering 'smoke' in connection with smoke and 'fire' in connection with fire, an organism can make the implicit behavior of uttering 'fire' when stimulated by the implicit behavior of uttering 'smoke.' Implicit responses are symbol-behavior. Once an organism has developed symbol-behavior the latter may be stimulated by any response, implicit or overt. The symbol-behavior can be carried on in the absence of further overt response. In this case the organism is thinking.

Meanings as ideas are universal in two respects: a) they are habits of responses which many people have, and b) as habits of response they can be stimulated by many individual things or events. For example, the habit of using the word 'dog' can be stimulated by this dog or that dog.[7]

The concept of meaning as idea or implicit response leads easily into that of meaning as *symbol meaning*. The meaning (symbol) of any symbol is another symbol. [Peirce, L., p. 55] For example, 'smoke' means (symbol) 'fire.' It is possible to speak of a relation between symbols as the meaning (symbol) relation. It is in virtue of this relation that we say, "Smoke means fire." Because of the symbol meaning Dewey says a word has meaning (symbol) only

[7] The explication of 'meaning' as implicit response or idea occurs in the following references: Q. for C., p. 151; Peirce; EinExL., pp. 51 and 432; E&N., pp. 187-8; also wherever Dewey discusses fixing and formulation, for he holds that symbols fix or formulate overt responses enabling them to "occur" as implicit responses. Put otherwise, implicit responses stand for overt responses.

We develop habits of implicit responses just as we develop other habits. For example, we have the habit of using the word 'table.' The distinction between type and token is the same as the distinction between habit of implicit response and a given implicit response.

It is interesting to observe that by means of the notion of the universality of ideas in Dewey's sense we have the beginning of an explication of "similarity," Russell's final universal. Consider, for example, that in speaking of the universality of a habit we do not have to say that a habit is universal because it can be stimulated by a number of *similar* things. The word 'similar' is unnecessary

in a system of words [L., p. 49] and claims that a symbol is a meaning (symbol). [L., pp. 51 ff]. And apparently Dewey prefers to use the word 'meaning' only in connection with symbols, and hence, implicit responses or ideas.

Strictly speaking, since the meaning (symbol) of a symbol is given by another symbol, meaning (symbol) is "expressed in" or is a property only of sentences. Thus, there are two kinds of meanings (ideas): an implicit response, and two implicit responses related to each other by a connection which is the organic analogue of the connection between thing-signifying and thing-signified. This organic connection is the meaning (symbol) relation. The meaning (idea) of a sentence is two responses connected by this relation. Dewey calls responses related in this way when they occur in the context of inquiry *propositions*. A sentence differs from a proposition because a sentence is a series of marks on paper or of sounds, whereas a proposition is a series of related implicit responses which originally produce the physical tokens. A sentence can occur in a book, a proposition cannot. [L., pp. 172, 225, 384 ff] A sentence can be removed from its original context, a proposition cannot. Since Dewey holds we can understand things only as parts of contexts, he holds that studying language merely by studying sentences will not be successful.

For analytic purposes it is important to notice that meaning *as* idea must be distinguished from the meaning *of* an idea. Meanings as ideas are implicit responses (*i.e.*, producing symbols). The meaning of an idea, the content, is the overt response or habit of response

---

in this connection because it can only mean that this group of things stimulate a given habit. That is, the notion of similar things can be replaced by the notion of things which stimulate *a* habit. And the only sense in which a habit is universal is the sense in which any individual object is universal.

Mention should be made of Dewey's use of G. H. Mead's concept of the significant symbol. This is the view that marks, sounds and gestures become symbols (linguistic media) by occurring in situations involving two or more organisms under such circumstances as to insure that the responses of all the organisms to the gesture are similar. [SS.] Dewey employs this concept to explain how sounds and gestures become words, and how it is that a given symbol can have the same meaning (as meaning *of* an idea, for which see below) for several organisms. A symbol can have the same meaning for several organisms because its initial uses occur in contexts involving several organisms. [WAU.]

for which an implicit response stands. Thus, the meaning *of* a proposition (Dewey's use) is a pair of related overt responses which "occur" implicitly as a proposition. It is the meaning of a proposition which non-Deweyans refer to by 'proposition.' Dewey uses 'proposition' so as to include the suggestion that it is a *proposal* because of his views concerning the essential function which language performs in inquiry.

Since the production of *any* sound, mark or gesture can become an implicit response (implicit responses as well as words as marks on paper or sounds are in this sense matters of convention), and since a sentence as uttered in the context of inquiry is the result of a group of implicit responses, different sentences can "express" the same proposition (ordinary uses). For example, the response which consists in uttering 'dog' might just as well have been associated by conditioning with overt responses to cats as the implicit response of uttering 'cat.'

The meaning (idea) of a sentence, *i.e.,* a proposition, must be distinguished from the meaning (symbol) of a sentence. The meaning (symbol) of a sentence is another sentence, just as the meaning (symbol) of a word is another word. We might call the meaning (idea) of a sentence *sentential meaning,* and the meaning (symbol) of a sentence *propositional meaning.* In this respect Dewey's theory of language shares with Peirce's a feature either ignored or inconsequentially treated by other theories of language and meaning. This feature is connected with that which Peirce called *Thirdness*. Symbols, according to Peirce and Dewey, differ from natural signs in the following respects. First, they are conventional. Secondly, they exhibit thirdness. Smoke means (signifies) fire not smoke. Similarly, 'smoke' means (symbol) "fire" not smoke. Meaning (symbol) is the analogue of signification. The characteristic of being a sign is reference to something else. Symbols differ from natural signs in having two relations of reference: designation and meaning (symbol). Natural signs have no analogue for designation.[8]

[8] In addition to the above explications of 'meaning' Dewey gives many others,

The explications of 'meaning' as meaning (idea) and meaning (symbol) enable Dewey to show how language functions in contexts of prediction and control which is one of the purposes of language as a tool for transforming some phase of the raw material

some of the more important of which are as follows.

"Meaning" is used in place of *'intention.'* We spean of meaningful activity having in mind intentional or purposeful activity. [Q. for C., p. 151; E & N., pp. 184-5; A. as E., p. 59]

Sometimes when we speak of the meaning of an utterance we might as well speak of its *purpose.* Thus, the meaning of a sentence, S, is to coordinate the behavior of speaker and hearer. One of the meanings (purposes) of language is the coordination of behavior. This is why the "utterances" of a phonograph are meaningless. They do not coordinate the behavior of speaker and hearer. [K. as SR., p. 354; E & N, pp. 184-5]

Sometimes in speaking of the meaning of a tool, we might as well speak of the *use* to which the tool can be put. We say a sentence has meaning (use) independently of particular circumstances. I can say, "This dog is brown" in the presence of Prince, Rover, etc. [WAU., p. 255] When we speak of the scientific meaning of a sentence we sometimes have reference to the fact that it is being used in inquiry. The æsthetic meaning (use) of an utterance is its use for expressing emotions or enjoyment.

A *consumatory meaning* is an idea whenever it occurs out of the context of inquiry; *i.e.,* when it serves a non-instrumental or non-sign function. [M. & E., p. 348; EinExl., pp. 13, 14] One of the meanings of an art object is the idea or ideas it causes in so far as they are not used inferentially or for purposes of prediction. Dewey says that consumatory meanings are not used. Consumatory meanings are sometimes called intrinsic meanings. It is possible that for purposes of aesthetics consumatory and intrinsic meanings might be distinguished.

Immanent meanings are ideas which have been repeatedly and successfully used. For example, when a sailor has repeatedly experienced the crack of bolt ropes and been led to expect that a sail has broken loose, the crack of bolt ropes has meaning (immanent) for him. We say that a thing has meaning in this sense when we recognize it. For a landsman the noise is a crack, for the sailor it is a sail broken loose. A crack and a sail loose are the respective meanings (immanent). [M&E., p. 349ff] Dewey uses 'object' technically to refer to things which have immanent meaning as distinct from those which do not.

Whatever ideas a situation stimulates are sometimes called the *meaning (suggestion)* of the situation. For example, flames mean (suggest) fire. However, we also tend to speak of a suggestion of which we are sure as a meaning, reserving suggestion for an idea of which we are not sure. When a suggestion occurs in the context of inquiry we sometimes use the word 'hypothesis' to refer to it. Sometimes hypotheses are called expectations or anticipations. [EinExL., p. 49; L., p. 109]

The emotion an art-object expresses or which it can help to bring about in a viewer is sometimes referred to as the *meaning (emotional)* of the art object. [A. as E., p. 73-4] Dewey explicitly denies that any linguistic medium has what Stevenson calls emotive meaning. [E. SM. and L.]

We say a thing or event has *meaning (extrinsic)* when it is one which stimulates ideas in us, *i.e.,* when it can be used as a sign. Dewey uses the term 'referential meaning' as a way of referring to its extrinsic meaning when a thing *is* used as a sign. 'Intrinsic meaning' is a way of referring to extrinsic meaning of a thing when it is not osed as a sign; *i.e.,* roughly, when the thing does not occur in a context of inquiry. [EinExL., p. 246] When intrinsic mean-of experience into new objects. Implicit responses (ideas) are ways of responding which enable an organism to control its experience in the sense that such responses do not commit the organism to further overt response as is the case if the organism responds overtly instead of implicitly. For example, if I respond to what seem to be flames in a building by running, no other overt response to the flame situation is possible in the situation in which I originally see the flames. If my response, however, is by implicit behavior (*i.e.*, symbol-behavior or thinking), my initial overt response to the flames may be either running away, approaching them, etc., depending on what my thinking about the situation indicates. Symbol behavior allows an organism to explore the possible consequences of a situation without participating actively in those consequences and thus losing control of its active response. Implicit response under certain conditions is prediction. Control of overt responses and hence of the total situation involves prediction.

Carnap has suggested that the traditional distinction between denotation and extension on the one hand and intension, connotation and meaning on the other contains two related distinctions. The first distinction is generally that between the value distribution of a propositional function and the function itself, more particularly and familiarly between a class and a property. The second distinction arises in connection with that which Carnap calls the *name-relation,* the relation between a name and whatever it names. This is the distinction of nominatum and sense or meaning. [M & N., pp. 126-7] I now wish to show that Dewey's analysis of language indicates that there are more than two distinctions involved, that they have been confused and that Dewey's analysis enables us to explicate whatever pairs of terms are required without referring to subsistent or abstract entities. We shall see that reference to such entities has resulted in part from confusing these distinctions and in part from ignoring the biological origins of language.

---

ings are involved in an æsthethic context, they are sometimes called aesthetic meanings. [A.asE., p. 73-4]

The *essence* or *essential meaning* of a thing or event, according to Dewey, is that sequence of ideas which an organism has selected by reason of interest from the total possible ideas a thing can stimulate as *the* meaning (idea).

We have found that Dewey makes the following distinctions in the types of meanings terms have. Generally, terms have two uses: concrete and abstract. They are used concretely when they are used to stand for existential things or events, in which case they either denote (stand for an individual thing) or mean extensionally (stand for a group of things). They are used abstractly when they stand for operational habits (connotation) or groups of related operational habits (comprehension). Thus, for the pair of concepts traditionally referred to by 'denotation'-'extension' and 'intension'-'connotation'-'meaning,' Dewey has the pairs denotation-connotation, extension-comprehension and the pair of uses: concrete and abstract.

It is the distinction between concrete and abstract use (without the refinements of Dewey's denotation, extension, connotation and comprehension) which present philosophers of language, such as Carnap, Church, Eaton, C. I. Lewis and Quine *sometimes* seem to have in mind when they write respectively of extension-intension, denotation-sense, denotation-connotation, denotation-intension and designation-meaning. Thus, Church [R.C., p. 301] holds that the denotation of a predicator is a class (*i.e.*, Dewey's extension); the sense of a predicator is a property (*i.e.*, Dewey's connotation); and the denotation of 'unicorn' is the null class (Dewey would say that 'unicorn' has neither denotation nor extension, it connotes). Carnap indicates that that which he has in mind by extension and intension is roughly the same as that which Church has in mind by denotation and sense. [M & N., pp. 23 and 125][9] I will show that the other authors seem to have this distinction in mind after I call attention to the other distinctions Dewey makes.

Dewey's analysis requires a further distinction in connection with the concrete and abstract uses of terms.[10] All terms designate or stand for something. Words concretely used designate existen-

---

* Dewey's distinction between denotation and extension is apparently given in Carnap's work by the distinction between, say, predicators and individual expressions which have their own kind of intension and extension. [N&N., p. 32ff]

[10] Terms are words which can be used concretely or abstractly. Logical constants are probably a different kind of word altogether. There is not space to discuss them here.

tial things or events and words abstractly used designate habits. Designation includes denotation, extension, connotation and comprehension in Dewey's use. Words in their concrete use, however, stand for something in two ways. They stand for an existential thing or group of things and they stand for an habitual response to those things. As implicit responses, that is, they replace the overt response to the thing, the response which would be made were the thing present in the experience of the organism in a non-linguistic context. Thus, words in their concrete use have, so to speak, an extra-organic and an organic "reference," whereas words in their abstract uses have only an organic "reference."

The distinction between concrete and abstract use is made with respect to the notion of designation or standing for something. Dewey's theory of language requires a further distinction between *designation* and something else which we have called symbol meaning, or what may hereafter be called *meaning*. The distinction between designation and meaning is exemplified in the case of a concrete word as follows: the designation of "smoke" is smoke, the meaning of 'smoke' is 'fire' (more strictly, *a* meaning of 'smoke' is 'fire'). All words which are used abstractly or concretely have both designation and meaning. Thus, designation and meaning constitute a second pair of explicata for the explicanda denotation-extension and intension-connotation-meaning in their traditional uses.[11]

[11] Although a traditional distinction has been made between this pair, no proof that the distinction was necessary was given till Frege [S&B.]. Generally Frege's argument is that we must distinguish the nominatum and sense of an expression to account for the difference between analytic and synthetic propositions. Frege evidently used 'nominatum' as Dewey uses 'denotation' and the use is clear. His use of 'sense' is, however, puzzling. I have shown elsewhere [F's S&B.] that the sense of a word may be interpreted within the limits of Frege's proof as the word itself as a mark on paper or a sound. Thus, the nominata of 'Morning Star' and 'Evening Star' are the same, but their senses differ. However, it will be seen that Dewey's analysis of language furnishes further possibilities for explicating sense. For the sense of a word may be the overt response for which it stands. Furthermore, it may be the symbol meaning. Since concrete terms designate in two ways, we have therein a further explanation for the confusion in explicating denotation-extension and intension-meaning-connotation in connection wholly with designation (Dewey's use). The *proof,* that is, that a distinction between the two sets is required will allow for a distinction either between two kinds of designation which we find in the case of concrete terms, or between Dewey's designation and meaning.

Designation and meaning as applied to words have analogues for sentences, referred to in Part I as sentential and propositional meaning.

The distinction between concrete and abstract use, and designation and meaning has been made clear only by Dewey. However, most explications of the connotation-meaning-intension member of the traditional pair imply Dewey's further distinction. The implication seems to have been confused by a view that any distinction has to be made wholly with respect to designation (Dewey's); in Dewey's terms, that words have designation but not meaning and "meaning" is a kind of designation.

Eaton [*Logic*, chp. vi] was close to avoiding the confusion, but apparently only because he was less explicit than more recent writers. He distinguished denotation and connotation and terms extensionally and intensionally used, and defined extension as the class of things to which a general term refers and the connotation of a general term as "all the other terms *necessarily implied* by it." [*Logic*, p. 243] The view of the connotation of a term as other *terms* is similar to Dewey's notion of meaning. However, the context of Eaton's writing in this connection does not make clear whether he is always aware of the distinction between designation and meaning; or *i.e.*, between a thing and a word. For example, he employs the word 'universal' indiscriminately to refer to words and universals, sometimes indicating a universal is a word and sometimes indicating it is something non-linguistic like a Platonic entity.

Carnap's concepts of extension and intension also embody the confusion between designation and meaning. He says, "two designators *have the same extension* . . . =df they are equivalent" and "two designators *have the same intension* . . .=df they are L-equivalent. . . ." [M&N., p. 23] He also writes that the extension of a predicator (say, 'white') is a class, its intension a property. The extension of a sentence is its truth value, its intension a proposition. The use of the concept of L-equivalence with its possible relation to "necessarily implies" suggests that Carnap has a view of intension which is similar to Eaton's connotation. However, the phrase "have the same intensions," Carnap's search for "suitable entities" which are intensions and his view that a proposition is a non-linguistic non-organic entity show that he does not make the distinction between designation and meaning. The phrase 'have the same intension' or referring to words as having the same intension suggests that the intension is something non-linguistic to which the words refer. This suggestion is supported by the search for suitable entities which are intensions and is confirmed by the view that the intension of a sentence is a non-linguistic, non-organic thing. Thus, since the meaning of a word as Dewey describes it *is* a word, it follows that Carnap's distinction between extension and intension is not that between designation and meaning.

C. I. Lewis' explanations of what he calls denotation and intension are similar to Eaton's distinctions. [A. of KV., pp. 39 ff and chp. vi] The intension of a term is "the conjunction of all other terms which must be applicable to anything to which the given term would be correctly applicable." He holds that the intension of a term is *other terms*. Thus, there is a resemblance to Dewey's concept of meaning. However, the view that *any* of the terms which is part of the intension of a given term "must be applicable to anything to which the given term would be correctly applicable" indicates a confusion between Lewis' intension and denotation. According to Dewey 'fire' is a part of the meaning of 'smoke' but it is certainly not applicable to anything to which "smoke" is applicable. The same observation must be made with respect to Eaton's "necessarily implied," Carnap's "L-equivalence" and W. V. Quine's 'synonymous,' which are used to explain "meaning."[12] These are all concepts connected with designation not meaning (Dewey's).

Furthermore, within intension Lewis distinguishes linguistic meaning and sense meaning. As far as I can make out this is similar to Dewey's distinction between a word (as the implicit response of uttering a sound) and the overt response or habit of response for which it stands (designates). The distinction between linguistic and sense meaning is essential, but the reference to both as a type of intension further indicates that Lewis' intension is not com-

[12] According to Quine "the meaning of an expression is the class of all the expressions synonymous with it." [N. on E&N., p. 120]

parable to Dewey's meaning and that it is in fact not clearly distinguished from Lewis' denotation.

It may now be seen that Dewey's analysis of language bears on the problem of nominalism *vs.* realism in three ways. First, his interpretation of linguistic, and hence intellectual activities as a continuation of biological activities furnishes explications for various uses of 'meaning' in terms of organic activities such as habits, responses and implicit responses. Further understanding of these terms is the task of the biologist and psychologist, but for ordinary purposes the terms are clearly and easily used.

Secondly, Dewey's analysis helps us with the puzzle about universals by placing it in a new context. It enables us to see at least in one way that the universals with which knowledge and discourse deal or which constitute knowledge and discourse are either habits of overt response or habits of implicit response. It illuminates the earlier nominalists' insistence that universals are words by showing us more clearly what words are. It replaces the search for an objective counterpart of concepts, things "outside the mind," with the study of the behavior of biological organisms, or contexts in which there is biological and linguistic activity. We see that the phenomena of universality and meaning, the traditional "objects of knowledge" are a type of organic activity; that there is no problem of an existential counterpart to mental activities conceived in isolation. The "objective meanings" are other organic activities. Knowledge and communicating knowledge have indeed "to do with universals" as Plato maintained, but the knowledge and communications *are* the universals.[13]

Finally, Dewey's distinction between designation and meaning helps us with the puzzle about universals in another way by clarifying the confusion with respect to denotation-extension and intension-meaning-connotation. Most writers making the distinction

[13] The change in attitude toward the problem of universals from the Platonic or realistic to the Deweyan is difficult. People will for some time be urged to ask, "But why does a table differ from a mountain? Dewey does not answer this." And it will continue to be difficult to see that this question, together with all of its variations which seem to require us to think of objective universals, is not significant. As long as we ask the question we shall be puzzled about universals. Dewey's analysis of language helps us to stop asking the question by finding that knowledge can be explained without asking it.

wholly in connection with designation have given confused interpretations of meaning by taking it as a kind of designation. In Peirce's terms they have overlooked thirdness.[14] Terms have been taken as standing for two kinds of entities, designations and meanings. This results either in overlooking meaning altogether (*i.e.*, the linguistic analogue of Dewey's signification), or in postulating all kinds of peculiar entities as the "meaning" of a term or sentence. The meaning "reference" of a word has been regarded as a non-linguistic entity just as denotations and extensions (Dewey's) are non-linguistic. Since words are universals in the sense that each stands for several things, the confusion between designation and meaning has required the possibility of existential universals which are the meanings of words.

[14] Taking meaning as a kind of designation is related to or responsible for the representative as opposed to the instrumental theory of knowledge. It is no coincidence that Dewey pays his respects to Peirce's theory of signs as well as his theory of knowledge.

BIBLIOGRAPHY

A. as E. — *Art as Experience*, John Dewey, Minton, Balch and Co., N.Y., 1934.
A. of KV. — *An Analysis of Knowledge and Valuation*, C. I. Lewis, Open Court, 1946.
E&N. — *Experience and Nature*, J. Dewey, Morton and Co., N.Y., 1929.
EinExL. — *Essays in Experimental Logic*, J. Dewey, University of Chicago Press, 1916.
E. SM. & L. — "Ethical Subject-Matter and Language," J. Dewey, *Jn. of Philosophy*, vol. 42, no. 26, Dec., 1945, pp. 701-12.
K. as SR. — "Knowledge and Speech Reaction," J. Dewey, *Jn. of Philosophy*, vol. 29, no. 21, Oct., 1922.
L. — *Logic*, J. Dewey, Henry Holt and Co., N.Y., 1938.
Logic — *General Logic*, R. M. Eaton, Scribners, N.Y., 1931.
M&E. — "Meaning and Existence," J. Dewey, *Jn. of Philosophy*, vol. 25 June, 1928.
M&N. — *Meaning and Necessity*, R. Carnap, University of Chicago Press, 1947.
N on E&N.— "Notes on Existence and Necessity," W. V. Quine, *Jn. of Philosophy*, vol. 40, Mar., 1943, pp. 113ff.
Peirce — "Peirce's Theory of Linguistic Signs, Thought and Meaning," J. Dewey, *Jn. of Philosophy*, vol. 43, no. 4, 1946 pp. 85-95.
Q. for C. — *The Quest for Certainty*, J. Dewey, Minton, Balch and Co., N.Y., 1929.
R.C. — "Carnap's Introduction to Semantics," Alonzo Church, *Philosophical Review*, vol. 52, 1943, pp. 298-304.
S&B. — *"Über Sinn und Bedeutung,"* G. Frege, *Zeitschrift für Philosophie und Philosophische Kritik*, 1892.
SS. — "The Significant Symbol," G. H. Mead, *Jn. of Philosophy*, vol. 19, p. 157.
WAU. — "What are Universals?", J. Dewey, *Jn. of Philosophy*, vol. 33, no. 11, May, 1936.
F'S&B. — "Frege's *Sinn und Bedeutung*," P. Wienpahl, *Mind*, April, 1950.

Language, Rules and Behavior*

by WILFRID SELLARS

MY PURPOSE in writing this essay is to explore from the standpoint of what might be called a philosophically oriented behavioristic psychology the procedures by which we evaluate actions as right or wrong, arguments as valid and invalid and cognitive claims as well or ill grounded. More specifically, our frame of reference will be the psychology of rule-regulated behavor, or rather, since such a science as yet scarcely exists, it will be such anticipations of a psychology of the so-called higher processes as can be precipitated from common sense by the reagents synthesized by the naturalistic revolution in psychology instituted within the memory and with the vigorous assistance of the man to whom this volume is dedicated. Within these coordinates I shall attempt to map a true *via media* (one which doesn't covertly join up with one or other extreme beyond the next bend in the road) between rationalistic a-priorism and what, for want of a better term, I shall call "descriptivism," by which I understand the claim that all meaningful con-

---

*The present paper has grown out of the stimulating discussions with my friend and colleague, Herbert Feigl, which it has been my good fortune to enjoy over the past three years. It was precipitated by a reading of an early draft of his paper, "De Principiis non Disputandum—?" which will appear in a volume of *Essays in Analytic Philosophy*, edited by Max Black, to be published in the fall of 1950 by the Cornell University Press. There the reader will find an exceptionally clear statement of puzzles relating to the justifiability of First Principles, together with a brilliant and original analysis of the various forms taken by the "appeal to Reason."

cepts and problems belong to the empirical or descriptive sciences, including the sciences of human behavior.

Those who deny the existence of such a *via media* offer the following argument: "How can one assert the existence of concepts and problems which do not belong to empirical science, without admitting the existence of a domain of non-empirical objects or qualities together with a mental apparatus of acts and intuitions for cognizing them?" The rationalists add a minor premise of the form, "Concepts and problems relating to validity, truth and obligation are significant, but do not belong to the empirical sciences," and conclude, "Therefore a domain of non-empirical qualities and a corresponding apparatus of acts and intuitions exist." The descriptivist, on the other hand, denying, as he does, the rationalists' conclusion while accepting their major premise, finds himself forced to deny the minor premise. Clearly he can do this either by maintaining that the concepts and problems to which the rationalists appeal are pseudo-concepts and pseudo-problems, or by claiming that, though legitimate, they are, after all, included within the scope of empirical science. In the field of moral philosophy, descriptivistically inclined philosophers characteristically divide into those who claim that the concept of moral obligation is a pseudo-concept, such words as "right" and "duty" serving merely to express attitudes and instigate actions, and those who accept some form of the venerable subjectivistic account now widely known as the "autobiographical analysis."

I can now bring my introductory remarks to a focus by supposing a suspicious pragmatist to ask: "Are you, perhaps, leading up to the following argument?

>Pragmatists are descriptivists
>Descriptivism entails Mill's philosophy of mathematics
>But Mill's philosophy of mathematics is absurd
>Therefore pragmatism is absurd

If you are indeed raising this old chestnut, it can be said right away that pragmatism is by no means committed to what it grants is an absurd interpretation of mathematics. The pragmatist merely insists that there is no aspect of *mathematical inquiry as a mode of human behavior* which requires a departure from the categories of naturalistic psychology for its interpretation. If this is what you call descriptivism, then the pragmatist is a descriptivist, but in that case, descriptivism does not have the absurd consequences with which you threaten us."

Let me reply to this challenge by immediately disavowing any intention of accusing pragmatism of being a descriptivistic philosophy *as a matter of principle*. Indeed, there are clearly certain areas, one of which is exactly the philosophy of mathematics, in which pragmatism has explicitly rejected the descriptivist account, while expressing sympathy with its naturalistic motivation. Notice that our suspicious pragmatist did not say

"The concepts and problems of mathematics belong to naturalistic psychology."

If he had, he clearly would be formulating a descriptivistic philosophy of mathematics. What he actually said was

"... there is no aspect of *mathematical inquiry as a mode of human behavior* which requires a departure from the categories of naturalistic psychology for its interpretation."

With this latter statement I am in full agreement. It must by no means be confused with the former. If it entails a descriptivistic philosophy of mathematics, it must be shown to do so by an involved argument of a type familiar to students of the rationalistic tradition. Needless to say, I do not believe that such an argument would be successful.

But if I do not accuse the pragmatist of being a descriptivist as a matter of principle, I do contend that pragmatism has been characterized by a descriptivistic bias. Thus, while it has defended the important insight that to reject descriptivism in the philosophy of mathematics is not to embrace rationalism, it has committed itself to descriptivism in other areas of philosophy (*e.g.* in its interpretation of truth and of moral obligation) with all the fervor of a

Dutch boy defending the fertile lands of Naturalism against a threatening rationalistic flood. Now it will be my contention in this paper that a sound pragmatism must reject descriptivism in all areas of philosophy, and that it can do so without giving one jot or tittle of comfort to what has so aptly been called the new Failure of Nerve. My point of departure will be an examination of the forms taken by our appeals to standards and principles when we *justify* something we have done.

What sort of thing, then, is a justification? Before attempting to answer this question, it will be worth our while to consider a familiar challenge to our right to raise it. Those who are alert to raise their voices on behalf of psychology will insist that to justify is to *do* something, to perform a mental action. To explain mental action is the business of the psychologist, and if he is not yet in a position to give a satisfactory acount, if the truth must wait until he is adequately grounded in the behavior of the *rattus albinus Norvegicus,* the question nevertheless belongs to him. It is not a more legitimate concern of the philosopher than, say, the question, What is gravitation? If the philosopher objects that this same argument would excuse the logician from examining reasoning and the philosopher of science from examining explanation, he is promptly told that these very parallels make it clear that his business is to explicate the *correctness* or *validity* of justifications, and not the causal structure of justifications as matters of psychological *fact.*

But is it so obvious that by concerning ourselves with the correctness or validity of justifications we have moved from one field called psychology to another called philosophy? If validity or correctness is a property of certain mental processes, then does it not fall within the province of psychology to tell us about this property and its opposite invalidity or incorrectness? Or shall we say that psychology deals with some but not all of the properties exhibited by psychological processes? And if not with all, then what distinguishes the properties with which it does deal from those with which it does not? Furthermore, must not the latter fall within the scope, if not of psychology, then of some branch of empirical anthropology?

Has, then, our philosophical problem turned out, after all, to be one of empirical science? Or shall we perhaps say that validity is a non-empirical property, and that, together with other non-empirical properties it falls within the scope of a non-empirical science of thought, a rational psychology? Is, perhaps, epistemology the non-empirical science of such non-empirical properties of thought as validity and truth? Could the propositions of such a science be anything but synthetic *a priori* truths?

How shall we choose between these alternatives? Or perhaps we have already made a mistake in speaking of validity as a property which can be exemplified by psychological processes; so that these alternatives do not even arise. If so, how could this be determined? Clearly we have come to the point where what is required is an exploration of some typical contexts in which the terms "valid" and "correct" appear to be properly, shall I say correctly, employed.

We began by asking "What sort of thing is a justification?" We should also ask "What sort of thing does one who justifies justify?" Consider the following exchange:

Jones: I stayed away from the meeting.
Smith (pompously): How would you justify your conduct?

Clearly, then, it is proper to speak of justifying *actions*. How is it done? The above exchange continues:

Jones: One ought to do what is conducive to the greatest happiness of the greatest number, and, as I could readily convince you, staying away from the meeting was so conducive.

We are thus reminded that to justify a piece of conduct is to argue concerning the conduct, and, what is more important, that at least the earlier stages of such an argument consist in subsuming the conduct under what used to be called a moral law. Characteristic of moral laws is the use of the word "ought" in its categorical sense.

Now, I must confess that I find the emotive theory of moral obligation as unacceptable as would be an emotive theory of logical necessity, or (*pace* Hume) an emotive theory of physical necessity. This is not to say that I agree with the intuitionists in finding a non-natural quality or relation to belong to actions over and above their empirical characteristics. As I see it, an inventory of the basic qualities and relations exemplified by this universe of ours, and, in particular, by the mental processes of human beings, would no more include obligatoriness than it would include either logical or physical (that is, "real") connections. Although I have felt ever since making its acquaintance that the intuitionism of Ross, Prichard and Ewing is the only contemporary philosophy of morals which is reasonably faithful to the phenomenology of moral thought and experience, I have been equally convinced that we must look elsewhere for an adequate insight into the nature of the *ought* which they so rightly find to be central to the moral universe of discourse. For a time I thought that this insight was to be sought in the direction taken by emotive theories. I now regard this as a mistake—not because the ethical "ought" isn't *essentially* an expressor and instigator, but because what it expresses and instigates is *the observance of a rule*. To make the ethical "ought" into even the second cousin of the "hurrah" of a football fan is completely to miss its significance. If I have become more and more happy of late about Kant's assimilation of the ethical "ought" to the logical and physical "musts," it is because I have increasingly been led to assimilate the logical and physical "musts" to the ethical "ought." But of this more later.

Let us now examine the process of justification in another type of context. Consider the following exchange:

Jones: It will rain shortly.
Smith: Justify your assertion.

Clearly it is proper to speak of justifying assertions, which are, in a suitably broad sense, *actions*. It is equally proper to speak of justifying beliefs, which are, at least in part, dispositions relating to assertion. Shall we say, then, that one does not justify a *proposition*, but the *assertion* of a proposition?—that one does not justify a *principle*, but the *acceptance* of a principle? Shall we say that all justification is, in a sense which takes into account the dispositional as well as the occurrent, a *justificatio actionis?* I am strongly inclined to think that this is the case. But if so, is not our new example of justification as much a justification of conduct as was the first? Or can we distinguish within action in the broadest sense, between action which is conduct and action which is not? and if so how?[1]

However this may be, Smith, in the above dialogue, has asked Jones to justify a certain assertion, and Jone's reply to this challenge is certainly relevant to our problem. The exchange continues:

Jones: Clouds of kind X cause rain, and there are clouds of kind X overhead.

Once again we have before us an argument of a familiar form. I want now to focus attention on three directions the argument might take if continued beyond this point.

(1) The justification will achieve its purpose only if Smith accepts the causal premise. If Smith should ask "Why *must* clouds of kind X be accompanied by rain?" Jones may either say, "Because they must, and that's all there is to it!" or, if he is in a position to do so, he may draw on his knowledge of meteorology in an attempt

[1] Certainly it won't do to say that that which is criticized as conduct is overt behavior, an individual's impingement on his environment, so that *public* assertion would be conduct, whereas the *private* assertion that is involved in thinking would not. For surely the mental setting oneself (Prichard) to stab an enemy would be conduct even though paralysis or a stroke of lightning prevented the occurrence of the intended sequence of events. Bearing in mind this obvious connection between conduct and *intention*, shall we say that what the moralist has in mind by "conduct" is basically a matter of the tendency of *thoughts about* sequences of events beginning with the me-here-now to bring about the actual occurrence of these sequences? Do not primitive and pictorial mis-conceptions of desire, motivation and the role of reward and punishment in shaping behavior stand in the way of a recognition of the true scope of "ideo-motor activity?"

to derive this law from other laws relating to atmospheric phenomena which are accepted by Smith. If Smith should challenge these new *musts,* and Jones is willing to continue the argument, but is unable to find still other laws which Smith will accept and from which they can be derived, he may attempt to persuade Smith to accept them (or the original law) by means of an argument from instances.[2]

(2) The justification will achieve its purpose only if Smith accepts the minor premise ("There are clouds of kind X overhead"). If Smith challenges this assertion, Jones, if he is willing to continue the argument, will attempt to find statements of particular matters of fact—let us call them *historical* statements—and causal laws which Smith accepts, and from which it would follow that there were (or that it was probable that there were) clouds of kind X overhead.

(3) Finally, the justification will achieve its purpose only if Smith accepts the logical *musts* embodied in the arguments Jones offers, as when he says "A and B, therefore *necessarily* C." If Smith challenges these, Jones is likely to say "It is necessary because it is necessary, and that's all there is to it!"

Now, when certain contemporary philosophers hear the words "must" and "necessary," particularly in such contexts as "It must because it must," or "It's necessary, and that's all there is to it," they immediately say to themselves, "Aha! Here we have something that is required by a rule of this fellow's language." And I am convinced that this is a very illuminating thing to say, though I am not certain that I know exactly what it means. As Augustine with

[2] In dealing with such situations, philosophers usually speak of inductive arguments, of establishing laws by induction from instances. For reasons which will manifest themselves in the course of my argument, I am highly dubious of this conception. I should be inclined to say that the use Jones will make of instances is rather of the nature of Socratic method. For Socratic method serves the purpose of making explicit the rules we have adopted for thought and action, and I shall be interpreting our judgments to the effect that A causally necessitates B as the expression of a rule governing our use of the terms '"A" and "B." But of this, more later.

Time, I knew what a rule was until asked. I asked myself and proceeded to become quite perplexed.

I suspect that my trouble with the concept of a rule is in large part due to my ignorance of the psychology of the higher processes. Yet certain things seem clear. In the first place, we must distinguish between action which merely *conforms to* a rule, and action which occurs *because of* a rule. A rule isn't functioning as a rule unless it is in some sense internal to action. Otherwise it is a mere generalization. Thus, if I train an animal to sit up when I snap my fingers, the animal's behavior conforms to the generalization "This animal sits up when my fingers snap," but we should scarcely say that the animal acts on the rule of sitting up when I snap my fingers. Clearly the type of activity which is rule-regulated is of a higher level than that which is produced by simple animal learning procedures. One way of bringing this out is to say that most if not all animal behavior is tied to the environment in a way in which much characteristically human behavior is not. Certainly, we learn habits of response to our environment in a way which is essentially identical with that in which the dog learns to sit up when I snap my fingers. And certainly these learned habits of response—though modifiable by rule-regulated symbol activity— remain the basic tie between all the complex rule-regulated symbol behavior which is the human mind in action, and the environment in which the individual lives and acts. Yet above the foundation of man's learned responses to environmental stimuli—let us call this his *tied behavior*—there towers a superstructure of more or less developed systems of rule-regulated symbol activity which constitutes man's intellectual vision. It is in terms of such systems of rule-regulated symbol activity that we are to understand an Einstein's grasp of alternative structures of natural law, a Leibnitz' vision of the totality of all possible worlds, a logician's exploration of the most diversified postulate systems, a Cantor's march into the trans-finite. Such symbol activity may well be characterized as *free*—by which, of course, I do not mean *uncaused*—in contrast to the behavior that is learned as a dog learns to sit up, or a white rat to run a maze. On the other hand, a structure of rule-regulated symbol activity, which as such is free, constitutes a man's understanding of *this* world, the world in which he lives, its history and future, the laws according to which it operates, by meshing in with his tied behavior, his learned habits of response to his environment. To say that man is a rational animal, is to say that man is a creature not of *habits,* but of *rules.* When God created Adam, he whispered in his ear, "In all contexts of action you will recognize rules, if only the rule to grope for rules to recognize. When you cease to recognize rules, you will walk on four feet."

If what I have just said appears to be rhetoric and not philosophy, I can only plead that it ought to be psychology, but that if an adequate psychology of rule-governed symbol behavior exists, I have not yet made its acquaintance. This, however, may well be just another example of the philosopher's characteristic ignorance of the science of his day (as opposed to the science of yesterday, with which he is notoriously well acquainted). But if what we have been saying belongs to psychology, then, once again, we must ask, "How does it concern us, who are philosophers and not psychologists?" What would be the relevance of an adequate empirical psychology of rule-regulated symbol activity to the task of the philosopher? Now, that psychology is neither the whole nor even a part of philosophy is granted. Yet bad psychology may give aid and comfort to bad philosophy. This is most clear in connection with the rationalistic pseudo-psychologies which we shall be criticizing in a moment. I want now to point out that if there is any truth in what we have said, then much of what (among philosophers) passes for tough-minded psychology is an over-simplified extension to the higher processes of the *dog—fingersnap—sit-up—sugar* schema of tied responses to environmental stimuli. Not that I should deny for one moment that animal learning theory provides the key to all psychological phenomena. On the contrary I am convinced that this is the case. And not that I should deny that the laws of animal learning (if we had them) would explain even the mathematician's behavior in developing alternative postulate sets for n-dimensional geometries. I am even prepared to endorse this promissory note. Yet the fact remains that the distinction between tied behavior and free, rule-regulated symbol activity, whatever they may have in common, is a fact of experience, one that the philosopher cannot afford to neglect.

We distinguished above between action which merely conforms to a rule and action which occurs because of a rule and pointed out that in so far as actions merely conform to it, a rule is not a rule but a mere generalization. On the other hand, we must not say that a rule is something completely other than a generalization. The mode of existence of a rule is as a generalization written in flesh and blood, or nerve and sinew, rather than in pen and ink. A rule, existing in its proper element, has the logical form of a generalization. Yet a rule is not *merely* a generalization which is formulated in the language of intra-organic process. Such a generalization would find its overt expression in a declarative sentence. A rule, on the other hand, finds its expression either in what are classified as non-declarative grammatical forms, or else in declarative sentences with certain special terms such as "correct," "proper," "right," etc., serving to distinguish them from generalizations. What do these special features in the formulation of rules indicate? They give expression to the fact that a rule is an embodied generalization which to speak loosely but suggestively, tends to make itself true. Better, it tends to inhibit the occurrence of such events as would falsify it—if it weren't already false, that is, for the generalizations which lie at the core of rules are rarely if ever true, and unless they *could* (logical *or* physical possibility) be false, they could scarcely function as rules. Thus, consider the moral rule, "One ought to tell the truth." The core-generalization on which this rule is built is "People always say what they believe" which is, of course, false.

Now, Kant saw all this quite clearly. He pointed out that moral action is action because of a rule, and said that to say this is equivalent to saying that to act morally is to act "so that I could also will that my maxim should become a universal law."[3] If he had said in-

[3] *Fundamental Principles of the Metaphysics of Morals*, p. 18 of Abbott's translation, included in his *Kant's Theory of Ethics*. The historically minded reader will observe that the concept of rule-regulated behavior developed in this paper is, in a certain sense, the translation into behavioristic terms of the Kantian concept of Practical Reason. Kant's contention that the pure consciousness of

stead that to act morally is to act as though the truth of the corresponding generalization depended only on the occurrence of that action, his claim would have been essentially identical with ours. As far as I can see, the basic fault of Kant's ethics is that he attempted (or seems to have attempted) to derive a specific code of rules from the definition of moral action as action because of rules together with a consideration of the basic traits of human nature.

Now, my chief purpose in making the above metaphorical and unscientific remarks about rule-governed behavior is to stimulate those philosophers who are always talking about rules— usually rules of language—to explain more fully what they have in mind. To urge that these are questions for the empirical psychologist to answer, and that we must wait upon his convenience, is to leave the field of cognitive and moral psychology to the rationalists. To content oneself with glib phrases about stimulus-response conditioning is to give the rationalist armor and armament. (In the good old days before the failure of nerve, when the climate of opinion was favorable to empiricism, the empiricist got away with murder. Today, he must use every weapon in his arsenal, and make doubly certain that it is sharp.) It is easy to shape the psychology of the higher processes as embodied in common sense into the direction of intuitionism and rationalism. Philosophers have been doing just that for over two thousand years. But common sense also contains cues which, when combined with the achievements to date of empirical psychology, can be developed into the outlines of an adequate psychology of rational behavior, and to do this is an urgent task for the embattled empiricist. In thus reconstructing common sense psychology, the empiricist will find that the outcome shows more *structural* kinship with the pseudo-psychologies of the rationalist than

---

moral law can be a factor in bringing about conduct in conformity with law, becomes the above conception of rule-regulated behavior. However, for Kant's conception of Practical Reason as, so to speak, an intruder in the natural order, we substitute the view that the causal efficacy of the embodied core-generalizations of rules is ultimately grounded on the Law of Effect, that is to say, the role of rewards and punishments in shaping behavior. The most serious barrier to an appreciation of Kant's insights in this matter lies in the fact that most discussions in philosophical circles of the motivation of behavior stand to the scientific account (whatever its inadequacies) as the teleological conception of the adjustment of organisms to their environment stands to the evolutionary account.

with much that passes today for psychology among empiricists. But the teeth will have been drawn. It is only by absorbing the insights of rationalism that a pragmatic empiricism can do justice to the facts. There are many signs that this is being done.

I have already indicated how I would approach this reconciliation of rationalism and empiricism in the field of ethics. I want now to turn to the problem of the *a priori* in the field of specifically cognitive activity. Here we note that where the *regulist* speaks of statements which exhibit the rules of the language in which they are formulated, the *rationalist* speaks of intuition or self-evidence. The regulist goes from object-language up to meta-linguistic rule, whereas the rationalist goes from object-language down to extra-linguistic reality. The regulist explains the significance of the word "must," as it occurs in arguments, in terms of the syntactical rules of the language in which it occurs; the rationalist explains it in terms of a non-linguistic grasp of a necessary connection between features of reality.

Now, certain overly enthusiastic regulists have spoken of the "sense meaning rules" of a language, arguing that the hook-up of an empirically meaningful language with the world is a matter of rules of linguistic usage. I am as convinced a regulist as any, and, as I shall indicate in a moment, a far more thoroughgoing regulist than most, but I regard this as a mistake. I have already argued above that the hook-up between rule-regulated symbol activity and the external environment rests on the *meshing* of rule-regulated symbol activity with what I referred to as "tied behavior." Now though this tied behavior is not *rule-regulated* symbol behavior, it is nevertheless customary to refer to certain forms it may take as "symbol behavior." Let us distinguish this symbol behavior by the phrase "tied symbol behavior." Thus we can say that picking up his dish is a tied symbol of food to a dog. Now, what misleads these regulists who speak of the sense meaning rules of a language is the fact that in order for the above mentioned meshing of rule-regulated language with tied symbol behavior to take place, *certain intra-organic events must function as symbols in both senses, as both free and tied symbols.* Thus, as children we learn to understand the noise "blue" in much the same way as the dog learns to understand the noise "bone," but we leave the dog behind in that the noise "blue" also comes to function for us in a system of rule-regulated symbol activity, and it is a *word,* a linguistic fact, a rule-regulated symbol only in so far as it functions in this linguistic system. The noise "blue" becomes a mediating link between what can suggestively be called a rule-regulated calculus, and a cluster of conditioned responses which binds us to our environment. Here we should note that the rules which inter-relate these mediating symbols *qua* linguistic symbols must mesh with the inter-relationships of these symbols *qua* tied symbols in the causal structure of tied sign behavior.[4]

Let me nail down the point I have been making as tightly as I am able, even though this means anticipating certain things I shall have to say later on. To think of a system of qualities and relations is, I shall argue, to use symbols governed by a system of rules which, we might say, *implicitly define* these symbols by giving them a specific task to perform in the linguistic economy. The linguistic meaning of a word is entirely constituted by the rules of its use.[5] A scientist who thinks of worlds which exemplify quali-

[4] Linguistic systems of the kind we are considering center around a structure of sentences which is, so to speak, a *map.* Thus, a language enables us to "find our way around in the world." Clearly this involves that in the employment of a language, not only must certain *predicates* in the language play the above double role, so also must certain *individual constants.* It is also obvious that the individual constants which do this must, from the logician's standpoint, be logical constructions from the basic individual constants of the language, since "recognizable individuals" are always "continuants" or "concrete universals." Thus, not only do "green" and "sweet" function both as linguistic symbols proper and as tied symbols, so also do "Jones" and "Picadilly."

[5] At this point, the reader will probably hurl the following challenge: "Are you not confronted by a dilemma? For surely the rules for a linguistic system are themselves linguistic phenomena. Therefore either you must hold that they, in turn, are rule-governed, or else admit that at least one linguistic structure exists which is not "rule-governed" in your sense. You can scarcely be prepared to adopt the latter course. If you take the former, you are committed, surely, to an infinity of rules, meta-rules, meta-meta-rules, etc." A full reply to this challenge cannot be given in the available space. The following remarks, however, may help. The reader is quite correct in predicting that we shall take the former course and grant that the rules are themselves rule-governed He is, however, mistaken in inferring that this "regress" is vicious. It would be vicious if

ties and relations not to be found in this world is making use of symbols which are, or may be, on a par with the symbols we use to think about *this* world *in every rule-regulated respect*. The "artificial" language with which the scientist is speculating does not, however, include— as does the language in which he speaks about the actual world—a sub-set of symbols which mesh in with his tied symbol responses to environmental stimuli.

If there were such things as sense meaning rules (as opposed to verbal conditionings) how should they be formulated? Perhaps: "When I have such and such experiences, I am to use the expression 'I see red' "? Unfortunately, the philosophers who speak of sense meaning rules are the same *moderni* who insist that there is no such thing as cognition unmediated by symbols. Whether or not such a rule as the above would be sensible given the non-symbolic intuitive cognition of the rationalist is another matter, but without it the rule obviously either doesn't make sense or doesn't perform the function for which it was invoked. In order for the rule to be intelligible, the person who is to obey it must already know when he sees red. But to know when he sees red he must, according to these same *moderni,* understand the meaning of either the symbol "red" or a synonym (which need not, of course, belong to any intersubjective language of *overt* utterance). In short, the very symbols whose possession of meaning is explained by these overly enthusiastic regulists in terms of sense meaning rules, must either already have meaning independently of the rules, or else the sole value of the rules is to serve as a means of acquiring synonyms for symbols which have meaning independently of the rules. This is but a sample of the confusion into which one gets by failing to

the infinity of rules which an organism would have to learn in order to exhibit rule-governed behavior constituted an infinity of rules which differed in the full-blooded way in which the rules of chess differ from the rules of bridge. That the hierarchy of rules is in a certain sense repetitious (compare a rule for naming a name with a rule for naming the name of a name) provides the answer to this difficulty. However, even granting this, the regress would still be vicious if in order for a type of behavior to be rule-governed, every instance of the behavior must be accompanied (brought about) by an organic event of which the *text* (to use Bergmann's term) is the core-generalization of the rule. If this were the case, then, obviously, an infinite hierarchy of events with texts would have to occur in order for any case of rule-governed behavior to occur.

distinguish the learning of tied symbol behavior from the learning of rule-regulated symbol activity.[6]

The above discussion enables us to understand why certain regulists who, owing to a failure to distinguish clearly between tied and rule-regulated symbol activity, push the latter beyond its proper limits are tempted to hold that the meaningful use of language rests on an intuitive cognition unmediated by symbols. Action on a rule presupposes cognition, and if confusion leads these philosophers to conceive of all symbol behavior as in principle—that is, parroting aside— rule-regulated, then they are committed to the search for an extra-symbolic mode of cognition to serve as the tie between meaningful symbol behavior and the world. This link is usually found, even by regulists who have been decisively influenced by behaviorism, in a conception of the *cognitive given-ness of sense-data*. It must, of course, be confessed that these tough-minded empiricists rarely formulate such a doctrine of cognitive awareness in so many words—and might even disown it—but the careful student can frequently find it nestling in their arguments.

Here we must pay our respects to John Dewey, who has so clearly seen that the conception of the cognitive given-ness of sense-data is both the last stand and the entering wedge of rationalism. Thus, since anything which can be called cognition involves classification, the conception of the cognitive given-ness of sense-data involves

[6] The stress laid by many empiricists on "ostensive definition" is on the one hand a sound recognition of the patent fact that a meaningful language system must tie up with the environment, and on the other hand a sad confusion between learning the *definition* of a word, that is to say, learning to use it in a rule-regulated manner according to socially recognized rules, and learning (being conditioned) to respond with the word-noise to certain environmental stimuli. This confusion is exhibited by the ambiguous usage of the phrase "ostensive definition." Sometimes it is used to refer to procedures typified by teaching a dog to understand the noise "bone." Sometimes it refers to procedures typified by leading an individual to adopt a rule by which he would use a new symbol "X" as an equivalent of the rule-regulated symbol "Y"—where "Y" is usually a complex symbol of the form "U and V and W. . . ." Thus a person might be led to adopt a rule by which he would use "sugar" as an equivalent of what corresponds in his intra-organic symbol economy to the "white and sweet and granular . . ." of the *language of overt utterance* which is English, by pointing to a piece of sugar (which he cognizes by means of this intra-organic symbol economy) and uttering the noise "sugar."

as a necessary condition the given-ness of universals.[7] But once the unwary empiricist commits himself to the given-ness of universals —even if only sense-universals—he has taken the first step on a path which, unless he shuts his eyes and balks like a mule, will lead him straight into the arms of the traditional synthetic *a priori*.[8] After all, if sense universals are given, and if there are real connections between them, must not these real connections be given? And who is so empirically minded today as not to make obeisance to real connections?

It is my purpose in the following pages to sketch a regulist account of real connections and of the "synthetic *a priori*" which preserves the insights of the rationalistic doctrine, while rejecting its absolutism as well as the pseudo-psychology of cognitive givenness on which this absolutism is based.

It is important to note that the classical doctrine of synthetic *a priori* knowledge distinguishes carefully between the *ontological* and the *cognitive* aspects of such knowledge. Ontologically there is the real connection between the universals in question— say, Color and Extension. It is here that the necessity is located. On the other hand there is the cognitive fact of the intuitive awareness of this real connection, the *Schau* of the phenomenologist. Since it is a necessary consequence of the real connection of the universals that any exemplification of the one (Color) must also be an exemplification of the other (Extension), to *see* this real connection is to have rational certainty that the corresponding universal proposi-

---

[7] Let me hasten to emphasize that the difference between the platonist and the nominalistic empiricist with respect to universals (and propositions) does not consist in the platonist's saying "There are universals" and the nominalist's saying "No, there are no universals," but rather in the platonist's speaking of psychological relationships between minds and universals, whereas the nominalist finds this to be nonsense. It is this way of speaking which constitutes the platonic hypostatization of universals, and not the making of triangularity into a super-triangle—which not even Plato seems to have done.

[8] But is this such a horrible fate? Already we find in the younger generation of epistemologically-minded philosophers—particularly among those who have been influenced by C. D. Broad's masterful *Examination of McTaggart's Philosophy*—those who argue that a carefully restricted synthetic *a priori* is not incompatible with the insights of logical empiricism.

tion "All colors are extended" will not be falsified by any future experience—or so the traditional doctrine goes.[9]

Now a philosopher who finds the notion of a real connection between universals to be a sensible one, and who approaches the problem of what is meant by "causal necessity," is likely to say that causal necessity consists in real connections between the universals exemplified by events in the natural order. On the other hand, unless he shares the rationalistic optimism of a Hegel, he will not claim that we are able—even in principle—to have a direct apprehension of these real connections and so achieve an *a priori* knowledge of the laws of nature. He may, however, as we have already suggested, make an exception in the case of certain real connections between sense-qualities and, perhaps, in the case of real connections between universals of a "categorial" nature, universals relating to the most pervasive features of the world. "Science," he will say, "is able to claim with ever increasing rational assurance that such and such *kinds of events* are connected, but with an assurance that is based on empirical evidence and induction, never on self-evidence."[10]

[9] In speaking of the "traditional" doctrine of the synthetic *a priori* I am, of course, referring to the rationalism characteristic of the Platonic-Aristotelian tradition, though only since Descartes and Locke has the distinction between analytic and synthetic necessity been explicitly drawn and given the center of the stage. Kant, who was aware—as his rationalistic predecessors were not—of the pitfalls of conceptualism, and who, in common with the overwhelming majority of the philosophers of the age, failed to see a possible way out along the lines of conceptual realism—later explored by Moore and Russell—gave his own peculiar twist to the notion of necessary synthetic truth. The regulist position we are formulating could equally well be developed against a Kantian background, but that is a story for another occasion.

[10] It must be confessed that it sounds rather queer to say that there are necessary connections between universals (kinds of events) and that we can understand scientific statements referring to these universals—as the rationalist understands "understand"—but that we cannot apprehend the real connections between them. For surely real connections are not so "external" to the connected universals that these can be apprehended without an apprehension of their connection! Sophisticated rationalists have invented plausible ways of circumventing this objection, the most popular of which rests on a distinction between the apprehension of a universal, and the thought of a universal by means of apprehending a definite description of the universal. Sense universals and perhaps a limited class of other universals, instances of which are *given*, can be directly apprehended. Other universals are accessible to thought only by means of descriptions. This approach, however, can only be consistently defended by denying that the universals one can apprehend have any *connection* with universals which one can not apprehend. But surely there are real connections (if we grant real connections

It takes but a moment to show that if there are real connections between universals, then universals are obviously not the kind of thing one would want to speak of apprehending. In the first place, the philosopher who asserts the existence of real connections can readily be seen to be committed to the existence of non-actualized possibilities. For in saying that all A's *must be* B, he clearly means to say more than that *in point of fact* all cases of A have been, are and will be cases of B. He is, in effect, saying that *there are no possible worlds in which there are non-B A's*. If there were possible worlds in which there are non-B A's, why shouldn't one of them be the actual world?[11]

The following obvious objection to the conception of real connections arises at this point: "If the connection between A and B is synthetic, then it *is* (*logically*) possible that there should be a world in which there are non-B A's. Why shouldn't this logically possible world be the actual one? Must not the rationalist admit that the assumption of a real connection between A and B doesn't *entail* that all actual cases of A are cases of B, and hence that the very concept of a synthetic necessary connection is a self-frustrating one?" Now, as far as I can see, the only reply open to the defender of real connections is that it is a *matter of ultimate fact* that there are no possible worlds which violate the generalization "All A's are B"—though he might explain this fact about A and B to the extent of subsuming it under a more general fact about the realm of the possible, namely, that for *every* universal there is at least one generalization which no possible world violates. A real connection, the rationalist must say, is *identical with* the non-existence of certain possible worlds, of possible worlds answering to a certain de-

---

at all) between sense universals and physical universals (the laws of psychophysics). Thus, the rationalist who takes this line is forced to underwrite either phenomenalism or neutral monism as an account of the qualities of physical objects.

The other approach is that of Blanshard, who speaks of *degrees* in the apprehension of universals and their internal relations. Induction is necessary for Blanshard, not because we cannot apprehend universals and their connections, but because only a grasp of the place of each universal in the total scheme would be a total grasp of any universal.

[11] For a detailed explication of the logical and physical modalities in terms of possible worlds, see my "Concepts as Involving Laws and Inconceivable without them," *Philosophy of Science*, 15, 1948.

scription. Should he be tempted to put this by saying that where A is connected with B it *makes no sense* to say "This is A but not B," he must hasten to add that this statement makes no sense *because* there is no possible world which violates "all A's are B." *Within his framework, the sense-ful reflects the possible and not the possible the sense-ful.*

If we are right in claiming that the defender of real connections is forced to hold that a real connection between A and B is identical with the sheer absence from the totality of possible worlds of worlds which contain A's which are not B, then it is obviously not open to him to speak of apprehending real connections. Real connections are no more possible objects of intuition or awareness than are families of actual and possible sense data.

But though it doesn't make sense to speak of intuiting real connections between universals (as this phrase is understood by the rationalistic philosopher), may not universals themselves be possible objects of awareness? But what would one be aware of in being aware of a universal? Since no universal exemplifies itself, to be aware of, say, *redness* is not to be aware of something *red*. Surely the rationalist is right in claiming that a universal is an item characterized by its place in a structure of universals and, indeed, that this structure is a system of real connections. If this is the case, then it is just as nonsensical to speak (in the philosopher's sense) of intuiting universals, as it has been shown to be nonsensical to speak of apprehending real connections.

Am I, then, claiming that it is nonsense to talk about real connections?—that the latest fashion in philosophy is just one more mistake? Far from it. I shall insist that it is just as legitimate and, indeed, necessary for the philosopher to speak of real connections, as it is to speak of universals, propositions and possible worlds. On the other hand, it is just as illegitimate to speak of real connections as possible objects of awareness or intuition or *Schau* (as these terms are used by the rationalist) as it is to speak of apprehending universals, propositions and possible worlds. I hasten to add that there is a context in which it is perfectly legitimate to speak of *grasping a possibility* or *seeing an alternative* or *apprehending the meaning of an expression*. This context is correct English usage in non-philosophical discourse. The rationalist makes the mistake of accepting the metaphors of common sense psychology as *analyses* of psychological facts. As Moore has pointed out, common sense knows what it knows, but doesn't know the analysis of what it knows. It is the regulist and not the rationalist who explicates the grammar of assent.

What, then, is the truth about real connections? What is the significance of modal words in logically synthetic sentences? The answer is the twin brother of the regulist conception of the logical modalities. Our use of the term "necessary" in causal as well as in logical contexts is to be traced to linguistic rules. Where Hume charged the rationalist (and before him, common sense) with projecting a subjective feeling of compulsion into the environment, we charge the rationalist with projecting the rules of his language into the non-linguistic world. Where Hume finds an example of the pathetic fallacy, we find the rationalist's (or rationalistic) fallacy, a pervasive mistake which has been bread and butter to the philosophical enterprise. Hume was on the right track, but since he failed to distinguish between rule-regulated mental activity and the association of ideas (an earlier form of the contemporary failure to distinguish between rule-regulated and tied symbol behavior) his account was necessarily inadequate, a fact which comes out clearly as soon as one realizes that he was unable to give even the germ of an account of *logical* necessity. From this perspective, Mill was wiser than most empiricists have realized. He, at least, saw the parallel between logical and causal necessity, and put them in the same category. Given the framework of psychological theory which he learned on his father's knee, what else could this category have been but the association of ideas? And does not his phrase "inseparable association" indicate a groping for a more adequate account?

But these historical asides are delaying the final stages of our argument. Our task is to give an account of the rules in terms of which, we have claimed, the causal modalities are to be understood.

What are these rules? and how do they differ from the formation and transformation rules which we have all come to recognize? I have elsewhere[12] called the rules I am going to discuss "conformation rules" and the phrase seems appropriate. In order to see that a language must have conformation rules as well as the familiar rules of formation and analytic inference, it is necessary to bear in mind the conclusions at which we arrived in the first part of this paper. The meaning of a linguistic symbol *as a linguistic symbol* is entirely constituted by the rules which regulate its use. The hook-up of a system of rule-regulated symbols with the world is not itself a rule-governed fact, but—as we saw—a matter of certain kinds of organic event playing two roles: (1) a role in the rule-governed linguistic system, and (2) a role in the structure of tied sign responses to environmental stimuli. But if the linguistic as such involves no hook-up with the world, if it is—to use a suggestive analogy—a game played with symbols according to rules, then what constitutes the linguistic meaning of the factual, non-logical expressions of a language? The answer, in brief, is that the undefined factual terms of the language are *implicitly* defined by the conformation rules of the language. These specify the proper use of the basic factual expressions of the language in terms of what might be called an axiomatics. Thus, for each basic factual word in the language there are one or more logically synthetic universal sentences which, as *exhibiting* the rules for the use of these words, have the status of "necessary truths" of the language. These sentences are those into which a user of the language would insert the words "must" or "necessary." He would say that what they express is *necessarily* so, as opposed to what *just happens to be so*.

Now it is clear that if the above account is correct, a language is essentially an axiomatic system. Here we run up against an obvious objection. "Is it not clear," it will be said, "that only logicians, mathematicians, and a few theoretical physicists behave in a way which we should call 'manipulating the expressions of an axiomatic system'? How, then, can we say that our ordinary use of language

---

[12] "Realism and the New Way of Words," *Philosophy and Phenomenological Research*, June, 1948; reprinted in *Readings in Philosophical Analysis*, edited by H. Feigl and W. S. Sellars, Appleton-Century-Crofts, New York, 1949.

is the manipulating of an axiomatic system? Furthermore, if our language is an axiomatic system, how shall we account for the fact that although the language has remained the same, yesterday's necessities are today's contingencies, and vice versa? If the language is the same, must not the rules be the same, and hence the necessities the same? If the rules of the language determine what is recognized as physically necessary, how make sense of the fact that we can meaningfully ask whether or not two kinds of event are causally related, and spend time and ingenuity seeking an answer? If what is causally necessary is merely a matter of the implicit definition of the corresponding terms by the rules of the language, could there be any sense to such a procedure?"

Fortunately, these questions admit of a straightforward answer. In the first place, knowing a language is a knowing *how;* it is like knowing how to dance, or how to play bridge. Both the tyro and the champion know how to dance; both the duffer and the Culbertsons know how to play bridge. But what a difference! Similarly, both you and I, as well as the theoretical physicist, can be said to manipulate an axiomatic system; but we are clearly at the duffer end of the spectrum. Again, in answering the second question we need only note that the identity of the empirical events used as symbols is at best a necessary and by no means a sufficient condition of the identity of a language. In a perfectly legitimate sense one language can change into another even though the noises and shapes employed remain the same. Indeed, modern man is not only constantly introducing new symbols governed by new rules, he is constantly changing the rules according to which old symbols are used. Thus, as science has progressed, the word "mass" as a class of visual and auditory events has remained, but the rules according to which it is used in the language of science have changed several times, and, strictly speaking, it is a new symbol with each change in rules, though each new implicit definition (conformation rule) has had enough in common with earlier implicit definitions so that the use of the same symbol has not seemed inappropriate. Indeed, the scientist in different contexts uses the term in different senses, according to different rules. In common sense contexts his language is of ancient vintage. Thus we can stick to English and yet be said to speak not one language but many.

In ancient time, changes in the rules of language were very slow. Man was content to be baffled. Since the birth of modern science, man has constantly remodeled his language; indeed, from the standpoint of the anthropologist, science consists exactly in the attempt to develop a system of rule-governed behavior which will adjust the human organism to the environment. If there are regularities in the world, it is only by means of regularities in behavior that we can adjust to them. This process of adjustment can be speeded up by the deliberate exploration of alternative linguistic structures. The recognition of this fact is the achievement of the philosophy of science since the Einsteinian revolution.

We have pointed out that most contemporary rationalists distinguish between those real connections which human thought cannot directly apprehend, which cannot, as they say, be *known*— so that we must be content with *probable opinion* concerning their existence— on the one hand, and those real connections (extremely limited in number) which we can directly apprehend and by apprehending gain synthetic *a priori* knowledge of the world. As examples of the latter we are offered such truths as "All colors are (necessarily) extended," "All tones have (necessarily) an intensity and a pitch," etc. The list is a familiar one. What is there, if anything, in our analysis which corresponds to this distinction? That there is *something* is suggested by the fact, which empiricists are surely sophisticated enough by now to recognize, that where there is rationalistic smoke there usually can be empiricist (regulist) fire.

We have interpreted the notion of real connection in terms of the conformation rules of languages. We thus make real connections, so to speak, entirely immanent to thought. They are the shadows of rules. What sense, then, can there be to a distinction between real connections which are *known* and real connections which are *accepted* but not *known?* The answer, as I see it, is to be found along the following lines. Modern man has been constantly modifying the rules of his language, and this resulted in an awareness of *alternatives* which keeps the reflective person from saying that he *knows*. Now, these modifications have occurred chiefly in a mid-region between two extremes which I shall now characterize. On the one hand, at least until recently, certain very general structural features of the axiomatics of our language have persisted through the changes due to the advance of science. Indeed, in spite of the dramatic changes of the past few decades, the axiomatics of the language has retained certain structural features from earlier science and even from common sense. These common features— and the extent to which there are any can easily be exaggerated— represent one portion of that which people are tempted to think of as real connections which are known, and which the rationalist claims to be synthetic *a priori* knowledge. These are features for which most of us have not yet been led to seek alternatives. Yet to the extent that one seriously looks for alternatives, they lose the feel of the "unconditionally known" and acquire a "hypothetical" character which is perfectly compatible with their performance of the *a priori* role which the regulist conceives them to have. As a matter of fact, then, the contemporary philosopher of science sees in this direction only structural features of our language for which we are more or less willing to consider alternatives.

In the other direction, however, we find those rules which even the most startling advances in science have not tempted us to abandon, rules which one who pays out any rope at all to the rationalistic doctrine of cognitive awareness will end by claiming to express insight into objective real connections. I have in mind the rules which concern those symbols which not only function in the language as rule-regulated symbols, but also are elements in the tied sign behavior of the organism, and which, by playing this dual role provide the link between language and the world. Here the rules mirror, so to speak, the structure of learned sensory discriminations and associated tied sign behavior. It is these rules that most forcefully present themselves to us as having no serious alternatives. Here is the locus of the most tempting claims to synthetic *a priori* knowledge.

Now it is one thing to recognize that these rules are *causally* in a privileged position, and quite another to make any concession to pseudo-psychologies of "seeing the universal in the particular" or of "intuitive induction." Here again we find rationalistic smoke which only the empiricist (regulist) can turn into illuminating fire. A useful test of one's thought in this connection is to ask oneself what happens when a person who has been blind from birth gains vision and, *never having heard color words used,* develops his own language about color experiences. Does one think of him as apprehending the universals Red, Green, etc., and as more or less deliberately fitting symbols to these universals and giving these symbols rules which correspond to the structural properties which these universals are apprehended to have? This is the way in which many philosophers would seem to think of the matter. And, of course, there is as much sense to it as there is to speaking of intuiting universals, apprehending meanings, envisaging possibilities, etc. It is a metaphorical way of speaking which, provided it is not taken to provide an *analysis* of the learning of rules relating to the use of sense predicates, is both useful and proper. Taken to be an analysis, on the other hand, it is one more example of rationalistic pseudo-psychology.

In the course of our argument we have analyzed the moral "ought," the logical "must" and even real connections or physical necessity in terms of the concept of rule-regulated behavior. The question arises, in each of these areas, "Why one set of rules rather than another? How is the adoption of a set of rules itself to be justified?" I should like to be able to say that one justifies the adoption of rules pragmatically, and, indeed, this would be at least a first approximation to the truth. The kinship of my views with the more sophisticated forms of pragmatism is obvious. Yet I should like to close on a note of caution. The more I brood on rules, the more I think that Wittgenstein was right in finding an ineffable in the linguistic situation, something which can be *shared* but not *communicated*. We saw that a rule, properly speaking, isn't a rule unless it *lives* in behavior, rule-regulated behavior, even rule-violating behavior. Linguistically we always operate *within* a framework of *living* rules. To *talk about* rules is to move *outside* the talked-about rules *into* another framework of living rules. (The snake which sheds one skin lives within another.) In attempting to grasp rules *as rules* from without, we are trying to have our cake and eat it. To *describe* rules is to describe the *skeletons* of rules. A rule is *lived*, not *described*. Thus, what we justify is never a rule, but behavior and dispositions to behave. The "ought" eludes us and we are left with "is." The skeletons of rules can be given a pragmatic or instrumentalist justification. This justification operates within a set of living rules. The death of one rule is the life of another. Even one and the same rule may be both living as *justificans* and dead as *justificandum,* as when we justify a rule of logic. Indeed, can the attempt to justify rules, from left to right, be anything but an exhibition of these rules from right to left? To learn new rules is to change one's mind. Is there a rational way of losing one's reason? Is not the final wisdom the way of the amoeba in the ooze, the rat in the maze, the burnt child with fire? The convert can describe what he was. Can he understand what he was? But here we are on Wittgenstein's ladder, and it is time to throw it away.

The Analytic and the Synthetic: an Untenable Dualism[1]

by MORTON G. WHITE

DEWEY HAS spent a good part of his life hunting and shooting at dualisms: body-mind, theory-practice, percept-concept, value-science, learning-doing, sensation-thought, external-internal. They are always fair game and Dewey's prose rattles with fire whenever they come into view. At times the philosophical forest seems more like a gallery at a penny arcade and the dualistic dragons move along obligingly and monotonously while Dewey picks them off with deadly accuracy. At other times we may wonder just who these monsters are. But vague as the language sometimes is, on other occasions it is suggestive, and the writer must confess to a deep sympathy with Dewey on this point. Not that distinctions ought not to be made when they are called for, but we ought to avoid making those that are unnecessary or unfounded. It is in this spirit that I wish to examine a distinction which has come to dominate so much of contemporary philosophy—the distinction between analytic and synthetic statements in one of its many forms. It must be emphasized that the views which will be put forth are not strict corollaries of Dewey's views; indeed, he sometimes deals with the question so as to suggest disagreement with what I am about to argue. But I trace the source of my own general attitudes

[1] The present paper is a revised version of one read at the annual meeting of the Fullerton Club at Bryn Mawr College on May 14, 1949. It owes its existence to the stimulus and help of Professors Nelson Goodman and W. V. Quine. My debt to them is so great that I find it hard to single out special points. My general attitude has also been influenced by discussion with Professor Alfred Tarski, although I would hesitate to attribute to him the beliefs I defend.

on this point to Dewey, even though my manner and method in this paper are quite foreign to his.

Recent discussion has given evidence of dissatisfaction with the distinction between analytic and synthetic statements. A revolt seems to have developed among some philosophers who accepted this distinction as one of their basic tenets a few short years ago. So far as I know, this attitude has not been given full expression in publications, except for a few footnotes, reviews, and undeveloped asides. In this paper I want to present some of the reasons for this decline of faith in such a pivotal distinction of recent philosophy, or at least some of the reasons which have led to the decline of my own assurance. On such a matter I hesitate to name too many names, but I venture to say, under the protection of the academic freedom which still prevails on such matters, that some of my fellow revolutionaries are Professor W. V. Quine of Harvard and Professor Nelson Goodman of the University of Pennsylvania. As yet the revolution is in a fluid stage. No dictatorship has been set up, and so there is still a great deal of freedom and healthy dispute possible within the revolutionary ranks. I, for one, am drawn in this direction by a feeling that we are here faced with another one of the dualisms that Dewey has warned against.

There is some irony in the fact that some of our most severely formal logicians have played a role in creating doubt over the adequacy of this great dualism—the sharp distinction between analytic and synthetic. It is ironical because Dewey has never looked in this direction for support; indeed he has shunned it. But such a phenomenon is not rare in the history of philosophy. Dewey has told of his attachment to Hegel's language at a time when he was no longer a Hegelian, and in like manner the contemporary revolt against the distinction between analytic and synthetic may be related to Dewey's anti-dualism. Perhaps this is the pattern of philosophical progress—new wine in old bottles.

There are at least two kinds of statements which have been called analytic in recent philosophy. The first kind is illustrated by true statements of formal logic in which only logical constants and variables appear essentially, *i.e.* logical truths in the narrowest sense. For example:

$$(p \text{ or } q) \text{ if and only if } (q \text{ or } p)$$
$$p \text{ or not-}p$$
$$\text{If } p, \text{ then not-not-}p$$

and similar truths from more advanced chapters of modern logic. With the attempts to define "analytic" as applied to these I shall not be concerned. Nor am I interested here in the ascription of analyticity to those which are derived from them by substitution of constants for variables. This does not mean that I do not have related opinions of certain philosophical characterizations of this type of statement, but rather that my main concern here is with another kind of statement usually classified as analytic.

My main worry is over what is traditionally known as essential predication, best illustrated by "All men are animals," "Every brother is a male," "All men are rational animals," "Every brother is a male sibling," "Every vixen is a fox"—Locke's *trifling propositions*. I am concerned to understand those philosophers who call such statements analytic, as opposed to true but merely synthetic statements like "All men are bipeds," "Every brother exhibits sibling rivalry," "Every vixen is cunning." The most critical kind of test occurs when we have a given predicate like "man," which is said to be analytically linked with "rational animal" but only synthetically linked with "featherless biped," although it is fully admitted that all men are in fact featherless bipeds and that all featherless bipeds are in fact men. The most critical case occurs when it is said that whereas the statement "All and only men are rational animals" is analytic, "All and only men are featherless bipeds" is true but synthetic. And what I want to understand more clearly is the ascription of analyticity in this context. What I will argue is that a number of views which have been adopted as papal on these matters are, like so many papal announcements, obscure. And what I suggest is that the pronouncements of the modern, empiricist popes are unsuccessful attempts to bolster the dualisms of medieval, scholastic popes. From the point of view of an anti-dualist, their distinctions are equally sharp, even though the moderns make the issue more linguistic in character. But the similarities between the medievals and the moderns are great; both want to preserve the distinction between essential and accidental predication and both have drawn it obscurely.

Quine[2] has formulated the problem in a convenient way. He has pointed out (with a different illustration) that the statement "Every man is a rational animal" is analytic just in case it is the result of putting synonyms for synonyms in a logical truth of the first type mentioned. Thus we have the logical truth:

(1) Every P is P

From which we may deduce by substitution:

(2) Every man is a man.

Now we put for the second occurrence of the word "man" the expression "rational animal" which is allegedly synonymous with it, and we have as our result:

(3) Every man is a rational animal.

We may now say that (3) is analytic in accordance with the proposed criterion. Quine has queried the phrase "logical truth" as applied to (1) and the phrase "is synonymous with" as applied to "man" and "rational animal," but I am confining myself to the latter.

Quine has said that he does not understand the term "is synonymous with" and has suggested that he won't understand it until a behavioristic criterion is presented for it. I want to begin by saying that I have difficulties with this term too, and that this is the negative plank on which our united front rests. I should say, of course, that the complaint when put this way is deceptively modest. We begin by saying we do not understand. But our opponents may counter with Dr. Johnson that they can give us arguments but not an understanding. And so it ought to be said that the objection is a little less meek; the implication is that many who *think* they understand really don't either.

[2] "Notes on Existence and Necessity," *Journal of Philosophy*, Vol. XL (1943), pp. 113-127.

Now that the problem is introduced, a few preliminary observations must be made.

First: it might be pointed out that we are searching for a synonym for the word "synonym" and we must, therefore, understand the word "synonym" to begin with. Now it *would* be peculiar to frame the thesis by saying that a synonym for "synonym" has not been found, for then it would appear as if I did not understand the word "synonym." Obviously, if I did not understand the word "synonym" and I formulated my complaint in this way, I could hardly be said to understand my own complaint. But such criticism is avoided by saying, not that there is no synonym available for the word "synonym," but rather that no one has presented even an extensional equivalent of it which is clearer than it. In short, rather weak demands are made on those who hold that the word "synonym" may be used in clearing up "analytic"; they are merely asked to present a criterion, another term which is extensionally equivalent to "synonym." In other words, a term which bears the relation to "synonym" that "featherless biped" bears to "man" on their view.

Second: whereas Quine appears to require that the criterion for being synonymous be behavioristic or at least predicts that he won't understand it if it's not, I make less stringent demands. The term formulating the criterion of being synonymous will satisfy me if I understand it more clearly than I understand the term "synonymous" now. And I don't venture conditions any more stringent than that. It should be said in passing that Quine's behaviorism would appear quite consonant with Dewey's general views.

Third: it is obvious that if the problem is set in the manner outlined, then the statement " 'All men are rational animals' is analytic" is itself empirical. For to decide that the statement is analytic we will have to find out whether "man" is in fact synonymous with "rational animal" and this will require the empirical examination of linguistic usage. This raises a very important problem which helps us get to the root of the difficulty and to ward off one very serious misunderstanding.

The demonstration that "All men are rational animals" is analytic depends on showing that it is the result of putting a synonym for its synonym in a logical truth. In this situation we find ourselves asking whether a statement in a natural language or what Moore calls ordinary language—a language which has not been formalized by a logician—is analytic. We find ourselves asking whether two expressions in a natural language are synonymous. But this must be distinguished from a closely related situation. It must be distinguished from the case where we artificially construct a language and propose so-called definitional rules. In this case we are not faced with the same problem. Obviously we may *decide* to permit users of our language to put "rational animal" for "man" in a language L_1. (For the moment I will not enter the question of how this decision is to be formulated precisely.) In that same language, L_1, which also contains the phrase "featherless biped" in its vocabulary, there may be no rule permitting us to put "featherless biped" for "man." Thus we may say that in artificial language L_1 "All men are rational animals" is analytic on the basis of a convention, a rule explicitly stated. In L_1, moreover, "All men are featherless bipeds" is not analytic. But it is easy to see that we can construct a language L_2 in which the reverse situation prevails and in which a linguistic shape which was analytic in L_1 becomes synthetic in L_2, etc.

Now no one denies that two such languages can be constructed having the features outlined. But these languages are the creatures of formal fancy; they are dreamed up by a logician. If I ask: "Is 'All men are rational animals' analytic in L_1?" I am rightly told to look up the rule-book of language L_1.[3] But natural languages have no rule-books and the question of whether a given statement is analytic in them is much more difficult. We know that dictionaries are not very helpful on this matter. What some philosophers do is to pretend that natural languages are really quite like these artificial languages; and that even though there is no rule-book for them, people do behave *as if* there were such a book. What some philoso-

[3] Even here, Quine asks, how do you know a rule when you see one? Only by the fact that the book has the word 'Rule-Book' on it, he answers.

phers usually assume is that the artificial rule-book which they construct in making an artificial language is the rule-book which ordinary people or scientists *would* construct, if they were asked to construct one, or that it is the rule-book which, in that vague phrase, presents *the* rational reconstruction of the usage in question. But suppose a logician constructs L_1 and L_2 as defined above, and now suppose he approaches L_3, a natural language, with them. Can he say in any clear way that L_1 is *the* rational reconstruction of L_3 and that L_2 is not? My whole point is that no one has been able to present the criterion for such claims. And the reason for this is that no one has succeeded in finding a criterion for synonymy.

The moral of this is important for understanding the new revolt against dualism. I hope it makes clear that whereas I understand fairly well the expressions "analytic in L_1" and "analytic in L_2," where L_1 and L_2 are the artificial languages mentioned, I do not understand as well the phrase "analytic in the natural language L_3."[4] More important to realize is that my understanding of the first two expressions in no way solves the serious problem of analyticity as I conceive it, and I want to repeat that my major difficulties will disappear only when a term is presented which is coextensive with "synonymous" and on the basis of which I can (operationally, if you like) distinguish analytic sheep from synthetic goats. I want to repeat that I am not doing anything as quixotic as seeking a synonym for "synonym."

Those who refuse to admit the distinction between "analytic in L_1" and "analytic in the natural language L_3" will, of course, disagree completely. But then, it seems to me, they will have to refrain from attributing analyticity to any statement which has not been codified in a formalized language. In which case they will find it hard to do analysis in connection with terms in *ordinary language*. They may say, as I have suggested, that people using natural languages behave *as if* they had made rules for their language just like those of L_1 and L_2, but then how do we establish when people behave *as if* they had done something which they haven't

---

[4] For many years Quine has also pointed to the unclarity of the phrase "analytic in L," where "L" is a variable even over formal languages.

done? As we shall see later, clearing this problem up is just as difficult as the one we start with, for it involves the equally vexatious problem of contrary-to-fact conditional statements. I suppose it would be granted that those who use natural language do not make conventions and rules of definition by making a linguistic contract at the dawn of history. What defenders of the view I am criticizing want to hold, however, is that there are other ways of finding out whether a group of people has a convention. And what I am saying is that philosophers should tell us what these ways are before they dub statements in natural languages "analytic" and "synthetic."

The point at issue is closely related to one discussed at length by Professor C. I. Lewis in *An Analysis of Knowledge and Valuation* (1946). We agree in seeing a problem here which is overlooked by what I shall call crude conventionalism, but differ in our conception of where the solution must be sought. Lewis is led to say that whether "All men are rational animals" is analytic in a natural language depends on whether all men are necessarily rational animals, and this in turn depends on whether the *criterion in mind* of *man* includes the *criterion in mind* of *rational animal*. Lewis has dealt with this matter more extensively than any recent philosopher who advocates a sharp distinction between analytic and synthetic, and his arguments are too complex to be treated here. In any case, his views are quite different from those upon which I am concentrating in this paper. He holds that I need only make what he calls an "experiment in imagination" to find out whether all men are necessarily rational animals. And when I try this experiment I am supposed to conclude that I *cannot* consistently think of, that I cannot conceive of, a man who is not a rational animal. But how shall we interpret this "cannot"? How shall we understand "thinkable"? I suspect that this view leads us to a private, intuitive insight for determining what each of us individually *can* conceive. How, then, can we get to the analyticity of the *commonly* understood statement? Lewis' most helpful explanation turns about the word 'include' in the following passage: "The question, 'Does your schematism for determining application of the term *"square"* include your schematism for applying *"rectangle"?* is one determined in the same general fashion as is the answer to the question, 'Does your plan of a trip to Chicago to see the Field Museum include the plan of visiting Niagara to see the Falls?' " The inclusion of plans, furthermore, is a sense-apprehensible relationship for Lewis. One either sees or doesn't see the relationship and that is the end of the matter. It is very difficult to argue one's difficulties with such a position and I shall only say dogmatically that I do not find this early retreat to intuition satisfactory. I will add, however, that in its recognition of the problem Lewis' view is closer to the one advanced in this paper than those which do not see the need for clarification of "analytic in natural language." My difficulties with Professor Lewis are associated with the difficulties of intensionalism but that is a large matter.

I want to consider now two views which are avowedly anti-intensional and more commonly held by philosophers against whom my critical comments are primarily directed.

1—*"Analytic statements are those whose denials are self-contradictory."* Consider this criterion as applied to the contention that "All men are rational animals" is analytic in a natural language. We are invited to take the denial of this allegedly analytic statement, namely "It is not the case that all men are rational animals." But is this a self-contradiction? Certainly looking at it syntactically shows nothing like *"A* and not-*A."* And even if we transform it into "Some men are not rational animals" we still do not get a self-contradiction in the syntactical form. It might be said that the last statement is self-contradictory *in the sense* in which "man" is being used. But surely the phrase "in the sense" is a dodge. Because if he is asked to specify that sense, what can the philosopher who has referred to it say? Surely not "the sense in which 'man' is synonymous with 'rational animal' " because that would beg the question. The point is that the criterion under consideration is not helpful if construed literally and if not construed literally (as in the attempt to use the phrase "in the sense") turns out to beg the question.

Let us then suppose that the criterion is not used in this question-begging manner. A self-contradiction need not literally resemble in shape "*A* and not -*A*" or "Something is *P* and not -*P*." All it has to do is to produce a certain feeling of horror or queerness on the part of people who use the language. They behave as if they had seen someone eat peas with a knife. Such an approach is very plausible and I would be satisfied with an account of the kind of horror or queer feelings which people are supposed to have in the presence of the denials of analytic statements. But on this I have a few questions and observations.

(a) Who is supposed to feel the horror in the presence of the opposites of analytic statements? Surely not all people in the community that uses the language. There are many who feel no horror at seeing people eat peas with a knife just as there are many who are not perturbed at statements that philosophers might think self-contradictory. Who, then?

(b) Let us remember that on this view we will have to be careful to distinguish the horror associated with denying firmly believed synthetic statements from that surrounding the denials of analytic statements. The distinction must not only be a distinction that carves out two mutually exclusive classes of sentences but it must carve them out in a certain way. It would be quite disconcerting to these philosophers to have the whole of physics or sociology turn out as analytic on their criterion and only a few parts of mathematics.

(c) If analytic statements are going to be distinguished from synthetic true statements on the basis of the degree of discomfort that is produced by denying them, the distinction will not be a sharp one[5] and the current rigid separation of analytic and synthetic will have been surrendered. The dualism will have been surrendered, and the kind of *gradualism* one finds in Dewey's writings will have been vindicated. The most recent justification of the distinction between essential and accidental predication will have been refuted. It may be said that sharp differences are compatible with matters of

---

[5] On this point see Nelson Goodman's "On Likeness of Meaning," in *Analysis* October 1949, pp. 1-7. Also W. V. Quine's forthcoming *Methods of Logic*, section 33 (Henry Holt, N.Y., probably 1950).

degree. Differences of temperature are differences of degree and yet we may mark fixed points like 0° centigrade on our thermometers. But it should be pointed out that a conception according to which "analytic" is simply the higher region of a scale on which "synthetic" is the lower region, breaks down the radical separation of the analytic and the synthetic as expressive of different kinds of knowledge. And this is a great concession from the view that K. R. Popper[6] calls "essentialism." It is reminiscent of the kind of concession that Mill wanted to wrest from the nineteenth century in connection with the status of arithmetical statements. Once it is admitted that analytic statements are just like synthetic statements, only that they produce a little more of a certain quality—in this case the quality of discomfort in the presence of their denials—the bars are down, and a radical, gradualistic pragmatism is enthroned. This is the kind of enthronement which the present writer would welcome.

2—*"If we were presented with something which wasn't a rational animal, we would not call it a man."* Such language is often used by philosophers who are anxious to clarify the notion of analytic in the natural languages. In order to test its effectiveness in distinguishing analytic statements let us try it on "All men are featherless bipeds" which by hypothesis is *not* analytic. Those who use this criterion would have to deny that if we were presented with an entity which was not a biped or not featherless we would not call it a man. But we *do* withhold the term "man" from those things which we know to be either non-bipeds or non-featherless. Obviously everything turns about the phrase "we would not call it a man" or the phrase "we would withhold the term 'man.'" Again, who are we? And more important, what is the pattern of term-withholding? Suppose I come to a tribe which has the following words in its vocabularly plus a little logic: "man," "rational," "animal," "featherless," and "biped." I am told in advance by previous visiting anthropologists that "man" is synonymous with "ra-

---

[6] See *The Open Society and its Enemies,* especially chapter 11 and its notes (Routledge, London, 1945).

tional animal" in that tribe's language, whereas "featherless biped" is merely coextensive with it. I wish to check the report of the anthropologists. How do I go about it?

In the spirit of the proposed criterion I must show that if anything lacked rationality it would not be reputed a man by the people in question. So I show them cocoanuts, trees, horses, pigs, and I ask after each "man?" and get "no" for an answer. They will not repute these things to be men. I must now show that there is a difference in their attitudes toward "rational animal" and "featherless biped" *vis-a-vis* "man." I originally produced things which lacked rational animality. But these very things also lack feathers and are not bipeds, and so the negative responses of the natives might just as well be offered as an argument for the synonymy of "man" and "featherless biped" as for the theory that "man" is synonymous with "rational animal." It would appear that such crude behaviorism will not avail. They don't call non-featherless-bipeds men just as they don't call non-rational-animals men. The criterion, therefore, is one that will not help us make the distinction.

We might pursue the natives in another way. We might ask them: Would you call something a man if it were not a featherless biped? To which they answer in the negative. Would you call something a man if it weren't a rational animal? To which they answer "no" again. But now we might ask them: Aren't your reasons different in each of these cases?—hoping to lead them into saying something that will allow us to differentiate their responses. Aren't you surer in concluding that something is not a man from the fact that it is not a rational animal, than you are in concluding it from the fact that it is not a featherless biped? If the savage is obliging and says "yes," we have the making of a criterion. But notice that it is a criterion which makes of the distinction a matter of degree. Not being a rational animal is simply a better sign of the absence of manhood than is the property of not being a featherless biped, just as the latter is a better sign than the property of not wearing a derby hat. It should be noticed in this connection that we are precluded from saying that the inference from "*a* is not a rational animal" to "*a* is not a man" is logical or analytic for them, since we are trying to explain "analytic." To use it in the explanation would hardly be helpful.

Probably the most helpful interpretation of this mode of distinguishing analytic and synthetic is that according to which we observe the following: when the natives have applied the word "man" to certain objects and are then persuaded that these objects are not rational animals, they immediately, without hesitation, withdraw the predicate "man." They contemplate no other means of solving their problem. But when they have applied the word "man" and are then persuaded that the things to which they have applied it are not featherless bipeds, they do not withdraw the predicate "man" immediately but rather contemplate another course, that of surrendering the hypothesis that all men are featherless bipeds. Now I suspect that this criterion will be workable but it will not allow us to distinguish what we think in advance are the analytic equivalences. It will result in our finding that many firmly believed "synthetic" equivalences are analytic on this criterion.

I am sure that there are a number of other ways of constructing the criterion that are similar to the ones I have just considered. No doubt students of language who have thought of this problem can develop them. But I want to call attention to one general problem that criteria of this sort face. They usually depend on the use of the contrary-to-fact conditional: if . . . were . . . then . . . would be . . . But in appealing to this (or any variety of causal conditional) we are appealing to a notion which is just as much in need of explanation as the notion of *analytic* itself. To appeal to it, therefore, does not constitute a philosophical advance. Goodman[7] has reported on the lugubrious state of this notion, if there are some who are not fazed by this circumstance. It would be small consolation to reduce "analytic" to the contrary-to-fact conditional, for that is a very sandy foundation right now.

After presenting views like these I frequently find philosophers

[7] "The Problem of Counterfactual Conditionals," *Journal of Philosophy*, Vol. XLIV (1947), pp. 113-128.

agreeing with me. Too often they are the very philosophers whose views I had supposed I was criticizing. Too often, I find, the criticisms I have leveled are treated as arguments *for* what I had supposed I was opposing. For example, there are some philosophers who construe the argument merely as an argument to show that words in natural language and scientific language are ambiguous—that "man" is synonymous with "rational animal" in one situation and with "featherless biped" in another—and who immediately embrace the views here set forth. But this is not what is being emphasized. Many philosophers who defend the view I have criticized admit that a word may have many meanings, depending on context. For example, John Stuart Mill, who admits that a biologist might regard as the synonym of "man," "mammiferous animal having two hands," and not "rational animal." But Mill also holds that in common usage "rational animal" is the synonym. Because of this admission of a varying connotation Mill regards himself (justifiably) as superior to the benighted philosopher who holds what has been called "The one and only one true meaning" view of analysis. If the benighted philosopher is asked "What is the synonym of 'man'?" he immediately replies "rational animal." If he is a Millian, he says it depends on the situation in which it is used, etc.

I am not concerned to advocate this view here, because it is quite beside the point so far as the thesis of this paper is concerned. The difference between the Millian (if I may call him that without intending thereby to credit Mill with having originated the view) and his opponent (I would call him an Aristotelian if such matters were relevant), is comparatively slight. The Millian takes as his fundamental metalinguistic statement-form: "X is synonymous with Y in situation S," whereas his opponent apparently refuses to relativize synonymy. The opponent merely says: "X is synonymous with Y." What I want to emphasize, however, is that by so relativizing the notion of synonymy he is still far from meeting the difficulty I have raised. For now it may be asked how we establish synonymy *even in a given situation*. The problem is analogous to the following one in mechanics. Suppose one holds that the question:

"Is x moving?" is unanswerable before a frame of reference is given. Suppose, then, that motion is relativized and we now ask such questions in the form: "Is x moving with respect to y?" But now suppose we are not supplied with a clear statement of how to go about finding out whether x is in motion with respect to y. I venture to say that the latter predicament resembles that of philosophers who are enlightened enough to grant that synonymy is relative to a linguistic context, but who are unable to see that even when relativized it still needs more clarification than anyone has given it.

I think that the problem is clear, and that all considerations point to the need for dropping the myth of a sharp distinction between essential and accidental predication (to use the language of the *older* Aristotelians) as well as its contemporary formulation—the sharp distinction between analytic and synthetic. I am not arguing that a criterion of analyticity and synonymy can never be given. I argue that none has been given and, more positively, that a suitable criterion is likely to make the distinction between analytic and synthetic a matter of degree. If this is tenable, then a dualism which has been shared by both scholastics and empiricists will have been challenged successfully. Analytic philosophy will no longer be sharply separated from science, and an unbridgeable chasm will no longer divide those who see meanings or essences and those who collect facts. Another revolt against dualism will have succeeded.

John Dewey and Karl Marx

by JIM CORK

> ". . . Probably my experimentalism goes deeper than any other 'ism'." —From a letter by JOHN DEWEY to the writer.

MARXIST CRITICISM, historically a part of the European intellectual tradition,[1] has been singularly opaque in regard to the great and progressive merits of John Dewey's philosophy. The critiques of Dewey's Instrumentalism, which have periodically come from the pens of Marxists of all shades of political persuasion, have been extraordinary documents, to say the least. Their consistently biased character was an inevitable outgrowth of the unexamined faith the Marxists yielded to the questionable methodological oversimplifications that had become imbedded in the Marxist tradition—viz., the inflexible overdriving of the sociological bent in its analysis, the over class-angling of cultural phenomena. It has been no uncommon tendency for Marxists to denigrate American cultural products merely on the basis of the bourgeois character of the society which gave them birth (a raw simplicism, incidentally, of which Marx himself was never guilty). An indication of the social setting, or the historical process which supposedly helped to inspire or shape ideas, seemed sufficient reason for these pundits to assign them to limbo, although, obviously, the purported social origin of

---

[1] America has no Marxist tradition of any significance. No theoretical works of major importance have been produced by any Marxist or socialist political organization, whether defunct or still in existence. The same can be said for the academicians. Sidney Hook and Lewis Corey practically exhaust the names of those who have produced significant works either of critical exegesis or original exposition.

an idea is hardly identical with a judgment of its possible validity. The first is cultural history. The second requires logical analysis and testing.

The worst offenders against decent canons of logical discourse in these matters have, of course, been the Russian Stalinists, whose claims to be the best descendants of Marx have acquired an increasingly strident, propagandistic tone down through the years. What their theoretical dogmatism and institutional authoritarianism has led to can be seen in the present Russian defamation of all Western culture, and the barbaric restrictions placed upon the natural development of art, music, literature, philosophy, and even science, in Russia itself.

The periodic respects the Russians have paid to Dewey present a fantastic, almost indescribable compound of political bias, cavalier disregard of the written word, outright fabrications, and violent name calling—that unusual blend of ideological discussion (recalling nothing so much as a court-room atmosphere) so peculiarly characteristic of Russian polemics since the Bolshevik ascendancy![2] We are treated to the unsavory spectacle of the use of the technical jargon of philosophy to squeeze and torture ideas into the preformed mold dictated by party and ideological loyalty.

The vices of this tradition, however, have been characteristic not only of the Stalinist "philosophers," Russian or otherwise. They attach in almost equal degree to those movements that were offshoots of Bolshevism (Trotskyism, Brandlerism, and other independent communist sects). They even extend, unfortunately, beyond these to many European socialists who, though never enamored of Bolshevism and able to dispute the findings of the Stalinists on the political and social fields, seem unable to completely disguise an unconscious snobbery towards American culture, per se, or to muster the necessary critical acumen to overcome the hypnotic hold that class-angling of cultural phenomena has acquired over them.

* See the latest example, the article by M. Dynnik in the November 1947 issue of *Modern Review*, a particularly horrendous specimen of what can only be called the "frothing-at-the-mouth school."

The favorite (and foregone) conclusion commonly arrived at by the Bolsheviks and their epigones is that Dewey is the philosopher of Western imperialism. August Thalheimer, for instance, a leading theoretician of the split-off Brandler wing of communists, had this to say about Dewey and Pragmatism in his *Introduction to Dialectical Materialism* (Covici-Friede, 1936): "It is therefore not so easy for the uninitiated [!] to recognize that the true character of this philosophy is reactionary and idealistic . . . that [like] all the various schools and sects of bourgeois philosophy after Feuerbach [it] revolves about just one problem, namely, how bourgeois society and the capitalist order can be defended against the socialist . . . it reflects the characteristic spirit of the American bourgeoisie . . . hence the distortion of cause and effect and the tendency towards commerce. Pragmatism is *literally* [my emphasis—J.C.] the philosophy of commerce. . . . Since it recognizes no reality external to the human mind it can have no touchstone for truth. For Pragmatism there is no objective measure for truth. . . ." etc. [pp. 241, 245 and 248]

This accusation against Pragmatism, that it has no objective touchstone for truth, that truth is what "works," what is useful, what gives inner satisfaction, hence is subjectively measured, represents one of the commonest and most persistent misconceptions about pragmatic logic (a misconception, incidentally, that is notoriously shared by Bertrand Russell, among others).

The test for truth is objective and is not concerned with ministering to subjective feelings, needs or desires. As Dewey says: "Truth is not verified just by any kind of satisfaction but only by that satisfaction which is born of the fact that a working hypothesis or experimental method applies to the facts which it concerns and effects a better ordering. No misconception concerning the instrumental logic of pragmatism has been more persistent than that one which would make of it merely a means for a practical end."

Or take one C. P. West, writing some years ago in *New Essays,* (an organ of independent anti-Stalinist communists whose moving spirit then was Paul Mattick) in an article whose very title gives the cue to the nature of the forthcoming treatment, "Pragmatism: The Logic of Capitalism." There the author says, among other gems of super-distortion: "Actually, Dewey does not provide us with a technique or logical method for thinking our way through our problems. We are given, rather, the psychology of a particular class behind the instrumentalist or class logic of Dewey and his fellow pragmatists ... instrumentalist logic—like the philosophy of Pragmatism itself—is the ally of the class in power today, safeguarding the vested interests of the capitalist preserves." [Vol. 6, No. 4—Winter, 1943]

The Trotskyites, on their part, have not been quite so crude. They have satisfied themselves in the main, in their periodic "notices" of Pragmatism, with the impassioned defense of the mystic mummeries of the dialectic, and an occasional attack on Sidney Hook for the latter's purportedly profane attempt to water down the revolutionary purity of Marxist philosophy by his espousal of pragmatic naturalism.

It was Hook who, after a thorough objective study of the original sources, made the assertion that allowing for differences in idiom and terminology, the broad philosophical positions of Karl Marx and John Dewey are basically similar. He first raised the question forcefully in his writings on Marx in the late twenties and early thirties in the *Modern Quarterly* and other publications. In 1935, in his essay, "Experimental Naturalism," in *American Philosophy Today and Tomorrow,* he claimed that ". . . their fundamental logical and metaphysical positions are the same . . ." In 1939, in his book *John Dewey,* he says: ". . . it seems to me that, were realistic Marxists prepared to submit their methods of achieving democratic socialism to serious scientific criticism, and were Dewey prepared to work out a more detailed program of political action with reference to the social and economic relations of the current scene, their positions would converge on a set of common hypotheses leading to common activities."[3]

[3] Hook's little book on Dewey, incidentally, provides the best single introduction to the entire span of Dewey's thought.

The persuasiveness of Hook's thesis has more to recommend it than the mere surface resemblances between elements of Marx's and Dewey's thought that various commentators have periodically pointed out. That his views have not been accorded the serious consideration they deserve is due to a combination of prejudice and indifference on the part of both professed Marxists and professional philosophers. Both sides seemed intent on preventing a favored doctrine from being contaminated by another, obviously regarded as foreign. Though the Marxists have been by far the greater sinners in this matter (as already indicated above), Dewey himself, unfortunately, has not been blameless in helping to foster mutual misunderstanding between the two doctrines.

Dewey's conception of Marx represents one of the rare occasions when he has forsaken the usual scientific caution and genial objectivity with which he deals with real or imagined opponents. He has paid more attention to Marx and Marxism in his *Freedom and Culture* than in any other of his works. In it, he does not reveal even to the extent apparent is some earlier references, first-hand knowledge of Marx's writings; does not distinguish between Marx's own ideas and encrustations upon them of subsequent interpretations; and delivers himself of criticisms which several reputable Marx scholars had already challenged as inadequate.

Dewey's main criticisms are:

1) Marx's ideas on the causal factors influencing historical change were *a priori* concoctions and not derived from empiric investigations: "This law [i.e. Marx's, on historical causation—J.C.] was not derived nor supposed to be derived from study of historical events. It was derived from Hegelian dialectical metaphysics."[4] This is an astounding charge in view of the historical parts of *Capital* and Marx's writings on 1848 in France and Germany, on the Paris Commune, Spain, the American Civil War, etc., all of which are concrete analyses of the actual historical events and served as testing ground for his theoretical constructions.

[4] *Freedom and Culture*, p. 79.

2) Marx denied social efficacy to human values, ideas, efforts: "The denial that values have any influence in the long course of events is also characteristic of the Marxist belief ... I shall criticize the type of social theory which reduces the human factor as nearly as possible to zero since it explains events and frames policies *exclusively* [my emphasis—J.C.] in terms of conditions provided by the environment. Marxism is taken as the typical illustration of [this] ... absolutism ... he [*i.e.* Marx—J.C.] also, in the name of science, denied moving power to human valuations."[5] That some Marxists mistakenly made of Marx's theory a doctrine of automatic inevitability that left completely out of consideration the instrumental behavior of men consciously working toward desired ends is undoubtedly true. But it is extremely questionable whether Marx was guilty of the same simplicism. He had too much respect for the dynamic creativeness of human thinking for that. Indeed, his theory of social change is inseparable from the social voluntarism (and possible social efficacy of their actions) of individuals: "Men make their own history."

3) The same considerations would raise some doubts concerning the validity of Dewey's charge that Marx claimed for his laws an inevitable and automatic certainty: "The Marxist has laid down a generalization that is supposed to state the law governing the movement and outcome of all the social changes."[6] Marx may not have sensed *all* the possibilities of alternative development. His view that complete laissez-faire capitalism and complete collective socialism exhausted the alternatives of social development was mistaken. He didn't see that mixtures of both were possible, and possibly desirable. And he certainly didn't anticipate the dangers of totalitarianism. But the whole tenor of his thought and action indicated that he did not believe that the "inevitable" success of socialism was guaranteed. Like most writers of the nineteenth century, especially those consumed by the sense of practical or historical mission, Marx does *not* use the term "inevitable" in a sense which makes it synonymous with "fated." He at least envisaged the pos-

[5] *Ibid.*, pp. 12, 75-76, 80.
[6] *Ibid.*, p. 53.

sibility of social regression if the forces making for socialism were not successful.

It is difficult to see why Dewey has so signally failed to distinguish between Marx's ideas and morals and those of the Stalinists. He seems to have been unduly influenced by the latters' tiresome claim that they were the only legitimate descendants of Marx. Accepting them at their word, his logical and moral critiques would undoubtedly seem to him to be imperative since he had seen these self-declared heirs of Marx violate every precious freedom, trample on all human rights and build in the Soviet Union the most powerful police state in history. As Chairman of the Commission on the Moscow Trials, he saw how the cynical lie and the frameup operated as essential elements in Soviet state morality. When, further, he saw Trotsky, himself the most celebrated victim of the Stalinist smear technique (i.e., all anti-Stalinists are against progress, are reactionaries, fascists, etc.), indulging in the same puerile illogicality, condemning all bourgeois democrats, social democrats, anarchists, humanitarians (*i.e.,* all anti-Trotskyites) as a common fellowship helping reaction to maintain itself and even acting as brothers in spirit to the Stalinists (". . . the democratic philistine and the Stalinist bureaucrat are, if not twins, brothers in spirit. . . . In the mechanics of reaction Stalinism occupies many leading positions. All groupings of bourgeois society, including the anarchists, utilize its aid in the struggle against the Proletarian Revolution . . .");[7] and the same Trotsky, the most brilliant of living revolutionaries, for all his brilliance, unable to break out of the narrow circle of faith and fanaticism, piling dogma upon dogma, unwilling to re-examine assumptions[8]—then he must have reasoned that there was something incipiently dangerous in the thought processes of the man commonly accepted as ancestor by both brutal victor and brilliant victim, and that that dangerous element had to be uncovered.

[7] See Leon Trotsky, "Their Morals and Ours," *New International,* June 1938.
[8] See Dewey's answer to Trotsky (see note 7 above) in the August issue of the same magazine, where the great philosopher convicts the great revolutionary of overlooking the integral character of the means-ends relationship.

Be my highly speculative psychological reconstruction what it may, the assumption, on Dewey's part, of a basic similarity between Marx's thinking and that of the Bolsheviks is a gratuitous one which is itself the product of that type of non-historical, uncontextual thinking Dewey himself so often criticizes, rather than the result of painstaking investigation at first hand of original sources. In both logic and morals, the Bolsheviks violated rather than followed basic, even decisive, elements in Marx's system of ideas. The history of thought reveals many analogues to this. It would be rash to lay at Plato's door the ideas of the Platonists of succeeding centuries. Indeed, it would be very risky to attribute to Dewey the notions of some latter-day educational followers of Dewey.

My statement of the similarities between Marx and Dewey will, of necessity, have to be expressed in brief, summary fashion.

1) Both find a common heritage in Hegel, who impressed them with the ideas of continuity and change and the organic nature of a society or epoch which, for all its disparateness, yet showed basic, underlying, unifying characteristics. As Hegel said: "The Constitution adopted by a people makes one substance, one spirit with its religion, its art and its philosophy, or at least with its conceptions and thoughts, its culture generally." Each in his own way emancipated himself from the idealistic heritage of Hegel without sacrificing the great insights of the German philosopher.[9]

2) Both consider philosophy as not "outside" this world and above common human practices, but a very important part of the general culture of any epoch, reflecting its common experiences, problems and needs. As such, philosophical ideas reflect also social divisions and conflicts and have been used for the purpose of buttressing dominant-class views: "The belief that a theory of knowing, which in its origin was inherently a leisure-class theory, has influence in justifying the state of society in which only a few are thus

[9] For Dewey's original allegiance to Hegelianism, see Morton G. White's *The Origins of Dewey's Instrumentalism*, Columbia U. Press, 1943.

privileged, hence in perpetuating the latter condition, *is* [Dewey's emphasis—J. C.] a part of my complete theory."[10]

3) The strong secular, naturalistic note in both philosophies. Both are opposed to all forms of irrationalism, mysticism and supernaturalism. Dewey was cool to James's religious vagaries and rejected F. C. S. Schiller's religious apologetics.

4) Both are in the materialistic tradition in philosophic thought, even though Dewey polemicizes against the use of the term "materialism" in favor of the word "naturalism" (see Schilpp, pp. 604 and 605). His argument against certain types of materialism would not hold against Marx, who was opposed to both mechanical materialism and reductive materialism. Dewey accepts the reality of the existence of the external world and the emergence of life and mind from physical (inorganic) matter and events. So much so, that in contradistinction to Russell and most modern philosophers, he refuses to regard the existence of the external world as a genuine problem. "Yet I cannot refrain from saying that (as Reichenbach's *Experience and Nature* clearly shows) upon his view the existence of the external world is a *problem* [Dewey's emphasis—J. C.] for philosophy, whereas according to my view the problem is artificially generated by the kind of premises we call epistemological. When we *act* [Dewey's emphasis—J. C.] and find environing things in stubborn opposition to our desires and efforts, the externality of the environment is a direct constituent of direct experience."[11]

5) Both are opposed to atomism, a-priorism, sensationalism, Platonic essences, and to the extremes of both organicism and formalism in understanding culture.

6) Both are opposed to the traditional philosophies of dualism (Descartes, Kant, etc.).

7) Both are opposed to absolute truths in favor of relative and provisional truths dependent for verification (and possible further extension) upon future inquiry: "The truth of any present propo-

[10] Schilpp, *The Philosophy of John Dewey*, Library of Living Philosophers, Vol. 1, Northwestern U., p. 529.
[11] *Ibid.*, p. 542.

sition is by definition subject to the outcome of continued inquiries; its truth, if the word must be used, is provisional; as near the truth as inquiry has yet come, a matter determined not by a guess at some future belief but by the care and pains with which inquiry has been conducted up to the present time."[12]

8) Both have a deep appreciation of the facts of biology and accept the philosophical implications of Darwinism with its central concept of the evolution of the organism (nervous system, brain, mind), developing in physical time, acting-in-and-reacting-to a natural environment in a series of interactions and transactions. Thus the dualism between mind and nature is resolved and human thought appears as continuous with the physical and biological activities of bodies.[13]

9) Both epistemological theories are practically identical. Both stress the unity of theory and practice. Both disagree with the conception of knowing as a passive, contemplative process and stress the knowing process as an active, constructive, practical, transforming activity. In his essay ("Dewey's New Logic," Schilpp, p. 143), Bertrand Russell, an ideological opponent of both Marx and Dewey on this question, says, "Allowing for a certain difference of phraseology, this doctrine [*i.e.* Marx's—J.C.] is essentially indistinguishable from Instrumentalism." Some evidence for this evaluation can be found in a comparison of extracts from Marx's *Theses on Feuerbach* with Dewey's statement of his Theory of Inquiry, both of which represent the heart of their respective epistemological positions:

Marx: "The chief defect of all previous materialism is that the object, the reality, sensibility is only apprehended in the form of the object or of contemplation, but not as sensible activity or practice, not subjectively. Hence it came about that the active side was developed by idealism in opposition to materialism (Thesis No. 1). . . . The question whether objective truth can be attributed to hu-

---
[12] *Ibid.*, p. 573.
[13] See in this connection the very illuminating essay, "Reconstruction of Logical Theory," by Ernest Nagel, re the influence of biological concepts on the logical theory of Dewey, in the volume, *The Philosopher of the Common Man*, Putnam, 1940.

man thinking is not a question of theory but is a practical question. In practice man must prove the truth, *i.e.* the reality and power, the 'this-sidedness' of his thinking (No. 2).... The philosophers have only interpreted the world in various ways, the point, however, is to change it" (No. 11).

Dewey: "Inquiry is concerned with the objective transformation of objective subject matter. . . . All thought contains a practical factor, an activity of doing and making which shapes antecedent, existential material which sets the problem of inquiry . . . the ultimate ground of every valid proposition and warranted judgment consists in some existential reconstruction ultimately effected" (*Logic*).

These nine items constitute an imposing list of agreements, sufficient to warrant investigation into a possible ideological rapprochement between the philosophical outlooks of these two influential figures.

The complexities of human history are too great to ever permit a completely successful, scientific account of historical development. It does not follow from this admission, however, that these complications are too involved to permit of *any* ordered resolution of events, that, consequently, past history can never be "recaptured"; in short, that a scientific *approach* to human history is impossible. One theory may be a more adequate explanation than another in that it permits of the ordering of a greater mass of phenomena. Marx undertook the necessary theoretical investigation of the relative weight to be assigned to the various historical factors (economic, political, cultural, psychological, religious, etc.) with the end in view of determining those relatively dominant and those relatively derivative and subsidiary (else only historical description, static historical "photography" becomes possible). Dewey's charge against Marx that " . . . the isolation of any one factor, no matter how strong its workings at a given time, is fatal to understanding and to intelligent action" (*Freedom and Culture* p. 23) is rather abstract criticism which overlooks the specific intent and the specific problem with which Marx was concerned as well as the spirit of his investigation. That spirit was to the highest degree empirical. Marx did not "isolate" the so-called economic factor (relations of production); rather did he attempt to assign it its relative specific weight in the entire congeries of factors. He merely viewed "the mode of economic production as the fundamental *conditioning* [my emphasis—J. C.] factor of only the general and most pervasive characters of a culture" (Hook). He neither denied nor failed to acknowledge the necessarily qualifying effects upon historical development of such factors as the weight of tradition, the unique in the development of specific countries, the accident of personality, the relatively autonomous development, especially in their formal aspects, of special cultural fields (law, science, poetry, say) although he did insist that the degree of independent impact generated by these factors was limited by the boundaries set by the relations of production. Above all, both Marx and Engels called attention to the reciprocal interaction of the various social factors.[14]

Whatever else may be said about Marx's theory of Historical Materialism, the above at least makes clear that it was not the narrow monistic theory misguided followers of Marx have made out of it, and that it takes cognizance of the factors making for causal pluralism. In the hands of the Soviet Marxists, the monistic conception has led to its most devastatingly negative results, ending up in a narrow sociological analysis of culture generally and a politicalization of art. It is in the field of culture especially that Marx's flexibility contrasts most sharply with the narrow dogmatism of Communist orthodoxy. He never thought of literature (or the writer) as subservient to narrow, utilitarian, socio-economic ends:

"The writer in no wise considers his work a means. It is an end in itself, and so little is it a means for him and for others, that he

[14] See in this connection Engels' "Four Letters on Historical Materialism," to Schmidt, Bloch, Starkenberg and Mehring, in the Appendix to Hook's book, *Towards the Understanding of Karl Marx*.

sacrifices *his* existence to *its* existence when necessary." [Debate on Freedom of the Press, 1843]

Marx stressed the historical continuity of art and art forms in spite of the sharply delineated and opposed economic and social wellsprings of the different epochs. He had a definite feeling for those universal aspects of art that transcended the social epoch which gave them birth. It was in the very book (*Critique of Political Economy*) where he formulated his masterly condensation of his theory of Historical Materialism that Marx penned the famous words on Greek art:

"It is well known that certain periods of highest development of art stand in no direct connection with the general development of society, nor with the material basis and the skeleton structure of its organization. Witness the example of the Greeks as compared with the modern nations or even Shakespeare. . . . The difficulty is not in grasping the idea that Greek art and epos are bound up with certain forms of social development. It rather lies in understanding why they still constitute with us a source of aesthetic enjoyment and in certain respects prevail as the standard and model beyond attainment." [Kerr Edition, pp. 309, 310-311, 312]

Compared to Marx's concrete analysis of capitalist society and his proposed program for social change, Dewey's remarks on politics appear as generalities, mostly value judgments as to what constitutes the good society. These have undoubtedly been excellent in themselves, and for Dewey the "Good Society" is obviously the end purpose of all philosophizing: "Is there anything in the whole business of politics, economics, morals, education—indeed in any profession—save the construction of a proper human environment that will serve, by its very existence, to produce sound and whole human beings, who will, in turn, maintain a sound and healthy human environment?"[15]

But this very praiseworthy end has remained an ideal, unimplemented (in very uninstrumentalist fashion) by a concrete pro-

---

[15] Quoted from Hook's *John Dewey*, p. 26.

gram of social engineering. This hiatus in Dewey's thought has been so apparent that even his most sympathetic critics have, perforce, had to refer to it.[16] There is point, therefore, in Hook's noting that Dewey's contribution to a desired (if possible) rapprochement between democratic socialism and Dewey's instrumentalism would be ". . . to work out a more detailed program of political action with reference to the social and economic positions of the current scene. . . ."

Ever since the derailment of the Russian Revolution, Marxian socialists have become increasingly sensitive to the means-ends relationship. It must be admitted that they were never sensitive enough to this question in the past. True, there were always important voices within the internationalist socialist movement which insisted on the necessary consonance of means and ends (within the different camps and in different connections, Rosa Luxemburg, and Martov and the Russian Mensheviks, for instance). But the realization of the central importance of the problem came late. It needed the last decade's experience with Russian developments to give the necesary jolt, especially to those who, in the earlier, more hopeful days, had given their unqualified allegiance to the November Revolution. If many socialists have painfully retraced their steps, they have but arrived at a position which Dewey has always occupied:[16] "If there is one conclusion to which human experience unmistakably points it is that democratic ends demand democratic methods for their realization."[17]

[16] John Herman Randall, Jr., for instance, in the Schilpp volume, p. 91. See in this connection also Hu Shih's very instructive essay, "The Political Philosophy of Instrumentalism," in the volume, *The Philosopher of the Common Man*, p. 205, for an illuminating discussion of Dewey's changing theories re the state, and for his conception of the instrumentality of violence. Hu Shih comes to the conclusion that: "After reading all the political writings of Dewey, I have come to the conclusion that he began to work out a truly instrumental political philosophy early in 1916, but, for some unknown reason, has apparently never taken up nor continued to develop this instrumentalist line of thought during the last quarter of a century." It is worthy of note that Dewey admits the justice of Randall's charge against him of relative neglect of the social engineering aspect in his summary essay answering his critics in the Schilpp volume (p. 592, footnoote).

[17] *Freedom and Culture*, p. 175.

Dewey's sense of democracy has been more pervasive than that of the Marxists. Democracy serves as the cement which binds the various aspects of his thoughts together. It underlies all his theoretical constructions. It suffuses his vision of the "Good Society." In short, democracy has been for Dewey a complete way of life. The same cannot be said for Marxists. On the whole, Marxists have tended to view democracy in too narrow a class sense, both historically, as well as in its present manifestations. They have suffered from a blind, almost teleological, faith in the automatic beneficence of the mere act of taking power, failing to realize that the problem of the extension of democratic values merely begins there and that its successful realization is impossible unless the movement has become thoroughly impregnated with faith in democratic values long before winning political power becomes a practical question on the agenda of history. Here too Dewey has had the longer-range viewpoint: "But the idea that the Revolution in its immediate occurrence, as of a given date, 1789 or 1917/18, is anything more than the beginning of a gradual process is a case of Utopian self-delusion. The method of intelligent action has to be applied at every step of that process in which a revolution 'runs its course.' Its final outcome does not depend upon the original abrupt revolutionary occurrence but upon the way intelligent action intervenes at each step of its course—as all history shows in spite of ex-post-facto 'inevitabilities' constructed after choice has manifested its effects."[18]

Marx's humanism is central and integral to his way of thinking. His supreme concern was man himself, and the possibility of man's attaining to full freedom and dignity. It was that concern which generated his explosive anger at the tyranny exercised over man by things (economic and social organization) and set him to search for a new society in which the proper administration of things would enable man to abolish the social exploitation of man and to permit the whole man to realize his best potentialities.

[18] Schilpp, p. 593.

Marx's periodic and eloquent defense of the *necessity* of human freedom forever sets him apart from the Soviet "Marxists" and would earn him the cognomen "petty-bourgeois decadent" in that unhappy land if he could survive long enough before being dragged before the tribunals of liquidation.

Marx never lost his concern for human rights and individual liberties which he inherited from the Enlightenment and the French Revolution. His early works especially are replete with eloquent testimony to this effect. At the very beginning, even in his doctoral thesis on the differences between the Democritean and Epicurean philosophies, he felt kinship with the rebellious figure of Prometheus who, himself the victim of the prejudice of the gods, braved their anger to bring aid to mankind. As early as 1844, when Marx was but 26 years old, he declared in his essay on the Hegelian philosophy of Right that ". . . man is the supreme being for mankind and . . .(it is necessary). . . to overthrow all conditions in which man is a degraded, servile, neglected, contemptible being. . . ." Soon thereafter, in his polemic against Bruno Bauer in *The Holy Family,* we read: "It is our business to order the empirical world in such a way that man shall have truly human experiences in it, shall experience himself to be a human being. . . . If man is formed by circumstances, we must make the circumstances human. . . . If man is unfree in the materialist sense (this meaning that he is free, not through the negative power of avoiding this or that, but through the positive power of fulfilling his own true individuality), it behooves us, not to punish individual offenses, but to destroy the anti-social foci of crime and to give every one social space for the manifestation of his life activities. . . ." The official journal of the Communist League, of which Marx was the moving spirit, which was published in 1847, reveals this dedication to civil rights and personal liberties: "We are not among those communists who are out to destroy personal liberty, who wish to turn the world into one huge barrack or into a gigantic workhouse. There certainly are some communists who, with an easy conscience, refuse to countenance personal liberty and would like to shuffle it out of the world. . . . But we have no desire to exchange freedom for equality."

What a contemporary ring this eloquent statement has! Here, though written a hundred years ago, is the essential critique from a democratic and humanist viewpoint of Stalinist totalitarianism. "The proletariat," Marx declared on another occasion, ". . . regards its courage, self-confidence, independence, and sense of personal dignity as more necessary than its daily bread."

It would be idle to deny a certain ambivalence in Marx's conceptions of democracy as a result of his later formulation of the principle of the Dictatorship of the Proletariat. But even here it is necessary to make the qualification that Marx's concrete picture of the dictatorship, of how it would take over and work, separates him fundamentally from the Bolshevik leaders. His conception had nothing in common with the concentration of all power in the hands of a small bureaucracy exercising a naked dictatorship over the entire population. For him a workers' democracy meant at first a dictatorship of the majority of the population exercised by organs responsible to the people below. Further, Marx envisaged the free organization of producers and consumers—*i.e.*, all the members of the community—democratically planning the entire productive machinery for the benefit of all. Granted that Marx underestimated the dangers of dictatorship generally, that he was unaware of his semantic confusions, that he did not sense the totalitarian potential inherent in a complete collectivism. Granted his other naivetés and misjudgments, the point to keep in mind is Marx's psychologic motivation. That is his desire to extend the democratic process to all areas of social life.

That is why Marx cannot be classed with the modern totalitarians. That would do violence both to his purpose and spirit, as well as to his written words. He stems from the liberal, humanitarian, democratic, radical traditions of Western thought and made, in turn, some important contributions to them. He is a genuine, if errant, child of the Enlightenment.

After this all-too-inadequate summary of mutual misunderstandings, similarities and differences, we return in a somewhat better position to judge the validity of Hook's thesis.

How does Dewey feel about his part of the projected "bargain"? Has he shown any indication of having been convinced by Hook concerning not merely the desirability but the feasibility of the projected ideological rapprochement? There is a puzzling duality in Dewey's attitudes here. On the one hand, in his *Liberalism and Social Action* (1935) he has formulated as eloquently as one could wish the heart of the democratic socialist ethic: "In short, liberalism must now become radical, meaning by radical, perception of the necessity of thoroughgoing changes in the set up of institutions and corresponding activity to bring the changes to pass. . . . Organized social planning put into effect for the creation of an order in which industry and finance are socially directed in behalf of institutions that provide the material basis for the cultural liberation and growth of individuals, is now the sole method of social action by which liberalism can realize its professed aims . . . the cause of liberalism will be lost for a considerable period if it is not prepared to go further and socialize the forces of production now at hand, so that the liberty of individuals will be supported by the very structure of economic organization . . . socialized economy is the means of free individual development as the end."

On the other hand, there is Dewey's resounding (and in some measure, unjustified) attack against Marx four years later in his *Freedom and Culture*. In addition, there has been on Dewey's part no forthright public espousal, to my knowledge, of democratic socialism.

I had always thought of Dewey as a left-wing Jeffersonian democrat with socialist tendencies. Puzzled by the seeming ambivalence of his attitudes, I wrote a note to him confessing my bewilderment and put the question directly to him. His answer is instructive. Although expressing certain reservations, and emphasizing the need for more critical and systematic study on the part of professed socialists, and stressing the fact that no "existing brand of socialism has worked out an adequate answer to the question of *how* [Dewey's emphasis—J. C.] industry and finance can progressively be conducted in the widest possible human interest and not for the benefit of one class . . ." he makes the following extremely significant admission: "I think that on the basis of *Liberalism and Social Action,* and to some extent *Individualism Old and New,* I can be classed as a democratic socialist. If I were permitted to define 'socialism' and 'socialist' I would so classify myself today. . . ." That "permission," it is safe to say, democratic socialists would be happy to grant. As an avowed socialist it would make it easier for him to redirect socialist thinking along the lines of 1) the necessary integration of socialism with democracy; 2) greater sensitivity to the means-ends relationship; and 3) the need for a more scientific, experimental approach to concrete matters. Dewey ends his letter with: "I think that the issue is not as yet sufficiently definite [*i.e.,* in respect to the "how"—J. C.] to permit of any answer save that it has to be worked out experimentally. Probably my experimentalism goes deeper than any other 'ism'."

As far as the proponents of democratic socialism are concerned, there can be no objection to submitting the methods proposed to achieve their ends to the sharpest scrutiny. In the light of recent experiences with Russian developments, democratic socialists have re-affirmed their rejection of the dictatorship principle, whether in the state or inside the party; have rejected the idea of the domination of the single monolithic party; have rejected the idea of the desirability of the working class being the sole active and directing group in social reformation; have rejected the narrow Bolshevik conception of the state as merely the executive committee of the ruling class; and finally, and most important, have increasingly stressed the desirability of a peaceful transition to socialism. Marx emphasized that possibility in the case of countries like England and America where democratic traditions were strong. The conquest of power by the Bolsheviks was achieved through violence and the result has been the opposite of socialism, its ghastly caricature, in fact. In England the Labor Party came into political control peacefully, and there exists, at least, the possibility of its achieving socialism, assuming the continuance of principles, vision and will.

However, we might be reckoning without our host. The socialist movement is hardly unanimous on these questions. Further, it has not yet taken Dewey to its heart, for the simple reason that too many of its adherents know too little of his philosophy.

Nevertheless, in spite of Dewey's criticisms of Marx and the opacity of the socialists (Marxist or otherwise) to Dewey, the movement for ideological rapprochement between democratic socialism and the philosophy of John Dewey is decidedly worth furthering. If the pragmatists would stop confusing Marx with some Marxists, recognize the hard, ineradicable, humanist-democratic core of Marx's thinking as akin to their own, and implement their praiseworthy, general value judgments with concrete instrumentalities applied to political and social questions; and if the socialists, on their part, would drop overboard the ludicrous excess baggage of the dialectic, rid themselves of the remaining shreds of inevitabilism, abandon their narrow class conception of democratic values, and learn to think experimentally in politics, there would seem to remain no major obstacles in the way of realizing Hook's hope that " . . . their positions would converge on a set of common hypotheses leading to common activities."

The ideological rapprochement between democratic socialism and the philosophy of Dewey, if it could but be achieved, would make socialism the heir to the deepest, most consistent and most generous radical-democratic strain in the entire American tradition. Without having to blunt its internationalist ideals in the slightest, democratic socialism could feel more at home on American soil.

Dewey in Mexico

by James T. Farrell

In 1937, I was urgently trying to convince a mid-western journalist about the historical significance of the Moscow Trials. Even though he rejected the official version of the Trials, he shrugged off my remarks with the question:

"What do the Moscow Trials mean in Kokomo, Indiana?"

At the time, these trials had little significance for many people. But for American liberals, and the American liberal movement, they constituted a test and a challenge.

For many years, American liberals had concerned themselves with world politics. They had taken many positions on essentially moral grounds, and they had repeatedly voiced their sympathies for the oppressed all over the world. They had rejected doctrines and practices of *Realpolitik,* and had defended the Irish, the Hindus, the victims of colonial imperialism, and others in the name of justice. Most American liberals had hailed the Russian Revolution. During the 1920's, they had sympathetically regarded the Soviet Union as a great social experiment. Then, with the onset of the American depression in 1929, their interest in the Soviet Union increased. For the depression shocked American liberal intellectuals as they had never been shocked before, and many of them went "left," as the phrase ran in the early 1930's. They viewed the Soviet Union as the country which was pointing the way out. In Soviet Russia they saw at least the beginnings of "planned economy." In capitalist America there was near chaos instead of a plan. Russia was supposed to have no unemployment, while millions were out of work in America. And in the Soviet Union, there was enthusiasm, when stark misery and fear were in so many American hearts. The future seemed to belong with the Soviet Union, rather than America, where the rich promises of American life were, apparently, blighted.

In addition, many American liberals applauded Soviet foreign policy. The United States had stubbornly refused to recognize the Soviet Union. The liberals, some of them conscience-stricken about the first World War, also feared another war. As a guarantor of peace, the League of Nations was a seeming failure. Treaties and agreements, such as the Briand-Kellogg Pact which formally outlawed war, began to look empty. Liberal moods were pacifistic, even bitterly so. And the Soviet Union, founded on ideals, was treated like an outcast. Whenever Litvinov made a statement, or proposed disarmament, the liberals hailed him. The enemies of the Soviet Union, both in America and on the world scene, were, also, the enemies of the liberals.

The rise of Hitler further attracted liberals to the Soviet Union. They were really unprepared to understand Nazism. They saw it largely as a consequence of the victors' peace at Versailles, as a result of the support for Hitler given by German industrialists, and, in addition, as being related to the "cowardice" of the Social Democrats. The failure of the Social Democrats, in particular, was like a failure of liberals themselves. Their own intellectual perspectives had been ruptured by history. They came more and more to look upon the Soviet Union as the leader in the international field.

From 1927 on through the early 1930's, the Communist International pursued a leftist line. This was in the so-called Third Period of the Comintern. In 1935, following the establishment of a military alliance with France—the Stalin-Laval Pact—the Communist parties of the world began to shift toward the adoption of the Popular Front tactic. This became official Communist policy in 1935. It seemed as though the failure of a United Front had led to Hitler's victory. While Trotsky and other Marxist opponents of the Communists distinguished between a United Front and a Popular Front, many liberals did not. They were not only admitted into Popular Fronts, but they were given new and added positions and prestige. The Communists began to outtalk the liberal in his own language, and, at the same time, to organize liberals. Liberals, in turn, began to feel that, thanks to their alliance with Communists, they were getting a new lease on life. Communists were helping many of them to revive their own declining and wearied faith.

In July 1936, the Spanish Civil War began. In August 1936, the first of the Moscow Trials was dramatically announced. The early news of the trials was bewildering and shocking. Zinoviev and Kamenev, two of Lenin's co-workers, made degrading confessions and their summary execution was promptly announced. Leon Trotsky, the organizing genius, the Danton—as it were—of the Bolshevik Revolution, was accused of plotting to murder Joseph Stalin. And these trials came when Spain was threatened by fascism. What position was to be taken on the Moscow Trials? What did these trials mean? An issue was posed for liberals.

Dewey was America's outstanding liberal: his ideas had influenced the entire liberal world. And he, himself, had shared somewhat in the attitudes held by liberals toward the Russian Revolution and the Soviet regime. He visited the Soviet Union with a group of educators in 1928, and in 1929 published impressions of *Soviet Russia and the Revolutionary World*. While in Russia, he saw schools and he met Russian educators. He did not meet Russian political figures. He tried to learn as much as he could about the life of the common people of Russia. His impressions, gathered on the streets of Leningrad and Moscow, at schools, and in meetings with Russian educators and teachers, were overwhelmingly favorable. In substance, he seemed to believe that in the Soviet Union, genuine advances were being made in the remaking of a socialized human nature. Especially for this reason, the Russian "experiment" was of the most profound importance and promise for the whole world.

Early in his book, he stated: "I find it impossible to believe that the communicated sense of a new life [among the common people of the Soviet Union] was an illusion." Because he had seen so much enthusiasm, energy, and promise of change in Russia, he wrote: "In spite of secret police, inquisitions, arrests and deportations of *Nepmen* and *Kulaks*, exiling many party opponents—including divergent elements in the party—life for the masses goes on with regularity, safety, and decorum." And he also declared that he had "never seen anywhere in the world such a large proportion of intelligent, happy, and intelligently occupied children."

He saw the Russian future revealed in what was being done in Russian education. In accounting for the importance of the new and promising educational agencies in Russia, Dewey thought that these could be used "as a magnifying glass of great penetrating power by which to read the spirit of events in their constructive phase." The intellectual and educational movement seemed to him to be the key to an understanding of Soviet Russia. For, he argued, the Russian political leaders, in their efforts to establish socialist instead of capitalist relationships, would have to substitute a collective and social type of mentality for the individualistic mentality of the bourgeois epoch. He objected to the introduction of so much propoganda in Soviet education, and made it clear that he did not sympathize with the doctrines of class war and world revolution. But he counted on the energy, the virility and growing intelligence and social awareness of the Russian people, living in this new and lively world where education was being revised so drastically and with such seriousness and intelligence, to outrun the appeal of Marxian and Bolshevik dogmatism. In education, he saw the possibilities of the future. Thus, " . . . the final significance of what is taking place in Russia is not to be grasped in political or economic terms, but is found in change of incalculable importance, in the mental and moral disposition of a people, an educational transformation."

Dewey was, he frankly admitted, glad that this experiment was happening in Russia, rather than America. He did not lose his sense of the value of freedom in America, but he did hail the

Soviet Union, and did remark that it should be studied. It could provide useful lessons. It was forging way ahead in education. And this educational advance promised to produce something more than a private culture from which many would be excluded.[1]

After the first Moscow Trial, a group of American liberals and radicals joined with American Trotskyites in organizing the American Committee for the Defense of Leon Trotsky. This Committee dedicated itself to two aims. One: to work so that Leon Trotsky would be given a hearing before world opinion. The principle underlying this aim was the old Anglo-Saxon one which affirms that a man should be considered as innocent until he is proven guilty. Two: to try to gain for Trotsky the right of political asylum. At that time, he was held incommunicado by Norwegian authorities. His personal situation, and that of his wife, were dangerous. It appeared as though he would receive no fair opportunity to defend himself against the charges made against him in the first Moscow Trials. John Dewey joined this Committee and became its honorary chairman.

Following his arrival in Mexico and the second of the Moscow Trials, Trotsky pressed impatiently for the organization of a commission of inquiry before which he could present his case. The major charges were that he and his son, Sedov, had allegedly organized terrorist attempts against the life of Joseph Stalin and other Soviet leaders, that he had allegedly plotted with the governments of Germany and Japan to foment a war against the Soviet Union, in order to permit the restoration of capitalism and the

---

[1] It would be exceedingly unfair to criticize Dewey's enthusiasm, from the standpoint of *ex post facto* historical hindsight. The period between 1925 and 1928 was, according to most students with an objective mind, the best one in the whole post-Bolshevik epoch. There was an increase in productivity, in wages, and in consumer goods. The enthusiasm of the Revolution remained. A new generation was coming forward after the Civil War, and for the most part, the members of this generation were the sons of workers and peasants. A large number of Mensheviks and other earlier opponents of the Bolsheviks, including Vishinsky, had made peace with the new regime. The Terror was not as all-pervasive then as now. The shock of hope and of new ideas, felt in 1917, was still felt. Russia seemed to be evolving. Dewey did note the play of counter tendencies in Russia: and in addition, he put down his impressions as impressions. He stated them with modesty.

ceding of Soviet territory to fascist countries, and that he had allegedly organized acts of sabotage in Soviet industries, resulting in the destruction of property and in the deaths of many workers.

In March of 1937, the American Committee for the Defense of Leon Trotsky organized a Commission of Inquiry. At first, the task seemed to be an almost hopeless one. It was a foregone conclusion that no one could get to any source of facts within the Soviet Union. Whether or not a good commission could be organized was, in itself, problematic. The American Communists were conducting a campaign of intimidation and slander and misrepresentation against the American Committee for the Defense of Leon Trotsky, seeking to break up the Committee. A few members did resign from it. One of those who did so, privately admitted that he had acted out of fear, and volunteered to make a secret financial contribution to the Committee. One liberal editor had sought to discourage the idea of having a Commission on the grounds that inasmuch as the officials of the Soviet regime would not cooperate with the proposed Commission, the work of the latter was doomed in advance to failure. This editor then proceeded secretly to employ a lawyer to investigate the trials and prepare a report which would make anti-climactic any investigation by the proposed Commission of Inquiry. The liberal press began to argue that it was impossible for almost anyone to be impartial concerning the issues involved in the Trials, and that, hence, an investigation could not produce an objective and impartial report. A committee of liberals and fellow-travelers had been formed to break up the Committee. *The Daily Worker* published a document, signed by a number of prominent liberals, which, in effect, charged the American Committee for the Defense of Leon Trotsky with intervention in the internal affairs of the Soviet Union, and with aiding the fascist drive for war against, and invasion of, Russia. Individual members of the Committee were offered trips to the Soviet Union. They were badgered, annoyed, pestered with telephone calls. They were cajoled and threatened. One writer was offered a bald-faced bribe, couched in the form of a guarantee of the sale of one of his own books. A campaign to damage the sales of writers who belonged to the Committee was begun. And the fact that ordinary Americans and many labor leaders were not especially concerned with the Trials gave added opportunities to the American Communists in this campaign. The integrity of the outstanding members of the Committee was what alone gave it protection, and helped to save it from being discredited and destroyed by the Communist campaign.

Such was the atmosphere in liberal and intellectual circles, when John Dewey agreed to serve as chairman of the Commission of Inquiry, and, with a sub-committee of the Commission, to go to Mexico where hearings would be held, permitting Trotsky to present his answer to Moscow. The Mexican trip was necessary, because Trotsky could not get a temporary visa anywhere for a public appearance before a court or investigating commission. At the time, Dewey was 78. He was engaged in work on one of his major books, *Logic, the Theory of Inquiry*: he put aside his own work in order to serve on the Commission. This fact speaks for itself.

John Dewey had no sooner committed himself to make this trip than the Communists intensified their campaign. Efforts were made to induce him to pay a second visit to the Soviet Union. Because of his age, members of his family opposed his journey to Mexico. He, himself, was pestered and badgered. The Communist press began to describe him as senile. But he was unswayed by all pressure. He was heedless of ridicule. He calmly dismissed all suggestions that he was placing himself and his health in jeopardy.

Early in April, 1937, Dewey left for Mexico with a small group. In this party were Benjamin Stolberg, the journalist, who was a member of the Commission, and of the sub-committee which would take Trotsky's testimony, Miss Suzanne La Follette, an art critic, editor and journalist, who was secretary of the Commission of Inquiry, George Novack, secretary of the American Committee for the Defense of Leon Trotsky, Miss Pearl Kluger, who served as secretary for the sub-committee, and myself. I made this journey merely because I was interested, and had no official task.

In one letter which I wrote at the time, I described John Dewey as follows: "He [Dewey] . . . did quite a bit of studying and reading . . . He also did everything for himself and would let no one help him . . . He always looked spic and span for meals. He is a very shrewd man, and a very wise one, and he gets the gist of things in a quiet and unobtrusive way. He does not get fooled by speeches, or tricks. . . . He states his impressions slowly, honestly, in a rather colorless language, but you see that when he does, he usually 'states' a point which goes to the gist of the question . . . Dewey has tremendous humility . . . Dewey has real fiber. . . ."

Everyone in this small group was aware of the meaning of the journey. Theirs was a mission concerned with truth and justice, and with making the historic record clear. Assume that Robespierre had escaped on the Ninth Thermidor, and had presented his case to history. Trotsky would be able to do what Robespierre hadn't been able to. But for Dewey, the issue was a question of truth and fair play. In speaking of his Mexican experience on his 83rd birthday, he remarked to me that he had not gone to Mexico because of Trotsky. He had seen an issue there. The issue contained a challenge to him as a man with democratic faith. The implications of the Trials were sinister. He did not fear these sinister implications. It was, let me add, this fear of the sinister implications of the Trials which caused some liberals to equivocate about them with dread. Their faith had been already become transposed from a democratic faith in their fellow men to one in the promises uttered by Soviet leaders. The sordid terribleness of the Trials frightened many humane minds. Dewey's reactions were simpler and braver than those of his fellow liberals. He would find out. He would seek the truth.[2]

[2] The following anecdote might further illuminate my point here. At the time, I, as well as others, posed this question: if the official version of the Trials were true, then, the co-workers of Lenin and leaders of the Bolshevik Revolution must be considered as one of the worst gangs of scoundrels in history; if the Trials were a frameup then the leaders of Soviet Russia were perpetrating one of the most monstrous frameups in all history. An outstanding and humane American, known for his anti-Communism and his utter honesty, wrote to me, stating that while he saw the justice of this question, he hated to face it.

Dewey had begun to prepare himself for the Hearings before he boarded the train for Mexico. He completed this task en route to Mexico. In fact, he amazed everyone on the train by the amount of work he was able to do. On the train, he finished reading the official versions of the first two Trials, and, also, he read from the writings of Trotsky. He spent many hours in his small compartment, alone, reading. He did not seem to take many notes, holding most of what he read in his head. Recently, when I asked him about his Mexican memories, he remarked that when he read the official reports of the Trials, he had made own logical analysis of these, and had found them to be utterly inconsistent. He was especially struck by one passage between Vishinsky, the Prosecutor, and the defendant Radek in which the latter gave "crucial" testimony implicating Trotsky. In this particular testimony, Radek said that he had seen two alleged Trotskyites on a Moscow street. He and they did not speak. These two men turned down a street. On the basis of this, Radek told Vishinsky what these men were thinking and plotting, what Trotsky had allegedly instructed them to do, and what these men were thinking of Radek, himself. In his close reading of the complete official records, Dewey found many inconsistencies. He had, prior to the Trials, always believed that Stalin's course was more sensible than Trotsky's. In particular, as his book describing his Russian impressions revealed, he had not been at all sympathetic with Trotsky's ideas of world revolution. His intelligence, his ability to think, his concern with truth and logic provided premises for the tentative conclusions he arrived at on the basis of his preliminary study of the official material. He was making this analysis on the train, while he read. His thinking here was much sharper and clearer than the thinking of anyone else in the group. The rest of us, when we talked of this material, talked more broadly, making comparisons with Thermidor and the French Revolution, and dealing with historical comparisons and analogies.

On the train, Dewey was very sociable. At meal times, he would listen and talk, and he would sit with us now and then, smoking a cigarette and drinking a glass of beer. Whenever anyone spoke, he would listen very attentively, sometimes leaning a little forward in order to hear better. It is an understatement to say that better listeners than John Dewey are rare. In these train conversations, the range of subjects referred to was wide. Usually, Dewey would allow others to talk and bring out whatever was on their minds: he would listen, would now and then comment in his modest but pertinent way, and he would always answer every question put to him, speaking in a slow and somewhat drawling way, letting the words, as it were, almost fall out of his mouth. His powers of attention, his dry wit, and his extraordinary keenness of mind were revealed with such modesty and simplicity that they come as a shock. But in such passing train conversations, it also became clear that he was a man with much temperament. I used to talk to him about American liberals, American philosophers, and education, and here, his expressions would be full of temperament. His estimations of men would be just, but not without sharpness. And as one talked to him, the years would seem to be stripped away from the man. One would lose some sense of the fact that this kindly old man was *John Dewey*. He was another human being, a member of this temporary group.

Possibly, a few more details concerning Dewey on the trip will fill out the picture. He was curious about everything. He was clearly learning and assimilating on the train. He would let none of us show him any special consideration because of his age and his prestige. Thus, he wanted to open the doors between cars himself, and wanted no other small acts of deference to be performed for him. He always seemed fresh, alert, and unruffled. Dewey's evenness of temper on the train was especially significant because there were possibilities of danger ahead. Violence is a Stalinist political tactic. And there were many rumors afloat to the effect that there was a strong concentration of Stalinist agents in Mexico. The verbatim records of the Trials were full of Machiavellian charges of intrigue and assassination. Dewey was en route on a mission of truth and fair play strange and unheralded in the annals of American philosophy. He was going into a world far removed from the library, the classroom, and the halls of a philosophical congress. He traveled to meet this new experience as calmly, as quietly, and with as little outward sense of excitement as though he might have been an unknown man journeying from one town to another in his native Vermont.

The Hearings in Coyoacan opened in the villa of Diego Rivera, on the Avenida Londres on the morning of April 10, 1937, at 10 A.M. The atmosphere was tense. There was a police guard outside. On entering, visitors were searched for guns and identified by a secretary of Trotsky who was, himself, armed. The room used was Trotsky's study. It was about forty feet long, and about twenty feet wide. It faced out on the street, and there were three French windows. These were covered, and behind each of them, there were six-foot barricades of cemented brick and sandbags so that no assassins might successfully shoot through the windows. These brick barricades had been completed the night before. Mexican workers, Trotsky's secretaries, American friends and sympathizers had all worked on these barricades. The writer visited Trotsky's home on the night before the Hearings opened and was also pressed into service carrying bricks. In and out of the room, Mexicans and Americans paraded, carrying bricks to be cemented onto the rising barricades. This work had gone on until late at night. Trotsky was still at work preparing his case. His final and brilliant summation of the Trials had not, as yet, been completed. Now and then he would appear, and stand for a moment or two, watching the work proceed, and passing a remark or two with someone. He was a well-built man of perhaps five feet ten or so, with lovely blue eyes. He was gray, and he gave the impression of being infinitely well-poised and seemingly relaxed, but with inner intensity. At moments, he would stand, watching the building of the barricades, and he would seem tired, concentrating on his work as he stood there. Then, he would turn and go back. Twilight changed to darkness. Trotsky went to bed, and the work went on. Although he was ready for the Hearings when these opened, he went on working while they were in session.

The rectangular room was partitioned off. Trotsky sat at his desk by the wall facing the street. He was flanked by secretaries, and Mrs. Trotsky sat near him on his left. The sub-committee, composed of John Dewey, Suzanne La Follette, Benjamin Stolberg, Carlton Beals, and Otto Ruhle, an old German socialist and exile, sat at one end of the room, on Trotsky's left. The press and visitors sat at the opposite end. Albert Goldman, Trotsky's lawyer, and the Commission's lawyer, John Finerty (after the first day's session), faced Trotsky. One side of the room opened onto a veranda and a courtyard.

There were photographers and newsreel cameramen. Pictures were taken. Then Dewey, wearing a blue suit, rose and opened the Hearings, speaking in a quiet voice. He said:

"The fact that hearings are being held in which a foreigner will defend himself before foreigners on Mexican soil is an honor to Mexico, and a reproach to those countries whose political system or current policy bars the holding of our meetings on their soil. . . . This Commission . . . believes that no man should be condemned without a chance to defend himself."

He described the functions and reason for being of the Hearings, observed that in the present case, there existed "no legally constituted court before whom the accused [Trotsky] might plead," and noted that Trotsky and his son, Sedov, had twice been adjudged guilty by the highest tribunal of the Soviet Union, without having had an opportunity to defend themselves.

"The simple fact that we are here is evidence that the conscience of the world is not as yet satisfied on this historic issue."

He concluded his remarks by saying in his own name:

". . . I have given my life to the work of education, which I have conceived to be that of public enlightenment in the interests of society. If I finally accepted the responsible post I now occupy, it was because I realized that to act otherwise would be to be false to my lifework."

Trotsky, speaking English with a pronounced accent, then made his introductory remarks. A group of Americans had given him his chance to answer Moscow's charges, and to allow him to defend his revolutionary honor as he saw it before world opinion and history. Wearing a gray tweedish suit, he gave the impression of a man who was immaculately but not ostentatiously put together. He also gave the impression of great simplicity, and of extraordinary control over himself. He was a decisive and non-casual person. He spoke with great precision. His manners were as impeccable as his clothes, and he was a man of charm. His gestures were very graceful. He was extraordinarily alert. At times, it seemed as though his entire organism were subordinated to his will. From day to day, as he talked, he revealed himself. His voice was anything but harsh or shrill. His temperament was most volatile. Thus, he was often quiet, and very controlled. But when Carleton Beals asked him questions which seemed to him provocative, he changed instantly, became sharp and taut. At other times, his irrepressible irony would break out.[3] His mind worked very rapidly.

At the close of one session, Trotsky approached me and asked what impression I had of the day's testimony. He was taut, as though he had been like a bow drawn as tightly as it could be. It would never snap, but it would vibrate at the slightest ripple of one's breath. His temperament was vibrant. He was a man of tremendous intellectual pride, and of self-confidence. He was intolerant of stupidity, of what he deemed to be stupid, and his simplicity

[3] I have not dealt in this article with Mr. Beals's resignation from the Commission before the sessions ended, because with the passage of time, this incident seems like a minor episode. The Western world has, since 1937, come more and more to associate the words: Moscow Trials and frameup. Many of those who accepted the official versions of the trials would now not defend them. Mr. Beals asked some improper questions which had no bearing on the issues of the Trials, and which could well have jeopardized Trotsky's status as an exile. Dewey and the other members of the Commission stated this as their opinion also. With the passage of years, the most charitable view to take of Mr. Beals's action is to assume that it was ill-advised. We have, or should have, learned, that there is no good to be gained by re-fighting dead issues. Mr. Beals's questions, Trotsky's answers, Mr. Beals's letter of resignation, the statement of Dewey about this letter, and the full verbatim record of the Hearings are available in *The Case of Leon Trotsky*, New York, 1938. The interested reader can find the full story there.

and extraordinary graciousness seemed like an acquisition of experience. He was a man of genius, of will, and of ideas. Perhaps, he might even be called an archtype of the civilized, highly cultivated and thoroughly Europeanized Western European. He was a man of the West, and, in this, so unlike the majority of the current men in power in the Soviet Union. And his Marxian faith was, also, a faith in ideas. We can properly say that Trotsky was a great man.

But John Dewey is also a great man. At Coyoacan, there was a contrast in the personalities of Dewey and Trotsky, but there was no competitiveness between them. Dewey subordinated himself to his role. He acted like a simple servant of truth. He tried to impress neither Trotsky, nor the audience as he put his quiet and searching questions. It must be remembered that Trotsky was a voluntary witness, and not a defendant, and also that the Commissioners were more investigators than they were judges. At the same time, Trotsky voluntarily placed his fate in the power of the Commission. A Commission abusing that power, could have ruined Trotsky in the eyes of world opinion, and have made his difficult life much harder. Dewey, as Chairman and as the outstanding member of the Commission, was in a delicate position, one requiring great tact as well as fairness. It is illustrative of Dewey's own sense of honor that he did not abuse nor step out of his position. The days were long, and the sessions were intense, suggestive, stimulating, and filled with the account of a terrible historic tragedy. Dewey's attention was unflagging. In a most unobtrusive way, he guided the proceedings when guidance was necessary. He was alert to see to it that all that was needed was put into the record. He would intervene when any point required clarification. When he cross-questioned Trotsky, his questions were apt, and they were part of a logical structure of questions which led to some clear and significant point or idea. He addressed Mr. Trotsky politely, and usually in the casual tone which marks so much of his conversation. Once or twice, in instances where Trotsky's own statements ran clearly counter to Dewey's own democratic ideas, there was a scarcely noticeable change of tone. In these rare instances, Dewey's own independence of mind, in the face of Trotsky's brilliance, was apparent. At the same time, there was here no violation of his role, no tactlessness. At these points, there was a revelation of temperament in intellectual exchange. Trotsky knew English less well than the other languages he commanded. He thought in Russian, French, or German, translated almost as he thought, and spoke in English. He had, however, an amazingly good use of English words. Dewey's words were often more colorless than Trotsky's. But in Dewey's talk as a whole, his choice of words is sometimes colorless: they take on color from the appositeness of his thought, and the capacity he has to give this thought a direct bearing on the point at issue. Dewey was more relaxed, more even-tempered than Trotsky, but then, their circumstances were so different that this specific contrast is not too significant. Trotsky was, however, not worried, and did not act like a hunted man. He was intent and concentrated. Dewey's relaxation here is a sign of an unsuspected strain of wordliness in his personality. He was as much at home in the world as Trotsky.

I have gone into detail here, presenting these two men because they so clearly and so dramatically represented two worlds. Trotsky himself, was interested in the contrasts and the relationships between Europe and America, and he believed that America was on the eve of a tremendous theoretical and cultural development, although he also believed that this would be guided by Marxian perspectives. It is doubtful whether Trotsky realized that the quiet and modest gray-haired man of seventy-eight, who sat in the room with him, listening, was the man whose influence had been and would continue for long to be a major one in creating the attitudes which would help toward the creation of such a cultural development in America, if this were to come. Trotsky did not understand pragmatism in the sense that Dewey is a pragmatist. He saw it as practically synonymous with British empiricism, and as such, undialectical. After the Hearings, he received some of Dewey's books. He was impressed neither by the style nor the thought in these works. His respect for and gratitude to Dewey were personal. He saw

Dewey's idealism as genuine. Also, he heard that Dewey had postponed a trip to Europe in order to see through the work of the Commission. And whether or not this was true, he believed it, and was touched. But I strongly doubt that he fully realized Dewey's intellectual, as distinguished from his moral, stature. And this is not peculiar to Trotsky, or to his revolutionary ideas. It is characteristic of many Western European intellectuals. In these two personalities, sitting in the room in Coyoacan, under such unheralded circumstances, two worlds were personified. They were contrasts, not open antagonists, although their basic ideas were full of antagonisms. No questions were posed in such a way as to bring to a sharp issue, the differing philosophies of the two men, although their differences were apparent.

In Mexico, Dewey remarked that Trotsky had spoken for eight days, and that he had said nothing foolish. And what Trotsky said exposed a world of terror, of tragedy, of degradations of the human spirit. "When people get accustomed to horrors," wrote the Russian poet, Boris Pasternak, "these form the foundation for good style." The horrors of history were a basic ingredient of Trotsky's style. His masterful irony is, like all great irony, a protest because the horrors of history loom so overwhelmingly in the face of the reason of man. And he was a man of history in the sense that most of us are not and can not be. His thinking was relatively pure Marxism and Hegelianism. He thought with categories in antithesis, and in accordance with what he accepted as laws, laws of motion, of society and history. And as he talked, his style, his thought, his irony gave the Hearings a tone which reduced the impact of the horrors of history which were revealed,—the tale of war, revolution, of idealisms turned to cynicism, of the breaking of brave men, the betrayals of honor, truth, and friendship, the perversions of truth, the sufferings of families and of the innocent, the revelation of how the revolution and the society which had become the hope of so many in the West was really a barbarism practically unparalleled in modern history. Read the cold print of his testimony, and all this is clear. Some of Trotsky's interpretive and causal explanations may vary from our own, but the facts, the revelations, the horrors are all there. And as Trotsky talked, accepting full moral responsibility for all of his own acts when he was in power, his style gave this testimony an almost artistic character. The historic tragedy unfolded in this testimony reveals this tragedy only in fragments. After having heard it stated by Trotsky, one needs to deepen one's sense of the horror by reading of it in black and white. This testimony, along with his eloquent summation, exposed the Trials as frameups. And, as is known, the full Commission, after checking every available source and clue declared that the Moscow Trials were a frameup, and that Trotsky and his son, Sedov, were not guilty of the charges made against them in these trials.

At Coyoacan, he told the story of his life. No man was expelled from more countries than he. As he recounted this story, he would say "expulsed" for expelled. He was "expulsed" from country after country. And in all the years, when he was not in power, what did he do in his exile? He wrote books, articles, letters. Again, he was expulsed. And he wrote more. The loss of children, his daughter a suicide after Stalinist persecution, his son, a non-political person, accused of poisoning workers, and given up as dead, another victim of Stalin's vindictiveness. Friends, followers, former comrades, imprisoned, dishonored, shot. Heroes, brave men forced to degrade themselves, and then, executed. Trotsky's dearest friend of thirty-five years, Christian Rakovsky, a man widely respected as truly noble and heroic, forced to give obviously lying testimony against Trotsky. When questioned about Rakovsky, Trotsky answered "Rakovsky is my old friend, my genuine old friend . . . . " Concerning another old comrade, Trotsky testified: "If a man such as Muralov—if he cries to be shot as a German and Japanese spy, he does his work to the end. He was arrested and remained eight months in prison without confession . . . . He [Muralov] was in the full sense of the word a heroic personality . . . . Muralov was a pure man, an absolutely pure personality." And after Trotsky was asked if there was documentary evidence for a statement of his asserting that "all the criminal proceedings, all the trials, and all the confessions are based upon the persecution of the members of the family" [of those accused—J.T.F.] he also said:

"Excuse me, it [his statement about the persecution of wives and children] is not an opinion. It is my personal experience. I paid for the experience with my two children."

Trotsky, at one point in his testimony, said:

"It is a witch's play, a very terrible one, but it is a combination of gunfire and what is necessary for Stalin."

The thirteenth and final session of the Hearings was held on April 17th. Trotsky's final summation was read in part by Albert Goldman, and in part by Trotsky himself. He sat, reading slowly and quietly. Everyone in the room was hushed, attentive. Trotsky concluded:

"Esteemed Commissioners! The experience of my life, in which there has been no lack either of successes or of failures, has not only not destroyed my faith in the clear, bright future of mankind, but, on the contrary, has given it an indestructible temper. This faith in reason, in truth, in human solidarity which at the age of eighteen, I took with me into the workers' quarters of the provincial Russian town of Nikolaiev—this faith I have preserved fully and completely. It has become more mature, but not less ardent. In the very fact of your Commission's formation—in the fact that at its head, is a man of unshakable moral authority, a man who by virtue of his age should have the right to remain outside the skirmishes in the political arena—in this fact I see a new and truly magnificent reinforcement of the revolutionary optimism which constitutes the fundamental element of my life . . . . Allow me, in conclusion, to express my profound respect to the educator, philosopher, and personification of great American idealism, the scholar who heads the work of your Commission."

There was applause. This was one of the greatest and most dramatic moments in the life of Leon Trotsky. Unlike his doomed ex-comrades in Russia, he had answered Stalin and Vishinsky.

Dewey said: "Anything I can say will be an anti-climax." Then, he made a formal announcement about the future work of the Commission. The Hearings ended.

Moved deeply, John Dewey immediately left. Most of those present thought that he had been so touched by the impact of Trotsky's speech. But they were mistaken. He had been watching Mrs. Trotsky, not only during Trotsky's final summation, but on and off, during the entire hearings. A faded, tired-looking, brave woman, dressed in a simple but distinctive and almost chic manner, she sat near Trotsky, looking, listening, watching intently. She did not understand English. But she remained absorbed from the moment the hearings opened until they closed. Her life had been bound up in Trotsky's for years. One of the children he had lost in Russia was hers. She had shared his triumphs, his exiles, his dangers. The entire tragedy unfolded in the long hearings seemed to have been stamped on this brave woman's face. What touched Dewey most deeply during the entire hearings was the sight of Mrs. Trotsky—a woman so brave and sad—sitting there, staunch and loyal at her husband's side. This was why he hurried out at the close of the hearings. He couldn't bear further to watch the bravery of a woman wounded who was continuing to bear her sorrows with such nobility, such courage, such loyalty to the man she loved.

During the Coyoacan Hearings, Dewey remarked on Trotsky's intellectual brilliance, but added his own feeling that Trotsky was a tactless man. And he commented on the character of Trotsky's thinking. This was extraordinarily fluid, within the framework of his fixed absolutes. In Dewey's estimation, it was seemingly pragmatic. Within the framework of his categories, in terms of what Trotsky accepted as laws of a fixed character, Trotsky exhibited a sense of the relativities and the inter-connections of events, and was able to defend and explain expediencies with extraordinary adeptness. He saw an inner contradiction here in Trotsky. He treated this in terms of his own conceptions of means and ends.

Trotsky in an essay, "Their Morals and Ours," printed in the magazine, *The New International,* February 1938, took the position that the supreme law of history was the law of the class struggle, and that the end of historic action in conformity with that law, should be the liberation of the proletariat so that all mankind could be freed and so that, in consequence of this, the power of man over nature could be increased, and the power of man over man abolished. This latter was, for Trotsky, the end which would justify any means necessary for moving toward that end. To a morality based on these conceptions, Trotsky counterposed abstract and formal conceptions, especially Kantian morality, and further argued that such a morality was *petit bourgeois,* the morality of intermediate layers and non-decisive groups in class society. He then counterposed this conception of the morality of the proletarian revolution to the morality of fascism, and he looked to the future for historic justification of his position.

On the invitation of the editors of *The New International,* Dewey wrote a critical comment on Trotsky's essay. Entitled "Means and Ends," it was printed in *The New International* of August, 1938. He observed that "the end in the sense of consequences provides the only basis for moral values and action, the only justification that can be found for means employed." While a means can only be justified by its end, the end, also, must be justified. Then, noting that Trotsky's stated end, or end-in-view, of increasing the power of man over nature and abolishing the power of man over man was not necessarily Marxist, Dewey pointed out how Trotsky used the word "ends" in two different senses. On the one hand, Trotsky used "ends" to mean the final justifying end; on the other hand, he used this word to signify the means applied for the attainment of the final justifying end. And while not ruling out class struggle *automatically* as a means, Dewey insisted that class struggle had to be judged as a means on the ground of the interdependence of means and ends. But, Dewey observed, Trotsky justified class struggle because it was the law of laws of history. And Trotsky's assumed scientific historical law of class struggle permitted Trotsky to establish his means deductively, instead of empirically in terms of consequences, and of the interdependence of means and ends. Here, Dewey technically pinned down the *a priori* character in Trotsky's thought. And with this, Dewey sounded a warning which we can now, with the value of much hindsight, see and take to heart. "The belief that a law of history determines the particular way in which the struggle is to be carried on certainly seems to tend toward a fanatical and over-mystical doctrine of the use of certain ways of concluding it [the class struggle]." And as Dewey saw the problem, the course taken by the revolution in the U.S.S.R. seemed more explicable "when it is noted that means were deduced from a supposed scientific law instead of being searched for and adopted on the grounds of their relation to the liberation of mankind." The implication of Trotsky's dual use of the word "ends" is thus illuminated. The "dictatorship of the proletariat," achieved by class struggle, becomes the end in place of the final justifying end.

In an interview granted to Agnes E. Meyer, and published in *The Washington Post* on December 19, 1937, Dewey said:

"The great lesson to be derived from these amazing revelations [at Coyoacan] is the complete breakdown of revolutionary Marxism. Nor do I think that a confirmed Communist is going to get anywhere by concluding that because he can no longer believe in Stalin he must now pin his faith in Trotsky. The great question for all American radicals is that they must go back and reconsider the whole question of means of inquiry about social change and of truly democratic methods of approach to social progress. . . . During the trial [the Coyoacan Hearings] I asked Trotsky whether there was any reason to believe that a proletarian revolution in any other country would be more successful than that of Russia. His reply was evasive. . . ." Dewey also said that he had always disagreed with Trotsky, and that after the Coyoacan Hearings, he disagreed more than ever. His critical comment on Trotsky's essay further illuminates these conclusions, and motivates them.

At Coyoacan, Dewey asked Trotsky a question concerning the August Bloc of Russian Revolutionaries. Lenin had designated those in this bloc as "lackeys of capitalism." Were, Dewey asked, the Mensheviks in this bloc "lackeys of capital?"

Trotsky answered: ". . . it is a designation for reformists. Lenin designated all reformists as lackeys of capitalism . . . It is a question of a political appreciation and not of criminal thought."

A little later, Trotsky was asked about the position in the Soviet government occupied by Kamenev and Zinoviev in 1923 when Lenin lay ill. Trotsky's answer was in part: ". . . they were both members of the Politburo, which is the genuine guiding center of the Party and of the country. The Government, the official Government, submits to the orders of the Politburo, and a member of the Politburo is incomparably more important than the highest minister."

Also, Trotsky was questioned concerning the structure of the Soviets and the relation between them and the Communist Party during the early days of the Bolshevik dictatorship. He was asked if, in fact, "the Party was supreme over the Commissars?" He answered "yes." The Commissars, he said, were elected by the Soviets. The Soviets were elected by the people with only "exploiters and moral compromisers" excluded from voting. He characterized the Soviets as more democratic than the Party. He also indicated that there had been full discussion and criticism before elections to the Soviets, and that, in voting for Bolsheviks as members of the Soviets, the workers and others knew the nature and program of the Bolshevik Party. Dewey asked if there had been any organized manner, aside from criticism and discussion, whereby the workers could control branches of the Party. Trotsky answered: "It was the right only of Party members to change the Party and to control the Party." A moment later, Dewey asked: "Under these circumstances [indicated above] how can you say that it was democratic?"

To this, Trotsky answered:

"I didn't say it was democratic in the absolute sense. I consider democracy not as a mathematical abstraction, but as a living experience of the people. It was a great step to democracy from the old regime, but this democracy in its formal expression was limited by the necessities of the revolutionary dictatorship." This meant, as Trotsky admitted in answer to another question a moment later, "democratic control . . . as . . . consistent with the dictatorship of the proletariat." Questioning and discussion was pursued further. Trotsky soon qualified this statement by distinguishing between a dictatorship with the O.G.P.U. for the people, and one where it was against the people. However, Trotsky here gave the essence of his views on the nature of the state in the period of a proletarian dictatorship, prior to the achievement of the final justifying end—the creation of a classless society.

Here, then, we have the political features of the different views of Dewey and Trotsky on means and ends. And in the hearings, as I have noted, part of the tragic story of how that state, founded by Lenin and Trotsky, and by many of their brave, noble and dedicated co-workers, evolved or was transformed (Trotsky at Coyoacan insisted on the word *transformed* in this context) into the Soviet totalitarian regime with which the world is now familiar. And also, when Trotsky told of the democratic slogans and of the struggle of the Left Opposition which he led against Stalin, and some of the men who were executed as "Trotskyites," his explanation of his defeat was, basically, necessitarian. Quoting from Trotsky's book, *The Revolution Betrayed,* Dewey asked Trotsky if the dictatorship, in its early stage, were "a matter of iron necessity." Trotsky's answer was: "To a certain degree, not an absolute degree, but to a certain degree it is an historical necessity."

Trotsky, one of the founders of the Soviet Union, was ambivalent in his theories about and analyses of that state. He unmasked the frameups of Stalin, refuted many of the lies of the Kremlin, and he broke decisively with political followers who refused to accept his view that the Soviet Union should be defended because it was a workers' state, though a degenerated one. The last words he wrote, as part of his unfinished biography on Stalin, were: "The machine [the bureaucracy] had grown out of ideas. Stalin's first qualification was a contemptuous attitude towards ideas. The ideas had . . ." When the murderer drove a pickaxe into his head, his blood spattered on parts of this uncompleted manuscript.

In his unfinished biography of Stalin, he also wrote: "I do not know of a single instance of any anti-Trotskyite writings that contain a single reference to incorrect sources by me." And at Coyoacan he said, very convincingly:

"I am not hungering for power personally. Power is a burden, but it is a necessary and inevitable evil. When your ideas are victorious, you must accept it. But the mechanics of power is a miserable thing. . . . During the time I was in office, the best time was on vacations when I wrote books. It is giving me full satisfaction. I am patient and await a new wave, a new revolutionary wave, and then, if I can serve the interests of the proletariat, I will do anything I can."

Shortly after his ninetieth birthday, I talked with Dewey about Trotsky. Dewey said: "He was tragic. To see such brilliant native intelligence locked up in absolutes."

He considered Trotsky as a writer to be the best of the dogmatic Marxists, but he looked upon him as a dogmatist. He also concluded that Trotsky's mind was of a legalistic order. And after hearing all of Trotsky's testimony, he disagreed with Trotsky's politics more decidedly than ever.

Further, his experience in Coyoacan was an educative one. I recall, for instance, how during a brief intermission in one of the afternoon sessions, he spoke with me in Trotsky's garden. His remarks are, in my opinion, especially significant. He said that he had made mistakes, but that he had done this going on the evidence which he had. He had made mistakes because he didn't know more. He was thinking then, not only about the direct material of the Moscow Trials, but also about his own views. He was testing his own ideas. He was correcting himself where he had been mistaken.

And in his interview with Agnes E. Meyer, he summed up his conclusions thus:

". . . the conclusion, or moral, or whatever you want to call it, is that we must depend on our own community, upon our own democratic methods for the working out of our problems, both domestic and international."

And he also explained his earlier attitude towards the Soviet Union. "These revelations have been a bitter disillusionment to me personally. . . . I did believe that a highly important social experiment was going on in that country [the Soviet Union] from which we and the other so-called capitalistic nations could learn a good deal. I looked upon the Soviet Union as a social laboratory in which significant experiments would be worked out. . . . Truth is the mainspring of human progress."

The final report of the Commission of Inquiry, *Not Guilty*, was published in 1938. It is a model for any future efforts of this kind. The bulk of this work was done by Miss Suzanne La Follette; Dewey did editing and editorial work, offered suggestions, and did a minor part of the writing. The report is an achievement in itself, and a monument to all who worked in this enterprise. It is an example of democratic thinking, reasoning, procedure and of Dewey's own conceptions of methods of free inquiry.

Dewey made two speeches at mass meetings in 1937, following his journey to Mexico. One, *Truth is on the March*, was delivered at Mecca Temple in New York City on May 9, 1937. In it, he reported on the work of the sub-committee in Mexico, and lashed out at those who were still conducting an organized campaign calculated to prevent the Commission from completing its task. And he said: "To hold Trotsky guilty of the specific charge upon which he was convicted because of his well known opposition to the present rulers of the Soviet Union is not fair or square." He accused some liberals of "an intellectual shirking that is close to intellectual dishonesty. . . . Treachery to the very cause of liberalism. For if liberalism means anything, it means complete and courageous devotion to freedom of inquiry."

And in conclusion, he declared:

"Lines are being drawn between devotion to justice and adherence to a faction, between fair play and a love of darkness that is reactionary in effect no matter what banner it floats."

And then in a speech, delivered at the Mecca Hotel in New York City on December 12th, Dewey announced the verdict of the Commission of Inquiry, declaring Trotsky and Sedov not guilty. He said in part:

"The implications of this finding are profoundly disturbing . . . the present regime [in the Soviet Union] is seeking to identify political opposition to itself with criminal activity against the Soviet

Union and people . . . shocking is the systematic use by the Communist parties throughout the world of the vicious 'Trotskyist-terrorist-fascist' amalgam as a means of destroying political opposition and even of justifying gross frameups and assassinations. . . . Even in this country, the Communist Party and its labor and liberal sympathizers have used this strictly amoral tactic, indistinguishable from the tactic of Fascism, to slander and persecute opposition, with a resulting confusion and disruption of the forces of economic and political progress which cannot be too strongly condemned."

And he explained this Communist conduct as a repudiation by a disciplined political organization, world wide in scope and influence, of the principles of truth and justice upon which the foundations of civilizations are laid. This signified an extraordinary corruption of the idealistic heritage of the Russian revolution and revealed "a danger against which our own people must guard themselves without illusion and without compromise."

After delivering the speech, John Dewey looked tired. He had talked simply, unpretentiously. As he concluded, his voice had thickened a trifle with fatigue. He had given himself to what he saw as truth, justice, fair play. He had put aside his own work in order to help a man whose ideas he opposed, gain a fair hearing before world history. He had given his mind fully to this cause. He practiced his own preaching in the face of scorn. At a time when so many American liberals were surrendering their best traditions to a new barbarism, he helped to vindicate those traditions.

In 1898, William James, at the State House in Boston, protested against a proposed medical license bill. He provoked criticism from his colleagues in the Medical School at Harvard. And in a letter to a friend, he commented:

". . . If Zola and Col. Picquart can face the whole French army, can't I face their [James's colleagues] disapproval? Much more easily than that of my own conscience!"

Dewey, the heir of James, also became the heir of Zola. He had stood up and declared to the world that a mighty and powerful empire had lied, and that it had framed innocent men. Since that time the pattern of its action has spread like a noxious blight to every part of the world in which, through its satellites, the Soviets have come to power. Those who thought that the Moscow Trials were a local episode, and not our concern, were mistaken. Dewey was right in his belief that they constituted a grave challenge to liberalism everywhere.

In a recent conversation, John Dewey remarked: "The only ends are the consequences." For John Dewey and for all those who share his faith in truth and in the spirit of free inquiry and in democratic standards of fair play, the consequences are really men. The only worth while ends in community life are free men who live and exemplify their freedom in a social and cooperative spirit. For totalitarians, the consequences are a different kind of man, a man physically enslaved by force and mentally terrorized by lies. The tradition which John Dewey vindicated and personified in Mexico was one which makes it possible for men to live a life of freedom based on truth. The methods which he vindicated were his own methods of free inquiry. In our age, many serious and liberal men of intelligence have despaired of truth, of the viability and effectiveness of truth in the struggle against totalitarian lies. The Moscow Trials produced one of the most monstrous of all totalitarian lies. And it was with Dewey's own method of free inquiry that this lie was exposed. In substance, John Dewey revealed here, as he has in his entire life, the great moral value of the liberal ideals of truth, freedom, fair play. As time goes on, men who cherish freedom will remember with love and warmth the memory of the seventy-eight-year-old, gray-haired philosopher who made this mission of justice to Mexico City, and who performed it with such simplicity, candor, courage, and intelligence.

Notes on the Contributors

GEORGE BOAS is Professor of Philosophy at the Johns Hopkins University and author, among other works, of *An Analysis of Certain Theories of Truth, The Major Traditions of European Philosophy, New Ways of Thinking*, and, together with A. O. Lovejoy, of *Studies in Primitivism*.

JOHN L. CHILDS is Professor of Education at Teachers College, Columbia University, and author, among other publications, of *Experimentalism as a Philosophy of Education*.

JIM CORK is an active figure in the American Socialist movement, and especially interested in philosophy, social theory, and musical criticism.

IRWIN EDMAN is Professor of Philosophy at Columbia University and Chairman of the Department of Philosophy. He is the author, among other works, of *Philosopher's Holiday, Candle in the Dark, and The Mind of St. Paul*.

JAMES T. FARRELL is the author of *Studs Lonigan, A World I Never Made*, and other major works of literature.

LAWRENCE K. FRANK is Director of the Carolyn Zachary Institute, a Leader of the New York Society of Ethical Culture, and author of *Society as the Patient, Projective Methods,* and other works.

HORACE L. FRIESS is Professor of Philosophy at Columbia University, co-author of *The World's Religions*, editor of Felix Adler's *Our Part in the World*, and of *The Journal of Religion*.

ALBERT HOFSTADTER is Associate Professor of Philosophy at New York University and the author of *Locke and Skepticism*.

SIDNEY HOOK is Professor of Philosophy at New York University.

HORACE M. KALLEN is Professor of Philosophy and Psychology in the Graduate Faculty of the New School for Social Research, and author, among other works, of *Art and Freedom, Why Religion?*, and *The Education of Free Men*.

FELIX KAUFMANN was Professor of Philosophy, Logic, and Methodology in the Graduate Faculty of the New School for Social Research. He was the author, among other works, of *The Methodology of the Social*

Sciences. He was one of the founders and contributing editors of the *Journal of Philosophy and Phenomenological Research*.

MILTON R. KONVITZ is Professor of Industrial and Labor Relations at the New York State School of Industrial and Labor Relations, Cornell University, and editor of the *Industrial and Labor Relations Review*. He is the author of, among other publications, *On the Nature of Values*, 1946, and *The Constitution and Civil Rights*, 1947.

ERNEST NAGEL is Professor of Philosophy at Columbia University and an editor of the *Journal of Philosophy*, and author, among other works, of *The Logic of Measurement*, and *Principles of the Theory of Probability*.

EDWIN W. PATTERSON is Professor of Law at Columbia University.

SIDNEY RATNER is Associate Professor of History at Rutgers University and author, among other works, of *American Taxation: Its History as a Social Force in Democracy*, and editor of *The Philosopher of the Common Man*.

HERBERT W. SCHNEIDER is Professor of Philosophy at Columbia University, an editor of the *Journal of Philosophy*, and author of *A History of American Philosophy*.

WILFRID SELLARS is Associate Professor of Philosophy at the University of Minnesota, Minneapolis, Minnesota.

MARK STARR is director of educational research of the International Ladies Garment Workers Union.

MORTON G. WHITE is Associate Professor of Philosophy at Harvard University, and author of *The Origins of Dewey's Instrumentalism* and *Social Thought in America*.

PAUL D. WIENPAHL is Associate Professor of Philosophy at Santa Barbara College, University of California.

A Selected Bibliography of Publications
by JOHN DEWEY

My Pedagogic Creed, NEW YORK: E. L. KELLOGG & CO., 1897
Psychology and Philosophic Method, BERKELEY: UNIVERSITY PRESS, 1899
The School and Society, UNIVERSITY OF CHICAGO PRESS, 1900; REV. ED. 1915
Studies in Logical Theory, UNIVERSITY OF CHICAGO PRESS, 1903
Logical Conditions of a Scientific Treatment of Morality, UNIVERSITY OF CHICAGO PRESS, 1903
Ethics, IN COLLABORATION WITH JAMES H. TUFTS, NEW YORK: HENRY HOLT & CO., 1908; REV. ED. 1932
The Influence of Darwin on Philosophy and Other Essays in Contemporary Thought, NEW YORK: HENRY HOLT & CO., 1910
How We Think, NEW YORK: HEATH & CO., 1910; REV. ED. 1933
German Philosophy and Politics, NEW YORK: HENRY HOLT & CO., 1915; REPRINTED IN 1942, NEW YORK: G. P. PUTNAM'S SONS; 1945, BOSTON: THE BEACON PRESS
Democracy and Education: NEW YORK: MACMILLAN & CO., 1916
Essays in Experimental Logic, UNIVERSITY OF CHICAGO PRESS, 1916
Creative Intelligence, DEWEY AND OTHERS, NEW YORK: HENRY HOLT & CO., 1917
Reconstruction in Philosophy, NEW YORK: HENRY HOLT & CO., 1920; NEW EDITION, BOSTON: BEACON PRESS, 1949
Human Nature and Conduct, NEW YORK: HENRY HOLT & CO., 1922
Experience and Nature, CHICAGO: OPEN COURT PUBLISHING CO., 1925
The Public and its Problems, NEW YORK: HENRY HOLT & CO., 1927
Characters and Events, EDITED BY JOSEPH RATNER, NEW YORK: HENRY HOLT & CO., 1929, 2 VOLUMES
The Quest for Certainty, NEW YORK: MINTON, BALCH & CO., 1929
Individualism Old and New, NEW YORK: MINTON, BALCH & CO., 1930
Construction and Criticism, NEW YORK: COLUMBIA UNIVERSITY PRESS, 1930
Philosophy and Civilization, NEW YORK: MINTON, BALCH & CO., 1931
Art as Experience, NEW YORK: MINTON, BALCH & CO., 1934
A Common Faith, NEW HAVEN: YALE UNIVERSITY PRESS, 1934
Liberalism and Social Action, NEW YORK: G. P. PUTNAM & CO., 1935

The Case of Leon Trotsky: Report of Hearings Made Against Him in the Moscow Trials, BY THE PRELIMINARY COMMISSION OF INQUIRY, JOHN DEWEY, CHAIRMAN. NEW YORK: HARPERS, 1937

Not Guilty: Report of Inquiry into the Charges Made Against Leon Trotsky in the Moscow Trials, JOHN DEWEY, CHAIRMAN. NEW YORK: HARPERS, 1938

Experience and Education, NEW YORK: MACMILLAN & CO., 1938

Freedom and Culture, NEW YORK: G. P. PUTNAM'S SONS, 1939

Logic: The Theory of Inquiry, NEW YORK: HENRY HOLT & CO., 1939

Theory of Valuation in *International Encyclopedia of Unified Sciences*, CHICAGO: UNIVERSITY OF CHICAGO PRESS, 1939

Intelligence in the Modern World, EDITED BY JOSEPH RATNER, NEW YORK: THE MODERN LIBRARY, 1939

"ANTI-NATURALISM IN EXTREMIS," *Partisan Review* (January 1943), Re-published in *Naturalism and the Human Spirit*, NEW YORK: COLUMBIA UNIVERSITY PRESS, 1944

"ETHICAL SUBJECT MATTER AND ETHICAL LANGUAGE," *Journal of Philosophy*, XLII (1945)

"THE CRISIS IN HUMAN HISTORY," *Commentary*, V, March 1946

Problems of Men, NEW YORK: PHILOSOPHICAL LIBRARY, 1946

"LIBERATING THE SOCIAL SCIENTIST," *Commentary*, VI, October 1947

"WILLIAM JAMES' MORALS AND JULIEN BENDA'S MORALS," *Commentary*, VII, January 1948

"PHILOSOPHY'S FUTURE IN OUR SCIENTIFIC AGE," *Commentary*, VIII, October 1949, 388-394

Knowing and the Known, IN COLLABORATION WITH ARTHUR F. BENTLEY, BOSTON: THE BEACON PRESS, 1949

"THE FIELD OF VALUE" IN *Value: A Cooperative Inquiry*, edited by R. LEPLEY, NEW YORK: COLUMBIA UNIVERSITY PRESS, 1949

Some Publications About John Dewey

Essays in Honor of John Dewey on the Occasion of his Seventieth Birthday, NEW YORK: HENRY HOLT & CO., 1929

ADOLPH ERICH MEYER, *John Dewey and Modern Education*, NEW YORK: THE AVON PRESS, 1931

W. T. FELDMAN, *The Philosophy of John Dewey*, BALTIMORE: JOHNS HOPKINS PRESS, 1934

SIDNEY HOOK, *John Dewey: An Intellectual Portrait*, NEW YORK: THE JOHN DAY CO., 1939

The Philosophy of John Dewey, EDITED BY PAUL SCHILPP, EVANSTON: NORTHWESTERN UNIVERSITY PRESS, 1939

The Philosopher of the Common Man, EDITED BY SIDNEY RATNER, NEW YORK: G. P. PUTNAM & SONS, 1940

FOLKE LEANDER, *The Philosophy of John Dewey, A Critical Study*, GOTEBORG: 1939

ORLIE A. PELL, *Value-Theory and Criticism*, NEW YORK: 1930

HENRY BAMFORD PARKES, *The Pragmatic Test*, SAN FRANCISCO: THE COLT PRESS, 1941

MORTON G. WHITE, *The Origin of Dewey's Instrumentalism*, NEW YORK: THE COLUMBIA UNIVERSITY PRESS, 1943

Social Thought in America, NEW YORK: VIKING PRESS, 1949

ROBERT DONALD MACK, *The Appeal to Immediate Experience*, NEW YORK: KING'S CROWN PRESS, 1945

MORRIS R. COHEN, *Studies in Philosophy and Science*, NEW YORK: HOLT, 1949

Wit and Wisdom of John Dewey, EDITED BY A. H. JOHNSON, BOSTON: BEACON PRESS, 1949

Value: A Cooperative Inquiry, EDITED BY R. LEPLEY, NEW YORK: COLUMBIA UNIVERSITY PRESS, 1949

"A Letter to Mr. Dewey Concerning John Dewey's Doctrine of Possibility, Published Together With His Reply," BY A. C. A. BALZ *and* J. DEWEY, *Journal of Philosophy*, 1949

ROCKMONT COLLEGE LIBRARY
34516